Routledge Revivals

The Communist Foreign Trade System

Originally published in 1963 but with lasting historical interest, this book was based on extensive research including many personal interviews with foreign trade officials and economists in communist East Berlin. It surveys the extent of economic integration between the European communist nations during the middle of the 20th century and pays particular attention to the problems of economic planning and decision making. The changing pattern of economic exploitation is revealed by the scrutiny of the foreign trade prices of these nations and the author also examines the economic motives behind the geographical pattern of trade.

The Communist Foreign Trade System

The Other Common Market

Frederic L. Pryor

Routledge
Taylor & Francis Group

First published in 1963 by George Allen & Unwin. Ltd

This edition first published in 2026 by Routledge
4 Park Square, Milton Park, Abingdon, Oxon, OX14 4RN

and by Routledge
605 Third Avenue, New York, NY 10158

Routledge is an imprint of the Taylor & Francis Group, an informa business

ISBN: 978-1-041-32998-5 (hbk)
ISBN: 978-1-003-78558-3 (ebk)
ISBN: 978-1-041-33000-4 (pbk)

Book DOI 10.4324/9781003785583

THE COMMUNIST FOREIGN TRADE SYSTEM

BY

FREDERIC L. PRYOR

London
GEORGE ALLEN & UNWIN LTD
RUSKIN HOUSE MUSEUM STREET

FIRST PUBLISHED IN 1963

PRINTED IN GREAT BRITAIN
in 10 *on* 11 *point Times Roman type*
BY SIMSON SHAND LTD
LONDON, HERTFORD AND HARLOW

To My Parents

LIST OF ABBREVIATIONS

CMEA	:	Council of Mutual Economic Assistance
CSSR	:	Czechoslovak Socialist Republic
DDR	:	German Democratic Republic (East Germany)
FTE	:	Foreign Trade Enterprise
FYP	:	Five Year Plan
I-O	:	Input-Output
MFT	:	Ministry of Foreign Trade

PREFACE

Academic research on the Communist Bloc presents some particular difficulties which, in light of my six-month imprisonment in East Berlin, deserve some comment.

Securing sufficient information to form a balanced picture of any aspect of Communist economies takes a good deal of time and patience. As I discuss in the text, information has been scanty and highly selective. Moreover, even serious Communist discussion on foreign trade issues has been, for the most part, marked by tendentious justifications of government policy, vacuous name-calling and imputation of motives, or assertions of spectacular growth and efficiency, substantiated by reference to the growing Socialist consciousness of the citizentry. Even a large number of academic articles on technical trade topics have been marked by a low degree of rigour and a surprisingly high degree of ignorance. Although the situation is now slowly changing, reading of the Bloc economic press is usually tedious and unrewarding.

At this point several alternatives are open to the Western economist. He can, for instance, analyse Communist foreign trade in the same way as Communist economists analyse ours. This would include such tricks as deliberate lies (e.g. the Bloc economist who claimed that US grants to underdeveloped countries were 'really' loans whose repayment dates had not been established); imputation of motives (e.g. the East German Assistant Foreign Trade Minister who recently asserted that the Communist Council of Mutual Economic Assistance was founded to promote peace while the European Economic Community was founded by the monopolists to unleash World War III); figures quoted out of context; and so forth. On the other hand, the Western economist can try to transcend this nonsense and employ standard research methods and statistical techniques in order to gain an accurate and objective view of the situation and to eliminate as much as possible any sources of political bias.

In carrying out this study I thought it important not only to thoroughly review the East Bloc economic literature on foreign trade but also to hold interviews with foreign trade experts in both East and West. In this way I could not only obtain more information but could also hear all sides of the various issues which I was trying to judge. Complete objectivity may be impossible; if there is bias in this study, however, it is in no way deliberate since I have taken all possible measures to avoid it.

Except for those few East Germans whom I met socially, I chose all my interview partners in East Berlin solely on the basis of their writings in technical journals or on the recommendation of other East Germans. For the most part these interviews lasted from two to four hours (which makes absurd an accusation against me that I interviewed these people to determine whether they would reveal State secrets). My relations with East Berlin economists and government officials were completely open; I made no attempt to hide my East Bloc contacts; and I drove around in a bright red car with a Western licence plate. Furthermore, I had shown various drafts of all my manuscripts to economists in America, West Germany, Poland, England, and Sweden, and was openly bringing several copies of the completed study to friends in East Berlin when I was arrested. I never had contact with any espionage organization; moreover I did not desire such contact.

As far as I know, none of the material in this study is a State secret. In my interviews with East Germans, I tried to pose questions only in non-sensitive areas of foreign trade. Most of my questions concerned the functioning of institutions and methods of planning rather than the state of foreign trade at that time. In other words, I focused the questions on how foreign trade was carried out rather than what was being traded or negotiated. Other materials in this study were gathered from published economic literature and unpublished Diplomarbeiten and Referaten which I had *official* permission to read at the Hochschule für Ökonomie in East Berlin.

I was held five and a half months incommunicado and interrogated almost every day by the East German secret police. Although they made many accusations, no formal charges were ever drawn up against me. Such treatment is quite inconsistent to the ideals of justice and democracy which the East German government proclaims its adherence. The reader can judge the nature of my 'spying' for himself; for this book is essentially the 'spy document' which was found in my car upon my arrest. Only minor changes in style, deletion of redundant materials, and additions to bring the study up to date have been made.

This study was completed with the help of many people and groups in both the East and West, to whom I would like to express my gratitude.

For patience and constructive guidance I want to thank Professors Lloyd Reynolds, John M. Montias, and Bela Balassa who served as my dissertation committee. For a research grant, I want to thank Yale University. For aid at various stages I want to thank Professor Karl C. Thalheim for the assistance of the Ost Europa Institut at the Freie Universitaet (West Berlin); Gerhard Abeken and Helmut Kupky for the use of the facilities at the Deutsches Institut fuer

Wirtschaftsforschung; Olivér von Gajzágó and R. P. Rochlin for translation of various Eastern European sources and for many interesting discussions; Hans G. Toenjes for help in selecting samples for making terms of trade indices; Professor Wolfgang Stolper and Tom Kronsjö for copies of their manuscripts and comments on a previous draft of this study; Professor Karl Deutsch, Dr Alec Nove, Professor Olin W. Blackett, Professor Thad P. Alton, Erich Klinkmueller, Maria Ruban, Geoffrey S. Shepherd, T. N. Srinivasan, and my parents for their suggestions for this manuscript; and finally, the librarians at the Ost Europa Institut, Annemarie Genske and Margarete Lehmann, and librarians at the Hochschule für Ökonomie for their invaluable help.

Naturally, these people do not necessarily agree with my interpretation of various facts and events although whenever possible I have tried to take their objections into account. I, of course, take full responsibility for mistakes and errors in this study.

CONTENTS

LIST OF TABLES

INTRODUCTION

In 1952 Stalin declared, 'The disintegration of the single, all embracing world market must be regarded as the most important economic sequel of the Second World War and its economic consequences. . . . The economic consequences of the existence of two opposite camps was that . . . we now have two parallel world markets also confronting one another.'[1]

Although many objections may be raised to Stalin's analysis, two trading spheres have crystallized since the war. Until recent years, however, Western economists trying to analyse the foreign trade of the Communist nations have faced great difficulties. The most basic foreign trade statistics were not published in the East; details on the new Communist foreign trade institutions were scanty; materials on the operation of these institutions were scattered and incomplete; and contact with foreign trade experts of these nations was negligible. It is no wonder that serious Western analyses of Communist foreign trade were limited and that Western opinions on various issues of this problem-complex were often very one-sided.

In the last few years, the European Communist nations have published a great deal more data and facts on their economies. The central purpose of this study is to use this new information to analyse the most important facets of Communist foreign trade in order to fill-in many of the gaps in our knowledge on this vital topic. Due to the current scarcity of information on the foreign trade of the Asian Communist nations, however, I have focused almost completely on the European nations of the Bloc.[2]

In attempting such a study several difficulties immediately arise, for many of the traditional methods of analysing foreign trade problems and decisions are inapplicable. In Soviet type economies the planners try to bring supply and demand forces into equilibrium by means of a system of centralized 'material balances' rather than relying on decentralized price-quantity adjustments, described by the classical Western economic models. Moreover, in each Communist nation a 'foreign trade monopoly' has been set up to act as a buffer between the world markets and the domestic economy.

[1] Joseph Stalin, *Economic Problems of Socialism in the USSR* (New York: International Publishers, 1952), p. 26. Since the twentieth Party Congress of the Communist Party of the Soviet Union, this proposition has been doubted by some East Bloc theoreticians.

[2] The best full length studies of the scanty materials on this subject are: C. F. Remer, ed., *Three Essays on the International Economics of Communist China* (Ann Arbor: U. of Michigan Press, 1959) and *Entwicklungshilfe innerhalb des Ostblocks* (Frankfurt/M and Berlin: Alfred Metzner Verlag, 1960).

Furthermore, prices and the money supply are centrally planned and the use of bank balances or credit by enterprises is controlled so that the well-known equilibration mechanisms to bring exports and imports into alignment, which we know in the West, have little place in Soviet-type economies.

In addition, plan-making presents some difficulties seldom discussed in the Western literature on decision making in foreign trade. For instance, foreign market prices do not usually affect most prices used within the various Communist nations; and internal prices often do not reflect production costs, or demand factors, or any type of equilibrium of supply and demand forces. Therefore, the problem of selecting an optimum commodity pattern of foreign trade with such a price structure is extemely difficult. Other factors, which I later discuss in great detail, complicate the problem even more.

Finally, the enterprises conducting foreign trade in the Communist nations are very different from the firms analysed in classical Western microeconomic theory. For instance, the range of activity of the enterprises is highly restricted by plans and directives which are handed down to the enterprises by the State Planning Commission, the Ministry of Foreign Trade, the Ministry of Finance, and other Ministries interested in foreign trade. Moreover, the rewards and incentives of the foreign trade enterprises in Soviet-type economies differ considerably from those in market economies; primary orientation is toward plan fulfilment and fulfilment of certain political and ideological goals.

Therefore, this study must be quite different from traditional foreign trade analyses because much greater attention must be given to organizational problems of the economy. This, in turn, requires special tools and I would like briefly to sketch the type of organizational analysis which I use in several chapters. Those who are impatient with discussions of methodology should skip the rest of this introduction.

In this study I define the foreign trade system as the total network of foreign trade decisions. More specifically, attention is focused on the decision makers and their place in the economic hierarchy; the information and values used in the making of decisions; and the co-ordination of the decisions into a consistent whole, on both a national and international level.

One major task is to examine the relevant decision-making processes within the various national economies, not only in terms of the 'rules of operation' of the institutions but also in terms of the most important structural aspects of the economy and planning system. I focus particular attention on three structural elements: centralization, specialization, and continuity. The specific application of these concepts to Soviet-type economies is limited by the materials available and my definitions are, for this reason, somewhat arbitrary.

I define centralization as the concentration of the decision-making function in the highest levels of the planning hierarchy. More specifically, given the sizes of the production and trade enterprises in the economy, centralization may be analysed from three sets of phenomena: the degree of detail of production and trade targets which are handed down from the State Planning Commission and the Ministries to the enterprises; the proportion of total production and trade which these plan goals cover; and the degree to which conflicts and problems between enterprises are solved by negotiation between the enterprises involved or by higher economic organs.

By specialization I mean the separation of the various economic functions from each other (e.g. trade from production) and the performance of the different functions by separate decision-making units. An increased specialization may be associated with an increasing centralization or decentralization, depending on the changes in the planning process. An increased specialization usually brings about an increased complexity of interaction between the different decision-making units and, therefore, causes additional problems of co-ordination.

I discuss two aspects of continuity of a structure: the permanence of a structure in time (external continuity); and the continuity of the decision-making process within the structure (internal continuity). More specifically, if the area of activity and legal identity of a firm are constantly changing, the firm exhibits external discontinuities. Similarly, if all the most important decisions within the firm are made at one point of time, rather than sequentially throughout the year, the firm exhibits internal discontinuities.

From the 'rules of operation' of the various institutions and from the three structural elements of the economy, I analyse the gathering of information for decision-making, the evaluation of alternatives, and the decision-making process within one nation.[1]

The interaction of the various national foreign trade systems must be approached in a different manner. There are some data (e.g. foreign trade price data) concerning this interaction directly, and I have used this information to illuminate the trade negotiation process and the choice of trade partners. Other aspects of the foreign trade system of the Communist Bloc as a whole must be inferred from analysis of decision-making in trade within a single country.

If I were to analyse the domestic foreign trade institutions of all

[1] My analysis of decision-making *per se* is derived from the more formal decision-making model of Herbert A. Simon, 'A Behavioral Model of Rational Choice,' Chapter XIV, *Models of Man* (New York: John Wiley & Sons, 1958) (Originally published in *Quarterly Journal of Economics* LXIII, February 1955).

Communist nations in detail, this study would be considerably longer and the reader would become thoroughly bored. Fortunately, the foreign trade systems of all these nations operate in fundamentally the same manner, since all were copied from the Soviet system. In trying to discuss planning and decision-making processes, it is best to choose one country to serve as a case study to illustrate most graphically the main problems facing the planners and policy makers in all nations. Since none of the nations in the Bloc is really 'typical' such a choice is difficult. Nevertheless, I have selected the DDR (East Germany) in spite of the fact that it is the most industrialized in the Bloc, for two reasons: Since it is economically the most advanced nation, its organizational and planning problems will be faced by the other nations in the future; and a great deal more information is available on trade problems and procedures than for other countries (although published trade statistics are still quite inadequate).

CHAPTER I

THE ROLE OF FOREIGN TRADE[1]

Until recently foreign trade was relatively neglected in the USSR. Symptomatic is its treatment in the Soviet *Textbook of Political Economy* where the subject is dismissed in a few scant paragraphs with the conclusion that foreign trade is merely '. . . a supplementary source of aid for the development of production. . . .'[2] Since the autarky of the USSR has been so often examined by Western economists,[3] I do not need to analyse it in detail in this study.

Except for China no other Communist nation has the huge mineral wealth or the large domestic market of the USSR. Notwithstanding this economic commonplace, the East Central European nations began to copy the autarkic Soviet development policies and productive resources of the Bloc have been considerably misallocated as a result. Since Stalin's death, however, Bloc policy makers have begun to pay increasing attention to problems of intra-Bloc trade and a specialization of production. Although important changes had been made by the late 1950s, the emphasis on autarky was not yet overcome.

1. AUTARKY IN THE CMEA BLOC

It is easy to detect both economic and political strands in the striving toward autarky in the Bloc. One political goal is quite clear: economic independence from any nation which is believed to be unfriendly. For instance, the DDR Prime Minister declared: 'We will make ourselves very quickly independent from the arbitrary measures of the American imperialists; the industry of the DDR will produce out of its own

[1] In the following chapters, I designate Albania, Bulgaria, Czechoslovakia (CSSR), the German Democratic Republic (DDR), Hungary, Poland, and Rumania as the East Central European nations; these nations plus Russia as the Bloc or the CMEA (Council of Mutual Economic Assistance) nations; and the CMEA nations plus the Asian communist nations as the East or Communist Bloc.

[2] Academy of Science of the USSR, *Politische Oekonomie Lehrbuch* (trans. from the first Russian edition, East Berlin: Dietz Verlag, 1955) p. 584. After protest from the East Central European nations, the section on foreign trade was considerably enlarged and the above quoted sentence was omitted in the next edition.

[3] See especially Baykov, *Soviet Foreign Trade* (Princeton: Princeton U. Press, 1946).

means the important products which we now import from . . . the capitalistic countries, or else we will import these goods from the countries of the camp of peace. That does not mean a drawing back from inner-German trade; quite the opposite, the Government of the DDR is at all times ready to raise the foreseen volume of trade contacts. But we do not need or will allow ourselves dependence (on the West).'[1] Given the post-war political tensions, this policy of the CMEA nations seems quite reasonable and, indeed, has played an important part in the general reorientation of the geographic pattern of trade (see Chapter VI). But this political goal does not explain why the volume of trade between the CMEA nations has not increased enough to compensate for the decline in East-West trade.

An ideological strand of the autarky policy is their belief in the economic benefits of autarky or, conversely, a complete disregard of the benefit of trade. It is common to find such unqualified statements in the Bloc economic literature as: 'A constant task of the planning . . . is the reducing of necessary imports.'[2] Moreover, up to 1953–4, Bloc economic theoreticians completely neglected problems of foreign trade theory or profitability of trade. In recent years, however, autarkic ideas have come under heavy attack[3] and problems of the profitability of trade are receiving increasing attention (see Chapter IV).

One facet of the autarky may be analysed from the data on domestic production and investment in each country. All Bloc nations geared their economy for rapid economic growth and during the period from 1950 to 1955 investment in every country (except the DDR) was 25 per cent or more of the gross national product.[4] More-

[1] Otto Grotewohl, quoted by Herman Makower, 'Wege zur Intensivierung des gesamtdeutschen Buchhandels,' *Der Aussenhandel*, I, 3/1951, pp. 79–80.

[2] Rudolf Brauer, *Die Planung der wirtschaftlichen Taetigkeit der volkseigenen Handelsunternehmen Deutscher Innen- und Aussenhandel in der DDR* (Doctoral Dissertation, Hochschule für Ökonomie, 1956), p. 44.

[3] The first major public attack in any Bloc nation was made in 1954 by two Hungarians, Tibor Liska and Antal Máriás, 'A gazdaságesság és a nemzetközi munkamegosztás,' *Kösgazdasági Szemle*, I, 1/1954, pp. 75–94. For a survey of trade theory in the Bloc, see my 'Communist Foreign Trade Theory', *Soviet Studies*, July 1962.

[4] 'The Planning and Finance of Investment in the Soviet Union and Eastern Europe', and 'Investment Programmes and Results in the Soviet Union and Eastern Europe', *Economic Survey of Europe in 1955*, pp. 198–247 (esp. Table 94). Aggregate data from national sources (and the Marxist definition of national income) were used here. Upon recalculating national income and investment aggregates with Western definitions and methods from disaggregate data from Bulgaria, the CSSR, Hungary, and Poland, the Columbia Project for Eastern Europe National Income Computations has tentatively concluded that investment during the 1950–5 period in these nations was over 30 per cent of national income. (Interview with Thad Alton, March 27, 1961.)

over, the overall investment policies were the same. Each nation planned and placed 40 per cent or more of all investment in industry, while neglecting agriculture and housing, and directed over 80 per cent of their industrial investment in 'heavy industry'. This may be compared with the situation in West Europe from 1950 to 1954, where industrial investment was 20 to 35 per cent of total investment and where heavy industry accounted for 40 to 60 per cent of total industrial investment.[1]

The first long-range plans of each Bloc nation were similar not only in their macroeconomic proportions but also in their planned composition of output. As one Western economist noted: '. . . in its main conception, each (plan) . . . looks rather like a copy, reduced in scale, of the Soviet classical model. Each seeks to provide the given country with a heavy industrial base comprising some metallurgy, some engineering and chemical industries, and electrification. The plans appear to follow Soviet precedent as closely in their substance as in their form and techniques of execution.'[2]

According to plan, each Bloc nation built giant iron-steel complexes: the Kremikowzi and Dimitrovo combines in Bulgaria; the Kosice and Nove Hute plants in the CSSR; Stalinstadt and Ost-Kombinat in the DDR; Sztalinvaros combine in Hungary; Nowa Huta and Czestochowa works in Poland; and the Roman combine in Rumania. Each nation also started or increased production of almost *all* major machine goods, chemicals, and other products of heavy industry. Analyses of this phenomenon have often been made in the West,[3] but do not, however, focus primary attention on foreign trade.

Examining the degree of autarky in the CMEA nations from the available trade data presents special problems. Perhaps the easiest way is to compare the foreign trade per capita of the various nations before and after World War II.

These data show that although per capita trade has increased considerably in every Bloc country except the DDR since the pre-war period, in many cases these increases have been lower than one might expect from the rapid increases of industrial production. Unfortunately, these data do not conclusively prove that the post-war economic development of the CMEA nations would have been more

[1] All data from Chapters 2, 3, 6 and 7, *Economic Survey of Europe in 1955*, supplemented by data from other issues of *Economic Survey of Europe* and UN *World Economic Survey for 1958*.

[2] Oleg Hoeffding, 'Soviet Economic Relations with the Orbit,' in Abram Bergson ed., *Soviet Economic Growth: Conditions and Perspectives* (Evanston and White Plains: Row Peterson and Co., 1953).

[3] See especially various issues of *Economic Survey of Europe* and *Economic Bulletin of Europe*.

TABLE 1–1

BLOC TRADE TURNOVER PER CAPITA FROM 1928 TO 1958[1]

Year	Bulgaria	CSSR	DDR	Hungary	Poland	Rumania	USSR
A. Current Dollar Estimates							
1928	28	139	—(165)	70	36	34	11
1938	20	42	314(62)	30	13	15	4
1950	37	114	48(40)	69	52	28	18
1958	95	217	206(183)	133	79	53	42
B. Constant Dollar Estimates (1954 Dollars)							
1928	25	143	—(170)	63	32	30	10
1938	56	102	872(151)	85	37	41	12
1950	40	132	52(44)	76	57	30	20
1958	97	217	206(183)	136	81	55	42

rapid if the countries had had a higher volume or different composition of trade. What is needed in this case is some concept of national 'trade potential', i.e., the volume of trade at the point where it is impossible to obtain a higher national income by a change in the volume and/or composition of trade. If the definition is to be 'dynamic', the 'trade potential' is the point where it is impossible to obtain a higher growth rate within a certain time period through a change in the trade volume and/or composition, with the consumption level remaining the same.

This concept of 'trade potential' is fraught with index number problems on a theoretical plane as well as computational problems on an empirical level. But, nevertheless, if we assume that market forces tend to push the foreign trade of market economies toward full utilization of their 'trade potential' (in a static sense, with the index number problems subsumed under the general theoretical problems of calculating a national income) then several rough methods are

[1] Pre-war data for Bulgaria, CSSR, Hungary, and Rumania from pre-war boundaries. Pre-war data for USSR includes Baltic nations; pre-war data for Poland, from pre-war boundaries plus Danzig. Pre-war data for DDR from current DDR area and includes estimation of pre-war inner-German trade; data in parentheses exclude inner-German trade. (Exact methods of estimating pre-war DDR trade are outlined in Statistical Appendix B.) Constant dollar estimates from current dollar data, deflated by unit price indices for trade of underdeveloped and developed nations. Because of the crudeness of method of deriving constant price data, these estimates must be considered indicative only of the general magnitudes.

Sources: Pre-war trade data for all countries except DDR from: League of Nations, *The Network of World Trade* (Geneva 1942); all post-war trade data from ECE, *Economic Survey of Europe for 1957 and 1959*, and various national statistical year-books. Population estimates from: League of Nations, *International Statistical Yearbook, 1929; Statistical Yearbook 1938–9; Statistical Yearbook 1940–1;* and from various issues of UN, *Demographic Yearbook;* and *Statistical Yearbook*.

available to estimate an approximate 'trade potential' of the various CMEA nations.

In an extensive statistical study of sixty market economies, Hollis B. Chenery found that trade per capita is very strongly correlated with per capita national income and total national population. Using more comparable production data of eight Western European nations, I found a correlation between per capita trade on one hand and per capita industrial production and total national population. It is possible to estimate a 'trade potential' (in a static sense) for the Bloc nations by using the results of these correlations from the non-Communist world. Because of the nature of the data, the results of this experiment must be considered very tentative, however, and simply indicative of the relative orders of magnitude of the various quantities.

TABLE 1–2

TRADE AND TRADE POTENTIAL OF THE CMEA NATIONS IN 1955[1]

Country	*Per Capita Industrial Production (dollars)*	*Population (millions)*	*Per Capita Trade Turnover (dollars)*	*Potential Per Capita Turnover* Chenery Formulae (dollars)*	*Potential Per Capita Turnover* My Formula (dollars)*
Bulgaria	99	7·548	56	160	256
CSSR	405	13·093	170	375	594
DDR	339	17·945	137	298	471
Hungary	189	9·805	117	236	350
Poland	215	27·278	68	188	240
Rumania	124	17·325	45	145	208
USSR	264	197·198	33	117	—

The results of this calculation are startling. In 1955, no CMEA Bloc nation realized even 50 per cent of its 'potential' trade per capita, using either of the formulae. Furthermore, the real 'trade potential' of the Bloc nations may be higher than the estimates in the table (and the utilization of 'trade potential' lower) because the actual 'trade potential' of the Western nations may be higher than actual trade, due to the influences of tariffs, etc., so that the formulae used in deriving Bloc 'trade potential' yield downwardly biased results.

Due to infant industries, 'trade potential' in a dynamic sense may be somewhat lower than 'trade potential' in a static sense. Nevertheless, the difference is not great enough to be able to begin to explain the contrast between actual and potential foreign trade in the Bloc.

[1] Due to the nature of the estimates of industrial production per capita and the use of the correlation formulae, the estimates of 'trade potential' must be considered as very approximate. For sources and methods of calculation, see Statistical Appendix B, Section 1.

From the data presented in Tables 1–1 and 1–2, it seems safe to conclude that the post-war economic development of all CMEA nations was autarkic to a significant degree through the late 1950s. One of the tasks of this study is to investigate the reasons behind this autarky.

2. RESULTS OF THE AUTARKY

During the post-war years, three interlocking results of the autarkic economic development of the Bloc nations appeared: All nations invested in uneconomic projects for which they had a comparative disadvantage; parallel investment and short production runs seemed to be the rule rather than the exception; and serious all-Bloc scarcities of major products occurred.

A. The over-exaggerated autarkic ideas of the policy makers and the semi-mystical notions that every nation must have certain industries, resulted in investment projects which were quite unprofitable from the standpoint of absolute cost. Perhaps the best known example of such a totally uneconomic investment by a Bloc nation is the case of the Hungarian steel industry, where the foreign exchange expenditure on the import of iron ore and coke required for the production of steel exceeded the cost of buying an equivalent amount of imported steel directly.[1] According to my calculations, a similar situation existed in the DDR for the production of pig iron. The following table makes this clear.[2]

In addition to investing in projects where the country had an absolute disadvantage, many Bloc nations also began producing goods where they were at a *comparative* disadvantage. For instance, with the large oil potential of the Bloc (in Rumania and the USSR) the investment in production of synthetic oil by the CSSR and DDR seems

[1] *Statisztikai Szemle*, 7/1957. For other examples of uneconomic Hungarian investments, see Bela Belassa, *The Hungarian Experience in Economic Planning*. (New Haven: Yale U. Press, 1960).

[2] DDR import data, USSR border, from *Vneshniaia Torgovlia SSSR za 1957 god*, Moscow, 1958; transportation costs from *Einheitliche Transittarif zum Abkommen über den Internationalen Eisenbahn und Güterverkehr, 1956;* data on coke needed per ton pig iron, *Statistisches Jahrbuch der DDR, 1958*, p. 361; data on Fe content in ore from USSR to DDR (55 per cent) from Herr H. G. Tönjes, Deutsches Institut für Wirtschaftsforschung. (According to the *Oxford Regional Economic Atlas: The USSR and Eastern Europe*, the average Fe content for ore in all Russia is 55 to 57 per cent; 2 to 3 per cent is less than 42 per cent Fe content and some of the ore from Krivoy Rog and Bahal is up to 68 per cent Fe richness. My 55 per cent figure may be somewhat low but I have assumed complete use of its iron content, a technical impossibility.) In the table I have omitted cost of limestone and other minerals used in pig iron production. The DDR can produce pig iron from its own iron ore (average Fe content, 28 per cent) and brown coal cokes but it is certainly cheaper to import Russian iron ore and hard coal cokes.

TABLE 1–3

1956 DDR IMPORT COSTS TO OBTAIN ONE TON OF PIG IRON

Imported materials to produce one ton of pig iron	*Cost at USSR Border* roubles	*Railway Costs* roubles	*Total Costs* roubles
a. Hard coal cokes	141	27	168
b. Iron ore	69	32	101
c. Total	210	59	269
One ton of pig iron imported directly	202	21	222

quite uneconomic. Similarly, the DDR development of a process for converting brown coal briquettes into coke, while interesting from a technological point of view, does not seem to be economically rational, taking into account the extensive coal reserves in Poland, the CSSR and the Soviet Union.[1] It seems a mis-allocation of Bloc resources for the various industrial countries with labour scarcities and poor soils to emphasize the production of highly labour-intensive agricultural products (such as fruits and vegetables) while a country like Bulgaria has concealed under-employment and very rich soil. Unfortunately, little information on production costs in the Bloc is available and although many more examples may be given, I cannot offer any more solid evidence than an appeal to the reader's intuitive knowledge of relative factor costs.

B. A second result of the autarkic foreign trade pattern was the increase of parallel investments in each country.

Imre Nagy summarized the situation in Hungary during the early 1950s when he declared: 'It must be pointed out that although the economic co-operation and mutual assistance between the socialist countries brought significant results, the activity of CMEA from the point of view of industrial production and development was extremely limited during the period of the (Hungarian) First Five-Year Plan (1949–54). This also contributed to the rise of inequalities of work distribution among the friendly countries. Despite the fact that agreements were made with some of the democratic countries with a view to assigning work in a way which would promote production and work distribution, parallel manufacturing, especially in

[1] For examples of uneconomical investments in the non-ferrous metals industry in the Bloc, see the public reports of the Central Intelligence Agency such as *Lead in the Sino-Soviet Bloc* (December 1961) or *Tin in the Sino-Soviet Bloc* (December 1961).

Concrete examples may be seen in each country. For example, in 1936 about 8,700 people were employed in the non-ferrous metal mining industry in the present DDR area; in 1957, about 26,000. In the second Five-Year Plan, investment between 460,000,000 and 500,000,000 DM in the area was foreseen. However, the average metal content of the ores is very very low. (See data presented in 'Der NE-Metallerzbergbau in der SBZ', *Wochenbericht*, XXV, 6/1958, pp. 21–3).

the field of machine industry, had an increasingly detrimental effect on our export opportunities and consequently on our foreign trade balance. Parallel manufacturing affected not only trade among the friendly countries themselves but led to an unhealthy competition among them in the capitalist markets as well. The exaggerated trend toward autarky within the socialist camp not only reduced our opportunities to export within the camp, but also deprived us of chances of importing basic and raw materials. . . .'[1]

Other Bloc officials had the same opinion. A Deputy Prime Minister of the CSSR declared that in 1957 Czechoslovakia produced about 80 per cent of all existing machine types, and he particularly emphasized the adverse effect on production costs which had been brought about by the quadrupling in the last ten years of the number of machine types made in the CSSR.[2] One DDR economist estimated that in 1959, the DDR produced between 85 and 90 per cent of all machine types.[3] The Bulgarians were also quite aware of the problem and in 1960 Grigor Popissakoff noted, 'The current state of the international division of labour among the CMEA nations which has been reached in the last two or three years in the area of machine building cannot be viewed as satisfactory. Quite the opposite. The success which has been made is only the first step and shows that for a more purposeful international division of labour the possibilities at hand in the different important branches have not yet been fully utilized and correspond neither to the demands of today nor to the level of development of economic relations between the Bloc countries. The gaps which can be seen in the specialization and co-operation of production in the machine building industry are visible by the excessively large number of machine types produced by the enterprises of this industrial branch in the various countries.'[4]

[1] Imre Nagy, *On Communism: In Defense of the New Course* (New York: Frederick A. Praeger, 1957), p. 189. Another Hungarian author, E. Illyes (quoted by ECE, *Economic Survey of Europe for 1954*, p. 128) noted, 'There was a considerable expansion in those transformation industries—particularly in engineering, for which no raw material basis existed in the country, while no account was taken of the fact that economic and historical conditions in one, or possibly more, of the countries in the socialist camp were substantially more favourable for the development of such branches of industry.'

[2] The Deputy Prime Minister concluded: 'This disproportional extension of types produced by the machinery industry influences unfavourably the efficiency of production, research, development, and construction of machines.' (Quoted by Jan Wszelaki, *Communist Economic Strategy: the Role of East Central Europe;* Washington, D.C.; National Planning Association, 1960; p. 116; from *Promyshlenno-Ekonomicheskaia Gazeta*, February 7, 1958.)

[3] Karl Morgenstern, 'Zu einigen Fragen der socialistischen internationalen Arbeitsteilung', *Einheit* XV, 4/1960, pp. 611–28. Any datum on the total number of machine 'types' produced in a nation is to be taken with caution.

[4] Grigor Popissakoff, 'Zur Entwicklung der internationalen Arbeitsteilung in Sozialismus', *Der Aussenhandel* X, 11/1960, pp. 22–5.

The effect of such duplication is, of course, non-economical short production runs. In the DDR one economist declared that in 1957, production runs for making office machinery were 5,000 to 30,000, compared with optimum runs in the range of 30,000 to 60,000 machines; he also noted that in 1958, 39,000 autos would be produced in several different factories, compared with an optimum production of 70,000 for any one make.[1] (These data for optimal runs are his; Western estimates, at least for autos, are higher.)

Khrushchev, in contrast to Stalin, appears very much concerned with this problem of parallel investment. For instance, in 1956 he stated: 'We already said a long time ago that a better (economic) co-operation should be established between our countries. It is impossible to have developed everything everywhere simultaneously. Unfortunately, we have often spoken in vain. Hungarians, Poles, Rumanians and also the others have tried to build up everything by themselves. Perhaps it is only small Albania which has not attempted this. . . . In the Soviet Union this is naturally not the same problem as elsewhere since Soviet industry produces for a vast demand. The same applies to China with its immense population. But for small countries, this creates very great problems, for which solutions cannot be found within national boundaries.'[2]

C. A third result of the autarkic trade pattern was the constant all-Bloc shortage of many vitally needed commodities, especially raw materials. In contrast to the situation in the private enterprise economies, the commodity problem in the centrally planned economies was one of persistent shortages rather than undisposed surpluses.[3]

This raw material shortage had two facets. The former Bloc suppliers of various minerals began to concentrate more heavily on other production. At the same time the former Bloc importers began to produce more of the minerals for themselves at high costs not only because of a policy of national self-sufficiency but because they were unable to rely on Bloc trade partners for continuous supply. A detailed UN analysis shows that for every important pre-war surplus raw material in the East Bloc (except one), domestic consumption in the various producer nations rose faster than domestic production, thus relatively decreasing the exportable surplus; and in every important pre-war deficit raw material of the Bloc, domestic production has increased faster than domestic consumption in the

[1] Karl Morgenstern, 'Die Industrie der DDR in der internationalen sozialistischen Arbeitsteilung', *Die Wirtschaft* XII, 49/1957, p. 6.

[2] Quoted by ECE, 'Developments in the Foreign Trade of Eastern Europe and the Soviet Union', *op. cit.*, p. VI–31.

[3] UN, 'Problems of Primary Commodities in Centrally Planned Economies', *World Economic Survey for 1958*, pp. 131–76.

various importing nations.[1] This fall in the export and import ratios reflects the increased autarky.

An economic crisis occurred in the Bloc from 1953 to 1956 when the most important raw material exporter, the USSR, barely increased these exports to the other CMEA nations and aggravated the raw material shortage.[2] In late 1955, committees of the Council of Mutual Economic Assistance made all-Bloc material balances for twenty or so critical materials for the coming Five-Year Plan period and found that by 1960, planned demand for hard coal in the Bloc would exceed planned production by about 10,000,000 tons; for rolled steel, by about 4,500,000 tons; for steel in bars, by about 3,500,000 tons.[3] Large deficits would also occur for copper, cement, cotton, sulphuric acid and many other raw materials because of the autarkic trade pattern.

3. SPECIALIZATION OF PRODUCTION IN THE BLOC: 1956–60

Since the death of Stalin in 1953, there has been an increasing realization among Bloc economists that foreign trade is a vital sector of the economy and that changes in the commodity structure and volume of trade could greatly increase economic growth for all nations. In 1953–4, several nations began to make 'Industrial Treaties' which specified certain products in which each would specialize and which each would export to the other. The reasons for such agreements lay in the unfortunate experience of several Bloc countries which found their export markets in other Bloc nations dried up as the latter suddenly began producing the imported items themselves. In 1955, Bloc economists began widely to discuss the idea of making all-Bloc production specialization agreements which would increase trade and which would allow each nation to gain the benefits of large scale production.

A. The Raw Material Sector

Planning a more rational Bloc division of labour in the raw material sector has been more difficult than first imagined. Early in 1956, the Council of Mutual Economic Assistance made recommendations for the development of Polish coal and Russian iron ore (from Krivoi Rog) for the whole Bloc. These measures were not only insufficient,

[1] UN *World Economic Survey for 1958*, pp. 131–76.

[2] Various issues of ECE, *Economic Survey of Europe* and *Economic Bulletin for Europe* present data on this matter.

[3] Interview on December 5, 1960, with Fritz Schenk, assistant to Chairman of DDR State Planning Commission from 1953 to 1957. Figures were from his memory.

but also the additional burden on Polish coal miners caused severe political problems in Poland in the summer and autumn of the year. In the late autumn of 1956, almost every nation sent delegations to the USSR to plead for more raw materials.[1] This led to the CMEA recommendation in 1957 that each nation begin making fifteen-year plans which would be co-ordinated with each other, because investment in mineral extraction often takes over five years to mature and any co-ordination for five-year periods would be insufficient to avert all-Bloc deficits. (By 1961 these fifteen-year plans had not yet been completed by all Bloc nations.[2]) Since 1957, the various CMEA Commissions have discussed problems of a more rational specialization in the various minerals. In the ferrous metals, Russia, Poland, and the CSSR will greatly increase their production of pig iron and steel. In most of the other Bloc nations emphasis will be placed on the second refining stage of steel. In the non-ferrous metals, Hungary will specialize in aluminium production; Bulgaria, copper and lead; Poland, zinc and sulphur; Albania, chromium.[3]

Already the new emphasis on production specialization in the raw materials sector is manifesting itself in different ways. First, a great many joint nation projects have been built, or are in the process of being built, on the sites of the richest mineral deposits or the best processing sites. For instances, a multi-national cellulose plant in the Danube delta will utilize the reeds in the area; and various nations are co-operating in the development of Polish coal and sulphur, Rumanian oil, and Hungarian bauxite. The current co-operative development of the Danube will not only facilitate transportation but will generate power for the chronically energy-short nations of the Bloc. Many nations are working on the oil pipeline which will deliver Soviet crude oil to the CSSR, DDR, Hungary, and Poland. This pipeline will eliminate the need for investing in costly synthetic oil plants in these countries, will reduce fuel bottlenecks, and will lower the current high costs of transportation of oil and petroleum products.

[1] According to Schenk and Lowenthal ('Khrushchev's Changing Empire', *The Observer*, November 9, 16 and 23, 1958) party leaders of the various East Central European countries refused to scale down their plans after the all-Bloc material balances showed increasing raw materials deficits, and Saburov, Chairman of the USSR State Economic Commission, refused to increase Russian exports of these minerals. In October 1956, delegations from the CSSR, DDR, Hungary and Poland came to plead for more raw materials almost simultaneously. This 'irregular meeting of the CMEA' did lead to some change in Russian policy and exportation of more raw materials.

[2] In the DDR, discussion on the desirability of making a 10-20 year plan 'following the example of the USSR' began in 1956. See J. Schir, 'Eine neue Etappe der Zusammenarbeit der sozialistischen Länder', *Der Aussenhandel* VI, 11/1956, pp. 368–9.

[3] For further details, see Appendix E.

Second, many of the most uneconomical investment projects in the raw materials sectors of the various Bloc nations have been either discontinued or reduced in scale. In the DDR, for example, the key project at the Schwartze Pumpe Combine to convert brown coal into metallurgical cokes has been deferred. Moreover, no new blast furnaces are foreseen and no further large-scale investments in iron-steel combines are scheduled, except for those at Stalinstadt, in order to secure the advantages of integrated production. The import ratio (imports/total domestic consumption) for pig iron was planned to rise from ·24 in 1958 to ·40 in 1965.

Third, a small multilateral credit programme in the raw materials industries has developed since 1958 when the CMEA recommended that various nations give Poland credits for investments in coal mining.

The extent of the various multilateral credit is, unfortunately, not known. The programme came about as Bloc economists became aware that investment in the raw materials industries had a longer gestation period and higher capital/output ratio than in most other industries, and that some way had to be found to develop mineral resources where they were most abundant.[1]

It is difficult to evaluate the overall effect of these efforts toward a more rational resource use. Bloc statistics reflecting many of these changes are not yet available since such investment projects take several years to come into operation. Moreover, many Bloc nations have been reticent in publishing production and trade statistics for the more strategic minerals and metals.

Nevertheless, some scattered data suggests that the planned specialization pattern in the raw materials sector leaves something to be desired. For instance, in the last few decades, the whole Western world has been changing from the use of solid fuels such as coal, to petroleum fuels. This change has been due to a rise in the costs of coal extraction, due to gradual depletion of deposits, and a fall in costs in oil extraction because of rapid changes in technology. One would expect the same shift in energy sources in the Bloc since large oil deposits exist, since coal mining costs seem to be rising, and since at least one Bloc nation, the Soviet Union, is following the world pattern. In the USSR the share of total energy consumed in the form of coal fell from 65 per cent in 1952 to about 55 per cent in 1960 and is planned to fall to about 45 per cent in 1965 and 32 per cent in 1972.[2]

On the other hand, in 1958, the share of energy from coal was over 90 per cent in the CSSR, DDR and Poland; over 80 per cent in Hungary;

[1] See, for instance, the remarks of N. Siluyanov in *Voprosi Ekonomiki* 1/1959, p. 21.

[2] T. Paul Schulz, *The Process of Adjustment to the Change in the Relative Prices of Oil and Coal: Case Study Poland* (unpubl. Swarthmore College Honours Programme Dissertation, April 1961) Chapter II.

and over 70 per cent in Bulgaria. Only Rumania and Albania seemed to be using oil as an energy source to any appreciable extent. Notwithstanding the pipeline from the USSR, Poland and the DDR *planned* to maintain about the same percentage of energy from coal in 1965, while Czechoslovakia and Hungary planned for a fall in their share of energy coming from coal by somewhat less than 10 percentage points.[1] In Bulgaria, the percentage of energy from coal has been rising steadily from 1954 and will probably rise even more. It seems to me that this continued emphasis on coal as an energy source by most of the East Central European nations is irrational in terms of Bloc resources and mineral extraction costs.[2]

Moreover, although the production of rolled steel forms was one of the first areas in which specialization agreements (both bilateral and all-Bloc) were made, the Economic Council for Europe noted that in 1956 less than 5 per cent of the combined output of crude and finished steel was exported.[3] This situation did not greatly improve in the next few years.

Finally, in the non-ferrous metal industry, extraction of very low yield ores continued even for metals for which the Bloc has had an overall surplus (e.g. tin).

B. The Manufacturing Sector

In December 1955, the CMEA made its first all-Bloc production specialization recommendations. Among other products, these covered steel forms, tractors, and several other types of agricultural machinery. In May of the next year the CMEA made similar recommendations for the production of some 600 machine goods. This enthusiasm was somewhat misdirected, however, and one high ranking DDR official declared, 'The lesson to be learned from the mutual (production) co-operation up to now is not to simply expand this work but to focus on the most important problems of the member nations. At the eighth Plenum of the CMEA in 1957, it was held to be useful . . . to abandon many details of the agreement (of the previous year) and to concentrate more fully on the most important questions. Of primary importance for all member nations are the important

[1] *Ibid.*, Figure 3, p. 28.

[2] It seems also strange that if the DDR planners continue their emphasis on coal as an energy source, they should also plan to increase their production of very high-cost hard coal at the same percentage as domestic consumption in the seven-year plan, rather than importing this coal in exchange for, let us say, precision goods and machines. The import ratio of cokes in the DDR is planned to remain constant until 1965 also.

[3] ECE, 'Developments in the Foreign Trade of Eastern Europe and the Soviet Union', *Economic Survey of Europe for 1957*, p. VI–12.

products of the basic materials industry such as rolled steel, fuels and non-ferrous metals.[1]

Since 1957, these all-Bloc specialization discussions have been slower and less spectacular but, at the same time, more thorough and systematic. For instance, specialization of production of chemicals was discussed in the Bucharest and Prague Plena (June and December 1958); specialization in machinery for making chemicals in the Tirana and Sofia Plena (May and December 1959). By 1960, specialization agreements had covered more than 500 chemical products, covering about 80 per cent of the Bloc gross production, and about 1,100 machine goods and equipment for producing chemicals.[2] Specialization in production of machines for other major production areas is said to be proceeding at a somewhat slower pace.[3] However, in the past several years, the Council has also made recommendations for machinery production in several small industries such as sugar refining, meat packing, and paper making.

Some idea of the great activity in making specialization agreements may be gained from the following data:[4]

These production specialization agreements have brought about some concrete changes. In the late 1950s, for instance, the DDR gave

[1] Kurt Gregor, 'Ergebnisse der 8. Ratstagung', *Die Wirtschaft* XII, July 4, 1957. According to Alexander Schalck-Golodkowski (*Der Export der DDR auf dem Gebiet der Kompletten Industrieanlagen unter dem Gesichtspunkt der internationalen Arbeitsteilung sozialistischen Typus;* Diplomarbeit, Hochschule für Ökonomie, 1957; p. 10.) 'Most of the recommendations of the seventh Plenum in 1956 were not possible to carry out since for many positions the necessary material and industrial pre-suppositions were not available in the various countries to maintain the agreements of the Council.' According to a Russian commentator (O. Bogomolov, 'Die internationale sozialistische Arbeitsteilung', *Die Presse der Sowjetunion*, 24/1960, pp. 523–5, from *Voprosi Ekonomiki* 1/1960) these recommendations were primarily for planned investment and not for changes in current production.

[2] Heinz Köhler, *East Germany's Economic Integration into the Communist Bloc* (unpublished PhD dissertation for University of Michigan, 1961) p. 130.

[3] One interviewee in East Berlin declared in 1959 that the Council is proceeding along the following lines: 'We are first working on the specialization in those branches of the machine building industry which are the most important means for the carrying out of the most important tasks of the long-range plans of the various Socialist nations. At the present time work is in progress to prepare for an extensive specialization in the area of production of chemical equipment and apparatus, as well as equipment for the metallurgy, mining, and refining industries.'

[4] Data from Walter Mostertz, 'Specialisierung und Kooperation im Maschinenbau zwischen den sozialistischen Ländern, '*Wirtschaftswissenschaft* IV, 5/1958. pp. 659–71 and ECE, Foreign Trade and Economic Developments in Eastern Europe and the Soviet Union', *Economic Bulletin for Europe* XI, 1/1959. The sources of the data do not specify if the USSR is included; I do not believe that it is, but I can not be sure.

TABLE 1–4

TYPES OF MACHINES PRODUCED IN CMEA COUNTRIES BEFORE AND AFTER STANDARDIZATION AND SPECIALIZATION AGREEMENTS

		Number of Machine Types Produced	
Products	*Countries*	*Before Agreements*	*After Agreements*
Diesel locomotives	All	42	27
Metal chipping machines	Bulgaria	25	13
	DDR	64	56
	Hungary	20	16
	Poland	40	35
	Rumania	14	6
	(Total)	(163)	(126)
Steam engines and turbines	All	149	80
Metal cutting machine tools	All	1,893	1,333
Non-metal cutting machine tools	All	1,454	1,007

up production of 291 types of machine tools, 89 types of wood-working machines, all heavy trucks and buses, and oil drilling equipment. It has initiated some new production, including 125 types of machine tools (mostly high-speed automatic equipment), 27 wood-working machines, rolling mill equipment, and ocean-going ships.[1] Various articles I have read in the DDR economic press indicate that the planners will be changing their emphasis from the mining, metallurgical, and heavy machinery industries and turning towards the precision machinery, electrotechnical, and chemical industries. Similarly, production patterns are supposed to be changing in the other CMEA countries. Hungary gave up the production of railroad freight and passenger cars; Bulgaria, large diesel locomotives and trucks. Each country has also started production of new products.

I have gained the impression from the Bloc literature and from an examination of the specialization agreements that the specialization of production is moving along several main lines. Those countries which use certain machines the most, will specialize in their production. Rumania will manufacture a great deal of oil drilling equipment; DDR, lignite mining machines; Hungary, wheat combines. Moreover, those countries with special labour skills are specializing in those manufactured goods where such skills are necessary for their production and are leaving the more simple types of manufacturing to the other nations. CSSR and DDR, the two East Central European nations with the most skilled labour forces, will especially increase their production of precision machines.

Although this sounds very impressive and although long lists of

[1] Köhler, *op. cit.*, p. 144.

production specialization agreements between the CMEA nations have been made,[1] it is difficult to draw firm conclusions from this discussion. First of all, it is not possible to find out how many of these specialization agreements were merely measures to stabilize existing trade patterns. Second, although the radical nature of these specialization agreements is often emphasized in the Bloc economic press, a close examination of some of these agreements reveals that in many cases the specialization concerned only particular product models.

For instance, in the transportation equipment field where specialization agreements were made as early as 1955, all CMEA nations except Bulgaria and Albania are to produce motor trucks; six nations, tractors; five nations, steam locomotives, electric locomotives and ships; four countries, railway freight cars, etc. Finally, no one knows how many of the specialization agreements have been actually carried out. The individual nations can ignore the agreements completely (see Chapter VII for some examples) or else only adjust their trade patterns without changing their investment and production plan. For instance, in June 1960, Gomulka reported to the Polish Workers' Party that although economic agreements between the CMEA nations covered foreign trade and exchange of technological information, it was still 'almost non-existent' so far as investment co-ordination was concerned. 'So far, everyone looks after his interest in this field . . . and loses by it,' he declared.[2]

Several isolated statistics show that the specialization of production in the Bloc has a long way to go in some areas. For instance, an important Soviet economist, N. Silujanow, complained that specialization in machine building in the Bloc was very unsatisfactory and gave several examples. Of the 70,000 metal cutting machine tools which were produced in the CMEA nations in 1957, only 3,412 (about 5 per cent) were traded; of 24,000 forge and pressing machines, only 622 (3 per cent) were traded; of 37,000 tractors, only 5,380 (15 per cent) were traded.[3] Another Soviet expert noted that only 3·5 per cent of the 200,000 metal-working machines produced in the Bloc entered into foreign trade.[4]

Unfortunately, no other recent all-Bloc trade/production ratios are available to make similar comparisons for other goods. However, with trade/production ratios of a single nation we can gain some in-

[1] For such a list see Appendix E: 'CMEA Specialization Agreements'.

[2] W. Gomulka, quoted by 'Comecon Looks Ahead', *Economist* CXCVI, August 6, 1960.

[3] N. Siluyanov, 'Eine neue Etappe in der Entwicklung der internationalen sozialistischen Arbeitsteilung', *Der Aussenhandel* IX, 8/1959, pp. 8–11.

[4] Bogomolov, cited by A. Zauberman, 'Economic Integration: Problem and Aspects', *Problems of Communism* VIII, 4/1959, pp. 23–9.

sight into the industrial sectors in which the specialization agreements have taken place.

If we were to assume that every change of the trade/production ratios for individual commodities of a single Bloc nation was due to intra-Bloc production specialization agreements, then a measurement of the *relative* movement toward a specialization of production in the various economic areas could be obtained. Since change in export and import ratios may have been due to other causes as well, the results of such an experiment should be viewed with some caution.

I have calculated export and import ratios in physical terms for 166-8 DDR exports and imports from 1955 to 1961. The average change in these ratios was about zero since the positive and negative changes cancelled each other out. By computing a standard deviation of change of these ratios for various industrial sectors, the problem of sign can be avoided and some idea of the relative change in trade ratios may be obtained. That is, the greater the standard deviation of change of export and import ratios for a given industrial sector from 1955 to 1958, then (according to the hypothesis concerning the cause of these changes), the greater the specialization of production in this industrial sector.

TABLE 1–5

CHANGES IN EXPORT AND IMPORT RATIOS OF THE DDR[1]

A = Average Change of Ratios

S = Standard Deviation of Change of Ratios

	1955–58			1958–61		
Industrial Sector	*No. of goods*	*A* %	*S* %	*No. of goods*	*A* %	*S* %
Raw materials	62	0·7	7·7	64	1·9	7·7
Industrial equipment	56	1·3	16·4	56	6·4	18·9
Consumer goods	48	1·9	8·6	48	2·5	8·7
All	166	1·3	11·6	168	3·6	12·8

A shift in trade ratios has occurred primarily in the industrial equipment industry in both time periods. Since a number of specialization agreements in these areas have been publicized, it is quite likely that the changes in the trade ratios reflected this phenomenon.

[1] Export ratios (exports of article A/total home production of article A) and import ratios (imports of article B/total home production + imports of article B) were computed for 168 items in physical terms from the trade and production data of the DDR for 1955 to 1958. If any article was both exported and imported, then the net export or net import was taken. The differences in these ratios for the various goods in the two years were taken. An unweighted standard deviation of these differences was computed since value or price data, with which weights could have been obtained, were not available. A more detailed picture may be

It seems quite reasonable that more specialization agreements occurred in the machine manufacturing sector rather than light industry, since the benefits of large scale production are greater in the former. However, the raw material industries, where specialization of production is probably most necessary, showed the least change in trade ratios.

C. The Agricultural Sector

According to a Yugoslav source: 'The specialization of production . . . in agriculture has been on the agenda of the CMEA several times. . . . Yet it is a fact that this question proves more intractable in agriculture than it does in industry.'[1] At the Conference of Party Secretaries in Feb, 1960, it was decided that for the present time each country should try to increase agricultural production of all major products in order to alleviate the all-Bloc shortages of agricultural goods.

Following this decision the CSSR has been planning to lower their import ratio of grains and meats, and the DDR is trying to meet all domestic demands for eggs, poultry, meat, milk, and butter.

Such moves notwithstanding, one can also discern several steps toward specialization of production of special goods which are being taken concurrently. The Soviet Union, which has the greatest crop land per capita of any Bloc nation is placing great emphasis on land-intensive products (such as grains and cotton) and is now exporting wheat to such a traditional grain exporter as Bulgaria. In the Bloc economic press one finds crude types of factor proportion arguments to support this development.

---

gained from the standard deviation of change in the various specific industrial groups from 1955 to 1958.

Industry Classification	*Standard Deviation of Change of Trade Ratios* %	*Number of Commodities in Sample*
General machine building industry	23	14
Vehicle manufacturing industry	20	7
Precision goods industry	18	9
Nourishment goods industry	18	14
Heavy machine building industry	16	27
Textile manufacturing industry	13	19
Wood goods industry	12	4
Metallurgy industry	12	14
Building materials industry	10	5
Metal goods and fabricating industry	10	3
Cellulose and paper industry	6	7
Chemical industry	6	32
Leather industry	5	3
Electrotechnical industry	4	5
Mining industry	3	6
Energy production industry	1	2

All data from *Statistisches Jahrbuch der DDR*, 1958.

[1] Cited by 'The Work of Comecon', *East Europe* IX, 4/1960, pp. 3–9.

The Danubian countries, with high density rural populations, are beginning to emphasize production of more labour intensive crops. The country with the most concealed unemployment, Bulgaria (which once exported workers to the USSR and the CSSR[1]) has greatly stepped up production of the labour intensive technical crops, tobacco, fruits, and vegetables.[2] In the future it is planned that Bulgaria will provide 55 per cent of Bloc exports of fresh fruits and 82 per cent of fresh vegetables. Hungary and Rumania have also been increasing their exports of fruits and vegetables and plan to continue this export drive.

Finally, various Bloc nations are specializing in production of agricultural goods for which climatic and soil conditions are especially favourable. Albania and Bulgaria are stepping up exports of early potatoes; Hungary is attempting to increase exports of rice.

Viewing the entire agricultural sector, however, two important Bloc economists recently concluded that it is 'too early for specialization at the present time.'[3]

D. Aggregative Measures of Production Specialization

It is possible to measure production specialization changes in many ways. However, examination of changes in distribution of labour and capital (or investment) or changes in the aggregate production pattern for each country is difficult because of lack of adequate data and non-comparability of statistics.[4] Other alternatives are fortunately available.

If the economic planners of a nation really wanted to increase the utilization of the trade potential, they could try to force foreign

[1] 'Manpower and Employment in Eastern Europe and the Soviet Union', *Economic Survey of Europe, 1957*, pp. VII–47.

[2] For a detailed analysis of the way Bulgaria has tried to wipe out disguised unemployment by a shift toward labour intensive agricultural products for exports, see Charles A. Cooper, *Agriculture, Labor Surplus and Foreign Trade in Bulgaria, 1925–60* (unpublished PhD Dissertation, Massachusetts Institute of Technology, September, 1960). Cooper interprets the rise in Bulgarian exports of fruits and vegetables to the other Bloc nations from 1955 to 1958 to be due to CMEA specialization agreements. I am inclined to believe that this increase of exports was due to an income effect in the other Bloc nations, i.e. as their national incomes increased, planners began to feel that they could afford to import these more expensive agricultural goods. Consumer demands unleashed by the New Course must have been a contributing factor.

[3] O. Bogomolow and J. Pekschew, *Sozialistische Planwirtschaft* 8 & 9/1962, pp. 1–6.

[4] Köhler, *op. cit.* (Chapter V 'A Survey of Criteria for the Measurement of East German Economic Integration into the Bloc) attempts such an analysis. He notes little change in the distribution of the labour supply between 1955 and 1959; finds the data on distribution of investment funds too poor for an interpretation; and decides that the changes in the production pattern are too inconclusive for any sure generalizations.

trade to grow as fast or faster than industrial production. In other words, comparison of the rate of growth of trade and industrial production is a rough measure of the changing specialization of production. Because of the nature of the data, such comparisons must be made cautiously.

Except for Bulgaria and perhaps the DDR, trade per capita from 1955 to 1958 did not increase significantly faster than industrial

TABLE 1–6

AVERAGE YEARLY INCREASES IN FOREIGN TRADE AND INDUSTRIAL PRODUCTION[1]

	1950–5		*1955–8*		*1958–65 (plan)*	
	Trade turnover per capita	*Industrial production per capita*	*Trade turnover per capita*	*Industrial production per capita*	*Trade turnover*	*Industrial production*
Estimate A: Current price trade data; constant price Bloc production estimates						
Country	%	%	%	%	%	%
Bulgaria	9·0	12·8	18·9	13·8	12·7[b]	9·9[b]
CSSR	8·4	10·0	7·3	9·2	8·1[c]	12·0[c]
DDR	24·6	14·2	14·6	9·6	8·3	9·4
Hungary	11·0	10·2	4·5	5·5	6·5	7·8
Poland	5·3	14·0	5·5	7·7	7·0[bc]	12·1[bc]
Rumania	10·1	13·9	5·9	8·0	12·3[b]	13·2[b]
Average	11·3	—	8·5	—	8·6[d]	—
USSR	13·0	11·2	7·9	7·8	10·5[e]	8·6[e]
Estimate B: Constant price trade data; Western estimates of Bloc production.						
Country	%	%	%	%	%	%
Bulgaria	7·6	—	19·6	—	—	—
CSSR	5·4	5·4	8·1	8·1	—	—
DDR	21·5	11·7	14·2	6·6	—	—
Hungary	9·2	—	5·0	—	—	—
Poland	3·6	5·7[a]	5·9	—	—	—
Rumania	8·2	—	6·8	—	—	—
Average	—	—	—	—	—	—
USSR	11·1	7·7	8·5	6·8	—	—

[a]=1949–55.
[b]=1960–5.
[c]=revised plan figures.
[d]=increase in intra-Bloc trade; revised upward from 17·9 per cent announced in 1959.
[e]=approximate.

[1] Foreign trade data are trade turnover (exports+imports). Constant price trade data derived from current price trade data, divided by unit trade price indices for developed and underdeveloped nations. DDR data has a special upward bias because reparations were not included in the export statistics at all and uranium exports were only included in 1957 and the following years. With these items included, Köhler (*op. cit.*, p. 316) estimates that DDR trade per capita rose at an average annual rate of 9·6 per cent from 1950–8. Treatment of reparations in Hungarian, Rumanian, and Bulgarian trade data is not known.

Production indices from Bloc nations are 'gross-gross' indices for all countries

production per capita. Even more strikingly, all nations except Bulgaria and the USSR foresee a more rapid rise in industrial production than trade in the current plan period. Both Poland and the CSSR, which raised the foreign trade goals of their preliminary long-range plans, raised the industrial production goals even more.[1]

The data on changes in trade and production from 1955 to 1965 are not inconsistent with the development of a somewhat more optimal intra-Bloc trade pattern and the elimination of the trade anomalies which developed during the Stalin era. It is also not inconsistent with a slight increase in the degree of utilization of the trade potential.[2] Nevertheless, these data also indicate that the specialization of production has not yet been, and will not in the near future be, radical enough to increase greatly the realization of the growing trade potential. No less an authority than N. S. Khrushchev has observed that when the production co-ordination work begins in earnest, the growth of foreign trade will outstrip the growth of output.[3]

Another aggregative indicator of the changes in production specialization is the percentage of 'single suppliers' in intra-Bloc trade. If production specialization has increased during the past years, then the percentage of imports of each country which is supplied by a single supplier in the Bloc should increase. For such a phenomenon to be accurately measured, we must have foreign trade statistics with a very fine division of products. Otherwise the specialization might occur with the products lumped together under one category, and the aggregate data would miss such details. The only country for

---

except Hungary.

Sources: for trade data, see Table 1–1. Bloc production indices from the various national statistical year-books. Plan data from *Economic Survey of Europe for 1959; Economic Survey of Europe for 1960;* and *Vneshna trgovya* VI, 6/1958. Western estimates of Bloc production from G. J. Staller, *American Economic Review* LII, No. 3, June, 1962, p. 392 (Czech data); Wolfgang Stolper and Karl Roskamp. *The Structure of the East German Economy* (Cambridge: Harvard U. Press, 1960); M. Ernst, *The Measurement of Polish Industrial Growth:* 1937, 1946–55, cited by Staller, *op. cit.:* N. M. Kaplan and R. H. Moorsteen. *American Economic Review* L, No. 2, June, 1960 pp. 295–318 (USSR data).

[1] In the preliminary plan, Poland planned an average annual rise of 5·7 per cent in foreign trade and 8·3 per cent in industrial production from 1958 to 1965; the CSSR planned an average annual rise of 7·9 per cent in foreign trade and 9·1 per cent in industrial production in the same period.

[2] According to formulae developed by H. Chenery (see my Statistical Appendix B, Section 1), trade potential increases with the increase of industrial production per capita and decreases with the growth of population. If we assume that population increases at 1 per cent a year, and industrial production per capita, 10 per cent, then 'trade potential' should increase about 6·8 per cent a year.

[3] N. S. Khrushchev, 'Vital Questions of the Development of the World Socialist System,' *Kommunist* Aug./1962, pp. 3–26, reprinted in *Current Digest of Soviet Press* XIV, 35 & 36/1962.

which we have data for an extended period is the USSR, which classifies its imports into some 325 categories. This does not seem fine enough for a completely unambiguous picture; nevertheless, such calculations should give us some evidence of broad trends in the 'single supplier phenomenon'. The results are quite surprising.

TABLE 1–7

'SINGLE SUPPLIER PHENOMENON' IN USSR IMPORTS FROM OTHER CMEA NATIONS [1]

	1955	*1956*	*1957*	*1958*
	%	%	%	%
Machines	—	25	24	22
Raw materials and fuels	—	45	43	37
Food and live animals	—	17	40	32
Consumer goods	—	5	7	4
Total	33	30	29	24

The relative amount of singly supplied imports decreased every year. Moreover, the relative amount of singly supplied imports decreased in each category except food and live animals, which counts for little in the total USSR import picture. Thus, examination of the single supplier phenomena suggests a decreasing specialization of production, occurring most markedly in raw materials and fuels and least markedly in production of machines. I do not believe that the degree of specialization of production did actually decrease from 1955 to 1958, but I have included these data to cast further doubt on the exaggerated claims of production specialization in the Bloc Press, covering the period up to 1958.

Analysing the degree of trade and production specialization from aggregate data on trade composition presents some difficulties. Several Bloc economists have claimed that the increasing proportion of machinery exports of all Bloc nations proves that production specialization in this sector is moving rapidly ahead. At the same time, however, the proportion of machinery imports has been decreasing in many of the same countries, which casts some doubt on such a one-sided analysis.[2] However, machinery imports of two of the

[1] See Statistical Appendix B, Section 3, for details of calculation.

[2] Some idea of this development may be gained from the following data. (Source: Gertrud Gräbig, *Internationale Arbeitsteilung und Aussenhandel im sozialistischen Weltsystem;* East Berlin: Verlag Die Wirtschaft, 1960; p. 64).

Percentage of Total Trade in Machine Goods and Machine Parts

	Export		*Import*	
	1950	1957	1950	1957
Albania	—	—	30·9	39·3
Bulgaria	—	7·5	36·5	29·7
CSSR	26·4	40·9	11·2	18·8
DDR	28·0	43·8	5·5	7·1
Hungary	22·5	38·5	20·8	12·7
Poland	7·8	20·0	32·4	23·8
Rumania	4·2	10·5	37·1	15·7
USSR	35·3	25·9	21·5	27·5

TABLE 1–8

STRUCTURE OF FOREIGN TRADE IN FOUR BLOC NATIONS[1]

A=machines, transportation vehicles, industrial equipment
B=raw materials, mining and timber products
C=foodstuffs and animals
D=consumer goods

Country	*Exports*				*Imports*			
	A %	B %	C %	D %	A %	B %	C %	D %
DDR								
1954								
CMEA Nations	—	—	—	—	—	—	—	—
Other	—	—	—	—	—	—	—	—
Total	57	30	3	10	3	57	34	6
1958								
CMEA Nations	52	35	1	12	10	62	23	6
Other	53	18	9	20	8	51	30	11
Total	52	29	4	15	9	58	25	8
1960 (Plan)								
CMEA Nations	64	21	1	15	11	60	24	5
Other	—	—	—	—	—	—	—	—
Total	—	—	—	—	—	—	—	—
1965 (Plan)								
CMEA Nations	66	20	0	14	12	71	14	4
Other	34	34	8	23	19	41	25	16
Total	55	25	3	17	14	60	18	8
CSSR								
1955	44	39	6	11	13	54	29	4
1958	50	30	3	17	22	49	25	4
1965 (Plan)	63	20	2	15	33	50	16	1
Hungary								
1955	29	24	31	16	11	68	18	3
1958	38	22	22	18	19	71	5	5
1965 (Plan)	46	21	20	14	30	64	1	5
Poland								
1955	14	63	16	7	39	45	12	4
1960 (Plan)	30	47	18	5	26	54	14	6
1965 (Plan)	39	36	18	5	29	53	13	5
1970 (Plan)	43	36	16	4	27	53	15	5
1975 (Plan)	47	32	17	4	24	54	17	5

[1] Sources: Structure of DDR trade with CMEA countries from Mirga Getthandt (*Die Widerspiegelung der internationalen Arbeitsteilung in der Entwicklung der Warenstruktur in Aussenhandel der DDR mit den sozialistischen Ländern;* Diplomarbeit, Hochschule für Ökonomie, 1960). Structure of total DDR trade from Sieglinde Fulde (*Probleme und Aufgaben zur volkswirtschaftlich richtigen Gestaltung der Warenstruktur des Aussenhandels der DDR im Siebenjahrplan* (Diplomarbeit, Hochschule für Ökonomie, 1960). 1955 data for the CSSR and Hungary from *Economic Survey of Europe for 1957*, pp. A–54 to A-56; 1958 and 1965 plan data for the CSSR and Hungary from *Economic Survey of Europe for 1959*, p. III–46. Polish data from M. Deniszcuk, 'Handel zagraniczny a perspektywy rozwoju gospodarczego Polski', *Handel zagraniczny*, 12/1959, pp. 514–17. Data may not add up to 100 per cent because of rounding. 1965 Polish export data adds up only to 98 per cent in the Polish text.

leading Bloc exporters have increased in the past years, which suggests that some specialization is occurring. More specifically, between 1955 and 1958, DDR machinery imports jumped from 5 per cent to 12 per cent of total imports; between 1958 and 1960, CSSR machinery imports increased slightly from 18·7 per cent to 21·6 per cent.[1]

A more valid conclusion about the effects of the production specialization may be made from aggregate data of the trade structure over a long time interval. Unfortunately, data are available for only four countries, which are shown in the table on page 45.

The changes in the trade patterns of the four nations are somewhat ambiguous but several features are noteworthy. The planned increase in the proportionate share of industrial equipment in Czech and Hungarian imports and exports suggests not only increased growth in this sector but also increased production specialization. However, no noticeable increase in the share of industrial equipment imports is foreseen for the DDR and Poland, nations which have the respective economic level of the CSSR and Hungary. Moreover, it seems natural to assume that the share of agricultural imports of the DDR and CSSR would increase since agricultural conditions are relatively less favourable here than in other Bloc nations. This is, however, not the case and, indeed, such imports are planned to fall in the CSSR.

It is remarkable that the overall trade pattern of the DDR is planned to remain about the same although considerable change is foreseen in the composition of trade with the Bloc. This suggests that for the DDR, at least, the Bloc 'specialization' agreements affect the geographical pattern of trade a great deal more than the underlying structure of trade and production.

4. SUMMARY AND CONCLUSIONS

The data of the trade per capita of the CMEA nations during the last thirty years and comparison of the trade potential of these nations with the actual conducted trade show that all CMEA nations have had an autarkic pattern of economic growth since the Second World War. Although foreign trade is not so important for the USSR because of the large domestic market and availability of most minerals, this autarkic policy in the East Central European nations has had three adverse consequences: many nations invested in production sectors which were extremely uneconomic; a great deal of parallel investment occurred and each country experienced high costs as well as

[1] Otto Hofmann, 'Die Waren- und regionale Struktur des Aussenhandels der DDR', *Der Aussenhandel* IX, 4 and 5/1959, pp. 16–18; and *World Economic Survey for 1960*, p. 230.

short production runs; great all-Bloc shortages of certain major products, especially minerals and raw materials, occurred.

Many difficulties faced the Bloc policy makers in trying to break down this autarky of each nation. One problem was the cold economic fact of the specificity of capital. Each nation had sunk vast amounts of investment funds into iron-steel combines, penicillin factories, and so forth; and, in the short run, it is very hard to convert the production in these factories to some other good. Another difficulty was the lack of any rigorous theory explaining the benefits of foreign trade and suggesting economic criteria for specialization. Other problems, especially in the process of planning, are discussed in later chapters.

Several trends in Bloc production specialization after 1955 are readily observable. Bloc planners seem to be paying much greater attention to the natural resources and factor endowments of the individual nations. That is to say, mineral extraction and refining are being especially encouraged in the countries with the richest deposits and production of labour intensive agricultural products is being greatly increased in the countries with the relatively largest rural labour reserves. In cases where such considerations are not important, the planners are using other criteria. For instance, in machinery production, the countries which use certain machines the most have begun to specialize in their production.

Nevertheless, some evidence suggests that this specialization of production did not proceed very far by the end of the 1950s. First of all, many anomalies in the Bloc trade structure still existed. Furthermore, comparisons of the growth of Bloc trade and production show that the degree of utilization of the trade potential by most of the individual nations was about the same in this period. Finally, analyses of the single supplier phenomenon and of certain all-Bloc production/trade ratios confirm this impression. Even taking the problems of the specificity of capital into account, it seems to me that many opportunities for higher economic growth by means of a different composition and greater volume of trade were missed at this time.

Although many changes in intra-Bloc foreign trade will occur in the near future, it does not appear that the degree of autarky will be very much lower because the planned growth of foreign trade is, in most cases, lower than planned growth of production. However, given the limited volume of trade, the intra-Bloc trade structure may well become more rational if some of the current specialization agreements are carried out. Nevertheless, certain anomalies in the planned structure of trade of four Bloc nations for 1965 may be seen. Furthermore, for at least one Bloc country, the production specialization agreements will affect the geographical pattern of trade a great deal more than the underlying structure of trade and production.

From all this scattered evidence, two main conclusions may be drawn. Most of the Bloc policy makers have not yet made a significant retreat from the old policies of autarky. And most of the far-reaching plans for specialization of Bloc production are still in the discussion rather than operational stage and will remain so for some time.

CHAPTER II

PROBLEMS OF PLANNING AND ORGANIZATION

Production and trade decisions in Soviet-type economies are co-ordinated bureaucratically rather than by some type of market mechanism. As a result, some institutional aspects of the planning apparatus and some organizational features of foreign trade operations have a very important influence in the volume and structure of trade which is actually carried out. Rather than survey the foreign trade systems of each communist nation, I use the DDR (East Germany) as a case study to analyse this inter-relation between trade institutions and actual trade.

In the early 1950s the greatest problems of foreign trade in the Bloc were unrealistic trade goals, neglect of profitability considerations in trade, and lack of flexibility in foreign trade operations. They may be traced, I believe, to the over-centralization of decision-making, a complete separation of trade and production institutions, a planning system which concentrated plan-making into one short period each year, and the clogging of intra-Bloc communication channels.

1. PLANS AND PERFORMANCE

All long-range plans of the DDR have foreseen rapid increases in foreign trade, industrial production and national income. The actual growth rates are impressive, even if Western estimates are used.

On the basis of the DDR trade data (current price data which contains an upward bias because of the rise in world market prices) the long-range plan goals in foreign trade seem to have been met, by and large, in both plan periods. However, according to Köhler estimates of the trade volume (constant price indices) the fulfilment of the foreign trade part of the first Five-Year Plan was 77 per cent; and of the second Five-Year Plan, 103 per cent.

Judging the fulfilment of the long-term plan goals for industrial production and national income presents similar difficulties. According to their own data, plan goals were met. According to Western estimates, however, actual performance fell slightly behind plan goals in every long-term plan.

D

TABLE 2–1

AVERAGE ANNUAL GROWTH OF DDR TRADE AND PRODUCTION IN THE LONG-RANGE PLAN PERIODS[1]

Aggregate	Period	*Plans*		*Performance*	
		Directives	*Law*	*DDR Data*	*Western Ests.*
Foreign	First FYP	—	23·7	22·9	18·2
Trade	Second FYP	11·2	10·3	13·4	10·6
Turnover	Seven YP	—	8·1	—	—
Industrial	First FYP	13·7	14·0	14·8	11·5
Production	Second FYP	9·2	6·7	9·5	5·4
	Seven YP	—	9·4	—	—
National	First FYP	9·9	9·9	10·2	8·7
Income	Second FYP	7·7	—	7·4	4·7
	Seven YP	—	6·8	—	—

Because the long-term plans in Soviet-type economies have not been the operational plans, examination of the degree of fulfilment of the short-term goals is, I believe, more meaningful.

From the table opposite, we see that increases in actual foreign trade did not begin to approach the plan goals until recent years. Plan goals for industrial production seem, by and large, to have been much more closely met.

Another interesting phenomena of DDR foreign trade is that this trade is not spread evenly throughout the year as the planners had hoped. Like industrial production, the export plan seems to be fulfilled in spurts of 'storming', occurring in the last month of a quarter or in the last quarter of the year.[2] One DDR economist com-

[1] First Five-Year Plan period, 1951–5; Second Five-Year Plan period, 1956–8; Seven-Year Plan period, 1959–65. DDR foreign trade data, current prices; Western estimates of foreign trade, constant prices. DDR national income and industrial data, constant prices from 1950 to 1955, and current prices from 1955 to 1958; Western estimates, constant prices.

Sources: Plan data, see Statistical Appendix B. DDR trade and production data from various DDR *Statistische Jahrbuecher* (national product and industrial production measured 'netto' in constant prices, 'Messwerte' from 1951–5 and in current prices from 1956–8; foreign trade measured in Roubles). Western estimates of foreign trade from Köhler (*op. cit.*, p. 481) who used 1955 West German foreign trade prices as weights for the DDR trade quantity data. The data in the above table are arithmetic averages of the annual average rise in exports (19·9 per cent from 1950 to 1955; 11·1 per cent from 1955 to 1958) and imports (16·5 per cent and 10·1 per cent in these respective periods). Western estimates of industrial production and national income from Wolfgang Stolper and Karl Roskamp (*The Structure of the East German Economy;* Cambridge, Mass.: Harvard University Press, 1960; p. 418), with 1950 West German prices as weights in the indices and the Marxist definition of national income.

[2] For discussion of this phenomenon, see Erich Klinkmüller, *Die gegenwaertige Aussenhandelsverflechtung der sowjetischen Besatzungszone Deutschlands* (Berlin: Duncker & Humblot, 1960) Chapter III ('Industrielle Produktionsschwankungen und Aussenhandel').

TABLE 2–2

ANNUAL GROWTH OF INDUSTRIAL PRODUCTION AND FOREIGN TRADE[1]

	Foreign Trade Turnover			Industrial Production		
		Actual Performance			Actual Performance	
Year	Plan %	DDR Data %	Western Ests. %	Plan %	DDR Data %	Western Ests. %
1950	90	—	—	21	—	—
1951	60	50·8	17·5	17·9	22·6	16·9
1952	(40)	14·5	14·3	13·7	16·1	9·5
1953	33	29·0	23·8	12·8(14)	12·2	16·2
1954	(48)	21·8	36·8	12·4	10·2	8·8
1955	5	3·2	3·4	5·1	7·7	6·4
1956	15	11·8	10·5	—	6·3	5·0
1957	25	25·0	13·0	6·0	7·5	6·7
1958	6·7	4·2	8·5	6·8	11·1	5·6
1959	10·7	15·4	17·2	11·1	12·3	—
1960	10	7·1	—	10·0	8·2	—

plained, 'When we look at the export plan, we can see that the overwhelming part of the yearly deliveries (up to 40 per cent and more) lies in the fourth quarter.'[2] Other DDR economists have claimed that in past years 30 per cent of the export plan was often filled in December.[3] But such 'storming' seems to have diminished lately as the data presented below shows. Unfortunately, no complete statistics are available for the earlier years.

In order to explain this lack of plan fulfillment and the annual 'trade cycle' as well as the autarkic economic development pattern discussed in the previous chapter, it is necessary to look beneath the surface of events at the underlying organization structure and planning system.

[1] DDR trade data in current rouble prices; Western estimates of DDR trade in constant prices. DDR data on industrial production is 'Bruttoproduktion' in constant prices; Western estimates of net industrial production in constant prices. Data in parentheses for foreign trade plans 1952 and 1954 are calculations based on a goal stated in absolute terms and trade turnover of the previous year. Datum in parentheses for industrial plan 1953 is a change in the original plan.

Sources: Plan data, see Statistical Appendix B. DDR trade and production data from various DDR *Statistische Jahrbuecher*. Western estimates of foreign trade are arithmetic averages of the changes in exports and imports calculated by Köhler, *op. cit.*, p. 481. (See Statistical Appendix B for the separate data of exports and imports.) Western estimates of industrial production from Stolper and Roskamp, *op. cit.*

[2] G. Schade, *Die Planung des Aussenhandels der DDR*, Lehrbrief of the Hochschule für Ökonomie, 1957, p. 18.

[3] G. Kohlmey 'Entwicklungsprobleme unseres Aussenhandels' *Der Aussenhandel* VII, 1/1957, pp. 16–18, and G. Gräbig *Der Aussenhandel im sozialistischen Reproduktionsprozess*, Lehrbrief of Hochschule für Ökonomie, 1959, p. 47.

TABLE 2–3

PERCENTAGE OF YEARLY EXPORTS FALLING IN SPECIFIC TIME PERIODS[1]

Period	1957 %	1957 %	1958 %	1958 %	1959 %	1959 %
First Quarter	17·3		19·3		19·9	
(March)		(10·5)		(9·8)		(9·2)
Second Quarter	24·3		25·9		24·5	
(June)		(10·8)		(12·4)		(10·7)
Third Quarter	24·3		23·9		24·8	
(September)		(16·6)		(10·3)		(9·8)
Fourth Quarter	34·1		30·9		30·8	
(December)		(15·8)		(12·8)		(14·4)

2. DILEMMAS OF ORGANIZATION AND PLANNING

A. Organization of Foreign Trade

According to the *Textbook of Political Economy*, foreign trade is a 'commanding height' of the economy and an absolute condition for the existence and the development of the socialist economy.[2] Origin-

[1] Sieglinde Fulde, *Probleme und Aufgaben zur volkswirtschaftlich richtigen Gestaltung der Warenstruktur des Aussenhandels der DDR im Siebenjahrplan* (Diplomarbeit, Hochschule für Ökonomie, 1960), p. 27. For Bulgarian data, see Statistical Appendix B.

[2] Academy of Science of the USSR, *Politische Oekonomie Lehrbuch, op. cit.*, p. 584. A great deal of traditional Marxist theorizing about foreign trade has concerned the 'functions of the foreign trade monopoly'. Such analyses have been extremely vapid.

According to current doctrine, '. . . the foreign trade monopoly in the USSR has, at the present time, two main functions: First, it secures economic independence from the surrounding capitalistic world market and protects the economy and domestic market from the invasion of foreign capital and from the influence of the economic crises and the anarchy of the capitalist world market. Second, it aids the economic co-operation of the USSR with the People's Democracies.' (*Ibid.*, p. 584.)

Other sources mention other economic 'functions'. For instance, according to one DDR author (Karl Hercher, *Die Zahlungsverkehr der DDR mit dem Ausland;* East Berlin: Verlag Die Wirtschaft, 1958; p. 13), the foreign trade monopoly not only protects the domestic economy from paying too much for imported articles, but also too little.

Bloc economists have always considered the political functions of the foreign trade monopoly important. One DDR commentator noted: 'The problem of the foreign trade monopoly . . . can only be correctly judged when we see and understand it from a class viewpoint. . . . It is an important instrument of our worker and peasant state for the leading of the class struggle within the DDR and in the relations with the capitalist countries. The foreign trade relations are always class relations that must be so organized by us . . . to strengthen the postion of the working class in the DDR and, with our trade partners, to contribute to the weakening of the position of the imperialists. For this reason we must view the foreign trade monopoly not only from its economic side but above all, its political character. . . .' (Franz Heiduschat, 'Die Notwendigkeit, die Funktionen und

ally the concept 'foreign trade monopoly' was interpreted to mean that all foreign trade was conducted by State-owned enterprises. During the past twenty-five years, however, the term has been increasingly used to designate a specific set of institutions and methods for the carrying out of foreign trade, which I call 'the Stalinist model of the foreign trade monopoly'.

In the economic Press of the Bloc there has been a great deal of arid theorizing about what organizational alternatives are consistent with the Stalinist model of the foreign trade monopoly. Indeed, debate concerning foreign trade institutions preceded and greatly overshadowed the discussion concerning problems of foreign trade theory and the planning of an optimal volume and composition of foreign trade. The policy makers of the East Central European nations set up the foreign trade institutions with an organizational structure rather than some concept of planning in mind.

The Stalinist model of the foreign trade monopoly has several main features. Most important, all foreign trade is channelled through State-owned foreign trade enterprises (FTEs). Planning and control is centralized in the Ministry of Foreign Trade which acts as the link between the FTEs and the State Planning Commission, sets general trade policy, and is responsible for the carrying out of the main foreign trade plan.[1] The Ministry employs direct instruments of control rather than the indirect trade controls, such as tariffs, which are used in the West.[2] The FTEs carry out most of the commercial aspects of trade; each is assigned a certain group of goods and does not compete against the others. Foreign and domestic aspects of trade are quite separate so that the FTEs have very little contact with the production enterprises except in the case of very specialized traded goods such as precision machinery. Usually the FTEs buy domestic goods from and sell foreign goods to the Ministries and the domestic trading organizations. Each FTE has a part of the overall foreign trade plan to fulfil.

---

die Sicherung des staatlichen Aussenhandelmonopols in der DDR und seine Bedeutung für die Weiterentwicklung des Aussenhandels', *Der Aussenhandel* VII, 15/1957, pp. 543–7.)

[1] The Ministry of Finance is responsible for some parts of the foreign currency portion of the plan; nevertheless, the trade plan in physical terms is the most important part of the overall trade plan and serves as the basis for the various financial plans.

[2] 'Trade tariffs are increasingly losing their meaning in the socialist nations. Foreign trade is carried on in a planned manner by the foreign trade organs so that tariffs have completely lost their economic-protectionistic function as a regulator of foreign trade between the socialist nations. Tariffs do, however, have a certain role in trade policy for the trade between socialistic and capitalistic nations.' (J. Nykryn, K. Herman, K. Stěpán, F. Heiduschat, *Organization und Technik des Aussenhandels;* East Berlin: Verlag Die Wirtschaft, 1956; p. 186.)

After World War II, each East Central European nation began to copy the Stalinist model of the foreign trade monopoly.[1] First, the sphere of action for the private foreign trade companies was gradually narrowed through nationalization and expropriation of private industrial and trade enterprises conducting foreign trade, imposition of licence systems for trade, and general denial of permission to trade in certain goods or with certain countries. Then State foreign trade enterprises (FTEs) began to crowd the private foreign trade companies completely out.

Due to the special political problems of Germany, events happened somewhat differently in the Russian Zone of Occupation; nevertheless, the first State FTEs were set up in 1948. The nationalization of foreign trade, as well as industry, was somewhat slower in the DDR than in the other East Central European nations but by 1951 the State FTEs accounted for 92·2 per cent of all exports and 100 per cent of all imports. In 1952, the export percentage had risen to 98·2 per cent.[2]

In 1948 the Central Administration of Foreign Trade was established and became the Ministry of Foreign and Inter-German Trade the next year. It gradually shucked off all important commercial functions of trade and concentrated on setting general trade policy, overseeing the operations of the individual FTEs, and carrying the responsibility of trade planning and plan fulfilment.

After the initial concentration of foreign trade in the hands of the State, certain measures were taken to make the FTEs semi-autonomous economic decision-making units and to separate domestic and foreign aspects of trade.

More specifically, the FTEs were converted into 'organizations of public law' in 1951 and, in line with the general legal reorganization of industry the next year, were given full legal identity and permission to act as trustees of the people's property. They were required by law to operate under the 'principles of personal responsibility', 'economic accounting' (khozraschet) and under the new 'general contract system' (a set of legal standards for contracts). The DDR policy-makers, who had previously focused their attention almost exclusively on the relationships between the enterprises and ministries ('vertical relationships'), tried through these various

[1] For a brief description of this process in each CMEA country, see Appendix C of my dissertation, *op. cit.*, N. Spulber, *The Economics of Communist Eastern Europe* (Cambridge, Mass.: Wiley and the Technology Press, 1957) or B. S. Vaganov, *Voprosy organizacii vnesny torgovli stran narodnoj demokratii* (Moscow: Vnestorgizoat, 1954). For a detailed description of events in the DDR, see Appendix C.

[2] Rudolph Brauer, *Die Planung der wirtschaftlichen Tätigkeit der volkseigenen Handelsunternehmen Deutscher Innenund Aussenhandel in der DDR* (Unpublished doctoral dissertation, Hochschule für Ökonomie, 1956), p. 8.

measures to untangle and systematize the relationships between one enterprise and another ('horizontal relationships').[1]

Up to 1952 the FTEs continued to exercise important functions in the domestic economy, partially assembling the import demands of the production enterprises and trying to coax export production from home manufacturers. Between 1952 and 1954, these domestic functions were gradually dropped. Requests for imports were assembled and processed by the State Planning Commission and the domestic marketing and supply organizations, and each production ministry was made responsible for its part of the export plan. As a result, direct contact between the FTEs and production enterprises considerably decreased. Foreign and domestic aspects of trade were thus separated and, with this development, the Stalinist model of the foreign trade monopoly was copied in toto.[2]

Another important structural feature of the DDR foreign trade system at this time was the continual changing of the number of FTEs and a shifting of the products which each was allowed to buy and sell. This phenomenon is not intrinsic to the Stalinist model of the foreign trade monopoly but, nevertheless, occurred in most East Central European nations.[3]

B. The Process of Planning

The system of material balances has been, since the introduction of total economic planning, the primary co-ordinating device for the planning of production and the distribution of goods and materials in all CMEA nations. The material balances have also been the primary planning link between domestic production and foreign trade. These balances are for both raw materials and fabricated products, and equate the supply of each goods available (production+imports +decreases in inventories) with the demand for these goods (consumption of households+consumption by government organs+use in further processing steps+increases in inventories+exports). They are an administrative instrument to aid in the allocation of re-

[1] The terminology 'horizontal' and 'vertical' relationships of an enterprise is borrowed from Janos Kornai, *Over-centralization in Economic Administration* (trans. by John Knapp, Oxford: Oxford University Press, 1959), pp. 191ff.

[2] For a complete description of the various institutions which make up the DDR foreign trade monopoly, see Appendix C.

[3] There was also a constant shifting of ministries, trusts, and other economic units. The classical case of such 'external structural discontinuities' in the DDR is the Mercedes Typewriter factory in Weimar which was converted in the late 1940s to the production of thrashers. In the New Course (1953–5) the factory began to make consumer goods such as iceboxes and vacuum cleaners. After 1955–6 the factory was converted to produce precision measuring instruments.

sources and goods, a function which, in the classical economic models, is filled by the market mechanism. The Soviet-type economies, the use of price changes as a means for equating supply and demand for a good is secondary and has occurred primarily in the consumer goods sector. Before turning to a specific examination of the foreign trade planning, several characteristics of the material balance system must be noted.[1]

(a) The key parts of the *system* of material balances are the technical coefficients which link the production of an article or set of articles with the inputs from which they are made (or, conversely, the production of the various articles to their uses). With such coefficients, determining a consistent production pattern has many formal similarities with solving an input-output problem. Without such coefficients, the planners have little idea of the effect of increasing production of one commodity on domestic or import demands for other products. A completely balanced material balance system, however, in no way guarantees that the optimal composition and volume of trade has been planned. This problem is discussed in detail in Chapter IV.

(b) The system of material balances and technical coefficients may be calculated solely in physical terms without the explicit introduction of prices or values. If a material balance is made in physical terms and includes more than one particular type of goods, then some method must be found to reduce these goods to a common denominator. Expressing the material balances in physical terms, which is most commonly done, greatly increases the difficulties in taking profitability considerations into account in decision-making.

(c) A system of physical planning may be used with a preference system coming from 'above' (planners' preferences) or 'below' (consumers' preferences). That is, the guidelines for planning may come from the consumer or consumer wishes, as imputed by the planners from market surveys, studies of consumer demand elasticities, and so forth. Or the preference guidelines could come from political goals from above, like maximization of national defence potential, or rapid growth of a heavy industry base, or production of some particular product like oil or coal. Or the preference guidelines could come, also, from considerations of profitable foreign trade (traders'

[1] For thorough discussions of planning with material balances, see Hans Hirsch, *Mengenplanung und Preisplanung in der Sowjetunion* (Basel: Kylos Verlag, 1957); John M. Montias, 'Planning with Material Balances in Soviet-type Economies,' *American Economic Review* XLIX, 5/1959, pp. 963–85; Herbert S. Levine, 'The Centralized Planning of Supply in Soviet Industry', *Comparisons of the United States and Soviet Economies* (Washington, D.C., Papers Presented to the Joint Economic Committee, Congress of the United States, 1959), pp. 151–75; or Bela Balassa, *The Hungarian Experience in Economic Planning* (New Haven: Yale University Press, 1960).

preferences). A combination of planners', consumers', and traders' preferences could also be used.

(d) Any unit of the planning hierarchy such as the State Planning Commission, the Ministries, the trusts, or the supply organs may use material balances for planning.[1] The greater the number of material balances made by the State Planning Commission, the greater are the number of plan possibilities and, simultaneously, the more difficult it is to balance the system. During the first Five-Year Plan period, the DDR State Planning Commission balanced over 1,000 different material balances and made many extra decisions concerning foreign trade for articles, primarily machine goods, falling within the different material balances[2] (or 'plan positions' which are the collection of goods grouped together in one balance).

The process of planning in Soviet-type economies is primarily the process of drawing up a consistent set of material balances for all products. Planning in industry and foreign trade have many similarities; the differences, however, are extremely important and very worthy of analysis. However, almost no materials, theoretical or descriptive, concerning foreign trade planning were published up to 1956. One reason was the xenophobia on the part of the trade policymakers; another was the serious neglect of the question.[3]

The State Planning Commission used two bases for the drawing up of the preliminary yearly foreign trade plan: the trade contracts (both long and short term) which were already signed, and the import needs which were determined from the preliminary material balances. The overall volume of exports was calculated by the addition of financial factors such as transportation costs of trade,

[1] According to Heinz-Werner Hubner ('Aktuelle Probleme der Industrieproduktion', *Sozialistische Planwirtschaft* I, 1/1960, pp. 8–15) in 1959 the State Planning Commission balanced 579 'plan positions'; the Unions of People's Industry (VVBS), 370 more plan positions; the Central State Marketing and Procurement organs, a further 2,000. For a theoretical discussion on the effect of the number of balances on the accuracy and difficulty of planning, see Hirsch, *op. cit.*

[2] H. Schmidt, 'Staatliche Plankommission antwortet', *Der Aussenhandel* IX, 3/1959, p. 14.

[3] 'In the past, the working out of a method for (foreign trade) planning, was treated as a stepchild. Scarcely anyone occupied himself exclusively with the problem. When the time for the drawing up of the plan came due, then someone had to wrestle with the problem out of necessity. Thus basic questions were not, and could not be, thoroughly treated; indeed, usually only a few changes were made in the nomenclature system. . . . Furthermore, another difficulty . . . was that a different person worked on this problem every year.' ('Neue Wege in der Aussenhandelsplanung', *Der Aussenhandel* VI, 22/1956, p. 787.)

debt servicing charges, and other invisibles, to the total import sum.[1] Then the planners drew up a very aggregate preliminary export plan. Although this 'import first' method of planning was severely criticized from 1955 on, it was still used until the late 1950s when several modifications were made.

The final trade plan was drawn up in two steps. First, the State Planning Commission sent its preliminary plans as 'control figures' to the Production and Trade Ministries five or six months before the beginning of the plan year. The Ministries would fill in some of the details of the control figures and pass them on to the enterprises below them.

On the basis of the production goals in the control figures, the domestic firms determined their needs for raw materials, intermediate goods and imports, and sent these revised requirements upward where they would be audited and aggregated and sent upward again. The State Planning Commission would recalculate the material balances and try to bring them into balance again. If it were impossible to eliminate the surplus of demand over supply through domestic measures (either lowering demand or increasing production) then the gap would be closed through additional imports and the Ministry of Foreign Trade would be sent revised 'control figures'.

When the FTEs received their original control figures they would step up their negotiation of import and export contracts with foreign trade partners. On the basis of the control figures and an estimation of trade possibilities, they would begin to draw up a 'goods/country plan' in which the broad trade directions (blocs of countries) would be decided for each plan position for both imports and exports. From the revised control figures and from detailed political directives they would draw up a 'country/goods plan' in which the broad categories of goods to be traded with each nation were listed. This country/goods plan, neglected until 1955, was supposed to be the basis of the negotiations for the global trade contracts with other East Bloc nations.[2]

Then, the State Planning Commission would enter into extensive negotiations with the Ministry of Foreign Trade and the various Production Ministries to bring their plans into agreement. At the end of this process, the most important plan figures would be sub-

[1] Brauer, *op. cit.*, p. 41. In 1954 two Hungarian economists wrote of the Hungarian experience: 'In our country today . . . an import plan is worked out on the basis of the production plan, and an export plan on the basis of the import and production plans. While the production plan, it is true, is supposed to take into account the international division of labour, no calculations have been made for this purpose. Thus planning does not start from the wrong end in theory but only in practice.' (Quoted by *Economic Survey for Europe in 1954*, pp. 131–35.)

[2] Brauer, *op. cit.*, p. 155.

mitted for the approval of the Council of Ministers, who would approve them as the 'state plan', which has the force of law. Sometimes, but not always, the legislature would also approve the plans. Finally, each FTE and production enterprise would receive its enterprise plan in which detailed plan goals were listed.[1]

One DDR economist schematized the order in which the various plans are drawn up in the following way:

DIAGRAM 2–1

THE STEPS IN DRAWING UP THE FOREIGN TRADE PLAN

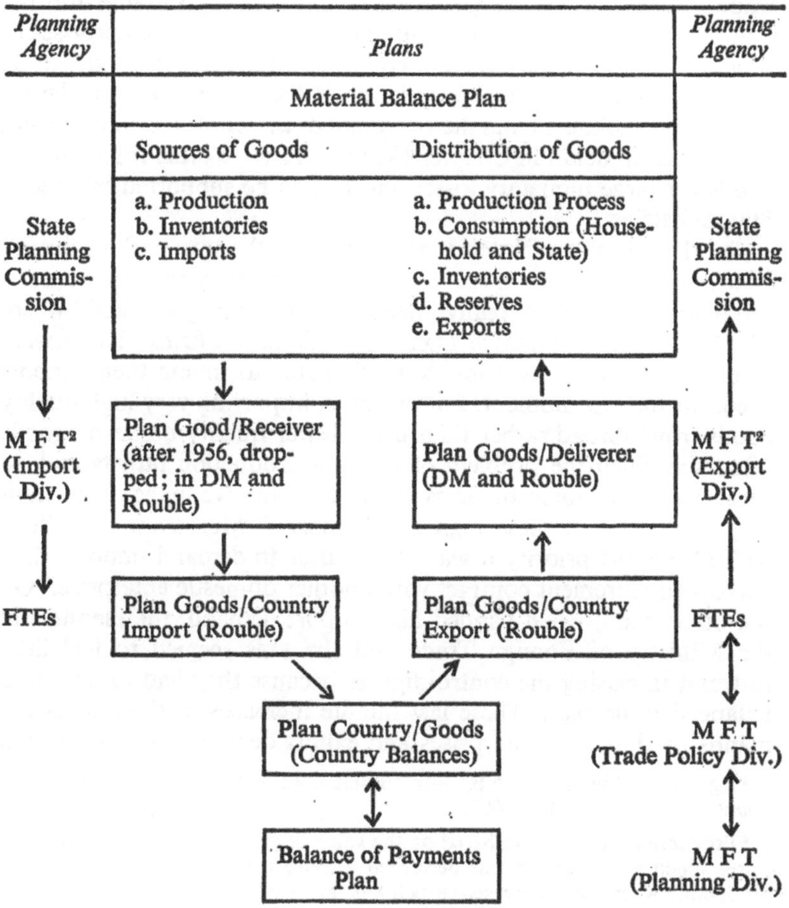

[1] For a description of the final foreign trade plans, see Appendix C.

[2] = Ministry of Foreign Trade. Diagram is from Brauer (*op. cit.*, p. 52) who pictures the planning process here as essentially linear. This is, of course, a great oversimplification and the diagram must be viewed, therefore, with caution.

This type of planning system had two main characteristics: First of all, planners tried to make all important planning decisions for the year in one short period of time. Second, there was an almost complete separation of production from trade, with communication going primarily from the State Planning Commission to the lower production units and back again, and thence to the FTEs and back again, and so forth. As a result of these features, special problems of co-ordinating and harmonizing decision-making between the production and foreign trade enterprises occurred:

(a) Many conflicts of interest arose between the production and trade enterprises. Some goods were extremely profitable for the FTEs to export, but were not profitable for the domestic enterprises to produce. For instance, there were cases recorded where domestic enterprises simply stopped production of these goods, even if the exports were profitable from the viewpoint of the whole economy.[1] And, as I discuss in detail in Chapter IV, the FTEs were often forced to sell goods for large monetary losses and had to be supported by special State subsidies.

Another conflict of interest arose because the FTEs had no overall view of the domestic market. On the one hand, they could not tell if a production enterprise really 'needed' a certain good and, if so, whether it was obtainable from other domestic firms. There were several major incentives for domestic firms to inflate their 'import needs' at the last moment. For example, importing very high quality goods from abroad rather than using lower quality domestic goods often simplified the problem of meeting production targets and, in some cases, the domestic firms would even receive higher bonuses if they could obtain these high cost imports![2] Moreover, for a firm with an import priority it was often easier to demand imports than make a procurement contract with another domestic enterprise.[3] On the other hand, when handed high import demand, the planners in the Ministry of Foreign Trade and the FTEs seemed to feel little restraint in raising the control figures because they had to present a balanced trade plan. These last minute increases in the import demands by domestic enterprises and export demands by FTEs were a

[1] e.g., see Wilhelm Rudolph, 'Rentabilität kontra Aussenhandel', *Der Aussenhandel* VIII, 19/1958, p. 657.

[2] Production premia were based on the value of gross production of an enterprise. When an enterprise was permitted to raise the official value of its gross production when costs increased (which was the case for enterprises working on a cost plus basis) then costs could be raised by buying high priced imports and higher bonuses could be obtained.

[3] J. Lyschik, 'Die Staatliche Plankommission hat jetzt das Wort,' *Der Aussenhandel* VIII, 23/1958, pp. 798–9. W. Schlitzer, 'Menge und Wert müssen eine Einheit bilden,' *Der Aussenhandel* X, 1/1960, pp. 30–1, has a discussion of this problem of inflated import needs.

major reason why the yearly foreign trade plans were seldom fulfilled.

(b) The FTEs were forced to make a great many decisions with very little information. They received control figures from the State Planning Commission covering about 80–90 per cent of imports and about 50 per cent of exports.[1] This presented several problems. First, the control figures covered groups of goods, rather than specific goods, except in special cases. Therefore, the FTEs did not have very many details for making trade contracts with foreign enterprises. Second, an additional uncertainty existed in exports, since the FTEs did not know what production capacity would be available. Therefore, the FTEs had either to obtain more specific information on domestic needs and production possibilities (which required a period of waiting), or to make trade contracts on the basis of past experience and present the domestic economy with a *fait accompli*.

(c) The domestic production enterprise often had little choice in signing a contract with an FTE for the delivery of some export item because of the importance of export production. Although production for export had the highest priority,[2] the domestic firms did not have complete assurance of obtaining the necessary raw and intermediate materials for this production.[3] Indeed, production of many export goods was dependent on imports, which caused additional headaches and some effort was made to reduce such exports (increasing the 'Heimatsintensität'). Furthermore, estimation of import needs of the production enterprises had to be made before the final production plan had been determined, which was another source of worry for the firms. In many cases, import needs were not sensitive to changes in the domestic production mix, but in other cases, the reverse was true.

(d) The final foreign trade plan was often late in being drawn up since it followed the production plan and the determination of import requirements. For instance, it was reported that the final trade plan of 1958 was not approved until March although the State Planning Commission had received the plan suggestions of the FTEs

[1] Horst Behr, 'Den Aussenhandel für 1959 rechtzeitig planen!' *Der Aussenhandel* VIII, 11/1958, pp. 386–8.

[2] The *Gesetzblatt der DDR*, 139/1953, p. 1,312, states: 'Export tasks are to be set equal in importance to the highest government tasks and are to be filled first, within the framework of the export quota of the yearly plans'. When a domestic firm did not fulfill its plan and could not fulfill all of its contracts, the FTE had one of the highest priorities on receiving what was produced. In many lawsuits in which FTEs and domestic firms with priority privileges were fighting to obtain some scarce product, the State Contract Board decided the issue. The Council of Ministers did not hesitate, in some cases, in overruling the State Contract Board when its decisions would have interfered with the export programme. ('Der Plan wird erfüllt,' *Der Aussenhandel* VII, 16 and 17/1957).

[3] This situation is well described by Theodor Hermes, *Der Aussenhandel in den Ostblockstaaten*, Hamburg: Cram-De Gruyter and Co., 1958, Chapter IV.

five months before. This happened because the production enterprises were so tardy in determining their import needs.[1] The lateness of the final approval of the trade plan led to great irregularities in production for exports and import deliveries and was one of the major factors causing the annual 'trade cycle'. As I discuss later in detail, the tardiness of the trade plan resulted in a late signing date for the annual global trade contracts with other Bloc nations. This lateness in both plans and global contracts contributed, in turn, to the difficulties in fulfilling the foreign trade plan goals.

(e) As a result of these factors, it was difficult for the State Planning Commission to bring every part of the plan into a consistent whole. Often the export plans of the production enterprises and the FTE plans were quite different, e.g., in 1958 these two plans for one branch of machine building varied by 23,500,000 Roubles (about $6,000,000)[2], Sometimes, the overall export and import plans did not balance, as in 1953.[3]

Some of the plan discrepancies could be corrected by the State Planning Commission, which would make the required changes in the FTE and enterprise plans.[4] However, since the enterprises had gone about making many contracts on the presupposition that their plans would be accepted, these changes caused a great many difficulties. Other discrepancies were not corrected until some crisis occurred during the plan year.

Looking over the planning process, one DDR economist remarked: 'Every year the fight between production and foreign trade enterprises concerning the product mix and quality of both imports and exports bursts into flame anew.'[5] Since a market mechanism was not used to resolve these conflicts and co-ordinate all decisions, a

[1] H. Schmidt, 'Staatliche Plankommission antwortet,' *Der Aussenhandel* IX, 3/1959, p. 14.

[2] 'Ökonomische Konferenz DIA Maschinen Export,' *Der Aussenhandel* VIII, 6/1958, pp. 200–1. One DDR economist (F. Fabian, 'Zuleinigen Fragen der neuen Planmethodik,' *Der Aussenhandel* VIII, 12/1958, pp. 435–7) declared, 'In the past it was often so, that the export plan was frequently changed from the production side. In the (final) yearly plan there was no guarantee that the production and foreign trade plans would be completely unified. . . .'

[3] Horst Joergens, 'Eine weitere kritische Stellungnahme zum Aussenhandelsplan 1953,' *Der Aussenhandel* III, 1953, p. 105. The State Planning Commission had to estimate a complete foreign trade plan in this case.

[4] According to a DDR author ('Zwischenbilanz der neuen Planmethodik,' *Der Aussenhandel* VII, 16 and 17/1957, pp. 619ff.): 'It often happened that after the Ministries had turned in their plan to the State Planning Commission, economic factors forced changes to be made, which made revision of the plan goals of the enterprises necessary. This, in turn, led to a situation where some enterprises received final plans which were greatly different from those which they had sent up to the Ministries.'

[5] 'Für 1958 gut vorarbeiten,' *Der Aussenhandel* VII, 15/1957, pp. 558–9.

special type of administrative bargaining process was substituted. The lower economic units (FTEs and production enterprises) would present their demands to their respective ministries who would either bargain the question between themselves or would present the case to higher authorities—State Planning Commission, the Council of Ministers, or the Politburo of the party—for judgment. Often the highest authorities had to use a heavy hand, as, for example, the time when the domestic production units demanded more imports of a particular item than total world production.[1] Disputes often became particularly heated when both of the lower economic units had gone ahead and signed contracts on the assumption that its foreign trade plan was correct.

C. Other Planning Problems

Two other major problems caused further difficulties in the planning system. First, the tools of operational planning such as data collecting and analysis were sadly neglected. Second, the fragmentation of planning in the FTEs brought about plan inconsistencies and confusion about plan goals.

Little attention was focused on the use of statistics in decision making. Before 1958 the science of statistics was sadly neglected and the few articles about statistics in the DDR journals usually concerned the 'essence of statistics' or very simple practical statistical exercises. There seemed to be a general disregard for the use of statistics, which was partly due to the low quality of the statistical materials[2] and partly to a basic apathy in their use.[3]

[1] Brauer, *op. cit.*, p. 54. I think he was exaggerating.

[2] According to Albrecht and Felber '(Über die Bedeutung der Statistik im Aussenhandel (II),' *Der Aussenhandel* VI, 9/1956, pp. 321–3): 'Many workers in foreign trade understand statistics only as the searching for or the collecting of numerical data. . . . The statistical analyses up to now have not rested on any really firm basis.' *Statistische Praxis*, the most important statistical journal in the DDR, has had several articles during the past twelve years on the computation of arithmetic averages. This reflects the training of personnel used in statistical work and, indirectly, the accuracy of early DDR statistics.

[3] According to Albrecht and Felber, *op. cit.*, 'The directors of the above mentioned FTEs unanimously declared that the Ministry does not react to the information contained in the analysis. . . . Hauptabteilung leader Steinbeck declared, "If I didn't have the (statistical) analyses of the FTEs, I would make my decisions exactly the same!"' According to F. Heiduschat ('Die Notwendigkeit . . .' *op. cit.*) 'The chief difficulty in the work of the Ministry . . . is that there exists no system of statistical evaluation of foreign trade activity which gives an adequate survey of the movements of goods and values in foreign trade. . . . The insufficiencies of our foreign trade statistics and reporting systems is also the main reason for the fact that the planning in the Ministry has not yet become the main instrument for the directing of trade in an economic manner, because administration is difficult when no one knows what's happening.'

One result was that only a few of the most simple statistical calculations were made. In 1957 a leading economist, Gunther Kohlmey, declared: 'One sees quite distinctly that not only the DM but also the Rouble data of our foreign trade has many deficiencies. We need volume statistics of our foreign trade . . . (as well as foreign trade) statistics on the basis of our domestic price level. Above all, we need . . . a development of the quantitative analysis of the structure and functions of our economy and the continual projections of the most important relations of the economic reproduction process. . . . That goes especially for foreign trade.'[1]

Another result was that the statistical reporting system was not unified because the different agencies drew up statistics using different definitions. As far as I was able to determine, the State Planning Commission worked out a balance of trade which included only 'normal' exports and imports. The Ministry of Finance drew up a plan which included trade on most but not all types of credit. The Ministry of Foreign Trade drew up another type of trade balance. It was difficult to compare plan goals with the actual trade which was carried out because of the different statistical definitions employed.

A great many of the statistics which were gathered were not available to the planners on lower levels because of a paranoic desire for secrecy. Until recently, little information concerning foreign trade was published. Moreover, according to a formerly high-ranking DDR economic official much important trade data was only available to the secretary of the Communist party and his top associates;[2] this was probably the case in other Bloc nations. Very few of my interviewees in East Berlin were able to answer questions on trade problems outside their very small area of specialization, although many expressed the desire to help me. The fact that only the leading functionaries have a broad view of the foreign trade situation has, of course, great disadvantages.

The other planning problem lay in the fragmentation of authority in the drawing up and fulfilling of the FTE plan. Although the FTES were responsible to the Ministry of Foreign Trade for their trade plan, they were responsible to the Ministry of Labour for the personnel part of their plan; to the Ministry of Finance for a part of their

[1] Gunther Kohlmey, 'Entwicklungsprobleme unseres Aussenhandels,' *Der Aussenhandel* VII, 2/1957, pp. 16–18.

[2] Fritz Schenk, *Magie der Planwirtschaft* (Köln: Kiepenheuer & Witsch, 1960), p. 88. My interrogator in prison in East Berlin told me that only ten men in the DDR know the balance of payments and that I had had an interview with the man who actually drew it up. The man in question worked ostensibly in the price research section of the foreign trade department of the State Planning Commission and had written several excellent articles in the foreign trade journals about planning, intra-Bloc prices, and so forth. When I spoke with him I did not know the true nature of his work.

financial plan, and so forth. This was not an essential structural element of the Stalinist model of the foreign trade monopoly but, nevertheless, occurred in several Bloc nations. In 1956, a DDR foreign trade expert wrote a searing critique of this divided responsibility in which he noted:

(a) 'With the present planning methods, there is no unified total plan of the FTE which brings together all facets of its economic activity.

(b) 'The drawing up of the various partial plans in the FTE is primarily the job of the specialists in each department, isolated from each other; the planning section plans . . . the (physical) movement of goods as well as the overall profit or loss (subsidy) of the enterprise; the finance department plans the domestic value side of trade (DM financing, administration costs, etc.); the foreign exchange comptroller plans the foreign exchange side; the personnel department plans the labour force, cultural activities, etc. . . . They all work on "their plans" quite isolated from each other. . . .

(c) 'This parallel and departmental planning of the single facets of the plan leads to discrepancies . . . between material and financial sides of planning, between the planning of the (physical) movement of goods and the plans of the domestic and foreign value of the movement of goods.

(d) 'As a result, everyone understands "plan fulfilment" to mean something different. . . .'[1]

3. LINKS BETWEEN FOREIGN AND DOMESTIC MARKETS

Foreign trade problems do not end with the development of an effective domestic planning system and organizational structure of foreign trade enterprises. Equally important is the development of a communication system between nations so that the most mutually profitable trade can be conducted. Such considerations are usually ignored in traditional economic analyses of foreign trade because, in the Western world, such problems lie in the realm of business administration of the trading company. In the East Bloc, however, the problem of communication has an important economic effect and, in this section, I briefly survey the most important communication channels for the exchanging of trade information.

A. Trade Negotiations and Contracts

Negotiations between the Bloc FTEs and foreign trade firms of the non-communist nations are not much different from trade talks between two capitalist trade enterprises, and have been widely dis-

[1] Brauer, *op. cit.*, p. 129.

cussed in the Western trade literature.[1] I concentrate below upon the relations between the foreign trade systems of the Bloc nations which are less well known in the West.

Up to 1955, the most important economic contact between the East Central European nations occurred in the bilateral negotiations for the long term (three to seven years) or short term (one year) global trade agreements.[2,3] The relationship of these contracts to the domestic planning system provides further insight into the influence of institutional factors on actual trade problems.

Because the major planning decisions are made in a short period of time, the planners face an important dilemma in the signing of global trade contracts. If a nation signs the global contracts before the material balances are balanced, it runs the risk of not filling some important import needs which are suddenly discovered, or of causing bottlenecks by contracting to export too much of a given good. If the domestic production plan is made first and the nation tries to fill the gaps in the plan (to equilibrate the unbalanced material balances) with imported materials and to pay for these with surplus goods, three dangers arise: it might get involved in some extremely unprofitable trade deals; it might not be able to obtain the needed imported goods after all, especially since some goods are in chronic scarcity on the 'Socialist world market'; it might be left with a surplus of unexportable and unusuable goods.

The global long-range bilateral trade contract was an important East Bloc innovation, dating from the USSR Poland Five-Year Trade Pact of December, 1947, and the USSR-CSSR Pact of January, 1948. In 1950, the Council for Mutual Economic Assistance recommended that such bilateral contracts be signed between all member nations and, within the next few years, most of the nations followed this advice. Between 1951 and 1953, the DDR managed to fix the amount

[1] e.g. American Management Association, *Aspects of East-West Trade* (New York, 1960); Trade Research Associates, *US-Soviet Trade: Facts for the Businessman's Appraisal* (Cleveland, 1960); Alec Nove and Desmond Donnelly, *Trade with Communist Countries* (London: Hutchinson, 1960). In German one magazine (*Osthandel*) is devoted to the problem.

[2] In the following discussion I omit considerations of the contracts for general trade standards, payment contracts, transportation agreements, and so forth. Information concerning these legal forms may be found in Eberhardt Pfuhl, *Das Recht der allgemeinen Lieferbedingungen in Zwischenstaatlichen Aussenhandel des Ostblocks* (West Berlin: Berichte des Osteuropa Instituts, Freie Universität, 1956), Erich Klinkmüller and Maria Ruban, *Die wirtschaftliche Zusammenarbeit der Ostblockstaaten* (West Berlin: Duncker & Humblot, 1960) or various issues of *Ost Europa Recht*.

[3] The relation of the various East Central European nations to Russia was somewhat different, due to Russian foreign trade banks in the DDR, Hungary, Rumania, and Russian advisors, and 'joint undertakings' in every East Central European nation except Poland.

(in physical terms) of about 30 per cent of the total value of all traded goods with Bloc countries by such long-term arrangements.[1]

A Hungarian official, Laszlo Hay stressed the importance of these contracts, and declared: 'At first the situation was such that, while a country with a planned economy could calculate for years ahead its vital import requirements and its export possibilities, it could not be sure for years in advance that it would definitely get everything it needed from the other countries with planned economy, or that it would definitely supply them with certain goods. Today, however, the long-term trade agreements serve as a solid basis for planning foreign trade for years in advance . . . by means of insuring supplies of certain goods over a period of several years.'[2] What he did not mention was that most of these contracts were signed after the long-range plans had been drawn up. These contracts probably served more as a form of insurance than as an integral part of planning.[3]

The long-range contracts specified minimum yearly deliveries, in value or physical terms, of various goods and groups of goods between the partners. For 'key positions' both value and physical amounts were set, i.e., an average unit price was set for the long-range. For the goods or groups of goods for which a target was set in value terms, a short statement was added, giving the criteria by which prices would be determined. An equality of imports and exports, modified by any credit agreements, was an explicitly stated goal of many of these contracts.

In the Stalin era, the negotiations for both long- and short-term

[1] Gisela Meier, *Die Aufgaben und Methoden der Bedarfsermittlung zwecks maximaler Erweiterung unserer Handelsbeziehungen mit den Ländern der demokratischen Weltmärkte* (Diplomarbeit, Hochschule für Ökonomie, 1956), p. 14. As far as I could understand, this 30 per cent figure was for goods traded with Bloc countries; if the base of this datum was total trade, then the long-range contracts fixed about 43 per cent of the trade with the Bloc nations.

[2] Laszlo Hay, 'Consolidating Economic Co-operation between Soviet Union and Countries of People's Democracy,' *For a Lasting Peace, for a People's Democracy*, November 14, 1952. Quoted by Nicolas Spulber, *The Economics of Communist Eastern Europe* (Cambridge, Mass.: John Wiley and Technology Press, 1957), p. 429.

[3] I doubt if some of these long-range trade contracts were actually honoured, although little information is available on this sensitive issue. However, according to Imre Nagy (*On Communism: In Defense of the New Course:* New York: Frederick A. Praeger, 1957; p. 189), the Russians and other CMEA nations cut their supply of 'essential products and raw materials' to Hungary by 50 per cent in 1955. This may have been an abrogation of long-term commitments.

The legal question of the consequences to a Bloc nation if it refuses to honour these long-term contracts has not, to my knowledge, been discussed in the CMEA Bloc press, and I was unable to get satisfactory information concerning the problem. In East Berlin I was told that since it is expected that yearly contracts will be substantially higher than the yearly quota in the long-range contract, there is usually no problem of abrogation of the long-term commitments.

trade contracts were conducted by only a few men, especially for the long-term agreements. Moreover, it appears that for the negotiations for the long-term contract, the Foreign Trade Ministers and top planning officials began discussions with very little previous consultation with the FTEs and very little preliminary staff work except for the exchange of lists of desired goods and goods available for export. The centralization of negotiations coupled with the heritage of a pre-war trade structure in which few goods were exchanged resulted in agreements with relatively few 'contract positions' (i.e. categories of goods for which quotas were set). For instance in the 1952–5 trade agreement between the DDR and the USSR, the contract included only ten to twelve positions for raw materials, twenty-two to twenty-five positions for machines, and a 'few miscellaneous positions'.

The trade of most of the CMEA nations during these early post-war years was quite concentrated in a few items. For instance tobacco exports constituted over 50 per cent of Bulgarian exports in 1948; and in 1950 coal, coke, and iron imports added up to over 20 per cent of DDR imports.[1] This concentration of the major trade negotiations in the hands of a few men had, of course, an adverse effect on the overall volume of trade.

Another type of trade contract between Bloc nations is the global, bilateral yearly trade agreement, which has been a prominent feature of intra-Bloc trade since the early post-war years. These contracts contain detailed lists of the physical amounts and the average unit prices of the goods to be traded. An overall value figure is given for the broad categories of goods for which further negotiations on the exact product mix are to be held. In the cases where the partners are unable to agree upon an average unit price for a particular good, a provisional price, subject to later negotiation, is set. From 1950 to 1955 these contracts, like the long-term contracts, were negotiated between the Ministries of Foreign Trade primarily on the basis of the exchange of lists of desired and surplus goods. The FTEs had little contact before the signing of the global contract, and had very little knowledge of economic events in other countries, as I discuss below.[2]

[1] For Bulgarian figure, *Statistcheski godishnik na Narodna Republika Bulgaria* (Sofia, 1957); DDR figure estimated from data in physical terms from *Statistisches Jahrbuch der DDR 1956* (East Berlin, 1957).

[2] In East Berlin I was told that the negotiations on the DDR side of the DDR–USSR trade contract were conducted by twelve men, assisted by various FTE representatives of the DDR in Moscow, experts in the Trade Policy Division of the DDR Embassy in Moscow, and 'hordes' of men flown in from Berlin. I have found some complaints in the DDR trade literature that the annual global contracts were not completely carried out. Although I have few data, I have received the impression that the deviations from these contracts have been usually small. See Table 6–12.

The lateness in signing these yearly global contracts was an important characteristic and the DDR foreign trade literature was filled with complaints about this situation. Up to 1959 the DDR signed the overwhelming majority of these global contracts after the beginning of the period for which they were to start; indeed, many contracts running from January to December were signed in March or April. In the short run as well as the long, it seemed as if the Bloc nations often 'balanced' their material balances in the hope that imports would be forthcoming.[1]

This lateness hindered trade in the first quarter of the year and was thus a casual factor in the yearly 'trade cycle'. Moreover, original plan goals were often not met because the global trade contracts diverged from the plans which were drawn up without specific knowledge of the foreign trade goals of the other countries.

B. Other Communication Channels

Bilateral trade negotiations are one means of communication of trade information but other more traditional channels of communication exist, such as advertising and market research, trade fairs, joint Chambers of Commerce, and so forth. These will be very briefly discussed below.

The sad neglect of market research in the DDR[2] was often graphically demonstrated. For instance, in 1954, DDR representatives went to a special technical exhibition in Sofia to sell to the Bulgarians certain types of high tension electrical apparatus, only to learn upon their arrival, that Bulgaria was an important exporter in this field.[3] The Secretary of the DDR communist party said a year later that they did not sufficiently know what kind of machines were wanted in which countries and in which branches of production of industrial equipment the DDR should concentrate.[4] In 1955 it was discovered that West German traders bought DDR chemicals such as sulphur and

[1] e.g. In 1956 the Russians complained bitterly that the DDR had 'planned' various imports from the USSR without getting Russia's permission or signature on a trade agreement. The Soviets resented having to bail out the DDR (Klinkmüller and Ruban, *op. cit.*, p. 165).

[2] In the DDR jargon, the term 'market research' (Marktforschung) is used only for research on the 'Capitalist world market' while the term 'research of needs' (Bedarfsermittlung) is used for market research on the 'Communist world market'. I will use the term 'market research' for both concepts.

[3] Ernst K. Stein, 'Erfolg und Lehren der DDR Fachanstalt in Sofia,' *Der Aussenhandel* IV, 37/1954, p. 805. One DDR foreign trader attributed the fact that every Bloc nation invested in penicillin production, as well as other products, directly to the lack of advertising and the ignorance in one country of the economic events in another. (Helmut Koch, 'Bessere Werbung in den Volksdemokratien,' *Der Aussenhandel* IV, 7/1954, p. 157).

[4] Walter Ulbricht, 'Stärkung der DDR als Bastion des Friedens und der Demokratie,' *Neues Deutschland*, June 10, 1955.

polyvinylchloride and resold them to other Bloc countries, and sold Polish and Czech chemicals like naphthalene to the DDR.[1]

DDR economists explained this indifference of market research as due to the lack of a Marxist-Leninist theory which explains why such activity is really necessary for trade.[2] It was generally assumed that the exchange of 'want-lists' between Ministries of Foreign Trade would solve all market research problems.

The disregard of market research may be seen in several ways. First of all, the DDR Market Research Institute was quite small for many years and less than four men were engaged in the study of plans and needs of other Bloc nations; the greatest attention in the Institute was paid to the 'Capitalist world market'. In the FTEs very few men were assigned to market research work. Finally, the network of trade representatives in foreign countries to gather information was very neglected. This function was left to a small economic staff in the countries where the DDR had embassies.[3] In the other countries trade representatives were appointed or occasional trade missions were sent. Although no quantitative measures are available I have gained the impression that this trade network has been very inadequate as a means of gathering information.

A parallel failure was the under-evaluation of the benefits of advertising to serve both the production and foreign trade enterprises as a means for increasing the effectiveness of imports and the volume of exports.

For instance, production firms had to receive special permission to import technical literature,[4] and it was forbidden by law for any domestic producer to receive advertising literature from abroad![5] Only Ministries, the Chamber of Commerce, FTEs, the official DDR Advertising Agency and trade representatives of foreign nations

[1] Heinz Friedländer, 'Chemie Export—ein wichtiger Bestandteil unseres Aussenhandels,' *Der Aussenhandel* VI, 24/1956.

[2] Gertrud Gräbig (*Internationale Arbeitsteilung und Aussenhandel im sozialistischen Weltsystem;* East Berlin: Verlag Die Wirtschaft, 1960; p. 77) noted that foreign trade officials neglected market research because they believed that it was solely the matter of the planners of each country to determine the trade needs and possibilities of their respective countries.

[3] The DDR had special problems which no other CMEA nation faced because it was not politically recognized by any Western nation and, therefore, had no embassies in these nations.

[4] Joachim Kaestner, *Die Finanzpolitischen Massnammen zur Exportfoderung* (East Berlin: Verlag Die Wirtschaft, 1959), p. 36.

[5] *GBl*, 16/1959, p. 176. Elfriede Heiduschat ('Importoperationen besser koordinieren,' *Der Aussenhandel* IX, 23/1959, p. 29) complains that this law was being violated. As far as I was able to find out, this measure has existed for some time (at least since 1953), although it was not formally written into the law until 1959. There is some doubt that the law was very strictly observed, since few of my interviewees in East Berlin were aware of such a measure.

could receive such literature. Since foreign advertising in DDR journals was minimal, advertising as a channel of communication for domestic producers to learn of foreign products was almost completely closed.[1]

Advertising in foreign journals or sending out of literature concerning DDR products was similarly neglected. First of all, it was very difficult for a DDR producing firm to place advertisements in foreign periodicals, as special permission was required from an FTE and from the Office of Literature and Publishing (later the Ministry of Culture). Export of samples was extremely difficult during the early years and permission for salesmen and technicians to travel abroad often required months to obtain.[2]

The FTEs seemed to do very little foreign advertising. For instance, one economist estimated that in 1955, only 3,746 advertisements were placed in the foreign Press and that the total FTE budget for export advertising (including, as far as I was able to determine, literature and catalogues sent by mail) amounted to only 25,000,000 DMs. (Total exports were 5,113,000,000 DMs.)[3] For the individual FTEs the advertising costs as a percentage of total exports appear quite low, although I have no comparable figures for the West.[4]

TABLE 2–4

ADVERTISING COSTS AS A PROPORTION OF TOTAL DDR EXPORTS IN 1955

FTE	%	*FTE*	%
Glas/Keramik	0·94	Invest-Export	0·2
Kulturwaren	0·6	Elektrotechnik	0·15
Nahrung	0·5	Maschinenexport	0·15
Feinmechanik/Optik	0·48	Stahl & Metall	0·12
Bergbau-Handel	0·44	Textil	0·09
Holz & Papier	0·41	Transportmaschinen	0·08
WMW-Export	0·41	Chemie	0·03
Chemieausruestung	0·35		

Moreover, although 75 per cent of total trade is with the East

[1] According to Nove (Nove and Donnelly, *op. cit.*, p. 22), Russian importers are responsive to foreign advertising in special Russian journals for this purpose.

[2] According to one DDR commentator (Walter Kresse, 'Die diesjährige Leipziger Messe und der Export nach dem kapitalistischen Ausland,' *Der Aussenhandel* III, 38/1953, pp. 917–19) DIA Maschinexport had to wait for fourteen months before receiving permission to send several of their representatives abroad for special work. The situation now is very much better.

[3] Franz Heiduschat, *Wirtschaftswerbung: Bedeutung und Nutzeffekt* (East Berlin: Verlag Die Wirtschaft, 1958), pp. 53 and 97.

[4] *Ibid.* Several foreign traders in West Berlin told me that these advertising costs were 'very low'.

Bloc, only a small percentage of advertising was directed towards the East:[1]

TABLE 2–5

TRADE AND ADVERTISING OF TWO FTES IN 1957

	DIA Glas/Keramik %	*DIA Maschinen-export* %
Planned Exports to East Bloc (as per cent of Total Export Plan)	37·6	90·3
Planned Funds for Advertising in East Bloc (as per cent of Total Advertising Plan)	5·3	8·0
Actual Advertisement Funds Spent in East Bloc by August 1, (as per cent of Total Advertising Plan)	0·2	2·0

This neglect of advertising was also explained as due to the lack of any political-economic theory to explain why advertising is necessary to a planned economy, or which would indicate its economic benefits as a channel of communication.[2] It is not strange that most experienced advertising men in the DDR left the country during the post-war years for the greener pastures of West Germany.[3]

Trade fairs were another means of communication, although one receives the impression from the Bloc literature that such a communication channel was not utilized to its fullest advantage in the early 1950s. Without more specific information it is impossible to make a judgment about this matter.

4. SUMMARY

The foreign trade system had three important structural elements and each had certain benefits and disadvantages.

A. The centralization of the foreign trade system had several advantages. First, by means of the material balances the State Planning Commission was the only economic institution which could select a trade pattern which would at least bring domestic production into some kind of consistent pattern. Since the price structure was distorted in every Bloc country, the FTES and production enterprises

[1] Mand Pielert, *Die Werbung als Mittel zur Erweiterung der Aussenhandelsvolumen der DDR mit den sozialistischen Staaten im II Fünfjahrplan* (Diplomarbeit, Hochschule für Ökonomie, 1957).

[2] Heidüschat, *op. cit.*, p. 5, discusses this lack of a Marxist theory of advertising and the adverse effects that such a theoretical lacuna has had on the economy.

[3] One sees evidence of this exodus of DDR ad men in copies of the DDR slick paper magazine, *Deutscher Export*, which has not only unimaginative ads but also frumpy models. Except for Poland and the CSSR, most CMEA Bloc nations have similarly neglected advertising.

could not make decisions on the basis of costs and prices which would be consistent with one another. Secondly, centralization permitted radical changes to be made in the structure of trade and production in a relatively short time. (This feature of centralization has proved very useful to wartime economies where the need for a high savings rate and a radical change in production is more important than achieving a static optimum allocation of resources.) Finally, in a situation where most employees in the foreign trade system were either untrained or politically suspect, centralization permitted a few trusted cadres to conduct large amounts of trade.

Centralization had several important disadvantages. First of all, the system lacked flexibility to meet new day-to-day opportunities and there were constant complaints in the foreign trade literature about this.[1] Second, information costs between the FTEs and higher organs seemed to run quite high. For instance, Walter Ulbricht declared that the Ministry of Foreign Trade gave out so many forms to complete in conjunction with exports that plant directors wasted most of their time just filling out the forms.[2] The Minister of Foreign Trade claimed that this communication was inefficient: 'Our comrades in the planning section occupy themselves with plan "methodology", i.e., with form sheets. They give these forms out to lower units; everyone fills them out; and they come up again to the top; this is what planning means to most people.'[3] Third, I doubt that the foreign trade experts in the State Planning Commission had the specific knowledge or the knowledge of details to make many decisions competently; resentment by the FTEs ran high and at a conference on planning in 1955, many foreign traders were heard to remark: 'We fulfil the plans in spite of the planning system,' or 'Just leave us alone with your . . . plans.'[4]

Finally, centralization, combined with the system of planning with material balances, had two adverse consequences. The strains in the material allocation system lead, as Western Commentators have noted in many Bloc countries, toward autarky within 'administrative empires' in the domestic economy. That is, economic units such as Ministries would often try to produce as many of the goods which they received from other sectors of the economy or imported from abroad in order to assure themselves of a *continuous* supply.[5] This

[1] e.g. 'Everyone who is active in foreign trade must have experienced how heavy and inflexible the whole planning apparatus is.' (G. Wiedemann, 'Neue Wege in der Planung des Aussenhandels,' *Der Aussenhandel* IV, 32/1954, p. 713.)

[2] Bernard Hein, 'Der IV Parteitag der SED weist uns den Weg,' *Der Aussenhandel* IV, 14/1954, p. 315.

[3] Kurt Gregor, quoted by Brauer, *op. cit.*, p. 169.

[4] Quoted by Brauer, *op. cit.*, p. 159.

[5] Nove and Donnelly, *op. cit.*, p. 21.

type of 'administrative autarky' was an important part of the overall autarkic tendencies. In addition, planning with material balances made it quite difficult for the planners to bring profitability considerations into decision-making.

B. The exclusive specialization in foreign trade by one set of decision-making units, the FTES, allowed the Ministries of Trade to control most easily the specific goods which were being traded. In an economy where the exchange rate is under- or over-valued, and where domestic prices do not reflect the relative scarcity of commodities, direct controls could prevent such adverse effects as exports of particularly scarce goods, a chronic imbalance of trade, and so forth. (I cannot see why a devaluation of the exchange rate, combined with certain types of indirect trade controls, such as tariffs, could not have been more effective.)[1]

The specialization had several disadvantages. First, as I have discussed, certain problems of co-ordination and harmonization of decisions between foreign trade and production enterprises occurred. Especially important were the conflict of interests between the two sets of enterprises. Secondly, the lack of continual contact between domestic producers and foreign markets led to the neglect of changing world market supply and demand conditions by the domestic producers. Production tended to lag behind the ever-rising 'world standard'. (See also Chapter VI.) Moreover, for certain traded goods, e.g., complex machinery, direct contact with the manufacturer is highly desirable in order to obtain goods meeting specialized requirements. Lack of such contact meant that some Bloc exports were discouraged and that the scarce import funds of the various Bloc nations were, in these cases, often used wastefully.

Finally, the informal contacts between citizens of Bloc countries

[1] DDR economists often argue that direct controls are necessary for the following reasons:

(*a*) To prevent capitalist crises from affecting the DDR economy. However, 75 per cent of the DDR trade is with East Bloc nations which supposedly have no crises. Moreover, this direction of trade can easily be maintained by means of a multiple exchange system or special tariffs. The business cycles and 'crises' in the West are going to affect the trade (and, thereby, the production) of the DDR with the West, no matter what direct controls are imposed by the DDR. Tendencies toward an adverse balance of payments, etc. caused by these business cycles and crises can be nullified by suitable indirect controls.

(*b*) To prevent gold flights or to stop foreign capital from coming in and controlling the economy. These, too, can be prevented by suitable indirect controls, as many Western nations have done.

(*c*) To prevent 'Capitalistic and Fascist elements' in the DDR from contacting similar elements abroad. However, the 'direct exporting' system (discussed in the next chapter allowed this to occur.

(*d*) To carry out special types of 'political-economic policies' of the government. If this phrase means economic warfare, then DDR economists are quite correct.

and foreigners, which might have been quite useful in expanding trade, went unused for the most part since all trade was funnelled through the FTEs. This was especially true for the DDR and its trade with West Germany.

C. The concentration of most yearly planning decisions into one short interval of time (a phenomenon which I name 'internal discontinuities') had few advantages as far as I can see, and two extremely important disadvantages. First, in the general rush to draw up the plan, profitability considerations were neglected. Second, as I discussed above, great disproportions sometimes arose since decision-making units in trade and production did not know or did not have time to find out what the others were doing.

These structural elements were combined with a great neglect of information gathering. The statistical reporting system was poor; many of the statistics which were collected were not seen by most of the workers in the foreign trade system because they were considered secret; and the statistics which were given to the foreign trade officials were often not used. The planners and foreign traders in one Bloc country had little contact with those of another; market research and advertising received little emphasis; and other intra-Bloc communication channels were not effectively employed.

The various disadvantages of the structural elements and the neglect of information gathering did not mean that the system broke down. However, they had four main adverse consequences:

A. The volume of trade was much smaller than the potential volume of profitable trade. This was caused by the centralization of trade decision-making and negotiations with other countries; the strains in the material allocation system; and the inadequate system of gathering information about profitable trade opportunities in other countries. Other reasons are discussed in the next chapter.

B. The plan goals for foreign trade were unrealistically set. This was due to the complete separation of foreign trade and production, which brought about conflicts of interest. Production enterprises would raise their imports at the last moment, which would force the Foreign Trade Ministry and the FTEs to raise the export goals. The lateness in signing the global trade contracts which diverged from the plan also contributed to the non-fulfilment of plan goals.

C. Trade was spread unevenly across the year. This was caused by the late approval of plans; the late signing of the global trade contracts; and the incentive system, which I discuss in the next chapter.

D. There was a great inflexibility in the foreign trade system, i.e., an inability to adapt to sudden changes in the domestic economy or world markets. Several factors contributed to this situation. The separation of foreign trade from production meant that communication from the production enterprises to the FTEs had to be channelled through the production ministries, State Planning Commission, and Foreign Trade Ministry. Second, the neglect of information gathering about foreign markets meant that the domestic foreign trade system was often unaware of changes which were occurring. Finally, there was a chronic shortage of reserves of gold and foreign currencies which could be used for sudden buying on the world markets. Reserves of goods which could be quickly exported seemed also to be quite small.[1] Unfortunately, a complete veil of secrecy was drawn over this subject.

[1] There are two types of 'reserves' which are important for foreign trade: the 'state reserves' which are stocks of important goods, such as steel and coal, and which serve to bridge any import irregularities; and the foreign trade reserves which are used not only to bridge import difficulties but also to export in emergencies to obtain cash for needed imports. For this latter purpose raw materials, which are easily sold on the world markets, are stockpiled. These reserves provide an escape valve for domestic difficulties.

CHAPTER III

REFORMS IN THE FOREIGN TRADE SYSTEM

In the doctrinal thaw during the New Course (1953–5) and afterwards, each Bloc nation began to re-examine and change its foreign trade system. The most important deviations from the Stalinist model of the foreign trade monopoly were decentralization, removal of the strict separation between trade and production enterprises, and a lengthening of the planning process so that more decisions were made sequentially instead of at one particular point in time. In addition, many Bloc nations such as the DDR started to pay a great deal more attention to problems of information gathering and statistical analysis.

1. CHANGES IN ORGANIZATION AND IN THE PLANNING PROCESS

From 1954 to 1957, DDR economists and policy-makers began important discussions concerning the planning and organization of all sectors of the economy. In foreign trade, a special commission examined the whole planning procedure from the lowest to the highest rungs and analysed such basic questions as decentralization, integration of trade and production planning, co-ordination of physical and value planning, as well as less important problems such as planning nomenclature, and so forth.[1] Another committee examined the pre-war organizational forms of foreign trade, the experience of trade in the other CMEA nations, and the various types of trade organizations in market economies. As a result, a series of measures were carried out between 1954 and 1958 which greatly affected the whole foreign trade system.

One of the first changes was a certain decentralization in the organization structure and planning system. It is difficult to examine rigorously this decentralization because few analytical tools and reliable data are available. DDR discussions of this problem in the foreign trade system are, for the most part, quite unenlightening

[1] 'Neue Wege in der Aussenhandelsplanung,' *Der Aussenhandel* VI, 22/1956, p. 787; and 'Auf der Suche nach neuen Wegen in der Planung des Aussenhandels,' *Der Aussenhandel* VI, 15/1956, p. 537.

since they are often conducted in terms of the volume of trade for each FTE, which can be a very misleading measure of centralization.[1] Some more useful information is, however, available.

The first important step toward decentralization in the foreign trade system (and a decrease in the separation of foreign trade and production) occurred in December, 1953, when the FTEs were permitted to give the production enterprises a global permission to export directly and in their own name to non-communist nations.[2] This permission was granted for three months, and extended up to 20,000 Roubles ($5,000) for each firm, with single shipments not to exceed 2,000 Roubles. The enterprises were not allowed to undercut a price established by the FTEs and received from the Central Bank only the domestic price of the good plus a bonus. This 'direct export' arrangement ('Eigengeschaft') was an innovation of the DDR and was not followed in this exact form by any other CMEA nation.[3]

[1] An example of how misleading such 'absolute coefficients' of centralization may be, can be seen by comparing the industrial structure in the DDR and the USA. In 1959 in the USA, the fifty largest firms accounted for 28 per cent of all manufacturing and mining production, and the 500 largest firms accounted for slightly over 50 per cent of this production. In the DDR, the 1,720 centrally directed companies accounted for only 68 per cent of DDR industrial production. From such measurements, it might appear that production in the USA is more centralized than in the DDR. (Sources: 'The Fortune Directory,' *Fortune*, LXII, July/1960, pp. 131–50, and *Statistisches Jahrbuch der DDR*, 1959, p. 297).

A better comparison may be made between the industrial production administration of the DDR and General Motors Corporation of Detroit, Michigan, both of which are about the same size:

'Coefficients of Size' in 1959	*DDR*	*GM*
Net industrial production (sales) (billion $)	$8–9	$11
Capital/output ratio	1·2	1·0
Employees (1,000s)	2,801	557
'Coefficients of Centralization' in 1959		
Kontingenttrager (Operating Divisions)	app. 110	45
Factories (DDR, only cent. administered; GM, only US and Canada)	1,720	134
Per cent of 'productive workers' (GM, hourly-paid employees)	71%	69%

On the basis of this type of analysis, using such 'coefficients of centralization,' it looks as if GM were more centralized than the DDR! Centralization is a great deal more complicated than sales or production per economic unit, and the DDR discussion of the matter has been very superficial.

Sources for 'coefficients of size and centralization': See Statistical Appendix B.

[2] *Gesetzblatt der DDR (GBl)*, 134/1953, p. 1,312. For an extensive history of the various measures to permit production enterprises to export directly, see Joachim Kaestner, *Die finanzpolitischen Massnahmen zur Exportförderung* (East Berlin: Verlag Die Wirtschaft, 1959), Chapter V.

[3] In some of the other Bloc nations, other arrangements were tried. In Poland, firms were allowed small deposits of foreign currency with which to buy and sell on the foreign markets, and one co-op, the PKO, was permitted to obtain dollars from Polish citizens at a free market rate and buy consumer goods in the West. In Hungary, nine large firms were permitted to export directly to the West in

In the next four years, these restrictions were loosened: the three months permission was lengthened to a year; the 20,000 Roubles limit was progressively raised to 50,000 Roubles and, in 1957, completely eliminated. As a result of such measures, these 'direct exports' became quite important for a few years:

TABLE 3–1

DDR 'DIRECT EXPORTS' AS A PROPORTION OF EXPORTS TO NON-COMMUNIST NATIONS[1]

	1955	1956	1957
	%	%	%
Heavy machinery	—	—	16
General machinery	—	—	37
Chemicals, mining, foodstuffs	—	—	26
Light industry	Est. 10	Est. 38	Est. 63
Total	Est. 5	Est. 13	—

Some economists demanded that 'direct exports' be extended to trade with the East Bloc and in 1957 two production enterprises were given this permission. At the same time, however, heavy attacks began against the whole policy of 'direct exports'.

Theoreticians claimed that even though global permissions were granted by the FTEs, the FTEs had little control over the 'direct exports' and, therefore, this trade was contrary to Lenin's concept of the foreign trade monopoly. Foreign trade officials also attacked the system of 'direct exports' for not bringing any additional benefits and, indeed, actually causing some losses. 'Direct exports' were said to have become a purpose in itself to obtain a higher foreign currency bonus.[2] Another foreign trade official argued that 'direct exports' only changed the selling agency and did not increase trade. He added that exports of machine goods were carried out much more poorly, payments from foreign customers were 70 per cent late, and DDR companies were often cheated, due to their inexperience.[3] These criticisms seem quite damning but, on the other hand, the Hungarian

their own names. In the USSR, the Sovnarkhozy were permitted to make small trading transactions and the Central Union of consumer operatives was allowed to trade in the West.

[1] Sources: Deiter Albrecht, 'Auch in der Leichtindustrie das staatliche Aussenhandelmonopol sichern!' *Der Aussenhandel* VIII, 1/1958, pp. 17–19; Franz Heiduschat, 'Die Notwendigkeit, die Funktion, und die Sicherung des staatlichen Aussenhandelsmonopols in der DDR und seine Bedeutung für die Weiterentwicklung des Aussenhandels,' *Der Aussenhandel* VII, 15/1957, pp. 543–7; Heiduschat, *Wirtschaftswerbung* (Berlin: Verlag Die Wirtschaft, 1958), p. 53.

[2] Albrecht, *op. cit.*

[3] Karl Haengekorb, 'Wie kann die Durchsetzung der handelspolitischen Ziele auf dem Auslandsmarkt verbessert werden,' *Der Aussenhandel* VII, 18/1957, pp. 645–6.

experiment of allowing nine large firms to trade directly with the West was successful enough for it to be still in operation. Without more specific information on the 'direct exports' it is impossible to tell whether the benefits of the greater decentralization and participation in trade by production enterprises were really outweighed by the factors mentioned above and the adverse trade deals induced by the distorted domestic price structure. I believe it noteworthy, however, that during the height of the 'direct export' period (1955–7) the exports to the West rose at an annual average of 17·6 per cent, which was considerably higher than the average annual rise of total exports. This may very well have been the result of the new export system.

After 1957, much stronger central controls were placed on the 'direct export' programme and domestic production enterprises were not permitted to directly export goods falling within any 'plan position'. The amount of 'direct exports' apparently fell considerably. I do not know for sure if the limiting of 'direct exports' contributed to the 2·7 per cent fall in DDR exports to the West in 1958, but I suspect that it played a major role.

A special type of arrangement for 'direct imports' also existed for a few years. In 1954, all enterprises fulfilling an export contract were offered a special foreign currency bonus, starting at 1 per cent of export sales and climbing rapidly for above-plan exports. The enterprise could use this foreign currency to import needed materials and machinery on its own account without special permission. This innovation lasted only until 1957, because, in the words of a DDR economist, '. . . goods were being imported which were unprofitable from the standpoint of the economy as a whole.'[1] This special export bonus to the production enterprises is still given, but the enterprises can use it only with the permission of the FTEs and only to import articles which increase export production or lower the need for other imports.

Another type of organizational decentralization was the increased emphasis on the 'horizontal relationships' between enterprises, which meant that many disputes between enterprises were settled by the parties involved or by special courts, instead of by higher economic organs such as the State Planning Commission or ministries.[2]

While this decentralization was occurring, a certain bureaucratization, following the guidelines of Parkinson's famous law of expanding bureaucracy, seemed to have taken place. In 1953, 60 per

[1] *Ibid.*, p. 32.

[2] Other organizational decentralization steps were taken, although they do not seem important enough to mention. The best account of the decentralization measures is: H. J. Nitz, W. Schneider, L. Benedikt, 'Zur Organization des Aussenhandelmonopols,' *Der Aussenhandel* VII, 19/1957, pp. 687–9.

cent of the personnel in foreign trade was 'operative' and in 1956 this percentage had fallen to 44·5 per cent.[1] Unfortunately, a breakdown of the composition of 'operative' and 'non-operative' personnel is not available so that it is impossible to decide whether or not this phenomenon acted as a counter-movement to the decentralization. (This bureaucratization occurred in other sectors of the economy as well.)[2]

Although the measures toward organizational decentralization received a great deal of attention, the quiet decentralization in the planning system was probably a great deal more far reaching and important. This came about through a reduction in the number of official 'plan positions' in the yearly plan from 955 in 1955, to 810 in 1956, to 440 in 1957.[3] However, the State Planning Commission continued not only to specify the overall trade volume and the trade

[1] As far as I have been able to understand, 'operative personnel' included all who were 'directly' concerned with foreign trade in the FTES, while 'non-operative personnel' included personnel in the market research, planning, employee relations, etc. departments. (Ministerial personnel were apparently excluded from these calculations).

It is not known how comparable the 1953 and 1956 data on 'operative personnel' are; and I was not able to obtain comparative data from the West. Therefore, no firm conclusions can be made. In the DDR foreign trade literature, one reads many complaints about the increasing bureaucratization (especially in the Ministry).

Sources: 1953 figure from Helmut Pabst, 'Neue Wege in der Planabrechung,' *Der Aussenhandel* III, 23/1953, pp. 535–6; 1956 datum from 'Was wissen wir von unserem Aussenhandel,' *Der Aussenhandel* VII, 24/1957, p. 877.

[2] According to Alfred Tomm, (Unsere Arbeitskraftlager—ein Erbe zweier Imperialistischer Kriege,' *Viertelsjahrshefte zur Statistik*, 1/1958, pp. 9–13) the structure of personnel in state enterprises had the following changes in composition:

	State Industrial Enterprises			*State Building Enterprises*			*State Agricultural Forestry and Water Enterprises*		
Year	*A*	*B*	*C*	*A*	*B*	*C*	*A*	*B*	*C*
1950	70·8	5·6	6·6	80·9	3·3	4·0	76·0	5·4	5·5
1951	68·3	6·0	6·9	78·4	4·0	4·6	69·3	5·3	5·3
1952	67·1	6·4	7·5	73·6	5·4	5·7	69·1	5·7	5·6
1953	66·7	6·6	8·1	69·0	6·5	6·5	73·8	6·0	5·0
1954	65·8	6·6	8·5	67·3	6·2	6·3	73·7	6·9	5·3
1955	67·5	6·6	8·4	67·0	6·1	6·1	74·0	7·0	4·2
1956	68·4	6·8	8·3	67·4	6·1	6·1	72·7	8·0	4·1
1957	67·5	7·0	8·3	64·6	6·3	6·2	71·5	7·9	3·9

A =per cent of production workers.
B =per cent of technicians.
C =per cent of administrative personnel.

[3] 'Zur Diskussion über die weitere Verbesserung der Leitung der volkseigenen Industrie,' *Wirtschaftswissenschaft* V, 3/1957, pp. 346–61. For the number of planning positions, quota materials and central material balances for previous years, see Statistical Appendix B.

volume with major nations for each plan position, but also to determine trade goals for many goods within the various 'plan positions'. In 1959–60 this procedure was dropped and the State Planning Commission restricted itself to specifying the trade volume only for the 'plan positions' and only for the broad geographical areas of trade ('Communist world market', 'Capitalist world market' and inter-German trade). Unfortunately, no other information on additional measures acting to decentralize the planning system has been published. However, I received the impression from the economic literature and from interviews in East Berlin that some other steps toward decentralization had been taken.

The decentralization of the organizational structure and the planning system did not, however, overcome the basic dilemmas of the foreign trade system and especially the problems of the co-ordination of trade and production. Indeed, the decentralization seemed only to focus attention on the necessity for a more fundamental attack on foreign trade problems.

A series of measures were carried out to break down the complete separation of foreign trade from domestic production and trade. The 'direct export' system was one organizational measure; another was the transfer in 1956 of many of the foreign trade 'accounts' (the administrative units in the FTEs which handled trade in various products) from Berlin to the location of the centre of production of a branch (e.g., for optics, Jena) or to the most important enterprise of the branch.[1]

In May, 1956, the basic roots of the problem of functional separation of trade and production were attacked by the adoption of a new 'simultaneous' planning system. The old way of channelling all communication between the production and trade enterprises through the State Planning Commission and the various ministries (who would also settle major disputes) and of drawing up the final trade plan later than the production plan, was dropped. Instead, the trade and production enterprises drew up their plans simultaneously on the basis of control figures and tried to co-ordinate these plans at a series of regional conferences before the plans were resubmitted to the State Planning Commission.[2] This procedure forced the FTEs to draw up plans with even less information than formerly about the exact domestic trade needs and possibilities. But, at the same time, it permitted the settling of disputes at a much earlier date in a free-

[1] Other methods of bringing together representatives from trade and production have also been used since 1953, e.g. the 'Export Committees' or the 'Hobby-horse Movement' (for above plan export production), etc.

[2] 'Zwischenbilanz der neuen Planmethodik,' *Der Aussenhandel* VII, 16/1957, pp. 619ff, and Fritz Fabian, 'Zu einigen Fragen der neuen Planmethodik,' *Der Aussenhandel* VIII, 12/1958, pp. 435–7.

for-all and fostered greater appreciation of mutual problems by the trade and production enterprises. This increase of 'horizontal communication' between trade and production enterprises, strengthened by the previously described organizational changes, decreased the role of the State Planning Commission and increased the flexibility of the whole trade apparatus. The 'simultaneous' planning also increased the role of foreign trade considerations in the making of investment decisions.

The new planning system still had its problems: FTEs had to make some decisions with very little information,[1] and co-ordination between production and trade planning, at least in 1958, left a great deal to be desired. Moreover, the system was not completely followed.[2]

The 'simultaneous' planning system also drew attention to discrepancies between trade and production plans brought about by the internal discontinuities, i.e., the 'explosion' type of decision-making, where all important planning decisions had to be made in a short period of time so that it was difficult to learn what other decision-making units were planning until it was too late.

In a sequential type of decision-making, major guidelines are already known; production and trade decisions are made all year round and, at any one point of time, are limited to only a small portion of total trade and production.[3] A completely 'sequential solution' would practically eliminate all yearly plans except an investment plan, and would bring about a type of market socialism which is ideologically repugnant to most DDR policy makers. One less radical substitute, however, entails placing greater emphasis on long-range planning so that the general guidelines become more visible and important to all decision-making units for their short-range planning. This compromise was being increasingly discussed by DDR economists after 1953.

The first Five-Year Plan of the DDR definitely did not serve as a guideline for decision-making by the various economic units since it was a crude affair which was greatly changed almost every year. Overall production goals of major groups of goods for the whole economy were specified, but the long-range plans of the major production enterprises were quite useless because the individual firms had too little time to draw up these plans and too little know-

[1] W. Schlitzer, *op. cit.*

[2] See, e.g. the complaints of W. Schulze, 'Formulartechnik und komplexe Planung,' *Der Aussenhandel* IX, 23/1959, pp. 18–19.

[3] This concept of 'sequential solution' seems a special part of the more general concept of 'incrementalism', defined by Robert A. Dahl and Charles E. Lindblom, *Politics, Economics, and Welfare* (New York: Harper & Brothers, 1953) and discussed in greater detail by Lindblom, 'Policy Analysis,' *American Economic Review* XLVII, June/1958, pp. 298–312.

ledge of the future sales possibilities of their particular products.[1] After the IV Parteitag in April, 1954, a frontal assault was made on developing long-range plans for specific sectors of the economy and by the end of 1956, 'sectoral economic plans' had been drawn up for several large economic sectors (brown coal, electricity, forestry, automobile and tractor, and water and rivers plans).[2] Plans for other sectors were being completed.

Two major difficulties occurred. Since so few of these long-range plans existed, the planners in the various sectors had little idea about future demands for their products and were forced to extrapolate, using assumptions which were not always consistent with each other. Second, few alternative possibilities were specified in the individual sectoral plans which, in turn, did not permit much experimentation in alternative product mixes by the central co-ordinators in the State Planning Commission.

Nevertheless, the increasing number of these 'sectoral economic plans' and the growing realization by DDR economic officials of the importance of long-range planning brought some important changes in planning methods for the Seven-Year Plan (1959–65). First of all, the long-range foreign trade plan received close attention for the first time.[3] Moreover, the plan was not exclusively drawn up by the State Planning Commission. Long-range control figures were given to each enterprise to be discussed and improved; and the trade and production enterprises were supposed to consult with each other before a final long-range plan was drawn up, a process similar to the procedure in making the yearly plans. Furthermore, as I later discuss, foreign trade agreements with other CMEA Bloc nations came before the final production plan had been drawn up. Finally, at the end of the planning process, each FTE and production enterprise received an approved long-range enterprise plan which was supposed to be consistent with the long-range plan for the whole economy.

Several difficulties in this new planning process occurred. First, the familiar co-ordination problems arose once again. Often, trade and production enterprises received different control figures, as we see from the data in Table 3–2 (see next page).[4]

[1] Alfred Lange, *Die Investitionen in der volkseigenen Industrie der DDR im ersten Planjahrfunf*, (East Berlin: Verlag Die Wirtschaft, 1958), p. 92.

[2] J. Rudolph and G. Friedrich, *Grundriss der Volkswirtschaftsplanung* (East Berlin: Verlag Die Wirtschaft, 1957), p. 105.

[3] A Gloeckner ('Zur Ausarbeitung des Perspektivplanes,' *Der Aussenhandel* IX, 2/1959, p. 6-9), and G. Grote, *op. cit.*, claim that the basis for many calculations in foreign trade for the DDR Seven-Year Plan was 1959, since no real long-range foreign trade plan in the second FYP period for 1960 had been made!

[4] G. Kallwut, 'Wohin im Siebenmeilenschritt, Textilmaschinenbauer?' *Der Aussenhandel* IX, 10/1959, pp. 21–2.

Since the planning period lasted eight months, production and trade enterprises had enough time to resolve some of these problems, although the final plan still contained many such discrepancies.[1]

TABLE 3–2

PLANS FOR EXPORT PRODUCTION AND EXPORTS OF TEXTILE MACHINES

Year	*Control Figures for Export Production by Trust for Textile Machines (from Machine Building Section of State Planning Commission)*	*Control Figures for Export of Textile Machines by FTEs (from Foreign Trade Section of State Planning Commission)*
1959	100	100
1960	96	143
1961	100	170
1962	115	186
1963	147	207
1964	185	242
1965	232	262

Second, because the Ministry of Foreign Trade did not send out very specific trade policy directions, many FTEs felt somewhat up in the air in making such decisions.[2] Third, these plans were often not co-ordinated with the work of the subcommissions of the CMEA.[3] Finally, as I discuss below, since market research was so neglected, some of the plans drawn up by the FTEs were of dubious quality. Nevertheless, the Seven-Year Plan seemed to have some operational significance, for better or worse, and provided a more visible framework for the drawing up and co-ordinating of the yearly plans.

I believe that the increasing operational nature of the long-run plans and the sequentialization of decision-making occurred in all CMEA Bloc countries. This opinion is also shared by Levine in his study of Russian planning methods[4] but is not universally held. For instance, the Economic Council of Europe claims that the long-term plans for 1959–65 were only general outlines of policy rather than directives to be followed in every detail, as was formerly the case.[5] They base this conclusion on the following facts: the recent decentralization measures in every country gave the enterprises more

[1] Hannelore Jahn, *Methoden und Wege der Erarbeitung des Perspektivplanes im VEH DIA Textil* (Diplomarbeit, Hochschule für Ökonomie, 1959)

[2] *Ibid.*

[3] Jochen Teubel, *Die Bedeutung der Perspektivplanung im Wirtschaftszweig Aussenhandel und ihre Auswirkung auf die Arbeitsweise im Aussenhandelsunternehmen, insbesondere auf die Jahres und Operativeplanung* (Diplomarbeit, Hochschule für Ökonomie, 1960), p. 14.

[4] Herbert Levine, *op. cit.*

[5] 'The Long-Term Plans in the Soviet Union and Eastern Europe,' Chapter III, *Economic Survey of Europe for 1959.*

authority over investment; and planners now speak of 'targets' rather than 'goals which, by law, must be made'. Such an analysis misses, I believe, three important factors.

A. Long-range planning in every country seems more detailed than formerly. Development is planned on a wider scale with emphasis on a broad range of goods rather than a few priority sectors.

B. Long-range planning is receiving a great deal more attention. For instance, in the USSR a system of 'rolling plans' has been introduced, in which the plan for the next five years is drawn up annually. Similar to the situation in the DDR, individual factories in other Bloc countries have participated more in the long-range planning process and, in the end, received their own five-year plan.

C. Greater emphasis has been placed on securing long-range trade contracts. Moreover, the discussion concerning the work of the Council of Mutual Economic Assistance has increasingly emphasized aspects of long-range planning.

In all CMEA nations it is possible to see deviations from the Stalinist model of the foreign trade monopoly through decreasing centralization, decreasing specialization of function, and decreasing internal discontinuities in decision-making. The speed at which these changes have occurred and the exact form the changes have taken in these various Bloc nations are somewhat different. Unfortunately, information is quite scanty on these organizational and planning features of other CMEA nations. More reforms of the foreign trade system seem to have been made in Poland and Hungary than in the USSR or Rumania.

Other less important changes in planning and organization of trade were also made in the DDR. After 1958 there was a decrease in the shifting of the number and area of activity of the economic units. This was a deliberate abandonment of further experimentation by the top policy-makers in order to allow a greater degree of efficiency to come about through greater structural stability.[1]

2. OTHER CHANGES IN PLANNING

The increasing attention paid to tools of operational planning, especially in the fields of data collection and analysis, paralleled the changes in organization and procedures in planning. Moreover, the physical and financial planning in the FTEs began to be done to-

[1] The greatest difficulties with the constant experimentation with the number and sizes of the enterprises were the problems of calculating any meaningful production cost data or the drawing up of any long-range plans. Other disadvantages included the impossibility of making intertemporal comparisons of performance, the anxiety among enterprise managers fearing a sudden change in their own area of authority, etc. The DDR economic literature is filled with complaints about this experimentation.

gether so that these plans were more consistent. More specifically, in the use of information in decision-making, several new measures were taken:

First, a much greater emphasis was placed on the use of statistics and more statistics began to be calculated. In 1958 the statistical department of the Foreign Trade Ministry finally started to make terms of trade analyses of DDR trade with various major nations,[1] and in the next year, calculated a volume index of trade. However, in the use of statistics and mathematical methods, the DDR seemed to be very far behind Poland, Hungary, the CSSR and the Soviet Union.

Second, greater attention began to be paid to the concepts behind foreign trade statistics. For instance, between 1957 and 1959 a fierce battle raged in the foreign trade journals concerning what should be included in the balance of payments and how this balance should be calculated, an incredibly low-level discussion with the most obvious errors in economic thinking. Nevertheless, the problem seems to have been finally solved although, of course, no actual balance has yet been published.

Third, great effort has been expended in unifying important elements of the accounting systems, the statistical reporting systems, and the planning systems in foreign trade so that a planned balance of payments could be compared with the reported balance of payments in a meaningful way. These measures included more careful cost accounting methods and a separation of the secondary costs of trade (transportation, insurance, packing, etc.).

Finally, there has been some attempt to make foreign trade statistics more comparable with production statistics. In 1957 there were almost no value coefficients in the statistics of industry and foreign trade which were directly comparable with each other.[2] Several DDR economists have been working on the problem in the late 1950s.

It is extremely difficult to evaluate the effect of these changes. Nevertheless, it seems as though these measures should have resulted in a saving of information costs and an increase in the efficiency of communication.

The special problems of planning in the FTEs, which were brought about by the existence of separate planning units within them and the split between planning in value and physical terms, were attacked in

[1] Walter Friedrich, 'Wie die Länderstruktur in unserem Aussenhandel zu verbessern ist,' *Der Aussenhandel* IX, 12/1959, pp. 26–7.

[2] Hans Metzgar, *Die Bestimmung von Kennziffern zur Ermittlung des Anteils des Aussenhandels und der Produktion* (Diplomarbeit, Hochschule für Ökonomie, 1957). Another economist (Hans Striegen, 'Koordinierende Bilanz der volkswirtschaftlichen Beziehungen zum Ausland,' *Statistische Praxis*, 8/1959, pp. 179–82) stated a year later, 'There is not yet an analysis of foreign trade relations which is comparable with the domestic economic data.'

1958–9 under the banner of 'complex planning'. The planning process within the FTES was reorganized so that a special planning unit would draw up both the physical turnover and the financial plans and would try whenever possible to do so at the same time. This planning unit would also oversee the plans from the other sections of the FTE. Second, in 1959 the main foreign trade plans began to be drawn up in DMs for the first time, which permitted a closer integration of the foreign trade with the production plan. Unfortunately, not enough information has been published to allow an evaluation of these new measures.

3. LINKS BETWEEN FOREIGN AND DOMESTIC MARKETS

A. Trade Negotiations and Contracts

After 1955 some major changes were made in the scope and procedure of the negotiations for both the long-and short-term global trade contracts. Most important, a great many more people (particularly representatives from the various FTES) began to take part in the negotiation process, expecially in the discussions about machine goods. This wider participation relieved the heavy burden from the few top officials at the annual bilateral negotiation periods, permitted the contracts to be a good deal more detailed, and encouraged a greater volume of trade.[1]

The long-range trade pacts, which lapsed in 1955–6 when all Bloc countries except Bulgaria began new Five-Year Plans, were not renewed until 1957–8 because of the confusions of the Hungarian and Polish disturbances and the specialization of production agreements.[2] The 1958–60 trade pacts of the DDR covered 100 to 200 positions (which was considerably more than the previous contracts and covered about one-fifth the positions of the second Five-Year Plan). In physical terms these agreements covered about 60 per cent of the expected trade with CMEA nations.[3] Nevertheless, the global trade contracts came well after the long-range plans had been

[1] The importance of more direct contacts between the decision-making units in the CMEA Bloc was especially stressed by Helfried Pech ('Neue Etappe der Zusammenarbeit,' *Die Wirtschaft*, November 1, 1956), who wrote: 'Only one way leads to a more flexible, more mutually advantageous, more purpose-directed (intra-Bloc) co-operation. This is when the production ministries, scientific institutions and, if possible, enterprises, have direct connections with similar institutions in friendly countries. Technology and production . . . are lively processes which one must certainly lead and plan but which one must not force into a narrow administrative-technical system.'

[2] Schenk and Löwenthal, *op. cit.* A great many long-range contracts for specific items were signed in 1956, however.

[3] The DDR-USSR Three-Year Pact for 1958–60, was said to contain specific provisions for 90 per cent of foreseen trade, although this figure seems a bit high.

drawn up, which indicates that considerations of foreign trade were not yet fundamental to the planners.

In 1958 the CMEA recommended that the long-range trade pacts up to 1965 contain provision for 70 per cent of the projected trade (in physical terms). This added emphasis was paralleled by two important new developments.

Except in the USSR, discussion on the trade pacts began before the plans or guidelines for the plans had been announced. This meant that the long-range trade discussions were for the first time an integral part of the planning process and that the old policy of 'balancing' the material balances on the hope that adequate imports would be obtainable was renounced. According to a Polish economist, the exchange of information on export possibilities and import needs, while the long-range plans were being drawn up, also made it more possible to define and co-ordinate the specific tasks of development which each nation faced, that is, to increase the Bloc specialization of production.[1]

Various Bloc nations initiated such negotiations in the spring of 1958 and the CMEA Plenum in Bucharest (June, 1958) recommended that the State Planning Commissions conclude these bilateral negotiations by the end of October, 1958. By and large this deadline seemed to have been met and these preliminary trade agreements gave the planners drawing up the national long-range plans a much firmer base than in previous planning periods.[2]

A year after the preliminary agreements had been made, the Ministers of Foreign Trade bilaterally negotiated the final global trade agreements.[3] Thus the long-range foreign trade discussions had two steps instead of one. In the period between these two steps the planners had time not only to discover additional bottlenecks in the plan which could be relieved through foreign trade but also to take into account the new CMEA specialization recommendations.

[1] Stefan Jedrychowski, 'On the Economic Relations among the Socialist Countries,' *Polish Perspectives*, 7–8/1959, pp. 3–9.

[2] According to a DDR source ('Zur Ausarbeitung des Perspektivplanes,' *Der Aussenhandel* IX, 2/1959, pp. 6–8): 'At the beginning of the second Five-Year Plan we did not have so many bilateral and multilateral agreements for the delivery of certain important raw materials such as hard coal, oil, rolled steel, etc. which we now have. Corresponding to our agreements with the USSR and other Socialist countries, we are today in possession of firm delivery commitments. The sales of the greater part of our production until 1965 is assured for the first time over such a long period.'

[3] These final bilateral trade agreements are apparently what is meant by the 'co-ordination' of the national plans which the Bucharest Plenum recommended to be completed by the middle of 1959. Various West German economists have asserted that a date for the 'co-ordination' of the long-long plans (20 year plans) was also set at this time but subsequent notices in the Bloc press indicate that such a 'co-ordination' did not take place up to 1961.

In the year between the preliminary and final trade agreements, some changes were made. This may be seen from the results of the USSR-DDR discussions. (See Table 3–3, below.)

An extending of the period of negotiation for the short-range trade contracts occurred also. More and more, the FTES began to meet before the signing of the global trade contracts to discuss the quantities and types of goods to be traded. These contacts between the FTES dampened the adverse effects of the late global contracts by permitting a certain amount of trade to be agreed upon beforehand. Moreover, since these trade negotiations and the drawing up of the yearly plan occurred at the same time, trade became a more integral part of the planning system in the short-run as well. Finally, the negotiations of top officials for the signing of the global contracts increasingly concerned prices rather than quantities of goods. Discussions between the DDR and USSR, which at one time lasted three months, were cut down to a period of several weeks.

TABLE 3–3

IMPORT AGREEMENTS AND PLANS OF THE DDR FOR 1965[1]

(1,000 Tons)

	Import Agreement with USSR		*DDR Import Plan*	
Commodity	*Preliminary Between State Planning Commissions 1958* (a)	*Final Between Foreign Trade Ministries 1959* (b)	*Preliminary Seven-Year Plan* (c)	*Final Seven-Year Plan* (d)
Met. cokes	1,550	—	—	—
Hard coal	—	5,670	—	8,850
Iron ore	—	2,180	—	—
Pig iron	1,600	1,400	1,635	1,435
Rolled steel products	1,560	1,450	2,000	2,265
Apatite concentrate	800	—	—	—
Crude oil	4,800	4,800	5,000	5,300
Aluminium	85	—	95	91
Copper	43	—	—	43
Wool	—	—	—	34
Wood (1,000m³)	1,200	1,900	1,545	1,545
Cars (number)	—	10,000	—	—
Cellulose	54	54	122	122
Phosphate (Fertilizer)	320	—	—	—
Cotton	—	100	152	147

[1] A dash (—) indicates that no information is available. The sources for these data are:

(a) Walter Ulbricht at the V. Parteitag, speaking of the USSR-DDR agreement of July 7, 1958, quoted by IWE, 'Der Aussenhandel der DDR,' *Tagesbericht* X, 113/1959, October 28, 1959.

It is difficult to gain a precise idea of the importance of these contracts between FTEs before the signing of the global agreements because data are scarce. In 1958 the following percentages of the 1959 DDR export plan were fixed in specific contracts:[1] by June 30, 1958, 30 per cent; by September 30, 1958, 45 per cent; by December 31, 1959, 65 per cent. However, the strong efforts to conclude the global contracts at an earlier date as well as the continual complaints that this aim was not achieved, indicate that an important amount of new trade was conducted at the last minute in the final negotiations for the global contracts.

Another type of trade agreement which seems to be gaining in importance is the 'additional contract', concluded in the late summer or autumn of the year for the immediate exchange of goods temporarily in surplus for goods which are urgently needed. These contracts, made between the Ministries of Foreign Trade, production ministries or domestic trade ministries of the Bloc countries, provide a flexibility over and above the yearly global trade agreement. For insta nce in 1958 Poland conducted over $50,000,000 worth of trade (about 3–4 per cent of its total trade turnover) through this escape valve arrangement.[2]

Thus the dilemmas of signing global trade contracts, which were listed in the last chapter, were solved by sequentializing the signing of trade contracts over the whole length of planning in five different steps. The basic core of trade for each year was agreed upon in the long-run bilateral agreements between the State Planning Commissions of each country. Additional goods were added to this basic core in the long-term bilateral trade contracts between the Ministries of Foreign Trade somewhat later. Then, as a Polish economist saw

(*b*) Franz Heiduschat, 'Zwei neue Handelsabkommen mit der Sowjetunion,' *Der Aussenhandel* IX, 23/1959, pp. 4-5.

(*c*) Quoted from *Neues Deutschland* by ECE 'Foreign Trade and the Economic Developments in Eastern Europe and Soviet Union,' *Economic Bulletin for Europe* XI, 1/1959.

(*d*) *Gesetzblatt der DDR*, 56/1959, pp. 703ff.

[1] From unpublished information supplied to me by Herr Albrecht, Statistische Abteilung Ministerium für Aussenhandel und Innerdeutschen Handel der DDR. He told me that the 1958 results represented a 'great improvement over past years' and scattered evidence in the DDR trade magazine *Der Aussenhandel* confirms this. In 1952 by the end of January only 50 per cent of the total export plan for 1952 had been fixed in operational contracts. By the middle of September, 1956, only 32 per cent of the exports for 1957 had been fixed in such contracts; by the middle of September, 1957, the figure was 26 per cent of the exports for 1958.

[2] ECE, 'Foreign Trade and the Economic Developments in Eastern Europe and the Soviet Union,' *Economic Bulletin for Europe* XI, 1/1959, p. 74. According to Jedrychowski, *op. cit.*, about $25,000,000 of this 'extra trade' was with the USSR. According to one DDR interviewee, such 'extra trade' accounted for about 3 per cent of total DDR trade.

the situation: '... Once the quantities of those goods which are the most important for a given state but, at the same time (are) usually most difficult to buy are fixed in the long-term agreements, the negotiators are able ... to direct their attention to problems which would have previously been considered secondary.'[1] The short-term contract-making occurred in three steps: the agreements made by the FTEs, based on the yearly breakdown in the long-term contracts, plus additional goods needed and available; the yearly contracts between the Ministries of Foreign Trade, which summarized and supplemented the contracts previously made and which provided the framework for more operational contracts between FTEs; and the 'additional contracts' which provided flexibility for the exchange of surplus goods for bottleneck goods during the plan year.

This sequentialization did not solve all problems by any means. The five-step process was still clumsy; contact between the various foreign trade-planning units in the Bloc nations was not constant and, as far as I have been able to ascertain, left much to be desired.[2] Several people in East Berlin mentioned that the clumsiness of the contract system encouraged autarkal tendencies and that some (unspecified) measures were taken to combat this.

B. Other Communication Channels

The development of effective communication channels between foreign and domestic markets presents many practical problems but few theoretical difficulties. It is primarily a matter of the business administration of FTEs and Ministry of Foreign Trade which has, for the most part, been shrouded in secrecy.

In the foreign trade literature the problems of market research have received increasing attention. Although more workers have been assigned to this work, much improvement needs to be made if we are to believe the evaluation of DDR foreign traders.[3] Among the Bloc nations, the DDR seems to pay less attention to market research than many others. For instance, in the DDR Market Research Institute, less than four men are engaged in study of plans and needs of other Bloc nations. In comparison with any FTE in the CSSR, even the FTE in the DDR with the most market research employees, placed a poor second.[4]

Greater appreciation is also being given to the benefits of advertising as a means of communication. An increasing number of

[1] Jedrychowski, *op. cit.*

[2] Recently a system of 'Rolling five-year trade contracts' has been proposed.

[3] See, for instance, *Der Aussenhandel* X, 12/1960, pp. 28–32.

[4] *Ibid.*

analyses concerning the need of greater advertising were made in the late 1950s.[1] Moreover, in December, 1957, an all-Bloc conference of advertising specialists resolved that each country should be allowed unlimited advertising privileges in the periodicals of other Bloc nations.[2] Although advertising of foreign firms has increased, it does not appear that any nation has taken real advantage of this measure.

Alternative communication channels have received greater emphasis. For instance, with the non-Communist nations the DDR has signed an increasing number of global trade contracts or bank agreements to facilitate trade. More and more trade missions and representatives are being sent to Western nations; and greater emphasis is being placed on co-operative arrangements with chambers of commerce of these countries. Without any data it is difficult to evaluate the extent of these improvements. As I note in Chapter VI, Bloc trade with the West has been continually handicapped by inadequate network of trade representatives and it seems that great improvement is still needed.

Within the Bloc the trade sections of the DDR embassies have become more active and their work is being supplemented by an increasing number of special trade missions sent out for particular purposes.[3] Trade fairs and technical exhibitions have also received much greater attention. Large annual or bi-annual fairs are held in Leipzig, Poznan, Brno (CSSR) and Plovdiv (Bulgaria), and bring together not only Bloc foreign traders, but also representatives from production ministries and State Planning Commissions to learn of production and economic conditions in other Bloc nations. Although many trade negotiations are carried out months before, these fairs serve as a meeting place for the signing of many contracts. Some ideas of the importance of the Leipzig Fair for the DDR may be seen from Table 3–4 on the following page.

Since the overwhelming majority of the contracts signed at the fairs were for deliveries in the next year, these fairs provided some escape from the dilemmas of 'explosion planning' which were discussed earlier. The growth of the activities of the Council of Mutual Economic Assistance since 1955 also led to the development of an

[1] e.g. see Heiduschat, *op. cit.*

[2] IWE, 'Aussenhandelswerbefachleute des RGW tagen in Prague,' *Tagesbericht*, December 10, 1957.

[3] From 1945 to 1956, Russia signed many international agreements which permitted Russia to have special independent trade missions in these countries, but did not permit reciprocal privileges. After 1956, however, reciprocity was finally granted. (E. Medvedev, 'Soviet Trade Agreements with Socialist Countries,' *Problems of Economics* III, August/1960; from *Vneshniaia Torgovlic*, 3/1960).

TABLE 3–4

DDR TRADE CONTRACTS SIGNED AT LEIPZIG FAIRS[1] (IN MILLION ROUBLES OR DMS)

Year	*Value of Export Contracts*	*Contracts as per cent of Total DDR Exports*	*Value of Import Contracts*	*Contracts as per cent of Total DDR Imports*
		%		%
1956	3,858 Rbls	69	904 Rbls	17
1957	2,661 DMs	37	593 DMs	17
1958	3,047 DMs	40	1,031 DMs	28
1959	4,054 DMs	48	1,479 DMs	30

alternative intra-Bloc communication network. Nevertheless, the work of the CMEA has primarily focused up to now on the exchange of technological information, the building up of common production standards, and the recommending of production specialization measures rather than on foreign trade *per se*. Although the Commission of Foreign Trade of the CMEA has worked on problems concerning the methods by which trade is carried out, the CMEA does not play a very great direct role in trade as far as I have been able to determine. (The CMEA is discussed in detail in Chapter VII.)

The importance of trade fairs, trade missions, CMEA work, and exchange of 'want lists' notwithstanding, I received the impression from my conversations in East Berlin and from reading the Bloc foreign trade literature that these measures do not serve as an adequate substitute for market research and advertising; and that money invested in both these areas might yield very high results.

4. SUMMARY AND CONCLUSIONS

Although many specific faults in the carrying out of foreign trade have been recognized in the DDR economic literature, most of their economists seem fairly content with the overall performance of the foreign trade system. The supposedly high trade turnover per foreign trade employee has been offered as proof of this claim. Some data are available.

In 1956 the average export sales per employee of the FTES were

[1] Sources: various communiques of the Leipzig Fair Administration appearing in *Der Aussenhandel*. To calculate the per cent of total trade, I used a conversion factor of 1 DM=1 Rouble for exports and 1 DM=1·8 Rouble (official rate) for imports. (See Chapter IV for justification of the procedure.) These data are not to be taken too seriously (especially the 1956 export figure, which seems out of line), but indicate in a general way the great amount of trade which is conducted. The fairs also have an important domestic function, bringing together buyers and sellers since domestic advertising is also neglected. When I was in Leipzig, the overwhelming number of visitors were DDR retailers.

about 700,000 Roubles ($175,000).[1] It was also asserted that trade turnover per foreign trade employee was three times higher for those handling trade with East Bloc nations than for those handling the accounts with Western nations.[2] This means that export sales per foreign trade employee in 'Socialist world market' sections were about 1,050,000 Roubles ($263,000) and for employees in 'Capitalist world market' sections, about 350,000 Roubles ($88,000).

Such data, while offering an interesting sidelight, certainly do not prove that the foreign trade system showed a good overall performance. The analysis of the previous chapter suggested that up to the middle 1950s the system had four principle faults: over-centralization in planning and decision-making; over-specialization of trade and production functions; great discontinuities in decision-making; and a neglect of information gathering. Since the death of Stalin some changes have been made:

A. The system was decentralized in several ways. First of all, the 'direct export' system allowed trade to be carried out by many more economic units. Moreover, the State Planning Commission began to specify the plan goals for the direction of trade in less detail, reduced the number of plan position, and dropped the practice of specifying trade targets for goods within the individual 'plan positions'. Furthermore, the introduction of the simultaneous planning system as well as the increased emphasis on the 'horizontal relationships' between enterprises gave the FTEs a greater degree of autonomy. Finally, a great many people were brought into the trade negotiation process with foreign nations.

B. The specialization in the carrying out of the foreign trade function by the FTEs was decreased in several ways. The 'direct export 'system allowed the production enterprises a limited amount of participation in foreign trading. Moreover, the increased contact between the FTEs and production enterprises, brought about by the transferal of some of the lower adminstrative units of the FTEs to the factories and by the introduction of the 'simultaneous' planning system increased the degree to which production representatives participated in foreign trade decisions.

[1] Datum calculated from 1957 exports (*Statistisches Jahrbuch der DDR*, 1958) and the number of FTE employees ('Was wissen wir von unserem Aussenhandel?' *Der Aussenhandel* VII, 24/1957, p. 877). Estimating the number of employees in the Ministry, the Chamber of Foreign Trade, the Market Research Institute, etc. as 1,000, the average export sales per foreign trade employee falls to 620,000 Roubles ($155,000). Comparable data for Western trade enterprises are not available, but one West German trader told me that 'this DDR figure was not in any way extraordinary.'

[2] 'Darüber muss auf der handelspolitischen Konferenz gesprochen werden,' *Der Aussenhandel* IX, 10/1959, pp. 8–10. Several of my DDR interviewees affirmed this statement.

C. The internal discontinuities in planning, that is to say, the practice by which all important decisions for the year were made at one time, were diminished through the greater operational nature of the long-range plans, and the making of trade contracts over the whole planning period from the long-run to the short in five different steps.

D. Much greater attention was paid to problems of information gathering. The statistical reporting system was improved; more aggregative statistics such as trade price and volume indices were made; and more emphasis was laid on the use of statistics in decision-making. The gathering of information of foreign markets was improved through the placing of greater emphasis on market research and intra-Bloc advertising as well as alternative channels of communication such as trade fairs and missions.

Some of the adverse aspects of Bloc foreign trade were modified through these changes. The data from the last chapter show that in the late 1950s the DDR finally began to fulfil its foreign trade plan. Moreover, the yearly 'trade cycle' was less pronounced. Through the increased emphasis on information gathering and the growing importance of 'additional trade contracts', the flexibility of the trade system was greater. However, as I noted in Chapter I, the relative degree of autarky remained about the same for most countries including the DDR in this period. Thus, the overall performance of the DDR foreign trade system was hardly ideal because a great many very profitable trade opportunities were missed. To explain this phenomenon, we must now turn to a closer examination of the making of trade decisions.

CHAPTER IV

CRITERIA FOR DECISION-MAKING

The classical argument against a highly centralized economic planning system is that it is impossible for the planners to make rational decisions optimizing the allocation of resources to achieve certain economic goals. Such an approach focuses attention on the decision-making process and especially on the criteria for decision-making.

In the early years, it was very difficult for the DDR planners to make decisions which would optimize the structure and volume of trade since the domestic price system was distorted. Profitability (in any sense of the word) considerations were neglected because the decision-makers had very little idea of domestic production costs After 1955, DDR economists began to attack the problem of setting up systematic criteria for making trade decisions and of working out 'profitability coefficients' of trade to guide the planners. By the end of the 1950s many criteria had been suggested and some empirical calculations were made. Although planning methods were thereby improved, these efforts to set up rational economic criteria for decision-making were marred by many unsolved theoretical and statistical problems and the whole programme has left much room for further improvements.

1. THE DOMESTIC PRICE SYSTEM OF THE DDR

In the first post-war decade, rational economic calculation in the DDR was extremely difficult since the domestic price system was so distorted.[1]

In the industrial sector there were three different sets of prices. Goods were sold at special 'factory prices' ('Betriebsabgabepreise') which were based on the irrational Nazi wartime prices and perpetuated through a 'stop-price' law which permitted only piecemeal changes for special factories. Industrial goods were bought by the

[1] I have omitted discussion of the special sets of prices which agricultural producers received or the three different sets of consumer prices. For a history of early price policies in the DDR, see Gerhard Thimm, *Die Preis- und Kostenstruktur in der Industrieproduktion der Sowjetzone* (West Berlin, Heft 24, Berichte des Osteuropa Instituts, Freie Universität, 1956).

enterprises at special transfer prices ('Industrieabgabepreise') which were the factory prices plus a differentiated turnover tax. Planning of production (as well as calculation of plan fulfilment on which bonuses were based) was carried out in an artificial price system ('Messwerte') which rarely reflected with accuracy relative production costs (e.g., the 'Messwerte' price for copper ingots was 4·25DM/kg; for copper wire of any diameter, 1·48 DM/kg; for simple copper cable, 1·26 DM/kg; and for complicated copper cable, ·88 DM/kg).[1]

The results were twofold. First, a system of State subsidies to enterprises whose prices were set below production costs became an important part of the post-war economy. In the early 1950s, for instance, the industrial sector received subsidies amounting to over 10 per cent of the total value of industrial production.[2] Furthermore, until 1955–6, prices for the same good were often quite different, depending on which enterprise produced the article. For instance, Ulbricht complained that factory prices for a particular type of wheel ranged from 338·31 DM to 771·79 DM.[3]

In February, 1953, a new price policy was announced: prices for each article were to be unified in the following years and were to be based on the average planned production cost.[4] These new prices would thus 'support' the profitability of State enterprises and would eliminate the payment of subsidies. To facilitate this new policy, the authority for price making was transferred from the Ministry of Finance to the State Planning Commission and the various production ministries and lower economic units. In the next few years this did not seem to make much difference, however.

In 1956 the pricing principles were amended so that prices were supposed to be based on 'socially necessary costs of production' which were defined as the average production costs for one of the most efficient producers of the good, plus a small profit (sales markup).[5] Depending on the size of the allowed profits, net subsidies to industry could be a permanent feature of the economy under this amendment which must, therefore, be considered a retrogressive step.[6]

[1] Fred Oelsner, *Ubergangsperiode vom Kapitalismus zum Sozialismus* (East Berlin: Akademie Verlag, 1956), p. 50.

[2] Helmut Meier, *Die Entwicklung des Haushaltswesen in der SBZD* (West Berlin: Duncker und Humblot, 1960), p. 127, has data for subsidies paid from 1951 to 1955. After that, only budget data are available.

[3] *Neues Deutschland*, 10/20/1955, p. 5, quoted by Wolfgang Stolper and Karl Roskamp, *The Structure of the East German Economy*, *op. cit.*

[4] *Gesetzblatt* (*GBl*), 22/1953, pp. 313ff. See also Thimm, *op. cit.*

[5] *GBl*, 58/1956.

[6] At least one Bloc nation, Poland, moved in the opposite direction and tried to base the prices of some goods on the cost of production of the least efficient

The various price reforms were carried out quite slowly and the price reform movement did not really gain momentum until 1957.[1] The 1958 budget foresaw State subsidies to industry of about 8 per cent of net industrial production; the 1959 budget, subsidies (State and local government) of about 5 per cent of net industrial production.[2] Although by this time, most DDR economists recognized the need to eliminate net subsidies to industry, the removal of the system of differentiated turnover taxes which also acted to distort producer prices was little discussed until 1958.[3] (In the DDR, turnover taxes on producer goods amounted to about 25 per cent of all turnover taxes[4] and were much more important in the tax system than similar taxes of producer goods in Poland or Russia.)

From this brief survey of the price system it is clear that rational economic calculation was impossible since the price structure was so distorted. Production costs, either marginal or average, were very imperfectly reflected in prices and demand factors had almost no influence on prices at all. Therefore, the planners could not use the

---

producers, thus introducing quasi-rents. See J. M. Montias, 'Price-Setting Problems in the Polish Economy,' *Journal of Political Economy* LXV, 6/1957; or 'Producer Prices in Poland,' *Value and Plan* (ed. by G. Grossman, Berkeley: U. of California Press, 1960), pp. 46–75.

[1] Some idea of the progress of the introduction of improved industrial prices may be gained from the following data (from Rudolph Lorenz, 'Zum Stand der Festpreisbildung in der Industrie,' *Wirtschaftswissenschaft*, Sonderheft No. 5, 4/30/1958):

Per cent of 'Warenproduktion' (without Agricultural Goods) with New 'Reform Prices' ('Festpreise')	%
1/1/1957	24
1/1/1958	36
1/1/1959	60

Per cent of 'Reform Prices' in the Various Ministerial Sectors 1/1/1958	%
Coal and Energy, Mining and Refining	84
Transportation	65
Building Materials	53
Machine Building	32
Light Industry	23
Foodstuffs	14

[2] *Gesetzblatt*, 5/1958, p. 66; *GBl* I, 4/1959, p. 52. These data are not completely comparable.

[3] This differentiated turnover tax did not receive real criticism until 1958, when one DDR economist (Gerhardt Richter, 'Die politische Ökonomie und unsere Preise,' *Wirtschaftswissenschaft* VI, 2/1958, pp. 201–20) remarked: 'We have become accustomed to view lower prices in the production goods industry and higher prices in the consumer goods industry as favourable for the development of the economy. Some disadvantages are obvious. We do not know what the producer goods really cost. Second, the lower prices do not provide any incentive to save raw materials.'

[4] Hans-Jürgen Nitz, 'Die Ausnutzung der Devisenrentabilitätsuntersuchungen bei der planung der Volkswirtschaft,' *Der Aussenhandel* X, 2/1960, pp. 7–9.

prices of the various commodities in planning an optimum allocation of resources or, indeed, even calculating the real costs of producing a good by means of alternative production processes.

In foreign trade an additional problem existed since the exchange rate had been arbitrarily set and did not in any way reflect a supply and demand equilibrium for foreign currency. This meant that even if domestic prices were 'rational', foreign and domestic prices could not be compared directly in order to decide whether a good should be exported or imported. The problem of choosing criteria which could be used in deciding the most profitable commodity structure of any volume of trade was one of surmounting these difficulties. In the following sections I focus primarily on the operational facets of decision-making although it is necessary to note several aspects of the DDR theoretical discussions of the various problems.[1]

2. CRITERIA FOR TRADE: BALANCING OF THE MATERIAL BALANCES

In Chapter II, I discussed how the State Planning Commission attempted to bring the material balances into equilibrium by means of imports and exports. This procedure for determining the structure of trade was not as irrational as one might think at first. To be sure, domestic prices could not be used by the top planners as an accurate guide for making trade decisions but this input-output balancing process did, in a very crude way, bring demand factors into account. That is to say, once certain domestic production and consumption goals were set, relative scarcities were indicated by the surplus of domestic demand over supply of the various goods in the material balances, and foreign trade served to relieve some of these deficits.[2]

It is well-known that such an input-output method of planning allows a consistent trade and production pattern to be achieved, although the probability of reaching an optimal solution by means of such a planning system is practically zero. Since the determining of the trade structure and volume through use of material balances neglected such factors as relative costs of production, alternative production processes and trade programmes, or relations between trade and investment, DDR economists began to search for methods by which these considerations could be taken into account.

[1] For a survey of foreign trade theory in the Bloc, see my 'Communist Foreign Trade Theory,' *Soviet Studies*, July 1962.

[2] Demand factors are, in the DDR literature, usually subsumed under discussion of 'use value' of a good. 'Use value' has several meanings: it seems to denote average (or sometimes marginal) utility of a good to 'society' or to an individual.

3. CRITERIA FOR TRADE: THE 'PREISAUSGLEICH'

The foreign trade enterprises during the first Five-Year Plan period paid little attention to overall questions of profitability, since primary emphasis was placed on meeting the high plan goals. When profitability considerations were brought into the foreign trade decisions, the FTES usually made a simple comparison of foreign and domestic prices by means of the 'Preisausgleich' (PAG) which was the special profit or subsidy accruing to the FTES as a result of trade. That is, the FTES bought goods at domestic transfer prices (Industrieabgabepreise = Betriebsabgabepreise + turnover tax), sold them abroad, and exchanged the foreign currency at the Central Bank at the official exchange rate. Similarly the FTES bought goods abroad with foreign currency obtained by giving the Central Bank the official equivalent in domestic currency, and sold these goods at domestic factory prices (Betriebsabgabepreise). According to the commodity structure of trade and the relationship between domestic and foreign prices, the FTES made an overall monetary profit or loss (measured in domestic currency units) even though trade (measured in foreign currency units) was balanced.

The PAG was in no sense a measure of real trading profitability for the economy as a whole, since it reflected not only the difference between the domestic production costs (for exports) or domestic prices (for imports) and foreign prices but also the influence of State subsidies to manufacturers, turnover taxes and, for the individual goods, the exchange rate. It was quite possible that an FTE could export an article it should really import (from the point of view of the whole economy) and import a good it should export, and make a very nice profit on both sides of the deal. For example:

Export		*Import*	
Value of export of A	$100	Value of import of B	$100
Value of export of A in DMs (at official exchange rate)	220 DM	Value of import of B in DMs (at official exchange rate)	220 DM
Domestic production cost of A	400 DM	Value of import of B in DMs (in domestic prices)	300 DM
Subsidy to enterprise	200 DM	(This price from domestic production costs of 200 DM plus 100 DM of net taxes and subsidies)	
Factory price of A	200 DM		
Turnover tax	10 DM		
Domestic transfer price of A	210 DM		
Preisausgleich (profit of FTE)	10 DM	Preisausgleich (profit of FTE)	80 DM

Although the real domestic production costs of export good A were 400 DM and of good B, 200 DM, the FTE made a profit by exporting A and importing B.

Several special features of the PAG are worth noting. First, although the exchange rate affected the PAG of exports or imports alone, as long as trade was balanced (measured in foreign currencies) the exchange rate had no effect on the overall PAG.[1] Second, the PAG in the DDR underwent three distinct phases:

The first phase, lasting until 1956, was marked by a relative neglect of the PAG, both by theoreticians and foreign traders. I received the impression in East Berlin that up through 1955 the FTEs had such difficulties in obtaining goods for exports and in making plan goals that PAG considerations were important for only a small area of decision-making in exports. Most public discussion of the PAG concerned the problem of whether it was a 'real' subsidy or not; almost no attention was focused on the factors which were reflected by the PAG or, in the process of maximization of the PAG, on the problem of what was really being maximized.[2]

The second phase began in 1956 with a new law permitting the FTEs to buy goods on the domestic market without paying the turnover tax at the last production stage.[3] The official justification of this measure was the elimination of the unnecessary circular flow involved when the FTEs paid the turnover tax and then received this money back in the form of a negative PAG (subsidy). Perhaps Ulbricht's announcement in 1956 that the net PAG was to be eliminated in the next few years caused the foreign trade officials to choose this very visible way to 'lower' the PAG. (Ulbricht's demand was, of course, quite impossible without a major overhaul of domestic prices as well as the whole foreign trade structure. Although prices were gradually being made more rational during the whole period and changes were being made in the structure of trade, this sug-

[1] This proposition may be easily proved.

Definitions: S=Preisausgleich; c=exchange rate

${}_{i}Q$=Quantity of imports; ${}_{e}Q$=Quantity of exports

${}_{i}p$=Domestic price of imports; ${}_{e}p$=Domestic price of exports

${}_{i}P$=World price of imports; ${}_{e}P$=World price of exports

Equations: Export $S=\Sigma {}_{e}Q\,[({}_{e}Pc) - {}_{e}p]$

Import $S=\Sigma {}_{i}Q\,[{}_{i}p - ({}_{i}Pc)]$

If trade is balanced: ${}_{e}Q{}_{e}P={}_{i}Q{}_{i}P$

With balanced trade: Total S=Export S+Import S= $\Sigma({}_{i}Q{}_{i}p - {}_{e}Q{}_{e}p)$. The exchange rate has completely dropped out of the expression.

[2] The major articles in this discussion are in *Der Aussenhandel*, 9–17/1954.

[3] *GBl* II, 3/1956, p. 18.

gestion was quietly ignored.) Such reasons notwithstanding, this new law permitted a slightly more meaningful comparison of foreign and domestic prices for exports since one part of one distorting element in the domestic price was removed.

I was told in East Berlin that the State Planning Commission at no time used the criteria of maximization of the PAG in making decisions concerning the overall commodity structure of trade and I have no reason to doubt this.[1] During this second phase the PAG seemed to be used by the FTEs for decisions concerning exports in two different ways:

A. A positive PAG was sometimes used by the FTEs to decide whether some article should be exported. Since the PAG for most exports was negative, due to the fact that the official exchange rate was greatly overvalued, this discouraged exports at a time when the DDR Government was trying to increase exports as fast as possible. This phenomenon is overlooked by those economists who state that Bloc exchange rates did not affect foreign trade.

B. Sometimes several articles in one plan category were compared, and the good with the highest PAG (or the lowest negative PAG) was selected for export. In this case the exchange rate had no effect since the PAG was being used only in a suboptimization process. Since the distorting effects of subsidies to producers, turnover taxes, etc., were often about the same when two similar goods were compared, such a suboptimization process had merit. By 1959, when the domestic price structure was more rational than formerly, there was a high correlation between the rank of profitability, calculated from special formulae for trade profitability (see next section) and from the PAG for goods of any one industrial sector, e.g., in the machine goods sector this correlation coefficient was about ·85.[2] However, distorting elements of the price system were not the same for goods from different industries and comparisons of such PAGs were often quite meaningless.

[1] If the PAG was used for overall trade planning, then there should be a correlation between the favourability of the PAG and the overall growth of trade for that industrial sector. However, I found no significant correlation of the 1951 PAGS for various industrial sectors (from Klinkmüller, *op. cit.* p. 102) with the growth of exports or imports of these sectors from 1951 to 1955. Another test of the hypothesis may be made on the micro-economic level. If the PAG was used by the State Planning Commission for the planning of trade of major goods, the articles whose domestic prices were relatively low in relation to world market prices should be exported and the goods whose prices were relatively high in relation to world market prices should be imported. Using West German (BRD) prices as 'world market prices,' and taking a comparison of 1955–56 BRD and DDR prices (from Thimm, *op. cit.*) for 39 important DDR trade articles, I found that this hypothesis could not be proven (chi square test, ·90 confidence limit).

[2] Hans-Jürgen Nitz, 'Die Ausnutzung der Devisenrentabilitäts-Untersuchung bei der Planung der Volkswirtschaft,' *Der Aussenhandel* X, 2/1960, pp. 7–9.

Maximizing the PAG was seldom used as a criterion for selecting imports because domestic prices for imports were even more meaningless than other domestic prices. In 1953 the FTEs took over the responsibility of setting these prices, and completely neglected the task.[1] Since imports were so desired, the State Planning Commission specified the import plan in detail, as I noted in the previous chapter, and gave the FTEs little room for independent decision-making in this area.

The third phase of the PAG came on January 1, 1959, when two PAGs were created.[2] PAG II was the same as the previous PAG, i.e., the difference between foreign price (converted to DMs via the official exchange rate) and the domestic price; PAG I was the difference between the foreign price, converted to DMs via a 'purchasing power exchange rate', and the foreign price, converted to DMs via the official exchange rate. The determination of the 'purchasing power exchange rate' has never been explained.

This new procedure had an advantage over the old PAG system, which may be illustrated by a simple example. Let us suppose

[1] The domestic prices for imported articles were set by the Ministry of Finance until early 1953; this arrangement was not entirely satisfactory since the personnel of the Ministry had little knowledge of production and production costs. In 1953 the Ministry of Foreign Trade and the FTEs received this price setting authority and were supposed to follow the following rules:

(*a*) For an article produced in the DDR, the domestic price was to be used.

(*b*) For an article not produced in the DDR, the price of an 'equivalent' good was to be used.

(*c*) If an 'equivalent' good was not available, the hypothetical cost of the good if it were produced in the DDR, was to be used.

(*d*) If this were impossible, the price was to be fitted 'harmoniously' into the rest of the price structure.

In 1954 it was realized that the domestic price of imported Sieman-Martin and Thomas steel was the same and did not encourage the use of the less expensive Thomas steel; therefore, some differentiation in these domestic prices was made. Since then, most authors in the foreign trade magazine have urged that import prices be 'fitted into the price structure' while acting at the same time as incentives or disincentives to import. I have seen no article which has rigorously faced the impossibility of always reconciling these two criteria.

In actuality, the FTEs paid little attention to the setting of import prices. One author (Werner Hafner, 'Die Inlandspreisbearbeitung in den Aussenhandelsunternehmen verändern,' *Der Aussenhandel* VIII, 12/1958, pp. 27–8) estimated that over 25 per cent of all imported articles had no legal price and noted that in one FTE no one was even in charge of the price setting work. Furthermore, the Ministry often arbitrarily changed the price suggested by the FTEs, adding markups, etc. In many cases it seemed that the FTE merely converted the foreign prices into DMs at the official exchange rate. Since the exchange rate was overvalued, this meant that imports were priced unduly low. I suspect that this practice was one of the causes for the introduction of the double PAG system in 1959.

[2] Edeltraut Drassado, *Der Preisausgleich und seine Aussagekraft auf den Warengebiet Heimtextilen unter Beruchsichtigen der Festpreisbildung* (Diplomarbeit, Hochschule für Ökonomie, 1959).

that the domestic price of an article was 80 DMs and the foreign price, \$30·00. The official exchange rate was \$1=2·20 DM; the 'purchasing power exchange rate' was \$1=4·20 DM. The world market price, multiplied by the 'purchasing power exchange rate' (30×4·20=126 DM) was supposed to represent the 'real world market price' for an article, i.e., the domestic equivalent of the foreign market price if the exchange rate reflected the real scarcity of foreign exchange. Assuming that the domestic price represented the true 'social costs' of producing a good, then the DDR should have exported the good since (126–80) 46 DM equivalents of foreign exchange would be gained in this way. If, however, the foreign price was converted to DMs by the current overvalued official exchange rate (30×2·20=66 DM) and compared with the domestic price, then it would have seemed profitable to import the good since (80–66) 14 DM equivalents of foreign exchange would have been gained in this way. In the first case, exporting yielded a positive PAG (PAG I+PAG II); in the second case, importing yielded a positive PAG II (which was equal to the former PAG).

Therefore, if no 'profitability coefficients' were available for a good, if the 'purchasing power exchange rate' really reflected the scarcity of foreign exchange, and if the domestic price reflected 'social costs', then the new PAG could be used to decide whether trade was really profitable from an overall point of view, i.e., when the distortions due to an unreal rate of exchange were eliminated. This may seem like an unnecessarily complicated system, especially since other methods were available to calculate 'foreign trade profitability' which did not rely on the assumptions that any 'purchasing power exchange rate' reflected the scarcity value of foreign exchange or that the domestic price represented true 'social costs of production'. Nevertheless, it seemed as though many foreign traders had a naïve faith in the power of the PAG to measure profitability and continued to use it.[1] The new system eliminated one major defect in this practice.[2] However, as the foreign traders began to gain familiarity with the profitability coefficients and as such coefficients began to be calculated in increasing numbers, the PAG was not used so often as a measure of profitability.

As far as I was able to determine, all other Bloc nations also used some type of PAG for making certain trade decisions. By the middle of the 1950s, however, the major defects of the PAG were slowly becoming apparent to economists all over the Bloc.

[1] This naïve faith by foreign traders in comparing domestic and foreign prices to measure real profitability is seen in many articles in the foreign trade literature.

[2] As I understand the new PAG system, the FTEs will receive PAG I from the Central Bank and PAG II from the state budget. Unfortunately, no official justification has been given for this procedure.

4. CRITERIA FOR TRADE: PROFITABILITY COEFFICIENTS

The public discussion in the Bloc of problems of foreign trade profitability began in 1954 in Hungary and the CSSR and shortly thereafter in Poland. In these countries a lively debate developed and, in 1956 and 1957, three all-Bloc conferences were held to discuss the subject.

The theoreticians in all Bloc countries started by analysing the distinction between 'normal profitability of trade' (Rentabilität), which is the relation of the average domestic cost of production of a good to the world market price; and 'total use of trade' (Nutzeffekt), which includes considerations not only of production costs but also of domestic demand forces and wider socio-political factors. Rentabilität coefficients can only be calculated for domestically produced goods; Nutzeffekt coefficients, however, can be calculated for all exported or imported goods.

Once this distinction had been drawn, discussion centred primarily on the problems of measuring Rentabilität of trade and, indeed, attention was usually focused only on exports. Foreign trade theoreticians viewed the problem of calculating Rentabilität as a problem of purifying the domestic prices, so that they represented the true 'social labour costs' of production, i.e., the direct labour and depreciation costs of production.

Up to 1957 little theoretical discussion concerning foreign trade profitability had appeared in the DDR economic journals. Nevertheless, the problem had been investigated by DDR economists in 1955 and 1956 who reported that 'in spite of the . . . relatively large number of people who have worked on the problem, the results have received very small support or understanding from the side of official institutions in the DDR'.[1] In 1956, a joint commission from the Ministry of Foreign Trade and the Hochschule für Aussenhandel discussed the problem, but very few results came from these talks. In 1957 a whole spate of articles appeared in DDR foreign trade magazines concerning the PAG and the problem of whether the FTES should pay the turnover tax when buying articles for export.[2] The confusion in this controversy lay in the hidden assumption as to what should be maximized in trade and what the concept of trade profitability really meant. In the middle of this discussion, the Czech theoretician Cerniansky published three path-breaking articles in DDR journals, which summarized many of the ideas which the Poles, Hungarians, and Czechs had been discussing for the last three years. Cerniansky pointed out that the function of foreign trade was to

[1] K. Bialecki, 'O badanéach rentownosći eksportu w krajach demokracj ludowy,' *Handel zagraniczny* II, 7/1957, pp. 22–3.

[2] The chief articles of this sterile discussion are in *Der Aussenhandel*, 1–10/1957.

maximize the saving of 'social labour' and gave formulae to measure overall 'Rentabilität' of production as well as 'Rentabilität' of the last stage of production.[1] From 1957 through 1960, the discussion in the DDR journals did not advance much further than these ideas; indeed, most of the discussion retrogressed from the high quality of the original articles. The great advances made in foreign trade theory in other Bloc nations, especially Poland, have received little mention in the DDR economic Press since then.[2]

Rather than review the shades and nuances of the twenty or so articles on foreign trade profitability which have appeared in the DDR journals up to 1961, it is perhaps easier to survey briefly what they have *not* discussed:

A. Only average costs of production have been analysed; the concepts of marginal production costs, or economic rents have not been brought into this discussion except in the most superficial way. Moreover, except for a Chinese contribution in the DDR foreign trade magazine, there has been no examination of the problems of adjusting the domestic costs of production to take into account the domestic demand for the resources or production factors used in the manufacturing of the traded good (e.g., adding a special rent for the use of capital or of a scarce labour skill). The problems of calculating profitability of foreign trade in cases of joint costs of production have not been rigorously attacked.[3]

B. The various economists have not analysed the whole production stage problem, i.e., the problem of how many production stages one should take into account in the calculation of the coefficients. For instance, two extreme types of coefficients are possible: a 'global coefficient' comparing the total production costs to the world market price; and a 'last stage coefficient' comparing the production costs at the last production stage to the world price at a similar production step (i.e., total world market price minus world market price of all goods going into the last production stage). Although both coefficients were used with modifications in the DDR, the merits of each have been left unclear. Moreover, the special theoretical problems of calculating a last stage coefficient, including the valuation of goods from previous production stages, have not been systematically examined.

[1] See Pryor, *op. cit.* for a review of Cerniansky's ideas.

[2] One reason for this neglect may lie in the fact that few DDR theorists can read Polish and that many more translations of Czech and Soviet articles were made by the translating bureaus, than of Polish and Hungarian material.

[3] This problem has, however, been discussed in the literature, especially by Rolf Hodam, 'Zur Devisenrentabilitätsuntersuchung,' *Der Aussenhandel* IX, 3/1959, pp. 24–5; and H. Jahn, 'Devisenrentabilitätsuntersuchungen,' *Der Aussenhandel* IX, 6/1959, pp. 17–18.

C. In the calculation of the coefficients, DDR authors have usually assumed that a constant world market price exists for the good or for the materials imported in order to make the good. In cases where no single world market price exists, DDR economists have suggested using various averaging procedures and using various types of terms of trade indices to determine where the good should be sold. The difficulties in this procedure have not yet been generally recognized in the West, but a Swedish economist has demonstrated mathematically that such averaging methods are inadequate, and that trade profitability can only be maximized by linear programming techniques in situations where different prices for the same good exist in different countries; where overall trade is limited by quotas for each category of goods in a global trade contract; or where the FTEs are allowed only a certain quota of goods to export and must balance exports and imports with various trade partners.[1] Although this problem has been discussed in private circles among DDR theoreticians, there has been no public examination of such optimization possibilities.

D. The effect of investment on foreign trade profitability and the possibilities of minimizing investment to obtain a unit of foreign exchange have not been analysed in the DDR economic literature, although a fierce battle over this problem has raged in Polish journals for many years.

E. Little attention has been paid to the future development of trade profitability brought about by changes in domestic production costs or in world market prices. The leader of the DDR programme for the calculation of trade profitability coefficients declared: 'Critics have demanded that estimation of trade profitability for the future be made, taking into account possible changes in foreign and domestic prices as well as domestic costs, the growing technical and qualitative level of our export goods in relation to the world standard, and the effect of these factors on foreign trade, These basic questions must be analysed. However, it seems to me that it is impossible to calculate such coefficients for the greater part of our exports and imports, at least at the present time. Even if it were possible, these should not replace the structural analysis of short-term coefficients but should supplement them.'[2]

[1] See Tom Kronsjö, *Optimization of Foreign Trade Policy for a Planned Economy by Mathematical Programmes* (Lund, Sweden: Institute of Economics, Lund University, mimeo., 1960). Kronsjö's manuscript has been read by DDR theoreticians.

[2] Hans-Jürgen Nitz, 'Die Ausnutzung der Devisenrentabilitäts-Untersuchungen bei der Planung der Volkswirtschaft,' *Der Aussenhandel* X, 2/1960, pp. 7–9, In a more recent article ('Untersuchung der Devisenrentabilität und der Preisentwicklung im Aussenhandel der Volksrepublik Polen,' *Der Aussenhandel* X, 30/1960) Nitz seems to have modified his position on this point.

Because these problems were not rigorously analysed in the DDR literature on foreign trade theory, the theoretical foundation of the programme for the actual calculation of the foreign trade profitability coefficients rested on a very shaky foundation.

Some calculations of foreign trade profitability coefficients were made in 1957 for special items, although it was not until January, 1958, that the State Planning Commission finally decided to start a general programme for calculating the coefficients for all exports. The DDR programme had few innovations and seemed to be based on the experience of other Bloc nations, especially the CSSR.[1]

The FTEs were given the task of calculating three coefficients for exports:[2]

$$D_e = \text{'foreign exchange coefficients'} = \frac{P_w}{P_i - A_i + S_i}$$

$$D_a = \text{'labour coefficient'} = \frac{P_w - R_w - S_w}{P_i - A_i - R_i + S_i}$$

$$D_m = \text{'material coefficient'} = \frac{P_w - S_w}{R_w}$$

where P_w=price received abroad (f.o.b. DDR border in Roubles)

R_w=world market prices in Roubles of raw materials, half-fabricated goods, and products of lower production stages

S_w=secondary costs and expenses (e.g., transport) abroad

P_i=domestic price (in DMs)

A_i=profit of firm at last production stage

R_i=domestic cost of raw materials, half-fabricated goods, and products from lower production stages

S_i=domestic secondary costs

All of these coefficients avoid the problem of the distorted exchange rate by comparing directly the world market prices with the domestic cost data. Each coefficient measures something different.

D_e is a global coefficient and compares the world market price of the good to a 'purified' domestic price, which should approximate the total 'social cost' of all stages of production. Since the effects of

[1] Eugen Faude, 'Zu den Rentabilitätsuntersuchungen im Aussenhandel der Volksrepublik Ungarn,' *Der Aussenhandel* X, 12/1960, pp. 21–22.

[2] Eugen Faude, *Die Notwendigkeit und Möglichkeit der Bildung eines Kennziffernsystems zur Charakterisierung der Rentabilität unseres Aussenhandels* (Diplomarbeit, Hochschule für Ökonomie, 1958). An alternative to D_e is also sometimes calculated:

$$D_e = \frac{P_w}{P_i - A_i}$$

profits or subsidies as well as turnover and other taxes from all but the last production stage are not eliminated, the 'purified' domestic price is not very pure. Furthermore, the costs of imported materials are not removed, which distorts the coefficient even more. For instance, in the case where a very cheaply imported raw material has a very high domestic price, exports would be discouraged because D_e would be low. Other Bloc nations circumvent this problem in the calculation of global coefficients, by subtracting the world market price of the imported raw materials from the numerator and the domestic price of these materials from the denominator. In actuality the D_e coefficient is merely a PAG coefficient with the inclusion of secondary costs of trade and the elimination of enterprise profits at the last production stage; as such, it suffers from many of the same defects of the PAG.

D_a is a 'last stage' profitability coefficient and involved some difficulties in calculation. World market prices for goods and materials from previous production stages often had to be estimated since no real international market existed for some goods. In several FTES, in order to simplify estimation problems, these goods from previous production stages were divided into four categories:[1]

A. Raw materials
B. Half-fabricated goods (castings, etc.)
C. Other parts used in manufacturing and construction
D. 'Supplementary materials' (grease, electricity, etc.)

In some of these categories, average world market prices were estimated by means of special coefficients. The DDR, unlike Hungary, did not have a standard 'world price list' for all FTES to use, which meant that the 'last stage' coefficients calculated by the various FTES were not completely comparable.

Instead of subtracting the domestic price of articles from previous production stages such as iron castings from the domestic price of the good and the estimated world market price of the castings from the world market price of the good, an alternative procedure was often used. The cost of making the casting was included in the last production stage and only the domestic and foreign prices of the iron in the casting were subtracted from the numerator and denominator of the coefficient. Such a procedure produced a coefficient which represented something between a 'global' and 'last stage' profitability coefficient.[2]

[1] Heinz-Rudolf Zopf, *Die speziellen Kennziffern zur Charakterisierung der Rentabilität des Exportes von Förderanlagen und ihre Bedeutung als Anhaltspunkt für die internationale sozialistische Produktionsabstimmung.* (Diplomarbeit, Hochschule für Ökonomie, 1959.)

[2] Some difficulties in calculating last stage coefficients are discussed by H. Trettin, 'Probleme der Devisenrentabilitäts-Untersuchungen,' *Der Aussenhandel* VIII, 24/1958, pp. 344–6.

The usefulness of a 'last stage' coefficient is also open to some doubt. For instance, the costs of manufacturing at the last stage of production might be quite low, due to some DDR technological innovation. If, however, the good was produced from domestic materials which were produced at extremely high costs (e.g., hard coal) or from foreign materials imported at very high transportation costs (e.g., iron ore), then it might be quite unprofitable from an overall viewpoint to export the good. To make an optimal decision, one must know the costs of the imported materials, domestic resources, and domestic production factors for alternative production methods for all the various stages of production.

D_m is the ratio of the net world market price of a good to the world market cost of the raw material in the good. This coefficient is discussed in the following section of this chapter.

The DDR programme for calculation of foreign trade profitability coefficients had several main faults:

A. Few coefficients were made for imports. At the end of 1957 the DDR did not even have a formula for calculation of such coefficients for imports,[1] although many articles in DDR journals pointed out the necessity for comparing export and import coefficients. In 1960, the head of the profitability coefficient programme declared, 'It is not possible at this time to take the development of the import structure into consideration in the analysis . . . of foreign trade profitability.'[2]

There were three reasons for this surprising failure:

(1) Theoreticians had ignored the problem.[3]

(2) Many of the imports of the DDR were not made within the country, and therefore, comparative production figures were not available. To be sure, production costs of substitute goods which were domestically produced could be used, but this procedure was not followed.

(3) For imports, demand considerations often played a much more

[1] Josef Horsky, 'Ein Nachtrag zur Einführung Gen. Ing. Jesbera betreffend die bisherige Entwicklung der Kennziffern der Rentabilität des Aussenhandels in der CSR,' *Sammelheft: Internationale Konferenz über die Rentabilität des Aussenhandels* (Liblice, CSSR: College of Economics, mimeo. 1957), pp. 483–95.

[2] H.-J. Nitz, 'Die Ausnutzung. . . ,' *op. cit.* In a later article Nitz speaks of calculation of some import coefficients. ('Untersuchung der Devisenrentabilität und der Preisentwicklung im Aussenhandel der Volksrepublik Polen,' *Der Aussenhandel* X, 20/1960).

[3] According to Winfried Fischer (*Die Möglichkeit der Bildung von Kennziffern zur Charakterisierung der Rentabilität des Imports;* Diplomarbeit, Hochscule für Ökonomie, 1959; p. 8): 'The investigation of profitability of imports is much less advanced (than for exports). In the scientific work concerning profitability problems there are only a few small theoretical hints on the periphery and in the DDR we have not yet begun with the practical research of import profitability. . . .'

important role than average production costs. For instance, lack of one small good might bring a whole industry to a standstill, and in such a situation it would be very advantageous to import this good, i.e., Rentabilität coefficients did not bring such factors as economic rent into consideration. Indeed, if the good were produced at a low average cost (although the marginal production cost might have been very high), the FTE might, on the basis of the Rentabilität coefficient, think it desirable to export the good. Since such important considerations could not be quantitatively taken into account by the FTEs, the State Planning Commission determined 80 per cent to 90 per cent of the import plan centrally with the aid of the material balances. (It is quite likely that the bargaining process for the distribution of the 10 per cent to 20 per cent of imports not covered by the central plan was a more effective allocating device because the system for obtaining such 'unplanned imports' was complicated enough to discourage almost all but the neediest cases.)[1]

B. The accounting methods in the FTEs were quite crude, especially the methods by which administrative costs were assigned to each good.[2] In the late 1950s these accounting procedures were much improved but I was told in East Berlin that they left much to be desired and still acted to distort the profitability coefficients.

C. Unlike other Bloc nations such as Hungary, there was no central agency to co-ordinate in detail the calculation of the coefficients between the FTEs and industry,[3] and co-operation between the two sets of enterprises was very limited in this area: 'In Hungary, unlike the DDR, there exists in the area of foreign trade profitability calculations an exceptionally close co-operation between the FTEs and industry. . . . In the DDR the enterprises producing export goods have not yet fully recognized the meaning of the profitability coefficients for the improvement of their own work. . . . The VVBs (trusts) and the

[1] According to *GBl* 33/1953, p. 409 and *MinBl* 31/1952, p. 105, the domestic enterprise must present proof to the Ministry of Foreign Trade that this desired import article is not available in the domestic economy and that no production possibilities exist. Failing this proof, the enterprise must obtain a special emergency certificate from his Ministry or Rat der Bezirke that the good is a vital necessity for fulfilling a special government priority task or the export plan.

[2] Until 1952, considerations of specific foreign trade selling costs did not enter the calculations at all, since an automatic percentage markup was added to all products. The new system for calculating selling costs was not much better. (See the various articles in *Der Aussenhandel* II, issues 2 to 5/1952.) In 1957 one author (Hans-Jürgen Nitz, 'Zu Fragen der Rentabilität im Aussenhandel,' *Der Aussenhandel* VII, 12/1957, pp. 433–5) noted: 'The current calculation system for our foreign trade does not include all the important cost elements for the making of trade prices . . . e.g. circulation costs (including interest on short-term loans) as well as costs of transport and transfer of goods within the DDR.'

[3] Faude, 'Zu der Rentabilitätsuntersuchungen im Aussenhandel der Volksrepublik Ungarn,' *op. cit.*

industrial sections of the State Planning Commission, which are responsible for the wants of industry, have had only the slightest influence on the calculation of the coefficients up to now. . . . Also a great amount of parallel work in the calculation of profitability exists. . . .'[1] Furthermore, many of the personnel in the FTEs seemed to view the calculation of the coefficients merely as 'extra work' and did not seem willing even to try to work more closely with industry.[2]

D. Although many coefficients were calculated, '. . . the lack of, or insufficient evaluation of the calculated profitability coefficients is the chief difficulty in the research of profitability of . . . foreign trade at the present time'.[3]

Many of these difficulties slowed down the calculation of the coefficients but, nevertheless, by the middle of 1958 coefficients for about 20 per cent of the total export volume had been estimated.[4] In 1959, special instructions were issued to accelerate the programme in order to aid in the preparation of the Seven-Year Plan, but by the beginning of 1960 these coefficients had been calculated for only about 50 per cent of the export volume.[5] However, by 1960 enough coefficients for one industry, machine building, had been calculated so that average 'condensed' coefficients for the exports of the industry as a whole could be estimated. Plans were also being made to make such 'condensed' coefficients for the chemicals and light industry.

The main use of the profitability coefficients in short run planning was in a sub-optimization process, i.e., each FTE was supposed to try to maximize the profitability of trade within each planning position or group of planning positions. This did not, however, insure a total optimization of trade because the degree of profitability of the trade of the various optimizing units was probably greatly different, and opportunities were missed for channelling more trade to the most profitable planning position or FTE. Nevertheless, the use of the profitability coefficients in the early 1960s represented a decided improvement over using the PAG.

It does not appear that the coefficients played a very important role in the drawing up of the main guidelines for the Seven-Year

[1] *Ibid.* One reason for the close co-operation in Hungary is the simple geographical fact that 50 per cent of Hungarian industry is located in the Budapest area which facilitates contact between the FTEs and industry (Zopf, *op. cit.*).

[2] Faude, 'Zu den Rentabilitätsuntersuchungen im Aussenhandel der Volksrepublic Ungarn,' *op. cit.*

[3] *Ibid.*

[4] Faude, *Die Notwendigkeit und Möglichkeit der Bildung eines Kennziffernsystems zur Charakterisierung der Rentabilität unseres Aussenhandels, op. cit.*

[5] Faude, 'Zu der Rentabilitätsuntersuchungen im Aussenhandel der Volksrepublik Ungarn,' *op. cit.* The CSSR was said to have such coefficients for 80 per cent of their exports.

Plan (1959–65), since so few were available. Nevertheless, the guidelines of the long-range plan were not completely rigid and in 1960 foreign traders were encouraged to finish making these calculations 'in order to improve' the structure of trade in the Seven-Year Plan.[1] I was unable to find out exactly how these coefficients were used in the making of the long-range plans or in the long-term trade negotiations, although I was assured in East Berlin that these coefficients did play 'a certain role'. To be sure, the material balance system was still the prime planning tool and the coefficients were probably used only in some long-term sub-optimization decisions. In other Bloc nations (e.g., Hungary) the profitability coefficients seemed to be a great deal more important, both in the drawing up of the long-term plans and in the trade agreement discussions.

From this brief survey, I must conclude that although the calculation and use of trade profitability coefficients were superior to the previous methods in trade decision-making, the programme had many faults on both theoretical and administrative levels. Undoubtedly many of these faults can be corrected; more sophisticated formulae can be devised; calculation methods can be improved; and the coefficients can be more extensively used. Nevertheless, some factors on the theoretical side which I have discussed (e.g., the problem of including demand factors or the problem of optimizing when certain limits are placed on trade and when alternative trade and production patterns are available) cast strong doubt on whether the profitability coefficients are the final answer to the overall problem of achieving an optimal volume and commodity structure of trade. Up to 1960 only economists in Hungary and Poland had experimented with the use of linear programming techniques to solve certain complex trade optimization problems, a signal advance over the crude algebraic 'methods of coefficients' of the other Bloc nations.

In addition to the profitability coefficients, a whole series of other criteria entered into the foreign trade decision-making process in the DDR.

5. CRITERIA FOR TRADE: NATURAL RESOURCES AND FACTOR ENDOWMENTS

A. Natural Resources

Although the area of the current DDR had about 22 per cent of the total population of pre-war Germany and about 24 per cent of total mining and industrial production,[2] these aggregates hide the fact

[1] H.-J. Nitz, 'Die Ausnutzung. . . ,' *op. cit.*

[2] Data for 1939 (excluding Berlin) from Bruno Gleitze, *Ostdeutsche Wirtschaft* (West Berlin: Duncker und Humblot, 1956), pp. 141, 173. This is the best study of distribution of pre-war German industry.

that the distribution of raw materials is quite uneven. The DDR is desperately scarce of important minerals such as iron ore, hard coal and petroleum but, on the other hand, has most of the German reserves of brown coal, copper and potassium salts. The raw material situation played a very important role in the structure of DDR post-war trade and economic development, and it was natural for DDR economists to analyse many trade problems in terms of domestic raw material supply.

One of the earliest published analyses of the foreign trade structure and the raw material scarcities came in 1951 when a pioneering economist urged a general reorientation of the export structure toward those goods made from materials produced cheaply in the DDR (e.g., glass, porcelain, paper, stone, and brown coal). He noted, however, that such goods were not always so easily sold on the world market.[1]

During the whole first Five-Year Plan period the general desirability of exporting goods which contained a minimum of scarce materials and of importing necessary raw materials at the lowest possible costs were constant themes of discussion, but trade and natural resource problems were never really analysed in any rigorous manner.[2] Indeed, vulgarization of these ideas reached incredible heights.[3]

In 1957, a very important study was made of the relative steel consumption of various exports. These coefficients, as far as I was able to find out, have played an important role in helping the State Planning Commission determine the general guidelines of future trade. Some of these coefficients have been published: See tables on the next page.

These coefficients had the advantage of being quite graphic. For instance, from a parallel investigation of the steel content in articles made in non-communist nations, it was proven that for almost every good, DDR producers used more steel than any major producer

[1] Ernst Frankfurter, 'Die Aufgabe der Marktforschung im Aussenhandel,' *Der Aussenhandel* I, 2/1951, pp. 45–57.

[2] e.g. see Heinrich Rau (former Minister of Foreign Trade), 'Zu einigen Fragen der volkswirtschaftlichen Rolle und Bedeutung unseres Aussenhandels,' *Einheit* XII, 2/1957, pp. 168–80, and Kurt Gregor (former Minister of Foreign Trade), 'Einige Probleme unserer industriellen Entwicklung,' *Der Aussenhandel* VII, 9/1957, pp. 311–12).

[3] Following the injunction that raw materials must be imported as cheaply as possible, two DDR economists demanded that the DDR import metallic ores to be domestically processed rather than importing refined metals. They completely omitted considerations of transportation costs, costs of new investment in equipment for refining these metals, and the acute DDR labour shortage. (Grünig and Ronneberger, 'Zweckmässiger und bedarfgerechter importieren,' *Der Aussenhandel* VII, 14/1958, pp. 509–10.) As I showed in Chapter I, it was cheaper for the DDR to import pig iron than iron ore and coke to make a ton of pig iron.

TABLE 4–1

STEEL CONSUMPTION (TONS) PER MILLION DM PRODUCTION VALUE[1]

	A	B
Mining and excavation equipment	350	342
Cement making plants	340	—
Machines for metallurgy and heavy industry	—	276
Boilers and turbines	274	—
Equipment for chemical and building materials industries	251	—
Machines for foodstuffs industry	—	108
Average for Ministry of Heavy Engineering	160	—
Textile machinery	86	79
Machine tools	85	91
Printing machinery	64	62

TABLE 4–2

AVERAGE EXPORT RECEIPTS PER KILOGRAM OF STEEL (ROUBLES)[2]

'Stahlbau'	2·00
Equipment for the printing industry	6·44
Single printing machines	17·00
Special machines of People's Enterprise Schobopack	45·00

in the West.[3] (This may have been due to the bonus system to management, which encouraged material intensive production.) The coefficients had the disadvantage of focusing attention solely upon steel and DDR foreign trade theorists searched for more general coefficients to indicate the use of raw materials.

In 1957 and 1958, the 'material coefficient' was developed, which showed the relation between the price received for an article on the world market and the world market price of the raw materials and half-fabricated goods contained in the product. (See previous section for formula.) From this coefficient the planners were supposed to be able to tell if the DDR was 'exporting vitally needed materials'. A similar coefficient showed the relation of domestic costs of raw materials plus depreciation costs to total production costs but was not in general use.[4]

Many theoretical and practical difficulties surrounded the use of coefficients measuring material use. Most important, since the various types of coefficients do not take foreign prices and domestic

[1] Data Set A: Hans Schönherr, 'Die Rohstoffbasis der Industrie der DDR (IX),' *Material Wirtschaft* V, 16/1957, pp. 14–16. Data Set B: Brass, *op. cit.* p. 100. Slightly different data are given by G. Grabig, *Der Aussenhandel in sozialistischen Reproduktionsprozess* (East Berlin, Lehrbrief of Hochschule für Ökonomie, mimeo., 1959), p. 18.

[2] Brass, *op. cit.* p. 100.

[3] See tables in Schönherr, *op. cit.*

[4] Lothar Rouscik, 'Die Ermittlung des ökonomischen Nutzeffektes der sozialistischen internationalen Arbeitsteilung,' *Der Aussenhandel* X, 15/1960, pp. 19–24.

production costs into account together, they were of little use as a measurement of comparative advantage. At best, a steel or copper consumption coefficient may be used in the place of some other type of disincentive for exports containing these materials (e.g. a high domestic price or a special rationing system); at worst, these coefficients might encourage unprofitable trade. That is, a good with a low 'material intensity' or 'steel intensity' might receive a price on the world market which would provide an extremely low return for domestic labour; similarly, a good with a high 'material intensity' might receive a price which would not only cover imported raw materials but provide a very generous compensation for domestic labour and capital.

DDR economists were aware of this dilemma and one complained: 'A substantial number of our foreign trade partners . . . have to give priority to development of basic materials industries and transport. They are, therefore, very interested in obtaining heavy equipment from us; and this limits the scope for the otherwise desirable changes in our engineering production patterns.'[1] Notwithstanding this insight, DDR economists have not really analysed the problems arising when the 'material coefficients' and the trade profitability coefficients suggest different courses of action.

Indeed, the whole theoretical examination of 'material intensity' in the DDR has been very superficial since problems of the meaning of 'material intensity' or the relation of 'material intensity' to the achieving of overall plan goals in the most optimal way, have been almost completely neglected.

B. Endowment of Production Factors

The high investment rate and forced development programme of the DDR focused great attention on problems of the scarcity of capital. In foreign trade, the discussion of the need to adjust the commodity structure of trade to conserve scarce capital was conducted primarily in terms of 'labour intensity' coefficients. Indeed, considerations of capital were seldom directly mentioned.

There were two different definitions of labour intensive goods in

[1] *Die Wirtschaft*, 14/11/1957, quoted by ECE, 'Developments in the Foreign Trade of Eastern Europe and the Soviet Union,' *op. cit.* pp. VI–18–19. Another economist (Kurt Lelansky, 'Der Schwermaschinenbau der DDR—Kernstück der Exportproduktion,' *Der Aussenhandel* VII, 4 and 5/1957, pp. 165–6) noted: 'In view of the high qualifications of our skilled workers and our limited raw material base, it is not our task to encourage the export of material intensive goods. On the other hand, because of the structure and tradition of our heavy building industry, we cannot fully give up production of material intensive goods. . . . The increase of exports of heavy machines must come primarily from labour intensive goods. . . .'

the DDR economic literature: one, in terms of the high ratio of wages to total production costs; the other, in terms of a low ratio of raw material costs to total production costs.[1] After 1955 various types of coefficients were calculated, such as work hours per 100 DM production value.[2] Some of these coefficients were inversely related to 'material coefficients':[3]

TABLE 4–3

MATERIAL AND LABOUR COEFFICIENTS FOR DDR PRODUCTION

	Wage Costs as a per cent of Total Production Costs %	*Tons of Steel per Million DM Production*
Printing machines	50·6	62
Textile machines	40·2	79
Machine tools	38·2	91
Machines for foodstuffs industry	34·5	108
Machines for metallurgy and heavy industry	30·5	276
'Förderanlagen und Stahlbau'	30·0	342

In 1959–60 the problem of conserving scarce capital was attacked more directly by the computation of output/capital ratios (production per 1000 DM capital) for some goods. These coefficients were criticized because of the general undervaluation of capital costs,[4] and have not, as far as I was able to find out, been used very extensively in foreign trade decision-making.

Investigation of factor proportions of production is extremely difficult for both conceptual and statistical reasons, and a vast literature on the various problems exists in the West. Disregarding the many nuances, several main theoretical and empirical problems exist.

First, of course, is the problem of defining a 'production factor'. Should we follow Ohlin and consider not only weather and climate as production factors but also the different qualities of land, labour and capital (if they do not have a constant elasticity of substitution with other units of the same aggregate factor)? Or should we follow Viner, Samuelson, and others and consider more aggregate units as 'production factors'?[5] This is an important analytical question which has been completely neglected in the DDR foreign trade literature.

[1] e.g. see definition of Frankfurter, *op. cit.*

[2] Rouscik, *op. cit.*

[3] Brass, *op. cit.* pp. 100ff. Brass is not very careful with his definitions, but I believe that the wage cost figure includes wages only in the final production step.

[4] H.-J. Nitz, 'Die Ausnutzung . . . ,' *op. cit.*

[5] For a discussion of this debate, see Richard E. Caves, 'The Meaning of "Factor of Production",' *Trade and Economic Structure* (Cambridge, Mass: Harvard University Press, 1960), pp. 93–101.

If a satisfactory definition of 'factor of production' is found, other problems arise in determining the relative factor endowment of a nation. According to a definition which is implicit in many Western discussions of the problem, nation M is relatively capital endowed if, for any factor price ratio, the capital/labour ratio of this nation is higher than for the nation N. However, it is quite conceivable that when factor price ratios shift, the supply of the factors in the two countries shift in such a way that nation M has a lower capital/labour ratio than nation N.[1] Secondly, when more than two factors are brought into the analysis, additional problems of defining factor endowment occur.

Although it is generally assumed in the DDR literature that the DDR is relatively labour endowed, this conclusion is difficult to confirm. Although data on the capital stock are not available, an examination of the population and labour force data and some general economic considerations permit certain tentative conclusions to be drawn.

TABLE 4–4

DDR POPULATION AND LABOUR FORCE DATA[2]

Year	*Population 1950=100*	*Per cent of Population in Working Ages*	*Number of Women per 100 Men*
1939	91·1	67·5	104
1950	100·0	63·3	125
1951	99·8	63·2	125
1952	99·5	63·1	125
1953	98·5	63·1	124
1954	97·9	63·2	124
1955	97·0	63·2	124
1956	95·7	63·0	124
1957	94·7	62·6	123
1958	94·1	62·3	123
1965[a]	95·2	58·4	121
1965[b]	99·0	57·2	120

The declining population, the high female/male ratio, the high use of male and female labour potential, and the low unemployment rate confirm the general Western opinion of the acute labour shortage in the DDR. The constant demand for more labour intensive exports by DDR economists seems, therefore, somewhat paradoxical, although it can be economically rational (see below).

Furthermore, the fact that the DDR has the highest industrial production per capita of any nation in the Bloc except the CSSR (see Table 1–2) and has had a high investment rate in the past years suggests that the DDR is probably relatively more capital endowed

[1] *Ibid.* Chapter IV.

[2] For sources, see Statistical Appendix B. For a much more sophisticated discussion of factor proportions, see Stolper and Roskamp, 'An Input-Output Table for East Germany with Application to Foreign Trade,' Oxford Stat. Inst. *Bulletin*, 4/1961, pp. 379–92.

Labour Force data:

Year	*Labour Force 1950 =100*	*Men in Labour Force as per cent of Male Labour Potential*	*Women in Labour Force as per cent of of Female Labour Potential*	*Women in Labour Force as per cent of Total Labour Force*	*Unemployment as per cent of Total Labour Force* Data	*Western Estimate*
1939	113·1	—	—	36·7	—	—
1950	100·0	—	—	37·0	4·2	—
1951	102·3	—	—	—	3·1	—
1952	105·3	87·0	52·3	42·3	1·3	—
1953	106·9	88·0	54·4	42·8	1·1	6·3
1954	110·8	89·6	58·2	43·8	0·7	—
1955	110·6	90·0	58·8	43·7	0·5	—
1956	109·9	90·3	59·5	43·6	0·5	—
1957	110·7	91·6	61·8	44·0	0·3	—
1958	109·9	92·1	61·7	43·5	0·2	—

(has a higher capital/labour ratio) than almost any other Bloc nation. I think that DDR economists have falsely evaluated the relative factor endowment of their nation.

Another difficulty arises in defining factor intensity of production of a good. Samuelson has used the following definition: Product A is 'capital intensive' relative to product B when, for each and any factor price ratio, the equilibrium capital/labour ratio for producing A exceeds that for B.[1] But, as some have pointed out, it is quite conceivable that when the factor price ratios change, the equilibrium capital/labour ratio for production of good A shifts in such a manner that A is now 'labour intensive' relative to B.[2] Changes in factor intensity of production brought about by a change in the overall factor endowment of a nation (caused by a change in factor prices) or addition of a third production factor into the analysis cause more analytical difficulties. Here again DDR theoreticians have not yet begun to scratch the surface of these problems.

Moreover, in a two factor world, it is quite conceivable for nation M, which is relatively 'capital endowed', to exchange 'labour-intensive' goods for 'capital-intensive' goods from nation N, which is relatively 'labour endowed'. This trade pattern could result from two nations having different production functions or different tastes; or the same tastes (community indifference curves) but different per capita national incomes.[3] This problem has never been discussed in the DDR economic literature.

[1] Paul A. Samuelson, 'International Trade and the Equalization of Factor Prices,' *Economic Journal* LVIII, June/1948, p. 182.

[2] Romney Robinson, 'Factor Proportions and Comparative Advantage,' *Quarterly Journal of Economics* LXX, May/1956, and August/1956, pp. 169–92 and 346–65.

[3] These propositions are proven by Robinson, *op. cit.*

Finally, in calculating whether production for good A is capital or labour intensive, it is necessary to look at all stages of production by means of some type of input-output analysis.[1] As far as I could determine, the DDR empirical investigations were often limited to the last few production stages and were, therefore, quite useless.

Although the fine points of theory were neglected by DDR theoreticians, many began to recognize intuitively that the factor proportion criteria for trade presented some difficulties in determining overall comparative advantage. For instance, one economist declared: 'We need to shift our exports more and more toward traditional and labour-intensive products: electrical equipment, precision and optical instruments, printing machinery, food processing machinery, vehicles, machine tools and certain products of light industries. But it is precisely in these fields that we have many serious shortcomings, and it happens that Japanese, French, British, West German and American competitors frequently surpass us in our own special lines, not only in the Capitalist countries but also in the Socialist countries such as China.'[2]

It is difficult to tell to what extent factor proportion criteria were ever used in trade decision-making. For drawing up the various long-range plans, they might have been one factor in determining the general guidelines of trade; if so, they probably hindered rather than aided the process of determining a profitable structure of trade. Since 1958, theoreticians have placed increasing emphasis on the profitability coefficients and have paid less attention to material or factor proportion coefficients. This shift in emphasis was, I believe, a forward step.

6. OTHER CRITERIA OF TRADE

A. Saving of Foreign Currency

When export targets were higher than realized exports and when planned imports had to be cut as a consequence, policy-makers of Bloc nations often began to speak of a 'shortage of foreign currency'. On top of difficulties in exporting enough to pay for vitally needed imports, the DDR faced several additional problems. First of all, the DDR had to pay a part of the occupation costs in foreign currency

[1] The first extensive statistical investigation of factor proportions in trade using input-output techniques, was made by W. Leontief, 'Domestic Production and Foreign Trade: The American Capital Position Re-examined,' *Economia Internazionale*, February/1954; and W. Leontief, 'Factor Proportions and the Structure of American Trade: Further Theoretical and Empirical Analysis,' *Review of Economics and Statistics* XXXVIII, April/1956, pp. 386–407.

[2] *Die Wirtschaft*, 11/14/1957, quoted by ECE, *op. cit.*, pp. VI–18.

up through the middle of the first Five-Year Plan period.[1] Secondly, the DDR has always had a passive service balance, due to the necessity to use West German harbours and foreign ships. For instance, in 1956 and 1957 the net passive balance for transportation amounted to $78,000,000 and $94,000,000 respectively.[2] Four times the USSR has had to bail the DDR out of trade difficulties through hard currency loans.

It was quite natural that a major goal of the second Five-Year Plan was the creation of an operative foreign currency reserve to supplement the small 'State reserves' (which were used for the highest priority imports). Trade difficulties in 1957 greatly intensified the problem[3] and DDR top policy-makers were extremely concerned about this whole situation.

This 'lack of foreign currency' and the high passive services balance were prime motives for the building up of the DDR merchant marine. Profitability considerations seem to have played a minor role: e.g., 'Between Rostock (DDR) and Odessa, the costs of sea transport are much higher than those of railway transport, to be sure; but one must consider that the transport by sea gives occasion to very little expenditure of foreign currency. . . .'[4] In 1958, 75 per cent of DDR foreign trade was carried by train (which necessitated foreign currency expenditures) and 9 per cent by ship. According to the Seven-Year Plan these percentages will become 49 per cent and 39 per cent respectively in 1965.[5]

Nevertheless, it is very difficult to tell the exact role of the criterion to save foreign currency in the actual choice of goods to be traded. A joint CSSR-DDR foreign trade textbook proposed a formal 'foreign exchange coefficient' which was simply the net export price (in foreign currency) divided by the cost of imported materials (also in foreign prices).[6] Although several DDR economists seriously ex-

[1] See 'Die Sowjetunion und wir,' *Der Aussenhandel* VII, 20/1957, p. 762. This was not mentioned in the DDR literature, to my knowledge, either before or afterwards and I do not know the extent of these payments.

[2] Eberhard Quietzsch, 'Verbesserte kommerzielle Dienstleistungen-geringere Devisenausgabe,' *Der Aussenhandel* VII, 11/1958, pp. 394–95, see also Quietzsch, 'Kommerzielle Dienstleistung im Aussenhandel der DDR,' *Der Aussenhandel* VIII, 4 and 5/1958, pp. 145–6.

[3] H. Beck, 'Die planmässige Schaffung einer operativen Valutareserve,' *Der Aussenhandel* VIII, 9/1958, pp. 332–34. Beck noted, 'Since we do not have any real gold reserve, we cannot build an operative foreign currency reserve from unplanned sources.' This may be one of the reasons why, in the Seven-Year Plan, the DDR has planned such a high export surplus.

[4] Ursel Mehlhahn and Eberhard Quietzsch, 'Wichtige Verkehrsprobleme sind in nächster Zeit zu lösen,' *Der Aussenhandel* IX, 15/1959, pp. 25–6.

[5] *Ibid.*

[6] J. Nykryn, K. Heřman, K. Štepán, Franz Heiduschat, *Organisation und Technik des Aussenhandels* (East Berlin: Verlag Die Wirtschaft, 1956), p. 304.

amined variations of this coefficient as possible criteria for trade,[1] such a formal coefficient does not seem to have been made by the FTEs. Nevertheless, the motive 'to conserve on foreign currency' played an important role in devising other formal criteria; the 'material coefficient', which I discussed previously, bears a great similarity to this foreign exchange coefficient.[2]

The saving of foreign currency seems to have been used more as an excuse for refusing certain import requests and increasing certain lines of domestic production than as a formal criterion in the decision-making process except in the decision to build up a merchant marine. I received the impression that a formal criterion of saving of foreign exchange had been once used by several Bloc nations.

B. Miscellaneous Economic Criteria

Since each FTE calculated its own set of trade coefficients (which were not published), it is difficult to survey completely the other criteria which entered into decision-making in foreign trade on the lower levels. Moreover, in the FTEs as well as in other enterprises in both the East and the West, many decisions were made on the sole basis of expediency. The most important *formal* economic criteria have been discussed.

C. Political Criteria

According to a former DDR Minister of Foreign Trade, 'Our foreign trade policy is an important part of the foreign policy of our worker and peasant state.'[3] The general Bloc political criteria in the choice of trade partners are analysed in Chapter VI; here, several special political motives peculiar to the DDR are briefly surveyed.

The first motive was the understandable desire of gaining political recognition through trade. The DDR was not recognized diplomatically by any Western nation, although in some cases, notably Egypt, the DDR trade mission served in the place of an embassy. In commenting on the signing of a bank agreement between the DDR and Turkey, one DDR author noted that this was a sign that more countries had begun to recognize *de facto* the sovereignty of the DDR.[4] Participation in international trade and trade fairs was

[1] See especially Hans-Jürgen Nitz, 'Zu Fragen der Rentabilität im Aussenhandel,' *Der Aussenhandel* VII, 11/1957, pp. 433–5; 13/1957, pp. 470–2.

[2] The main difference is that in the 'material coefficient,' the world market price of all raw materials in the good, whether imported or produced domestically, are included in the denominator.

[3] Heinrich Rau, 'Begründung des Aussenhandelsgesetzes,' *Der Aussenhandel* VIII, 3/1958, p. 102.

[4] 'DDR-Turkei Handelsabkommen,' *Der Aussenhandel* IV, 17/1954, p. 382.

an excellent means of bringing the DDR case to other nations.[1]

The second special political motive was tied up in the struggle between the East and West German Government for the loyalty of the German people; the weight of propaganda concerning inter-German trade was probably greater than the actual trade. Both nations criticized the other for allowing political considerations to enter trade,[2] stealing patents,[3] and importing on credit.[4] (Neither German State seemed willing to finance the trade or economic development of the other). The German Federal Republic (BRD) accused the DDR of dumping and sending inferior goods; the DDR accused the BRD of encouraging German militarism by hindering trade.[5] Both sides hindered the flow of books, although it is much easier to obtain DDR books in the BRD than the reverse.[6] In order to nullify the bargaining strength of the DDR foreign trade monopoly, the BRD set up a special bureau to distribute export and import licences to West German firms. To counteract this move, the DDR recently forced all West German firms to deal through two special FTEs to increase the bargaining strength of the DDR.

[1] Rudolf Brauer, 'Wachsende Erfolge unseres Aussenhandels im kapitalistischen Ausland,' *Der Aussenhandel* IV, 19/1954, pp. 419–20.

[2] One interesting question is the degree to which inter-German trade is tied with the status of West Berlin. For instance, in September, 1960, after the DDR refused to grant permission for West Germans freely to enter East Berlin (which, *de jure*, was still under four-power administration), West Germans claimed that this was a violation of the original trade agreement and threatened to stop all trade until the withdrawal of this measure. This crisis was solved by a compromise.

[3] The German patent situation is a mess, since it is an open question whether a patent belongs to the DDR or the BRD (West Germany) when a pre-war Germau firm had branches in both parts of the country. A more difficult question was posed by the Zeiss camera patents. Zeiss was originally located in Jena, DDR. During the post-war years, a great many Zeiss employees took the 30-mile trip to the BRD and set up their own factory, claiming that they, rather than the DDR government which nationalized Zeiss (without compensation), represented the true Zeiss enterprise.

[4] The official statistics of the inter-German trade in the BRD statistical yearbook show an export surplus of the BRD for almost every year; the official statistics of inter-German trade in the DDR statistical yearbook show an export surplus of the DDR for almost every year.

[5] Premise 1: Militarists in the BRD want political tension so as to have an excuse to invade the DDR. Premise 2: Hindering trade increases political tensions. Conclusion: Hindering trade encourages militarism. The DDR government has never tired of repeating this sylogism.

[6] According to Herman Makow ('Wege zur intensivierung des gesamtdeutschen Buchhandels,' *Der Aussenhandel* I, 3/1951, pp. 79–80), the DDR forbids the imports only of those books 'which glorify war and remilitarization, which are slanted toward the hindering of German reunification, which glorify the American way of life and "culture."' In actuality, the DDR has prevented the import of all BRD books on economics or sociology, most fiction, and many philosophy books, such as the works of Karl Jaspers, as well as almost all West German newspapers.

Inter-German trade is a sad story of propaganda, hypocrisy, and calumny. I will leave the problem to the Germans themselves to discuss and solve.

7. INCENTIVES FOR FOREIGN TRADE

Formal criteria for foreign trade decision-making were not the only factors guiding foreign trade. Different incentives were offered to the traders and producers which encouraged their activities into various channels. Although these incentives were not formal decision-making criteria (as profitability coefficients were), they influenced decision-making in trade and acted as implicit criteria. Several different types of foreign trade incentives were offered to the FTES and production enterprises.

The foreign traders were granted premia through various programmes and competitions throughout the year, where total bonuses were sometimes as high as a million marks. The criteria for granting premia were quite complex, and were determined not only by the guidelines of the State laws concerning premia, but also by special policy instructions from the Ministry of Foreign Trade, which they refused to give me. Since the whole question has not been systematically discussed in the economic literature, my analysis must, of necessity, be sparse and based on material from several interviews from East Berlin.

Originally, premia were granted for the fulfilment of the trade turnover plan (in Roubles). This was unsatisfactory since it placed sole emphasis on a high volume of trade at any cost. In the middle of the first Five-Year Plan period, fulfilment of the PAG plan was made an additional requirement for receiving a bonus and, since then, premia have become partially conditional on other factors such as surpassing the targets of the 'cash-turnover plan', saving of selling expenses, etc. In 1955, payments to the director funds were also made conditional on the fulfilling of the PAG plan. Both the premia system and director fund system have been in constant flux during the past years with different weights placed on the different factors mentioned above.

An additional bonus was given in the various competitions. In the early years, one FTE would challenge the others to see who could save the most administrative costs, sign the earliest contracts, overfulfil the plan, etc. Since 1952, there have been general competitions for the fulfilment of trade volume plans, foreign currency plan, and so forth. Saving of PAG has also been a feature of the competitions.

For domestic enterprises producing export goods, a series of special incentives were set up. After 1953, the main financial incentive was the general 'foreign exchange bonus', which was granted to any enterprise producing export goods and which amounted to 1½ per cent of the foreign exchange obtained for planned exports (or equivalent in DM) and up to 30 per cent of the foreign exchange received for over-fulfilment of the plan for export production.[1] Between 1954–7, this money could be used by the enterprise to import on its own account. After 1957, the secondary suppliers were also given a share of this export bonus.

Another type of incentive was freedom from certain types of taxes. Since 1953, the enterprises producing export goods were exempted from having to pay turnover taxes on these goods, and since 1954 received reduction in income and licence taxes. Special expenses involved in foreign trade work were allowed to be deducted from income in the corporation tax. No special credits were given to producers of export goods, but these firms received especially favourable treatment under the regular credit regulations. A special bonus for outstanding work in producing export goods was also given from 1956 on. If a company could demonstrate that the current domestic price did not allow it to make a profit on goods which could also be sold abroad, the Ministry of Finance had the power to change the domestic price to encourage such production.

Finally, special bonuses were granted to the winners in special contests or actions for fulfilment of various parts of the plan by May 1st, or the birthday of the Republic, or Stalin's birthday, etc.

These various incentives and bonuses to production and trade enterprises had several common features:

A. The incentives were arranged to encourage a high volume of trade rather than achieving the most profitable structure of exports and imports or obtaining the lowest world market prices for imports. This was especially true for the bonuses to the production enterprises. For the FTEs, the introduction of additional factors (such as fulfiling the PAG plan) into the various types of bonuses improved the situation, although my interviewees stressed that the main emphasis was still on over-fulfilling the physical trade plan and increasing the trade volume, regardless of domestic cost.

This focus on trade volume was not, I believe, completely irrational for two reasons. First of all, trade was at a low level and most of the imports had an extremely high value to the planners in relieving bottlenecks. Due to this economic rent factor, the marginal value of imports could have been much greater than the losses incurred in dumping almost any good onto the export market (at least during the first Five-Year Plan period). Second, until 1958–9 when profitability coefficients began to be calculated, the planners

[1] For a complete description of the whole bonus system for production enterprises, see Joachim Kästner, *op. cit.*

had little idea of 'profitability' on which to base any new type of bonuses.

In 1959–60, Hungary tried to set up a foreign trade bonus system, based on the profitability coefficients, which would encourage a more optimal structure of trade.[1] In the DDR in 1960, there were conferences on the problem of new types of foreign trade bonuses, but I do not know the final results of the discussions.

B. The planners made little conscious use of the bonuses to encourage a certain direction of trade. Some bonuses acted in this way, e.g., the bonus for 'direct exports' (which could only be carried on with Western nations), but most of the qualitative effects of the bonuses seemed unplanned.[2] In the CSSR, on the other hand, foreign traders were given extra high bonuses for fulfilling the export plan with the Western nations.[3]

The crudeness of the incentive system of foreign trade was a manifestation of the general neglect of indirect controls (or, in Marxist terminology, 'economic levers') to guide production or trade decisions. Any type of piecemeal overhaul of the incentive system of foreign trade would still leave one fundamental difficulty untouched, the conflict of interest between the trade and production enterprises (which I discussed in Chapter II).

In order to induce domestic manufacturers to make decisions which would meaningfully take foreign trade considerations into account, the incentive system should have as a pre-condition a realistic exchange rate (or a realistic shadow rate for foreign currencies) and domestic prices of traded goods which are related to world market prices. In order to induce foreign traders to make decisions which would meaningfully take into account considerations of comparative advantage, the incentive system should have as a pre-condition a domestic price system which allows expression of domestic supply and demand forces.

However, the idea of relating domestic prices of traded goods to world market prices has only been discussed in Poland; and the price discussion in most Bloc nations has been seriously handicapped by lack of adequate concepts of marginal costs, economic rents and marginal utility. Another unsolved problem of Bloc policy-makers is deciding the optimal mixture of direct and indirect controls.

[1] Faude, 'Zu den Rentabilitätsuntersuchungen im Aussenhandel der Volksrepublik Ungarn,' *op. cit.*

[2] Since the official exchange rate with the West German DM was, in terms of the other exchange rates, overvalued, exporters had a special incentive to export to West Germany and to exchange the foreign exchange bonus into domestic DMs. Since the overvalued exchange rate existed long before the bonus, this special incentive was not specifically planned.

[3] Faude, '*Die Notwendigkeit und Möglichkeit . . .*,' *op. cit.*

Up to now discussion of this problem in the economic Press of all countries has in all Bloc countries except Poland, been seriously handicapped by the inviolable Marxist condemnation of 'economic spontaneity'.

8. FOREIGN TRADE AND INVESTMENT CRITERIA

In the previous sections of this chapter, analysis has primarily concerned short-run considerations, i.e., given a certain domestic structure of production, how the most profitable commodity structure of trade might be obtained. Equally important is the relation between investment and trade, i.e., the relation of a changing commodity structure of trade and production, so that trade would become more profitable in the future. The increasing emphasis on long-range planning and long-range trade contracts in the Bloc after 1955 focused greater attention on this problem and, in the different Bloc nations, a great variety of measures were taken.

In Poland, analysis of special investment criteria which brought in considerations of foreign trade, preceded the discussion in all other Bloc nations. Coefficients of the profitability of foreign trade for certain investments and foreign exchange received per unit of investment were made for many goods and with relatively sophisticated formulae and statistical techniques. In the DDR, both theoretical and statistical analyses of these problems lagged far behind; indeed, as I noted before, the simple capital/output ratios, which were calculated for some export goods, did not seem to be very highly regarded.[1] However, lack of formal criteria and formulae does not mean that foreign trade considerations were not taken into account in the investment programme. In Hungary, for instance, a foreign trade representative participated in every one of the joint councils making investment decisions. In the DDR there were four links between trade and investment.

A. The State Planning Commission was ultimately responsible for the long-range planning in both these areas and it is reasonable to assume that a good deal of informal communication occurred between the separate groups planning trade and production. As I indicated before, formal trade profitability criteria did not seem to be extensively used by the State Planning Commission for long-range planning.

B. FTES were sometimes invited to send to the production ministries special suggestions for new investment.[2] In the beginning this move-

[1] A complete revaluation of capital was carried out in 1960 and capital/output ratios should in the future become a more useful tool of planning.

[2] 'Aus den Entschliessungen der Fachtagung der Aussenhandelskonferenz,' *Der Aussenhandel* VI, 14/1956, pp. 503–6. One of the conclusions of the foreign

ment was not very extensive or successful, but after 1958 such suggestions began to be made on an increasingly greater scale. Moreover, production enterprises could receive investment credits from the banks a great deal more easily with a 'letter of recommendation' from the Ministry of Foreign Trade.

C. Since 1957 or 1958, the Ministry of Foreign Trade has had direct control of a small amount of investment funds.

D. The late Heinrich Rau, Minister of Foreign Trade from 1955 to 1961, was one of the most respected economic administrators in the country. East Germans told me that he wielded a great deal of influence in the Council of Ministers in the making of investment decisions, and that Rau and a minister or trust (VVB) director made 'an unbeatable combination in obtaining investment funds'.

Such informal methods were better than none and provided flexibility in the system. Nevertheless, lacking a general system of trade profitability coefficients for investment, it seems likely that a great many opportunities for investing in industries which would have produced highly profitable export goods were missed.

9. SUMMARY AND CONCLUSIONS

The formal criteria for decision-making in foreign trade, such as the profitability or the material-intensity coefficients, had several main weaknesses. First of all, they were very crude and could not, for the theoretical reasons which I have discussed, lead to any kind of optimal commodity structure of trade. Indeed, some criteria, such as the factor proportion arguments, might have encouraged trade which, in the final analysis, was disadvantageous. Moreover, there were many different types of coefficients which were used and problems of reconciling the conflicting courses of action determined by these criteria arose. The head of the DDR programme for the calculating of the coefficients noted: 'One should concentrate on analysis of several important coefficients, instead of calculating a great number of coefficients, which in the long-run are confusing and which mask the essential aspects of foreign trade profitability.'[1] Nevertheless, the problem of reconciling decision-making criteria was not rigorously attacked. Furthermore, due to the specialization in production and foreign trade by different sets of decision-

trade conference was: 'In order to take the needs of foreign trade more strongly into account in investment, the FTEs should give investment proposals to the Ministry. . . . The specialist departments of the Ministry will discuss these proposals with the proper production ministry and the State Planning Commission and will make agreements with the production ministry concerning the realization of the demands of the FTEs. The Ministry of Finance is to be informed.' Very little seems to have come from this very good idea for several years.

[1] H.-J. Nitz, 'Die Ausnutzung . . .,' *op. cit.*

making units, conflicting types of incentives and decision-making criteria were used in these two functional areas, which added to the general confusion. Finally, theoretical understanding of the benefits of trade, especially for the long-run, was at such a low level that discussion in the economic literature has not brought out the vast untapped foreign trade potential.

These factors led to a certain schizophrenia in foreign trade policy-making. On one hand, top DDR officials publicly have recognized the need for a much higher volume and for a more profitable commodity structure of trade. On the other hand, foreign trade has been relatively neglected. For instance, in the Seven-Year Plan (1959–65) greater relative emphasis was placed on industrial production than foreign trade (see Table 1–6) and no radical change in the overall commodity structure of trade was planned. Furthermore, it was planned for the personnel in foreign trade to remain constant throughout the period[1] although in other 'priority sectors' a rise in personnel was foreseen. As far as I could determine, no effort has been made to attract high calibre personnel into foreign trade by means of high salaries.

The split between recognized need and relative neglect lies, I believe, in the fact that the foreign trade planners failed to demonstrate concretely to the top policy-makers the actual trade potentialities. They failed to show, for instance, that the DDR could grow economically much faster with a few more trained foreign traders and a greatly increased volume of trade than through the opening of a new (high cost) hard coal mine or the construction of a new addition to the Wartburg car factory (when almost every other nation in the Bloc had also planned to increase car production). In other words, they did not gather adequate information on foreign market conditions and domestic production costs; and they did not apply adequate criteria to evaluate the information at hand. The result was a relative neglect of foreign trade and an autarkic economic development.

[1] Otto Hofmann and Fritz Enderlein, 'Die Aufgaben des Siebenjahrplanes erfordern neue Formen der Masseninitiative,' *Der Aussenhandel* IX, 22/1959, pp. 1–4.

CHAPTER V

THE PRICE SETTING PROCESS

Price setting in foreign trade between the European communist nations is a boiling stew of propaganda, ideology, economic forces and self-delusion. In this chapter I isolate and analyse some of the economic ingredients.

Since the early post-war years, the formal basis for setting intra-Bloc foreign trade prices has been the structure of prices on the Western markets. Nevertheless, conflicting sources in the Bloc indicate that other criteria have been used, although it is impossible to derive any firm conclusions from the Bloc discussion. From a description of the way in which prices are negotiated, it seems quite likely that they are set in very heated bargaining sessions. In an extensive statistical analysis of intra-Bloc trade prices, I conclude that although intra-Bloc foreign trade prices are related to Western market prices, traditional economic forces may be used to explain some of the deviations. In the analysis I pay particular attention to the economic factors behind the price discrimination practiced by the Soviet Union. The results of this statistical investigation provide some perspective on the differences between the pricing criteria suggested by Bloc theoreticians and the actual pricing practices.

1. INTRA-BLOC FOREIGN TRADE PRICES: A BLOC VIEW

Although proletarian internationalism is the ideological basis for the resolution of all conflicts within the Bloc, it is impossible to derive specific prescriptions for the settling of actual disputes from this idea, especially in such a politically sensitive area as foreign trade prices.[1] To guide negotiators in setting these trade prices,

[1] According to the Soviet Academy of Science, *Politische Ökonomie Lehrbuch* (first ed. East Berlin: Dietz Verlag, 1955), p. 693: 'In the Socialist camp the relations between the countries are an embodiment of the principle of proletarian internationalism—the international solidarity of the daily worker. The relationships are based on selfless mutual support as well as considerations of national sovereignty and national interest. The brotherly friendship and the close mutual co-operation of the nations of the Socialist camp are extremely important factors in the unconquerable strength of the camp and a critical factor for the successful building of Socialism in these nations.'

formal pricing criteria have been written into the bilateral global trade contracts. However, informal pricing criteria and modifications of the formal criteria seemed to be also used. The Bloc discussion of this whole problem is confusing because the distinction between pricing criteria, formal and informal, and actual pricing practices is usually blurred.

Four different formal price criteria for intra-Bloc trade have been used in the bilateral global contracts in the post-war period:[1]

A. 1946–50

In these years the trade contracts usually stated that intra-Bloc trade prices should be based on the 'average world market price at the signing of the contract'. No explanations were given on how such prices were to be determined.[2]

B. 1951–53

This was called the 'era of stop-prices' for the contracts usually specified that 'average world market prices of 1950' were to be employed, in order to avoid the distorting price influences of the Korean war price-boom. By 1953, however, world market prices became increasingly out of line with these prices and several Bloc countries began to feel that they were discriminated against.

C. 1954–57

In this period so-called 'adjusted prices' were used and the formal price criterion varied between contracts. In some contracts, arrangements were made to 'adjust' in some unmentioned way the 1950 stop-prices in order to eliminate the greatest discrepancies between these prices and current prices. In other contracts, specific emphasis was placed on determining prices from the 'average world market prices

[1] This material was gathered from interviews and confirmed in articles by Josef Mervart ('Některé otázky působení zákona hodnaty na světovém socialistickém trhu,' *Politiká ekonomie* V, No. 7; reprinted in *Czechoslovak Economic Papers*, Prague, Nakladatelství Ceskoslovenskí akademie věd Praha, 1959; pp. 85–111); S. Polaczek ('Odrebny uktad cen w handlu zagraniczym dia krajow socjalistycznck,' *Ekonomista*, 1/1960); or Mikhail Bolabanoc ('Prices in Trade Between Socialist Countries,' *Vneshna trgoviya* VI, 10/1958, pp. 8–12); Günter Kohlmey, *Der demokratische Weltmarkt* (East Berlin: Verlag Die Wirtschaft, 1954), pp. 267–8.

[2] Fritz Schenk, former assistant to the Chairman of the DDR State Planning Commission, told me that the USSR and DDR often used pre-war 'stop-prices'. I have found no confirmation of this statement in the Bloc economic literature or from East Berlin interviewees. For a sample foreign trade contract of this period, see Nicolas Spulber, *The Economics of Communist Eastern Europe* (Cambridge, Mass. and New York: Wiley and the Technology Press, 1957), pp. 455–7.

for the previous year on the chief markets of the goods in question'.[1]

D. 1958–61

It is difficult to determine exactly what the formal pricing criterion was in this period. In its ninth Plenum (June, 1958) the CMEA recommended that the average world market prices for 1957 be used as the basis for setting intra-Bloc prices.[2] [3] However, several DDR officials told me that raw material prices were supposed to be based on world prices over a longer period, while, on the other hand, several DDR foreign traders seemed unaware of these recommendations and told me that in 1960 prices in intra-Bloc trade were based on 1959 world market prices.

There have also been many conflicting reports concerning the informal pricing criteria.

In 1957 one Russian author declared, 'In the trade between the Soviet Union and the Socialist countries, as well as in mutual trade among all Socialist states, prices are fixed on the basis of world prices on the basic commodity markets for a given period which is mutually agreed upon by foreign trade organizations. . . . Prices at which the Soviet Union and the countries of the Peoples' Democracy supply goods to one another . . . are stable, and . . . adjustment [of the Capitalist world market prices] excludes the factor of temporary price changes, which are connected with the speculative machinations of Capitalist monopolies, the military-inflationist business cycle, and so on. . . . The commercial relationships have no casual character but are based upon a planned and systematically widening economic collaboration.'[4]

In the same year, the Polish Ministry of Trade issued a statement which read, '. . . this year's agreements with the Soviet Union have been for the first time based upon current world prices. These prices have been fixed for one year with the provision that, in cases of some

[1] A Polish economist, Polaczek (*op. cit.*) emphasized the adjustment of the 1950 stop-prices. An article in *Notatnik Agitatora*, 17/1956 (this citation was given to me by John M. Montias) confirms this view. On the other hand, my DDR interviewees emphasized the use of world market prices of the previous year as the principal formal pricing criteria.

[2] Franz Heiduschat, *Deutsche Aussenpolitik* (East Berlin) 11/1958, pp. 1084–92; Gomulka, on the other hand, said the price basis for the period was 1958 world market prices (see *East Europe* XI, 9/1962, p. 45). Gunther Kohlney (*Sozialistische Planwirtschaft* 8 & 9/1962, pp. 34–40) said that the 1957 price basis was obsolete in 1962.

[3] See Appendix A for a price contract between the DDR and USSR in 1958.

[4] V. Zolatarev, 'Trade Relations of the USSR with Socialist Countries,' *Vneshniaia Torgovlia*, November/1957, quoted by Jan Wszelaki, *Communist Economic Strategy: The Role of East Central Europe* (Washington, D.C.; National Planning Association, 1959), p. 63.

considerable fluctuation on the world market, each party has the right to give notice as to the suspension of fixed prices.'[1]

A Bulgarian source, on the other hand, said that although world market prices were used as a basis for determining sale and purchase prices since 1956, these prices were 'adjusted to the specific cost level in the selling country or to the possibilities of the purchasing country.'[2]

One DDR authority explained to me that '. . . for goods which have a special meaning for the Socialist world system, the trade partners in the trade contract can, in exceptional cases, set an incentive price which still stimulate the development of production of the particular good.'

On the other hand, another important DDR economist wrote that '. . . for some time there has been an increasing tendency to choose the [domestic?] prices of the USSR as the basis . . . for price setting on the CMEA market.'[3]

Finally, a formerly high DDR official told me that prices for goods which had no real world market price (such as very complex machinery, ships, and uranium) were based on domestic costs plus a specified profit, converted to Roubles by the official exchange rate.[4]

All of these statements suggest that the informal pricing criteria might have been more important than the more formal criteria.

In the foreign trade literature of the CMEA nations, one also finds a curious disagreement as to whether foreign trade prices for particular goods were the same between the various CMEA nations. Almost all USSR authors state categorically that intra-Bloc trade prices for the same good were about the same: 'One characteristic of price building in the mutual trade between the countries of the democratic camp . . . are the unified prices. This means that each country sets the same price for the same good, with no regard to which nation in the

[1] Witold Trampczynski, *Tribuna Ludu* 4/19/1957, quoted by Wszelaki, *op cit.* p. 62. A DDR author (Helmut Schneider, 'Einige Gedanken zur Ermittlung von Weltmarktpreisen,' *Der Aussenhandel*, VIII, 2/1958, pp. 54–5) also stated that actual use of world market prices was a relatively recent development. He did not say what prices were used before.

[2] *Vneshna Trgoviya*, 10/1956, pp. 6–13, quoted by ECE, 'Developments in the Foreign Trade of Eastern Europe and the Soviet Union,' *Economic Survey of Europe in 1957*, p. VI–27.

[3] Kohlmey, *Der demokratische Weltmarkt, op. cit.* p. 267. See also, P. K. Figurnov, *Stroitel'stve socizlisticeskoj ekonomiki i razivike vnešnej torgovli evropejskich stranach narodnoj demokratii* (Moscow: Vnestorgizdat, 1955), Chapter IV.

[4] Interview with Fritz Schenk. According to the East Berlin radio (cited in *Neue Zürcher Zeitung*, March 21, 1957) uranium was sold to Russia on a cost plus basis, thereby confirming Schenk's statement. I have found nothing on this topic in the Bloc press.

democratic camp the article will be exported. A price difference for a good occurs only because transportation costs are added.'[1]

On the other hand, DDR economists complained that this was not so. For instance, in a book which won a National Prize (similar to a Stalin prize in the USSR) in 1954, one author wrote, 'The prices for the various goods are not yet unified in the trade agreements on the democratic world market.'[2] One DDR economist told me that the unifying of foreign trade prices was a long-range problem which could not really begin to be solved until 1965. He said that the most important short-range problem was the improvement of the existing prices in the trade between the Bloc nations and the elimination of the largest price deviations.

From this brief review of the criteria to set intra-Bloc foreign trade prices, it should be quite clear that no firm conclusions may be drawn about actual trade prices. However, on this topic direct evidence is fortunately available.

2. THE PROCESS OF SETTING INTRA-BLOC FOREIGN TRADE PRICES

Price setting in foreign trade in the Bloc has two characteristics which differ from Western practices. First, prices for different goods are made at three different levels of negotiations. In the long-range bilateral contracts, an average unit price is set for a few 'key positions' (a few important raw materials) for a period from three to seven years in advance. For some goods, however, only a 'temporary' average unit price is set for the last few years of the contract. In the bilateral governmental negotiations for the annual global trade contracts, prices are set for the remaining important items, often for two or three years in advance. For the less important goods and for many types of machinery, the prices are either established by negotiations between the various foreign trade enterprises (FTES) of the two countries or set in governmental negotiations at a later time.

Second, negotiations concerning the quantities and prices of the traded goods are often separated by a period of months.[3] This has

[1] I. Dudinski, 'Festigung und Entwicklung des demokratischen Weltmarkts,' *Über die Entwicklung des Aussenhandels der Länder des Weltfriedenslagers* (East Berlin: Verlag Die Wirtschaft, 1953), p. 53 (originally printed in *Voprosy ekonomiki*, 6/1953). For similar sentiments, see N. Ivanov, *Vneshniaia torgovlia*, 10/1952 or, more recently, F. Bystrow, *Voprosy ekonomiki*, 2/1960.

[2] G. Kohlmey, *Der demokratische Weltmarkt*, *op. cit.* p. 266. See also G. Kohlmey, 'Entwicklungsprobleme unseres Aussenhandels,' *Der Aussenhandel* VII, 1/1957, pp. 16–18.

[3] This phenomenon was first noted by Margaret Dewar, *Soviet Trade with Eastern Europe* (London: Royal Institute of International Affairs, 1951), p. 8, and has continued up to the present day.

come about through the practice described in the previous chapters, where the foreign trade enterprises of the various Bloc nations meet before the governmental negotiations for the global contract and arrange certain trade deals in physical terms. The annual negotiations for the global trade contracts have increasingly centred on problems of price, rather than quantity.

There are some similarities to trade practices of 'capitalists' in the negotiations between Bloc nations if we are to believe the testimony of witnesses in two well-known show trials: one in Sofia in December, 1949, against T. Kostoff, the Secretary of the Central Committee of the Bulgarian Communist Party and Assistant Prime Minister; the other in Prague in November, 1952, against R. Slánsky who held similarly important positions in the CSSR.[1] Although such evidence is to be taken with a large grain of salt, it confirms the statements of officials from Bloc nations who have fled to the West.

First, it seems that prices have not been 'objectively set' but have been bargained. For instance, the Bulgarian foreign trade adviser in Moscow reported: 'The Soviet Union had a certain interest in our tobacco. Since we knew about this, we decided to offer a smaller amount [than expected] and in this way to cause difficulties in the negotiation and to frustrate, as far as possible, the conclusion of the agreement. The second question was . . . the price question. We decided to demand excessively high prices for our tobacco and pulp and offer low prices for Soviet goods. . . . The discussions proceeded quite slowly and difficultly. The Soviet representative was astonished at why the Bulgarian delegation demanded such high prices for their goods and asked such low prices for Soviet goods when such prices did not exist on the world market.'[2] The Assistant Foreign Trade Minister of Czechoslovakia confessed, 'The foreign trade enterprises, according to my instructions, asked the USSR for prices quite high above the prices on the world market. They demanded, with my approval and according to my instructions, prices 30 per cent higher than those which we received from the Capitalist countries for our exports of crankshafts, generators, electric motors, and oil pipes.'[3] Another Assistant Foreign Trade Minister admitted, 'I know that

[1] For the following citations from the Kostoff and Slánský trials I must thank Erich Klinkmüller.

[2] Leon Nebenzahl, trans. (from Russian), *Traitscho Kostoff und seine Gruppe* (East Berlin: Dietz Verlag, 1951), p. 212. In connection with the 1948 Bulgarian-USSR negotiations (to which the above statement probably refers), the Bulgarian statistical yearbook shows that for tobacco this ruse was not successful.

[3] CSSR Ministry of Justice, *Prozess gegen die Leitung des staatsfeindlichen Verschwörenzentrums mit Rudolf Slánský an der Spitze* (Prague: Orbis, 1953), pp. 394–5.

this parasitical work [offering goods only at extra high prices] is most observable in those sectors of machinery building which are the most important link between Czechoslovakia and the countries of the democratic (CMEA) camp. The Kovo company, for instance, demanded that the USSR pay prices for electric motors which were about 400 per cent higher than the prices at which these goods . . . were offered to the Capitalist nations.'[1]

The negotiations have contained more difficulties than mere price bargaining: market information seems to have been scarce and a source of some power. Kostoff admitted: 'Without being the head of the state but nevertheless acting as such, I let myself be carried away to precipitous and thoughtless behaviour in which my nationalistic convictions and my hostile attitude to the USSR often came to light. Such thoughtless and careless actions on my part were [promulgations of] regulations through which I, using the Bulgarian laws for the protection of State secrets, deprived the Soviet representatives of information which was necessary for the wider development and consolidation of economic regulations between the USSR and Bulgaria. I also directed the leading officials of the Ministry of Foreign Trade to keep secret from the USSR trade representatives the prices which were the basis of some of the trade agreements with the Capitalistic lands. In this way I attempted to repeat . . . the same activities which Tito in Yugoslavia had used in his breaking away from the USSR and the People's Democracies.'[2] Before his sentence was announced, the adviser for trade policy in the Bulgarian embassy in Moscow confessed to the crime of revealing USSR State secrets: 'Immediately after the conclusion of the negotiations [for the USSR-Bulgarian trade agreement] I was visited by Ziberna [the Yugoslavian Embassy official in charge of trade policy]. He demanded that I give him exhaustive information concerning the types of imported and exported goods. He further asked for information about the amount, the assortment, the quality, and the price of the goods. I gave him all the desired information.'[3]

Negotiations have finally been hindered by 'tie-in' and other dubious sales devices. An Assistant Foreign Trade Minister of the CSSR reported: 'Moreover, I also sabotaged the relations . . . with the People's Democracies by the way I created four commodity categories . . . in the CSSR import and export lists, and insisted that each single category balance. . . . In 1947, I forced the USSR . . . to accept many miscellaneous goods from the CSSR for which the USSR had absolutely no interest and with this device I reserved valuable

[1] CSSR Ministry of Justice, *op. cit.* p. 435.

[2] Nebenzahl, *op. cit.* p. 140.

[3] *Ibid.* p. 213.

goods for export to Capitalist countries.'[1] Such 'tie-in' arrangements are still used.[2]

Due to the nature of these show trials, none of the bargaining tactics of the Soviet Union were brought to light. However, some information is available from other sources. A top DDR defector told me that the Soviets had knowledge of every important price agreement which the DDR made with other Bloc nations since the results of these negotiations were written up on Russian-German form sheets with one copy going to the DDR Ministry of Foreign Trade and another to the Russian Embassy.[3] This practice lasted through 1956 and may still be in use.

In Poland in November, 1956, Gomulka summarized the foreign economic relations between Bloc nations in the following manner: 'The mutual relations between the parties and states of the Socialist camp should not give any cause for any complications. This is one of the main features of Socialism. These relations should be shaped on the principle of international working class solidarity, should be based on mutual confidence and equality of rights; on granting assistance to each other; on mutual friendly criticism if such should become necessary; and on a rational solution, arising from the spirit of friendship and from the spirit of socialism, on all controversial matters. Within the framework of such relations, each country should have full independence, and the rights of each nation to a sovereign government in an independent country should be fully and mutually respected. This is how it should be and—I would say—this is how it is beginning to be.

'In the past it was unfortunately not always like this in the relation between us and our great and friendly neighbour, the Soviet Union.

'Stalin, as the leader of the Party and of the Soviet Union, formally recognized that all of the principles enumerated should characterize the relations between the countries of the camp of Socialism. Not only did he recognize them, but he himself proclaimed them. In fact, however, these principles could not fit within the framework of what makes up the cult of personality.'[4]

[1] CSSR Ministry of Justice, *op. cit.* p. 395.

[2] According to Werner Förster (*Die Notwendigkeit der Koordinierung der Produktion bei Werkzeugmaschinen zwischen der Volksrepublik Polen und der DDR und ihre Auswirkung auf den Aussenhandel;* Diplomarbeit, Hochschule für Ökonomie, 1958, p. 32) in a recent trade contract with the DDR, the Poles demanded that each of several broad commodity categories be balanced. Förster added. 'This point of view is very advantageous for the Poles, but the carrying out of this arrangement with raw-material poor nations like the DDR would cause great difficulties.'

[3] Interview with Fritz Schenk.

[4] Quoted by Zinner, ed. *National Communism and Popular Revolt in Eastern Europe* (New York: Columbia University Press, 1957), pp. 227–8. Radio Peking

These statements suggest that the price negotiation sessions between the Bloc nations have not always been ruled by the harmony doctrine of proletarian internationalism. Indeed, it seems that a heated bargaining situation has arisen in which participants have acted quite like stereotype 'Capitalists' and where questionable economic and political practices have been employed to achieve strong bargaining positions. Although more can be said about these negotiations, I believe it more useful to turn to a statistical analysis of the prices which were actually set.

3. EMPIRICAL ANALYSIS OF INTRA-BLOC FOREIGN TRADE PRICES

The following analysis will centre on three basic questions: First, what are the relationships between intra-Bloc trade prices and trade prices between Western nations? Second, what are the relationships between the prices which each Bloc nation receives from the various other Bloc nations and can these be explained as due to the action of economic forces? More specifically, is there price discrimination and, if so, can this discrimination be explained by considerations of bargaining power? Finally, are there other 'capitalistic' price phenomena which occur in intra-Bloc trade pricing?

A. Level and Movement of Prices

Although the formal basis for setting intra-Bloc trade prices was supposed to be the foreign trade prices in the West, it is important to know whether this has really been the case or not. Comparing intra-Bloc and Western foreign trade prices presents, however, several knotty statistical problems. First of all, it is extremely difficult to use average unit price data from both Bloc and non-Bloc countries together, since the trade nomenclature systems are quite different and comparability is doubtful. Second, it is difficult to obtain adequate samples of intra-Bloc prices.

Four Bloc nations have published average unit price data of trade with both Communist and non-Communist nations, and comparison

---

in November, 1956, noted, 'Because of the unanimity of ideology and aim of struggle, it often happens that certain personnel of Socialist countries neglect the principle of equality among nations in their mutual relations. Such a mistake, particularly the mistake of chauvinism by a big country, inevitably results in serious damage to the solidarity and common cause of the Socialist countries.' Cited by Zbigniew K. Brzezinski, *The Soviet Bloc, Unity and Conflict* (Cambridge: Harvard University Press, 1961), p. 276.

of these prices may be made with a standard index formula.[1] Because some important export goods accounted for 'a large percentage of the sample and dominated the indices, I computed the indices both with and without these goods. (These may have been the goods whose prices were negotiated in the long-term agreements.) In the table below, a figure over 100 per cent indicates that higher average prices for the various exports were received from non-Communist countries than from Bloc nations.

TABLE 5–1

EXPORT PRICES RECEIVED BY BLOC COUNTRIES FROM NON-COMMUNIST NATIONS COMPARED WITH EXPORT PRICES RECEIVED FROM OTHER BLOC NATIONS[2]

	1952 %	*1953* %	*1954* %	*1955* %	*1956* %	*1957* %	*1958* %	*1959* %
USSR	—	—	—	86	89	95	87	—
Bulgaria-whole sample	167	135	96	87	81	—	79	77
Bulgaria-sample without tobacco	117	85	76	84	79	—	68	68
Hungary	88	81	82	88	59	85	75	—
Poland-whole sample	—	—	—	—	—	—	76	—
Poland-sample without hard coal	—	—	—	—	—	—	83	—

[1]
$$\frac{\sum_{a}^{n} P'_j Q_j}{\sum_{a}^{n} P_j Q_j}$$

where P' is the average unit price (border of exporting nations) which the Bloc nations received on the Western market,

P is the average unit price received on the CMEA market, and

Q is the quantity of the good exported to the CMEA countries.

[2] In the indices I have used only homogeneous goods or goods for which quality differences could be expected to cancel out. This meant that most machinery exports (and goods whose prices were determined on a cost-plus basis) were not included. For 'Western markets' I have used only nearby Western trade partners so that transportation cost differences would be minimized. By these methods I have tried to meet the objections of making price comparisons which were outlined in 'A Blatant Attempt of an American Magazine to Slander Soviet Foreign Trade,' *Vneshniaia Torgovlia*, 11/1958, pp. 56–8. The sizes of the samples varied from an average of 10 per cent of total exports (early Bulgarian samples) to an average of 45 per cent of total exports (USSR). For sources and further statistical details, see Statistical Appendix A.

The pioneer studies in the field of East-West price level comparison are: Horst Mendershausen, *Terms of Trade Between the Soviet Union and Smaller Communist Countries, 1955–7* (Santa Monica: RAND Corporation Paper, January 18, 1959) and *The Terms of Soviet-Satellite Trade: A Broadened Analysis* (Santa Monica: RAND Corporation Paper P-1,873, January 7, 1960). All the data in this and the following sections, unless specifically noted, are my calculations.

From these data it appears that prices on the Western markets were, on the whole, lower than the intra-Bloc prices (i.e. that the 'CMEA foreign trade rouble' was overvalued); that in 1955 this differential amounted to about 15 per cent; and that by 1958 this differential had increased slightly.

Examining import prices with the same statistical methods should lead to similar conclusions; unfortunately, the import samples are much smaller than the export samples and yield mixed results. In the table below, a figure over 100 per cent indicates that higher average prices for the various imports were paid to non-Communist countries than to Bloc nations.

TABLE 5–2

IMPORT PRICES PAID BY BLOC COUNTRIES TO NON-COMMUNIST NATIONS COMPARED WITH IMPORT PRICES PAID TO OTHER BLOC NATIONS[1]

	1952	*1953*	*1954*	*1955*	*1956*	*1957*	*1958*	*1959*
	%	%	%	%	%	%	%	%
USSR	—	—	—	101	115	122	108	—
Bulgaria	160	112	93	107	125	—	114	92
Hungary-whole sample	93	111	73	104	117	107	95	—
Hungary-sample without cokes	93	85	67	90	—	—	—	—
Poland	—	—	—	—	—	—	106	—

For the USSR, import prices paid to Western nations were higher than those paid to other Bloc nations. In about half of the other cases, prices paid to non-Communist nations were higher than those paid to other Bloc countries.

The data from these tables can be interpreted in two quite different ways:

1. The prices on the CMEA market were somewhat higher than the foreign trade prices on the Western market.[2] The lower prices (in the import samples) came from a systematic bias in the data, due to the importation of higher quality goods from the West than from the Bloc nations.[3] The lower import prices which Russia paid to the other

[1] Size of samples varied from an average of 5 per cent of imports (early Bulgarian samples) to over 30 per cent (1958 and 1959 Bulgarian samples). For sources and statistical details, see Statistical Appendix A.

[2] This is also the conclusion of the ECE (*Economic Survey of Europe for 1957*, p. VI–28) which states: 'There is plentiful evidence [sic] that sellers of goods that are particularly scarce within the region frequently manage to obtain more than the "basic world market price".'

[3] John M. Montias suggested to me that there might have been a systematic bias in exports because CMEA nations exported higher quality goods to Western nations than to their Bloc partners, which would mean that relative prices on the CMEA market were even higher than indicated in Table 5–1.

Bloc nations could also have been due to Russian exploitation of the East Central European nations.[1]

2. Or else, the prices on the CMEA market were approximately the same as 'world market prices' and the differences were due to the fact that Bloc nations received or paid prices which were different from the 'world market prices' in trade with the West. For instance, one might suppose that the Bloc nations were disadvantaged on the Western markets (due to various reasons which I discuss in the next chapter) received relatively low export prices, and paid relatively high prices for imports.

Neither of these explanations alone is completely satisfactory,[2] and until Western data have been closely examined, a final answer to this problem cannot be given. However, it is important to note that the deviation of the general level of intra-Bloc trade prices from the general level of prices achieved on the Western markets was seldom greater than 25 per cent. Intra-Bloc prices are not unrelated to Western market prices and I believe that 'Capitalist world market' prices have been used in intra-Bloc price negotiations as starting-off points in the bargaining sessions.

[1] Mendershausen, *op. cit.* tries to prove that the Soviet Union exploited the East Central European nations by showing that the terms of trade between the USSR and the other Bloc nations were more advantageous than with the West. However, this is also the case for every other Bloc country (see Table 6–4). You can't prove trade exploitation between the Soviet Union and the Bloc by comparing Soviet trade price data with the Bloc and the West any more than you can prove trade exploitation by looking only at export prices (which Mendershausen also does).

[2] Franklyn Holzman ('Aspects of a Theory of the Soviet Bloc Customs Union: Soviet Price Discrimination Reinterpreted,' *Review of Economics and Statistics* XLIV, Summer/1962) has an alternative interpretation. If the prices of traded goods between two nations in a customs union are determined by splitting the differences between domestic production costs of the two countries, then trade prices could result which, in comparison to world prices, would look discriminatory against one nation but which are, nevertheless, fair. More specifically, if this price rule is followed in the Bloc and if the Soviet Union exports a good to the other Bloc countries for which the Bloc has a comparative disadvantage in trade (in relationship to the rest of the world) and imports a good for which the Bloc has a comparative advantage, then the Soviet Union has more advantageous terms of trade with the Bloc than with the rest of the world. Moreover, this type of explanation can also be used to justify the fact that Bulgaria gets better terms of trade from the Bloc than from the West.

I have two objections to these arguments. First of all, although I've seen several proposals for this type of pricing rule, it is *not* yet used in intra-Bloc trade. Second, *each* country in the Bloc cannot export goods to the other Bloc nations for which the Bloc has a comparative disadvantage and import goods from other Bloc nations for which the Bloc has a comparative advantage.

Holzman also uses the 'customs union effect' to explain the phenomenon that the Soviet Union and Bulgaria do not receive higher than World market prices for all of their exports to other Bloc countries. However, this phenomenon may also be due to a stochastic element in the price bargaining sessions.

Comparing the relative level of CMEA and Western average market prices is only a static view of the situation; it is equally important to compare the changes of prices in both markets. Although the dynamic relationships of the prices in both markets can be analysed on a macroeconomic level, terms of trade indices are needed for quite a few years. The price comparisons in the above tables were computed with different commodites in the samples for each year and cannot, therefore, be used for this purpose; computation of standard terms of trade indices from the raw data of the longest series (Bulgaria or Hungary) presents some great statistical difficulties. Only one country has published terms of trade data for both Communist and non-Communist nations; unfortunately these indices also cannot be used.[1]

It is more practical to analyse the relationships of changes in foreign trade prices between Bloc nations and between non-Communist nations on a microeconomic level, and research with this approach has been carried out by Horst Mendershausen.[2]

From charts of price changes for various raw materials in both 'world markets' Mendershausen demonstrates that changes in the London price of various goods were reflected in the Russian trade prices (exports and imports) with the Bloc, but in a damped manner and with a one-year lag.[3] He concludes that the one-year lag was caused by the fact that prices for the whole year were set in the negotiations for the annual global contract which occurred at the beginning of the year. The price changes were damped because the Bloc negotiators attempted to eliminate 'speculative' price movements. Because Mendershausen's analysis of this point is extensive, there is no need here to present further data.

[1] According to a Czech source cited by the ECE, *op. cit.* p. VI–27, the terms of trade of the CSSR from 1949 to 1956 were: (1949=100)

	Overall Terms of Trade		*Exports*		*Imports*	
Year	*With All Communist Countries*	*With All Non-Com. Countries*	*With All Communist Countries*	*With All Non-Com. Countries*	*With All Communist Countries*	*With All Non-Com. Countries*
1949	100	100	100	100	100	100
1950	92	86	87	78	95	92
1951	84	74	92	91	110	124
1952	82	76	93	82	114	108
1953	84	80	95	69	112	85
1954	88	68	93	63	104	95
1955	80	74	89	63	110	85
1956	79	77	85	68	109	87

Since the commodity structure of trade with the West was quite different from the commodity structure with the East, these indices cannot be compared.

[2] Mendershausen, *The Terms of Soviet-Satellite Trade: A Broadened Analysis*, *op. cit.*

[3] Other Westerners have also found this one-year lag, e.g. ECE, *op. cit.* p. VI–27 and Table VI–Q.

B. Price Discrimination in the Bloc

Economists in the West have often claimed that price discrimination exists in intra-CMEA trade (especially by the USSR) because there are great differences in prices which various Bloc countries receive from the other Bloc nations for specific exports. Although Soviet economists have proclaimed loudly that this is not the case, these price differences may be seen by examining the average unit prices of some chief exports of several Bloc nations.[1]

TABLE 5–3

PRICES FOR IMPORTANT EXPORTS RECEIVED BY BLOC COUNTRIES FROM VARIOUS TRADE PARTNERS

	1950	*1951*	*1952*	*1953*	*1954*	*1955*	*1956*	*1957*	*1958*
Bulgaria: tobacco, leva/ton									
USSR	—	—	7069	7261	7516	7968	6380	—	—
Other CMEA nations	—	—	7105	9355	8607	10040	9390	—	—
Capitalist nations	—	—	13390	13610	8822	7634	5760	—	—
Hungary: bauxite, forint/ton									
USSR	66	62	57	88	136	90	—	—	—
Other CMEA nations	148	146	141	131	129	122	—	—	—
Poland: hard coal dollars/ton									
USSR	1·25	1·25	1·25	1·25	—	—	—	—	15·53
Common market nations	——12·00–16·00——				—	—	—	—	11·45
Russia: coke, rouble/ton									
Albania	—	—	—	—	—	81·0	80·2	113	93·5
Bulgaria	—	—	—	—	—	87·9	87·9	113	82·5
DDR	—	—	—	—	—	80·7	92·2	113	107·3
Hungary	—	—	—	—	—	82·1	80·0	102	104·4
Rumania	—	—	—	—	—	80·9	80·8	111	100·8

[1] Quality differences may account for some differences in price, but I doubt that such differences would cause a systematic bias. Russian, Bulgarian, and Polish exports were valued f.o.b.; Hungarian exports were valued at point of change of ownership. For sources, see Statistical Appendix A. Polish data 1950–53 from John M. Montias, 'Unbinding the Polish Economy,' *Foreign Affairs*, April/1957, pp. 479–80. It is not known what prices Poland received from the West from 1950–53 but World market prices varied between $12 and $16. In 1956 Russia cancelled all Polish debts, which was supposed to make up for this low coal price of previous years. For specific cases of other price manipulations by the USSR, see Fritz Schenk, *Magie der Planwirtschaft* (Köln: Kiepenheuer and Witsch, 1960), p. 87; or Alfred Zauberman, *Economic Imperialism: The Lesson of Eastern Europe* (London: Ampersand Ltd, Bellman Books, 1955).

Quality differences, domestic transportation costs, packing expenses, etc. might have caused some of the differences in the average unit prices, but in many cases the differences seem too great to be accounted for by these factors. However, a higher price received from one purchaser than from another should not be regarded *ipso facto* as price discrimination or exploitation for two reasons: some prices might not have followed the changes in World market prices because they were fixed for a certain length of time in the long-term agreements. Or import and export prices between two Bloc nations could have been both higher or lower than World market prices so that their deviations would have cancelled each other out.

This first consideration is, I believe, not very important. Although I cannot empirically evaluate the influence of the long-term fixed prices from 1950 to 1953 because of lack of adequate data, their influence afterwards was not great. In 1954 and 1955, many of the long-term 'fixed prices' were adjusted when they became too far out of line with World market prices; between 1955 and 1958, no global long-term contracts were signed between Bloc nations, so few, if any, long-term prices existed in this period.[1] The second consideration can be easily handled by analysing the import and export prices together by means of trade indices.[2]

[1] Some long-term contracts for individual goods were signed but I received the impression from an East German economist that these contracts specified only the quantities to be traded.

[2] In the calculations, I have used the following formulae and definitions:

(1) Two markets a and b; commodities traded=1. . . .n (all commodities used in the indices were relatively homogeneous goods).

(2) P_j^{ea}=export price in market a of good j; Q_k^{ib}=imported quantity of good k on market b.

(3) Percentage advantage (or disadvantage, if under 100 per cent) of importing from market b rather than market a='import relation'=

$$\frac{\sum_1^n Q_j^{ib} \; P_j^{ia}}{\sum_1^n Q_j^{ib} \; P_j^{ib}}$$

(4) Percentage advantage (or disadvantage if under 100 per cent) of exporting to market b rather than market a=1/'export relation'=

$$\frac{\sum_1^n Q_j^{eb} \; P_j^{eb}}{\sum_1^n Q_j^{eb} \; P_j^{ea}}$$

(5) Percentage advantage (or disadvantage, if under 100 per cent) of balanced trade='import relation'/'export relation'='combined import and export relation.'

The problem of transportation costs immediately arises. Does nation A exploit nation B (in relationship to nation C) if it offers a certain good to B at a higher price than C, although with transportation costs included, B would pay a

Assuming that price discrimination was the most important factor causing the price differences, it is possible to measure this price discrimination which Russia practiced between the other CMEA nations by taking the average Russian export and import prices with the six largest East Central European nations (market a in the formulae on previous page) and comparing these to the Russian trade prices with each nation separately (each nation used as market b). Any percentage over 100 per cent indicates that the nation was *relatively* discriminated against (in relationship to the other CMEA nations):[1]

TABLE 5-4

RELATIVE SOVIET TERMS OF TRADE WITH THE EAST CENTRAL EUROPEAN NATIONS ('COMBINED EXPORT AND IMPORT RELATIONS')

1955	%	*1956*	%	*1957*	%	*1958*	%
CSSR	108	Hungary	108	Hungary	107	Hungary	106
Hungary	106	CSSR	105	CSSR	105	CSSR	105
Rumania	103	Rumania	103	Rumania	102	Poland	103
Bulgaria	99	Bulgaria	99	Poland	97	Rumania	102
Poland	96	Poland	98	Bulgaria	95	Bulgaria	99
DDR	93	DDR	96	DDR	93	DDR	90

The results are surprising. First they are a good deal more consistent from year to year than one would have suspected. Second, the relative order seems somewhat strange. For political reasons I would have guessed that Czechoslovakia would have been lower on the list (less discriminated against) and Bulgaria, higher.

Three main interpretations of the data are possible. The discrimination could have been the result of pure economic forces such as relative bargaining strengths. Or the discrimination could have come

lower total price? In a perfect market, nation A would offer a good to other nations at the same price f.o.b. border, and would import a good at the same price c.i.f. from all countries. But there was not a perfect market in the Bloc and the handling of transportation costs might affect the results of the indices. I calculated most of the indices both with and without transportation costs and found that in actuality they did not really affect my conclusions or correlations. The data presented are, with several exceptions, f.o.b. border of the exporting country (which is the price that is negotiated in the various bilateral contracts between Bloc nations). For further statistical details, see Statistical Appendix A.

[1] Countries are arranged in order of decreasing discrimination. Size of export samples range from an average of about 26 per cent (Bulgaria) to an average of about 61 per cent (CSSR). Size of import samples range from an average of 4 per cent (DDR) to an average of 33 per cent (Rumania). It is doubtful if there are any systematic biases due to different qualities of traded goods. For further statistical details, see Statistical Appendix A. Mendershausen, *op. cit.* calculated USSR price discrimination for exports alone; his calculations and mine (for exports alone) differ because my samples are smaller but more select.

about as the outcome of political decisions by the USSR to favour certain East Central European nations. Or the above results could be merely the result of my statistical methods and have little actual meaning.[1] Rejecting this last interpretation, the problem becomes one of deciding the relative influence of economic and political factors. Since I believe that economic forces were decisive, it is incumbent upon me to isolate the forces which could have brought about such results.

Two general hypotheses come to mind. The degree of price discrimination might be related to the mutual trade dependence of the trading partners; that is, the greater the degree of dependence of nation A on the USSR, the more this nation was discriminated against; and similarly, the more the USSR was dependent upon nation A, the less this nation was discriminated against. Or else the degree of price discrimination might be related to the degree of monopoly power which each nation had in trading with the other; i.e. the more one nation acted as a 'single supplier' of certain exports to the USSR, the more this nation was able to tie other trade deals to these monopolized goods and obtain more favourable prices; and similarly, in regard to the degree to which the USSR acted as a 'single supplier' of exports to the other Bloc nations. (A previously cited quotation from the Slánsky trial suggests the importance of this monopoly hypothesis.) These hypotheses may be tested with correlation techniques; the reader is, however, warned that the data leave much to be desired and that any conclusions must be considered only as tentative.

The 'trade dependency' of nation A on nation B may be measured by the ratio of the trade turnover between these nations to the total trade turnover of nation A. The trade dependency hypothesis may be tested by calculating a multiple regression of the following type: $D=A+Bx+Cy$, where D=degrees of discrimination ('combined export and import relations' of Table 5–4); x=percentage of USSR trade with the various East Central European nations: y=the percentage of trade of the various East Central European nations with

[1] Two main objections can be raised. My samples were based on average unit prices of only relatively homogeneous goods (e.g. raw materials). The price differences in the goods which were not included in the samples (e.g. machines) might have compensated for the differences in the prices of the goods in the samples, i.e. for two different sets of goods, two different sets of economic (or political) factors entered the price negotiation process. Somehow this does not seem very likely. Another objection is that the *inter*-Bloc price differences swamped the *intra*-Bloc price differences. It is impossible to test this hypothesis since transportation costs played a much more important role in trade with the West. (Because Denmark was close to West German coal mines Russia would have had to offer an especially low f.o.b. coal price to meet the c.i.f. price the Gernans offered.) Unfortunately I could find no estimates of East-West transportation costs.

the USSR (see Table 6–10); and A,B,C=regression coefficients. The following results are obtained:[1]

Year	$R^2_{D.XY}$
1955	·29
1956	·70
1957	·61
1958	·81
Pooled data for all years	·57

The first question is whether the regression coefficients for each year come from the same universe, i.e. whether the variation between the regression coefficients was due to random factors. From an examination of the unexplained residuals of the regression for the single years and of the regression for the pooled data with an F test, it was found that this indeed was the case and, therefore, the regression from the pooled data can be used for any further statistical tests.

The second question is whether the regressions are statistically significant (·95 confidence limit), i.e. whether the independent variables contributed significantly to the variance of D. By means of an F test I found this to be the case, i.e. the trade discrimination may be explained by trade dependency factors.

Calculating the coefficients of the regression from the pooled data, the following formula is derived:

$$D = 111{\cdot}45 - {\cdot}59\,X - {\cdot}27\,Y$$

(all the coefficients are statistically significant, ·95 confidence limit). This means that the discrimination was inversely related to the trade dependency of the USSR on the individual East Central European nations; however, discrimination was also inversely related to the trade dependency of the individual East Central European nations on the USSR, which is quite unexpected. (Similar results occur in the regressions for each year.) Because of lack of further information about the price negotiations between the CMEA nations, I am unable to explain this latter result. And, because of the limited nature of the data, it is not advisable to perform further statistical tests.

Testing the 'monopoly hypothesis' is more difficult since it is impossible to obtain comparable data concerning the degree to which the USSR acted as a single supplier to the East Central European nations. Therefore, only a regression of the following type can be calculated: D=A+Bx, where D=discrimination in USSR import

[1] The regressions were calculated from the unrounded data which were the bases for Table 5–4. I would like to thank Mr T. N. Srinivasan for his help and great patience with the calculation and testing of these hypotheses; he is, however, not responsible for any errors. I tested also a series of hypotheses explaining total trade discrimination or discrimination in exports or imports alone by means of the trade dependencies of the various nations alone. None of these correlations yielded statistically significant results.

prices (USSR 'import relation'); x=the ratio of 'singly supplied imports' of the USSR from each Bloc nation (in per cent); A and B= regression coefficients. The following results are obtained:[1]

Year	r^2_{DX}
1955	·61
1956	·43
1957	·29
1958	·10
Pooled data for all years	·31

Using the same techniques described above, I found that the coefficients are all from the same universe. Nevertheless, the pooled coefficient is not quite statistically significant (·95 confidence limit) and therefore the 'monopoly' hypothesis cannot be considered proven.[2]

Due to the nature of the available data, the exact roles of the trade dependency and monopoly effects in the intra-Bloc price negotiations cannot be discovered. Nevertheless, the analysis of these factors suggests that economic factors are important. This does not preclude, however, the influence of political factors as well.

Thus far I have analysed only the *relative* price discrimination of the USSR between the various East Central European nations. A more interesting question, which has been discussed without much data for years by anti-Communists, is the degree of *absolute* price discrimination practiced by the USSR.

Although there are many ways to analyse the absolute price discrimination, I believe that this can be best measured by comparing the terms of trade which the various East Central European nations obtain from the USSR to the terms of trade which these nations receive from each other for the same goods. From the proceeding discussion about economic influences in trade prices it seems quite likely that the USSR has been able to obtain an absolute price advantage from the other Bloc countries because of the trade dependency effect (the USSR has been the largest trade partner of all other Bloc nations since the early post-war years) and also because the USSR has been, in all probability, the largest 'single supplier' in the Bloc. In Table 5–5 any figure below 100 per cent indicates that trading with the Soviet Union was less advantageous than trading with the other Bloc nations.

The hypothesis that the USSR had a trading advantage over the other CMEA nations seems, in the main, confirmed by the data in the table up to 1956. The 1958–59 Bulgarian data, which come from very

[1] For details of calculation of the 'single supplier' phenomenon, see Statistical Appendix B.

[2] The full correlation was D=105·25—·16 x, i.e. the degree of monopoly power was, as expected, inversely proportional to the degree of discrimination.

TABLE 5–5

TERMS OF TRADE OF THE EAST CENTRAL EUROPEAN NATIONS WITH THE USSR COMPARED TO TERMS OF TRADE OF EAST CENTRAL EUROPEAN NATIONS WITH EACH OTHER ('COMBINED IMPORT AND EXPORT RELATIONS')[1]

	1952	*1953*	*1954*	*1955*	*1956*	*1957*	*1958*	*1959*
Bulgaria	%	%	%	%	%	%	%	%
Whole sample	98	85	87	76	72	—	85	84
Sample without tobacco	90	96	90	85	92	—	96	97
Hungary								
Whole sample	82	95	91	97	(123)	(131)	(123)	—
Sample without bauxite	100	105	87	101	—	—	—	—
Sample without cokes	—	—	—	—	(116)	(128)	(125)	—
Poland								
Whole sample	—	—	—	—	—	—	102	—
Sample without coal	—	—	—	—	—	—	105	—

adequate samples also substantiate the hypothesis. However, 1958 Polish data, which also come from a large sample, show the reverse situation to a very slight degree. It is not necessarily inconsistent that Bulgaria received a relatively higher terms of trade than Poland in the trade of the Soviet Union (Table 5–4) while, on the other hand, it received relatively lower terms of trade from the USSR than from the other Bloc countries when exactly the reverse was true for Poland (Table 5–5). This could be due to the fact that while Bulgaria's bargaining power was relatively stronger than Poland's *vis-a-vis* the USSR, it was relatively weaker *vis-a-vis* the rest of the Bloc. The 1956–58 Hungarian results are placed in parentheses because their validity is doubtful; the basic data were taken from later Hungarian statistical year-books which conveniently omitted mentioning those goods for which trade with the USSR was disadvantageous during the years 1953–55.[2]

With these mixed results, it is impossible to draw a completely firm conclusion after 1956. However, it is safe to say that although absolute price discrimination by the USSR cannot be seen in every

[1] Data in parentheses are of dubious quality for reasons discussed in the text. I do not believe that any of the above results were complicated by any systematic biases due to quality differences. Bulgarian and Polish prices were valued f.o.b. exporting country; Hungarian, at point of change of ownership up to 1956 and f.o.b. exporting country thereafter. See Statistical Appendix A for further details.

[2] 1955 was the only year in which the indices calculated from the 1949–55 year-book and the 1957 and 1958 year-books overlapped, and there was a great discrepancy in the two series here. Since the samples for 1955 from the 1949–55 year-book were larger, I used these data for the overlap year. See Statistical Appendix A for details.

case after 1956, the East Central European nations certainly did not receive any great price advantage in trading with the USSR in comparison to trading with other Bloc nations.

Very blatant discrimination by the USSR may be seen for those goods whose prices were set on a domestic cost-plus basis, converted to Roubles at the official exchange rate. Here the problem of discrimination is the problem of the relation of the official exchange rates to the exchange rates which 'would have occurred' if they had been determined by market forces, Of course, it is difficult to calculate such exchange rates but, as a first approximation, the relative 'purchasing power' of these currencies can be used. That is, if the currencies of the East Central European nations were relatively undervalued (in terms of 'purchasing power') to the Russian Rouble, then Russia discriminated against these nations.

No serious study of the relative purchasing power of the various Bloc currencies has yet been made in the West. In the Bloc, however, special non-commercial exchange rates were set up in 1957, based on relative purchasing power calculated from the prices of seventy-five or so items weighed in a standard manner.[1] Although this market basket consisted primarily of consumer goods and services, it was the only comparison of currency values which I could find. Since the non-commercial rates remained about the same from 1957 to 1960, the 1960 rates could be used to estimate the relative purchasing power of the various national currencies in 1957.

TABLE 5–6

OFFICIAL GOLD AND NON-COMMERCIAL EXCHANGE RATES (1960)[2]

Country	*Official Exchange Rates*		*Non-Commercial Exchange Rates*	
Albania	100 Lek	= 8·00 Roubles	100 Lek	= 10·00 Roubles
Bulgaria	100 Lewa	= 58·82 Roubles	100 Lewa	=112·4 Roubles
CSSR	100 Crowns	= 55·56 Roubles	100 Crowns	= 86·21 Roubles
DDR	100 DM	=180·00 Roubles	100 DM	=258·0 Roubles
Hungary	100 Forint	= 34·10 Roubles	100 Forint	= 71·43 Roubles
Poland	100 Zloty	=100·00 Roubles	100 Zloty	= 66·84 Roubles
Rumania	100 Lei	= 66·67 Roubles	100 Lei	=103·09 Roubles

Up to 1957 it seemed as if the USSR received an extremely favourable deal in non-commercial (tourism, services, costs of embassies) and cost-plus transactions with every country except Poland. Hungary was the most discriminated against, followed by Bulgaria, the CSSR and the DDR. This discrimination was not entirely past history after the introduction of the system of non-commercial rates in 1957 because some services were still bought at domestic prices converted to Roubles at the official gold rate, and some cost-

[1] For further details, see Appendix B.

[2] For sources and details, see Appendix B.

plus goods were still being traded. The devaluation of the Rouble (January 1, 1961) was a step to eliminate this type of exploitation by the Soviet Union.

It is noteworthy that Poland, a nation which received more advantageous terms of trade when trading with the USSR than with the rest of the Bloc, derived the greatest advantage from the manipulations through the official exchange rate. It is also interesting that the order of discrimination against the various nations through the official exchange rate bears some semblance to the order of relative terms of trade with the USSR (Table 5–4). Because of the tentative nature of the non-commercial exchange rates as a measure of relative purchasing power, it is not worthwhile to perform any statistical tests on the data.

From these various statistical results the nature of the price bargaining between the CMEA nations becomes clearer. Although the formal bases of intra-Bloc prices were the prices existing on the Western markets, these were difficult to determine for those goods for which transporation costs or quality differences were important or for those goods whose prices fluctuated a great deal. In these cases a price indeterminacy existed, and factors of economic power became important. Bargaining advantages were also secured by political methods as well.

Although Bloc trade officials played sweet tunes of proletarian internationalism in public, they practiced price discrimination in private. This took several forms. For the goods whose prices were theoretically based on World market prices, it was more advantageous for the East Central European nations to trade with each other than with the USSR, up to 1956, and this situation continued for some nations through 1959. Moreover, in the trade with the USSR, Hungary was the most discriminated against and the DDR, the least. The results of the correlation analyses suggest that mutual trade dependency was an important factor here. For those goods whose prices were based on internal costs converted to Roubles at the official exchange rate, all East Central European nations except Poland were heavily discriminated against by the USSR until 1957. Thereafter, this discrimination continued for some goods until 1961.

I was told that although DDR officials grumbled for years about the price disadvantages in trade with the USSR, an official study of the problem was not made until 1956.[1] Aside from the economists working on the project, only the Minister of Trade, the Chairman of the State Planning Commission and the Secretary of the Party, Walter Ulbricht, saw the report. No known action was taken, but undoubtedly high level pressure was exerted on the Soviet Union.

Due to the general political difficulties in the CMEA Bloc in late

[1] Interview with Fritz Schenk.

1956, it seems likely that Russian foreign trade policy with the East Central European nations was changed. This might explain the introduction of the non-commercial exchange rate system as well as the fact that at least one nation received more favourable terms of trade with the USSR than with the other CMEA nations. This change in Soviet trade policy was paralleled by other changes in economic policy toward the Bloc.[1]

Before turning to the problem of price leadership in intra-Bloc trade, it is worth noting that the economists from the CSSR and Hungary, the two nations most discriminated against by the USSR, were also the most vociferous in demanding that CMEA foreign trade prices be more closely related to world market prices, while Bulgaria and DDR economists, from the two most favoured nations, did not seem so receptive to this idea and offered various alternatives.[2]

C. Price Leadership

In the CMEA Bloc economic press one finds several vague hints concerning price leadership. For instance, in 1954 one DDR economist wrote: 'In the foreign trade of the People's Democracies [with each other] the various nations have increasingly based their prices ('supported themselves') on the prices which the Soviet Union has used in its trade with these nations.'[3] A joint DDR-CSSR foreign trade textbook declares, 'Since 1948 the average price on the democratic World market has begun to approximate the prices which the Soviet Union uses for its deliveries to the People's Democracies.'[4] When questioned about this, one DDR economist told me that Soviet prices, while not determinant for the setting of prices between the other Communist nations, have been very important.

[1] In the period 1953–56, most of the Soviet and mixed Soviet firms in the Bloc were liquidated; the USSR cancelled over five billion Roubles of debts to Albania, DDR, Hungary, Poland and Rumania and granted new credits to almost every Bloc country; the Danube Commission was also re-activated.

[2] One DDR author (Horst Behr, 'Die Preisbasis auf dem sozialistischen Weltmarkt,' *Der Aussenhandel*, VIII 11/1958, pp. 401–3) noted that the nations which foresaw a rise in World market prices for their principle exports demanded a closer observance of intra-Bloc prices to World market prices; but when the same World market prices were falling, these nations would plead for other pricing criteria. (This was, for instance, the case with Polish coal.) Behr is, in essence, saying that the 'theoretical suggestions' for intra-Bloc pricing were based on national economic interests and that the people who made these suggestions (primarily economists) were paid lackeys of the national interest. This is a rather interesting sentiment for a Marxist to express in public.

[3] Hans Strobel, 'Einige Bemerkungen zu den Fragen des Preisausgleiches und der Subvention im Aussenhandel der DDR,' *Der Aussenhandel* IV, 7/1954, pp. 200–4.

[4] Nykryn, *et. al., op. cit.*, p. 310.

Examining the price statistics of the various Bloc nations for this price leadership is very difficult since only the Soviet Union and Poland have comparable data. Out of the hundreds of import and export items, only about twenty-five relatively homogeneous traded goods could be found for which meaningful comparisons could be made.

In none of these cases did Poland and the USSR pay about the same average unit prices to the exporting countries or receive about the same average unit prices from the importing nations. Nevertheless, I found that in many cases whenever Poland received a higher price from one nation than from another, so did the USSR. A similar situation existed for imports.

In order to examine this 'relative price leadership' more thoroughly, I computed an average unit price (border exporting country) for each good in the sample and then ranked these prices in order of increasing expensiveness to Poland and the USSR. For instance, for a certain good Poland might pay the lowest price to Country 1, and increasingly higher prices to countries 2, 3, and 4, while for the USSR the ranking might be 1, 3, 2, and 4. These rankings for the different goods were then recorded on a contingency table. In this example both the first ranking and fourth ranking trade partners were the same, while the second and third ranking partners were reversed.

TABLE 5–7

PRICE LEADERSHIP COMPARISONS[1]

Imports

		Rank of Increasing Expensiveness: USSR			
		1	2	3	4
Rank of	1	10	1	—	—
increasing	2	1	10	—	—
expensiveness:	3	—	—	2	—
Poland	4	—	—	—	—

Exports

		Rank of Increasing Expensiveness: USSR			
		1	2	3	4
Rank of	1	7	1	1	1
increasing	2	2	7	1	—
expensiveness:	3	—	—	2	1
Poland	4	1	1	—	—

[1] For statistical details and sources, see Statistical Appendix B. One objection to the above analysis is that the 'relative price leadership' was due to the general bargaining strengths of the countries involved and that one country might have a relatively weaker bargaining strength than another country with both Poland and the USSR. However, this did not seem to be borne out by my sample. That is, for some goods (goods A and B) the same two countries (countries 1 and 2) were involved. It occurred that for good A, Poland and Russia would receive better prices from country 1, and for good B, better prices from country 2.

If there were perfect 'relative price leadership,' then only the diagonal (north-west—south-east) would be filled. Although this is not the case it is possible to test whether the ranks of discrimination for Poland and the USSR were significantly correlated by means of an ordinary chi-square test of independence. Because the samples are so small, I had to collapse the matrices into two-by-two matrices before making the tests. With the collapsed matrices the hypothesis of independence had to be rejected (·95 level of significance), i.e. price leadership seemed to exist in intra-Bloc trade.

How did this price leadership come about? As I discuss in the next chapter, it was the general practice for a nation to begin price negotiations (as part of the negotiations for the annual global trade contract) first with its largest trade partners. After a country had negotiated annual trade prices with these countries (especially the USSR), it is quite likely that these prices were used as agreement points or as limits to the bargaining process with other countries, in order to save the time and tempers of the negotiators. Further support for this view may be gained from details of price negotiations between two Communist countries with very little mutual trade. In a recent DDR-Mongolia trade agreement, the contract specified that prices would be based on the foreign trade prices 'valid in the Socialist camp.' If this meant the prices given to and received from the USSR by the DDR and Mongolia, then formal price negotiations between the two countries could be almost entirely eliminated. Price leadership in the Bloc (and also for American oligopolies) reduces friction and the frazzling of nerves. It was not irrational for an East Central European nation to use the prices received from or paid to the USSR as limits to the price bargaining negotiations with other trade partners unless the nation was greatly discriminated against by Russia.

4. THEORETICAL AND PRACTICAL PROBLEMS IN PRICE SETTING BETWEEN BLOC NATIONS

Since intra-Bloc prices were bargained, rather than negotiated from 'objective criteria,' several general considerations need to be mentioned before turning to a brief survey of the Bloc theoretical discussion of the pricing problem.

A heated bargaining situation does not always insure that the highest possible volume of trade will be conducted. From the previously cited quotations by Gomulka and others, it seemed as though Russian political pressures were a stabilizing element in trade in the early years by providing a method for resolving economic conflicts, although this stabilization method had many disadvantages for the East Central European nations. Once these political pressures were removed, an explosive situation could have developed and intra-

Bloc trade could have suffered as a result. It was, therefore, imperative for the Bloc to find some criteria for the resolution of such price setting problems so that both partners could benefit from trade.

Such a *modus operandi* could be based on theoretical considerations, deduced from general principles recognized by all, or on practical considerations, derived from a frank recognition of the forces of necessity. Both theoreticians and foreign trade practitioners in the Bloc have been concerned with the problem of foreign trade pricing and the contribution of both groups will be briefly examined.

The most difficult ideological problem was the justification of the use of prices from the 'Capitalist world market' for intra-Bloc trade after Stalin had proclaimed the existence of two world markets.[1] With very few exceptions, this question was completely avoided. Instead, theoretical discussions of the principles for pricing in intra-Bloc trade focused on completely different sets of considerations. Three main schools of thought have arisen:

A. One school of thought, represented most vociferously by the prestigeous Russian economist K. Ostrovityanov and by many Bulgarian economists, believed that intra-Bloc prices should be based on the costs of production of an item within the Bloc.[2] They criticize the use of 'Capitalist prices' on the grounds that great uncertainties were introduced into foreign trade planning when the 'wild price movements' of the Capitalist world market were imitated. More-

[1] Joseph Stalin, *Economic Problems of Socialism in the USSR*, *op. cit.* declared the *complete* separation of the 'Capitalist world market' and the 'Socialist world market' in 1952. After 1956 this proposition was questioned by some Bloc theoreticians, e.g. Gunther Kohlmey, *Entwicklungsprobleme des sozialischen Weltwirtschaftssystems* (East Berlin: Akademie Verlag, 1958), p. 31.

[2] See speech by Ostrovityanov at twenty-first Party Congress (*Pravda*, February 6, 1959, p. 9); D. Toscheff, 'Zur Preisbasis auf dem sozialistischen Weltmarkt,' *Der Aussenhandel* IX, 9/1959, pp. 22–3); Mikhail Balabanov, 'Prices in the Trade between Socialist Countries,' *Vneshna trgoviya* VI, 10/1958, pp. 8–12; or M. Horovitz, 'Despre unele particularitati, si limite ale actiunii legii volorii in comertul exterior socialist,' *Probleme Economice*, XI, 4/1958, pp. 10–20; or Gertrud Gräbig, 'Das Wertgesetz und die Preise auf dem sozialistischen Weltmarkt,' Chapter III, *Internationale Arbeitsteilung und Aussenhandel im sozialistischen Weltsystem*, *op. cit.* At an all-Bloc conference, a Yugoslavian (Dragoslav Todorvic, 'Referat,' *Sammelheft: Internationale Konferenz über die Rentabilität des Aussenhandels;* Liblice; College of Economics, 1957; mimeo., pp. 159–64) suggested a labour-hour-of-production price basis for intra-Bloc trade and a Rumanian (Tiberiu Pavel, 'Referat,' *Sammelheft*, *op. cit.*, pp. 213–21) proposed a complicated intra-Bloc price system which would equalize the production labour hours saved through trade for each country. This idea was suggested again by L. B. Shaynin, 'Proportions of Exchange,' *Economic Journal* LXX, December/1960, pp. 769–83. (I do not exactly understand why he chose to present his views in an English economic journal. Furthermore, he seemed quite unaware of much of the discussion on the matter in the East Central European countries. Nevertheless, this is the best Bloc discussion of the problem I have seen.)

over, Capitalist market prices are not 'equivalent'[1] and they caused inequities within the CMEA Bloc when they were employed. The members of this school differ among themselves on how costs of production should be measured in a single country, and how different costs of production in the various producing nations should be averaged to derive one unified Bloc price. Indeed, the present disparities between domestic price structures of the various nations complicate the problem of calculating an average Bloc production cost almost beyond solution.

B. Another school of thought on intra-Bloc pricing, represented most strongly by some Czech theoreticians (although this view is not universal in the CSSR), believes that prices on the CMEA market should be attuned as closely as possible to the prices on the World market: '. . . The more the prices on the Socialist world market correspond to Western foreign trade prices, the more the [Socialist] prices will lead to increasing trade and the development of that production which serves the common interests of the whole Socialist world market; if, for example, some Socialist country continually asks and receives higher prices than the price on the chief international trade market for a certain good, it must necessarily lead to the situation where the Socialist buyer, sooner or later, will buy the article on the Capitalist market.'[2] More bluntly, one contributor declared, 'No country should be forced to buy an item for more than what it can pay for the good in another country. . . .'[3] The adherents to this viewpoint differ among themselves on the following questions:

1. Over how long a period should Western market prices be

[1] 'Equivalence' is a term with several meanings. In its most important meaning, articles produced in two different countries have 'equivalent prices' when equal amounts of domestic labour hours are exchanged when the goods are traded. For a more extensive discussion of the theoretical issues surrounding 'equivalence', see my 'Communist Foreign Trade Theory,' *op. cit.*

[2] V. Cerniansky, 'Die Preibasis auf dem sozialistischen Weltmarkt,' *Der Aussenhandel* VIII, 4 and 5/1958, pp. 153–5; see also Mervart, *op. cit.*

[3] V. Kaigl, quoted by Karl Morgenstern, 'Zur Preisbildung auf dem sozialistischen Weltmarkt,' *Wirtschaftwissenschaft* VI, 3/1958, pp. 442–9; see also Jan Vaněk, 'K některým otázkám zbozi a působeni zákona hodnoty na kapitalistickém a socialistickém světovém trhu,' *Politká ekonomie* VI, 1/1958, pp. 1–17. Josef Mervart ('Ceny na svĕltevem socialistickém trhu,' *Nová mysl*, 9/1958, pp. 818–28) says simply, 'I believe that one must start in the setting of price on the Socialist world market from the . . .working of the law of value and should not try to get around the category of an international value . . . . A disunity of price basis (between 'Socialist and Capitalist world markets') would disturb the planned operation of exchange between Socialist countries.' As noted in the text, most of the backers of this view seem to be Czechs. I have found only one Russian, V. S. Alchimov ('Referat,' *Sammelheft*, *op. cit.*, pp. 261–7) who seems to recognize the validity of these arguments. The most important ideological point involved is the question of the distortion of the 'Capitalist world market' prices due to international cartels, etc.

averaged? Proposals have varied from a one-year period to a ten-year span.

2. How often should the prices (derived from Western foreign trade prices) be changed? Proposals have varied from once a year to once every five or seven years.

3. What type of 'irrational capitalistic disturbances' (monopolistic, speculative, inflationary, cyclical, etc.) should be eliminated and how should this be done?

4. How should the problem of transportation costs be handled?

5. What type of criteria should be used for choice of the 'chief world market' of a good to derive a 'world market price?'

Aside from the introduction of 'Capitalist price fluctuations' into the CMEA market, several other major objections have been levelled against this position. Since capital has been so scarce in the Bloc, capital intensive investments must receive very high returns to induce a country to make such an expenditure. Use of 'Capitalist prices' has discouraged certain types of necessary Bloc investments, particularly high capital-output, long maturing investments such as mineral extraction, or new products which have involved high development costs, since the investing countries have had other less capital-intensive investment outlets and have been quite willing to let another Bloc nation make these investments.[1] In addition, some authors maintain that the current 'Capitalist' foreign trade prices in intra-Bloc trade discouraged specialization apparently because the cost savings have not always been visible, and no country has wanted to risk investing in unprofitable directions.[2]

C. A third group of contributors straddle the fence between these two schools of thought and suggest that most prices in intra-CMEA Bloc trade be set from World market prices but that certain relatively high cost products necessary for Bloc autonomy should be subsidized by a cost-plus method of pricing.[3] Such industries would be

[1] This objection is valid only to the extent which the planners took considerations of capital use into account. In some Bloc nations capital/output (capital turnover ratios) or special cost coefficients of capital (in place of an interest rate) have been directly employed in investment planning. In other nations, these formal methods have not been used but it is hard to believe that capital cost considerations have not entered in some informal way into the decision-making process.

[2] See Gerd Friedrich and Lothar Roucik, 'Die Specialisierung und Kooperation der Produktion im sozialistischen Weltwirtschaftssystem,' *Wissenschaftliche Zetschrift der Hochschule für Ökonomie*, 3/1958, pp. 189–97.

[3] See, for example, Imre Vajda, *Der Aussenhandel* VIII, 22/1 1958, pp. 775 ff; or Polaczek, *op. cit.* In August, 1962, Khrushchev spoke of the necessity of special credits and preferential prices to producers of goods of special interest to the entire Bloc; unfortunately, he did not specify exactly how such a system was

the strategic raw materials industries whose costs lay above World market prices (e.g. Hungarian aluminium), infant industries which would reduce the Bloc's dependence on the West, or goods whose prices had suddenly fallen on the Capitalist markets, due to the introduction of new production techniques which had not yet reached the East. Many of these arguments have been the same as those used in pleading for higher tariffs in Western nations.

Since the production cost structure in the Bloc is quite different from the production cost structure in the West, a great many Bloc goods are 'relatively high-cost products.' The greatest objection to a subsidy system has been that the criteria for such aid have been vague enough so that special interest groups might demand such subsidies for almost every export article they produced. (It does not seem accidental that it was a Hungarian who pleaded for subsidies for Hungarian aluminium).

Each of these three positions has merit; each can also be attacked on theoretical or ideological grounds. The by-products of the dispute have been fruitful, e.g. a subcommittee of the CMEA started to investigate the pricing and accounting procedures for each country in order to examine the feasibility of a production cost basis for intra-Bloc trade prices. The intra-Bloc pricing dispute also encouraged the various member nations to calculate trade profitability coefficients and to investigate prices on the Capitalist markets much more thoroughly. Indeed, the emphasis on trade profitability induced several countries (notably the DDR) to start computing terms of trade indices, a gap in the statistical reporting which had been glossed over before.

Nevertheless, if the problem of pricing in intra-Bloc trade had been left to the East Bloc professors, there is some doubt whether there would have been any agreement on pricing at all. However, there have been some important practical necessities for agreement and some heavy pressures on the hapless Bloc foreign trade officials who have had a plan goal to fulfill (and a healthy bonus for overfulfilment) and who have had somehow to come to an agreement over prices with their partners from other East Bloc nations.

Game theorists tell us that in a bargaining situation in which both sides will benefit from a settlement, the most unambiguous criteria for a solution will most readily be used, even though one partner may benefit much more than the other.[1] This is to avoid the possible

to operate. (See 'Vital Questions of the Development of the World Socialist System,' *Current Digest of the Soviet Press*, 35 & 36/1962.)

[1] See especially Thomas C. Schelling, 'Bargaining, Communication, and Limited War,' *Journal of Conflict Resolution*, 1/1957; or Schelling, 'An Essay on Bargaining,' *American Economic Review*, 3/1956.

stalemate which could occur in searching for a fairer solution. Furthermore, in this price dilemma, any pricing criteria used must take into account that the nation which is disadvantaged might place national economic interests above the political interests of the Bloc and trade with the West. However, there has been a leeway of at least 10 per cent from this price since the CMEA nations have been in a weak bargaining position *vis-a-vis* Western nations and have received unfavourable prices. (See Tables 5–1, 5–2 and 6–4.)

The average price on the 'chief capitalist market' of a product, while not unambiguous, has the advantage of an obvious starting point. It avoids the problem of comparing one irrational price structure with another; it avoids the problem of determining what Bloc products are really strategic and should be subsidized. Therefore, in spite of the fact that Stalin's notion of parallel world markets was the official doctrine in all CMEA nations from 1952 through 1956 (and later), some variant of the Capitalist market price has been used as the officially stated pricing criteria. This necessity for an unambiguous pricing criteria was also realized by Bloc theoreticians, e.g. by the DDR economist who complained: 'In spite of the fact [that prices on the "Capitalist world market" are distorted], the Socialist foreign trade must use the World market price [since] . . . it is the only accessible criteria of equivalent exchange.'[1]

Some Bloc theoreticians have also discussed the problem of who should bear the transportation costs in trade. Most theoreticians seem to agree that once the price (based on the price on the chief world market) has been set, the transportation costs should be split in some way. In actual practice the solution has been simpler and less ambiguous—the importer has borne the entire cost. This would seem to confirm the 'game aspect' of the situation.

The average World market price on the chief market of the good in question for the previous year, as I have noted, is not completely unambiguous, and this has resulted in a curious split in the foreign trade literature. On one hand, some writers have actually believed that there is one 'real World market price' which is an objective fact and which is divorced from 'irrational Capitalist market manifestations'. For instance, one DDR lawyer suggested that an international (intra-CMEA) price court be established to settle price disputes with 'objective norms'.[2] On the other hand, more practical men in the Bloc have seen the price criteria problem as an exercise in setting up

[1] Rudolf Thiele, 'Der sozialistische Aussenhandel als potentielle Akkumulationsquelle bei äquivalentem Warenaustausch,' *Der Aussenhandel* IX, 4 and 5/1959, pp. 53–5.

[2] Helmut Wagner, 'Zu einigen Rechtsfragen aus den Preisklauseln im Aussenhandel zwischen den sozialistischen Ländern,' *Der Aussenhandel* VIII, 16 and 17/1958, pp. 569–70.

unambiguous criteria which would not cause any re-direction of trade to the West and yet which would eliminate the indeterminacy in the concept of 'World market prices'. Thus the DDR and USSR Foreign Trade Ministries signed a very detailed agreement setting up a series of rules to be used, e.g. that 'chief market' be defined as the largest non-Communist market *available* to a country if it had to buy or sell on the Capitalist market; and that certain types of very specific documentation be used as proof of the World market price.[1] These specific rules have resulted in the DDR using West German machine prices in their price negotiation with other Bloc nations, rather than the higher English machine prices, because adequate documentation has been more readily available.[2]

No matter how precisely the price rules are stated, a degree of indeterminacy exists if the bargainers from both sides are trying to obtain the highest prices possible within the framework of the rules.[3] Damping of the bargaining process depends on the efforts to narrow the degree of bargaining indeterminacy through arbitrary rules.

5. FUTURE TRENDS IN INTRA-BLOC FOREIGN TRADE PRICING

As I have shown, many Bloc theorists are unhappy that 'Capitalist world market prices' are used as a basis for intra-Bloc trade prices. Almost all Bloc economists who have written on the subject believe that sooner or later the Bloc will have its own foreign trade pricing system. More and more frequently in the Bloc economic literature, such statements appear as: 'With the growth of the Socialist world economic system, the foreign trade prices between the Socialist nations will become increasingly based on factors which take into account the fact of the existence of the two World markets.[4]

Certainly it is quite reasonable for Bloc economists to want an intra-Bloc pricing system which would more accurately reflect

[1] See DDR-USSR Contract in Appendix A.

[2] One DDR commentator noted: 'The World-market price (in intra-Bloc trade) must be documented by the seller of the good. The buyer has the right in each case to present counter-documents. If, in this process, different "chief markets" of a good are determined, the average price is valid. . . .' (Heiduschat, 'Die Handelsbeziehungen der DDR mit der Sowjetunion,' *Der Aussenhandel* VII, 21/1957, pp. 784–5).

[3] On this point the former DDR Minister of Foreign Trade wrote: 'Our Socialist foreign trade has the task and the duty with all countries, Capitalist or Socialist, to carry through equal valued exchange of goods and to achieve for our economy the most favourable results.' (Heinrich Rau, 'Zu einigen Fragen der Volkswirtschaftlichen Rolle und Bedeutung unseres Aussenhandels,' *Einheit* XII, 2/1957, pp. 167–80.)

[4] Karl Morgenstern, 'Zu einigen Fragen der sozialistischen internationalen Arbeitsteiling,' *Einheit* XV, 4/1960, pp. 611–28.

supply and demand forces within the Bloc. More specifically, assuming that the Council of Mutual Economic Assistance does not become a supra-national planning commission with coercive powers, some way must be found to encourage changes in the Bloc production pattern to eliminate all-Bloc deficits and surpluses and to develop the Bloc as an economic unit.[1] Moreover, it is difficult to compute intra-Bloc prices from Western market prices where quality differences are important (e.g. machinery) or where the prices fluctuate a great deal (e.g. raw materials).

However, until the identity of economic interests between Bloc nations becomes greater so that a nation will not be tempted to export to the West when the intra-Bloc price is lower, and until the CMEA develops some adequate methods by which relative production costs and productivity in each country can be compared, the old system of basing intra-Bloc prices on Western prices will doubtless be used.

No one knows when the Bloc will finally use foreign trade prices appreciably different from Western prices. However, I would heavily discount any rumours of impending changes.

[1] According to a Polish interviewee of John M. Montias, several Polish and Russian economists have proposed basing intra-Bloc trade prices on the shadow prices of goods of a gigantic linear programming model of the whole Bloc. Indeed, some such shadow prices have already been worked out by Polish economists although it is doubtful that they will be accepted by Bloc foreign trade policy-makers.

CHAPTER VI

THE CHOICE OF TRADE PARTNERS

According to the *Great Soviet Encyclopedia:* 'The policies of the Soviet Union in the area of foreign trade correspond to the principles of foreign policy of the USSR which Stalin . . . had formulated. The development of Soviet foreign trade is of first rank importance for (Soviet) political relations. . . .'[1] Almost all important Bloc officials have made similar statements at one time or another, and, therefore, Western commentators have paid almost exclusive attention to the political factors behind the choice of trade partners by Bloc nations. It is my opinion that such analyses are too one-sided and in this chapter I show that Bloc foreign trade decision-makers have not been as indifferent to economic factors in choosing trade partners as commonly believed in the West.

In order to analyse thoroughly the choice of trade partners, political and economic factors must be separately examined although, of course, both are present in many trade decisions. Since the political side of Bloc trade has been often discussed, I limit my analysis in this chapter to only the most important political factors such as the Western foreign trade embargo.

On the economic side I first examine the pattern of trade of the CMEA nations between the East and West and show the economic factors such as terms of trade consideration which have influenced and shaped the Bloc decision to limit trade with the West. I then discuss the Bloc choice of trade partners between developed and underdeveloped nations within the 'Capitalist world market' in order to place in perspective the additional economic forces which have been present here. Finally I consider several economic aspects of the choice of Bloc trade partners within the Bloc to show that some factors, such as bilateralism, have been overemphasized in the West.

1. THE PATTERN OF CMEA TRADE BETWEEN EAST AND WEST

In major Bloc documents and speeches of political leaders, the policy of the CMEA nations to trade primarily within the East Bloc is stated

[1] G. S. Roginski, B. T. Rolpakow, S. N. Bakulin and M. J. Paromow, *Grosse Sowjet Enzyklopaedie: Der Aussenhandel* (East Berlin: Verlag Die Wirtschaft, 1953), p. 28.

often and in very unambiguous terms.[1] This policy decision was made at the very highest peak of the power pyramid and called for a radical change of the pre-war trade pattern in the early post-war years. The redirection of trade may be easily seen in the Tables on the following page.[2]

Several important conclusions may be drawn from these data. First, the change in direction of trade occurred a great deal more quickly in the ex-enemy countries (Bulgaria, DDR, Hungary, Rumania) than in the former Allied countries (Poland and the CSSR). Second, the entire process hit a peak in 1953, the first year of the 'New Course', after which the percentages of trade within the Bloc fell to the 1951 level.

A. Political Factors

Perhaps the most important factor behind the change in the direction of trade from the West to the East was the desire of the Communist Governments to be economically independent of the West.[3] The increased trade of the East Central European nations with the USSR formed the major part of this redirection of trade (see Tables 6–9 and 6–10) and was facilitated, in the four ex-enemy countries, by the Russian occupation and the subsequent need of exports from these nations to help the USSR with its reconstruction programme. These initial changes have received extensive comment in the Western economic literature and need not be further analysed here.[4]

[1] e.g. according to the first DDR FYP: 'The basis of the foreign trade of the DDR is the trade with the USSR; the People's Democracies and China. The foreign trade relations with these countries are to be developed in order to insure the fulfilling of the import needs of the Republic . . .' (*Gesetzblatt der DDR*, 128/1951, p. 987).

[2] Data in parentheses exclude inter-German trade. Albania is omitted because of lack of data although Albanian trade is included in the trade of the other countries. For 1938 the foreign trade of the DDR area and German area east of the Oder-Neisse was estimated. For specific estimation procedures and for sources, see Statistical Appendix B.

[3] See Klinkmüller and Ruban, *Die wirtschaftliche Zusammenarbeit zwischen den Ostblockstaaten*, *op. cit.*, pp. 81ff. This desire for economic independence from the West has usually been stated in somewhat muted tones since it clashes with the East-West trade propaganda. The whole concept of 'economic independence' has not been, as far as I know, analysed carefully in the Bloc economic literature and what this policy meant for, let us say, machine imports from the West, is impossible to ascertain. Köhler (*op. cit.*, p. 117) notes that the Foreign Trade Standing Commission of the CMEA recommended that before a Bloc nation exports something to the West, it should make offers to other Bloc nations 'to avoid unnecessary transit trade and preserve the independence of the Socialist from the Capitalist world'.

[4] See especially A. Zauberman, *Economic Imperialism*, *op. cit.*, and Margaret Dewar, *Soviet Trade with Eastern Europe*, *op. cit.*

TABLE 6–1

PROPORTION OF THE TRADE TURNOVER OF CMEA NATIONS WITH THE ENTIRE EAST BLOC

Year	*Bulgaria* %	*CSSR* %	*DDR* %	*Hungary* %	*Poland* %	*Rumania* %	*Average* %	*USSR* %
1938	30	22	4(16)	23	13	25	8(19)	13
1948	78	32	75(—)	34	41	71	44	—
1950	85	53	72(86)	61	59	84	64	81
1951	90	60	76(81)	67	57	80	67	—
1952	89	71	75(79)	73	66	85	73	—
1953	86	78	78(83)	76	70	84	77	—
1954	87	74	76(84)	71	70	80	75	—
1955	87	69	72(81)	61	64	79	69	78
1956	80	65	73(82)	61	62	78	68	74
1957	83	67	73(82)	68	59	76	69	72
1958	84	69	73(82)	67	56	77	69	73
1959	80	71	75(84)	67	61	79	71	69
1960	80	70	73(81)	66	61	72	69	66
1965 (Plan)	—	75	75(—)	75	65	—	—	—

TABLE 6–2

PROPORTION OF THE TRADE TURNOVER OF CMEA NATIONS WITH OTHER CMEA NATIONS

Year	*Bulgaria* %	*CSSR* %	*DDR* %	*Hungary* %	*Poland* %	*Rumania* %	*Average* %	*USSR* %
1938	30	19	3(13)	23	13	25	7(17)	7
1948	78	32	75(—)	34	41	71	44	—
1950	85	53	72(86)	61	59	84	63	50
1951	90	57	74(78)	61	55	79	63	—
1952	88	66	70(74)	67	63	85	69	—
1953	83	71	71(77)	69	67	83	72	—
1954	84	67	69(75)	65	66	79	68	—
1955	84	63	64(72)	54	60	74	64	53
1956	77	59	66(74)	54	57	72	62	50
1957	81	60	67(75)	62	55	72	63	54
1958	82	61	65(74)	60	51	72	62	52
1959	79	64	69(77)	62	56	73	65	47
1960	79	64	68(75)	62	57	67	64	49
1965 (Plan)	—	70	—(—)	—	—	—	—	—

In 1948, intra-CMEA trade received two major stimuli. First, as I have noted before, each East Central European nation began to copy the Russian foreign trade system and the 'foreign trade monopoly' of each nation was practically completed by 1950. This centralization of trade permitted a small number of trusted officials from CMEA Bloc nations to conduct a relatively large amount of trade with each other (at the price, however, of realizing only a fraction of the total 'trade potential').

Secondly, the Western nations began systematically to restrict exports to the CMEA nations, the first step toward an extensive blockade. In March, 1948, the United States instituted an export licensing system for American exports to the entire Bloc in order to prevent their receiving 'armaments and strategic goods'. Moreover, Western trade with the Soviet Occupation Zone in Germany was almost entirely stopped between August, 1948, and May, 1949, to retaliate for the cutting of land transportation routes to West Berlin by the Soviet Military Administration. In the autumn of 1948, the United States began bilateral negotiation with various Western European nations to receive their co-operation for the embargo of strategic exports to the Bloc.

The security export controls were of three types:

(1) Denying to the CMEA Bloc those goods which could imperil Western security;

(2) Limiting export of goods which could be turned rapidly from civilian to military use;

(3) Establishing a surveillance list for certain key commodities such as rubber.

'Thus the emphasis was placed from the beginning on the composition and not the volume of this trade.'[1] The tensions before and during the outbreak of the Korean War in June, 1950, led to the forming of the Consultation Group Co-ordination Committee (COCOM) of fifteen Western powers to enforce the embargo more strictly. The 'Battle Act' which came into force in January, 1952, stopped US foreign economic grants and loans to any country which would not apply adequate security export controls to the Bloc.[2] The continuing discussions in COCOM resulted in a steady expansion of the embargoed goods up to 1953 when the list included 260 commodities and commodity groups which were completely forbidden (list A) and ninety others which were limited (list B).

The important question is, of course, what constitutes a 'strategic export', and the definition has varied considerably over the years. In 1949, the list included 'metalworking machinery, chemicals and petroleum equipment, precision instruments, metal (some) chemicals, petroleum and rubber products'.[3] At the peak of the embargo, one

[1] N. Spulber, *The Economics of Communist Eastern Europe* (Cambridge, Mass. and New York: The Technology Press and Wiley, 1957), p. 446.

[2] A complete list of documents concerning the embargo has been collected by Hans Jürgen Lambers, *Das Ost Embargo* (Frankfurt a.M. and West Berlin: Alfred Metzner Verlag, 1956). One law which perhaps has been as effective as the export control laws in limiting US trade with the East is the Johnson Act which forbids US companies to extend long-term credits to any foreign entities in default of debts owed to the US government.

[3] 'East-West Trade,' Chapter IX, *Staff Papers Presented to the Commission on Foreign Economic Policy* (Washington, D.C.: US Congress, February 1954), p. 443.

non-official US Government publication described strategic materials as those which 'may contribute directly or indirectly to industrial growth and hence to war potential'.[1] Although this seems an exaggeration of the official US policy position, the list in 1953 was still impressively long and included not only the items mentioned above, but also many non-ferrous metals and special alloys, electronic equipment and special machinery. In the early months of 1954, after the London Tripartite Conference in March, list A (completely forbidden exports) was shortened to 170 and list B (limited exports) to twenty. Further cuts have been made since then; in August, 1958, list A was reduced to 100 and list B was completely dropped.[2] The US Government has maintained, however, a somewhat longer list than the COCOM list for US exporters to most Bloc countries.

The effects of the blockade and the deliberate policy of the East Bloc policy-makers to redirect trade with the East is reflected in the following data from the Bloc nations:[3]

TABLE 6–3

VOLUME INDEX OF CMEA IMPORTS FROM NON-COMMUNIST NATIONS (1950=100)

Year	*East Central Europe*	*USSR*	*Total CMEA*
1938	313	217	287
1948	96	—	—
1950	100	100	100
1951	109	—	—
1952	90	—	—
1953	86	—	—
1954	111	—	—
1955	140	190	153
1956	147	260	177
1957	172	316	210
1958	187	376	238
1959	206	383	254

One must be careful in interpreting these data for both statistical and analytical reasons:

(1) The statistics must be used cautiously since the methods to change current price data to constant price data were crude. Moreover, these data are incomplete since they do not show the apparently great amount of contraband trade which was carried on during the period.[4] (It is interesting to note that Eastern statistical sources

[1] *Ibid.*, p. 443.

[2] 'Die neuen Embargolisten,' *Ost Handel* 8 and 9/1958, p. 1.

[3] Statistics in current prices from Bloc sources listed in Statistical Appendix B, deflated by world trade average unit price indices for imports.

[4] One DDR interviewee bragged to me, 'With dollars we can, and could, buy anything,' Although this was probably an exaggeration, Desmond Donnelly (Alec Nove and Desmond Donnelly, *Trade with Communist Countries, op. cit.*, p. 112) reports one example where the Chinese were able to circumvent the American blockade with apparent ease.

show a higher amount of East-West trade, measured in dollars, than Western sources.)[1]

(2) It is difficult to separate the effects of the blockade from the effects of the deliberate trade redirection policy by East Bloc politicians. In essence this is the problem of determining the adverse effects of the blockade, a problem which has been extensively discussed in the economic literature of both the East and West.

The East Bloc analyses of the blockade generally follow the interpretation of Stalin, who wrote that although the 'Socialist world market' would have arisen anyway: '... it should be observed that the USA and Great Britain and France themselves contributed—without desiring it, of course—to the formation and consolidation of the new, parallel World markets. They imposed an economic blockade on the USSR, China and the European People's Democracies, which did not join the "Marshall Plan" system, thinking thereby to strangle them. The effect, however, was not to strangle but to strengthen the new World market.'[2]

Western experts, although disagreeing with Stalin's analysis of Western motives, usually agree with his conclusions concerning the end results. 'Limitation on the exports of these (strategic materials) ... probably has slowed up the industrial growth of the Soviet Union to a modest extent during the past few years (before 1954). But it would be too much to say that these measures have, or ever would, really hurt the all-over Soviet Bloc economy in any vital way.'[3] 'What the embargo policy has actually prevented is the further development of the Soviet industrial machine on the basis of Western deliveries of heavy equipment or vehicles on long-term credit.'[4] 'The trouble with the embargo is simply that the more efficacious it becomes with respect to the small countries of the Soviet orbit, the greater becomes the bargaining position of the USSR in its intra-Bloc trade relations ... and the indications are that the stronger nations of the orbit will be able to push a large share of the burden of the embargo onto the weaker nations in Eastern Europe.'[5]

[1] For a more extensive analysis of East-West trade from Western statistics, see Nicolas Spulber, 'Effects of the Embargo on Soviet Trade,' *Harvard Business Review*, 6/1952, pp. 122–8; US Department of Commerce, *Free World Imports from and Exports to Soviet Bloc Countries by Commodity Groups*, various years, and ECE, *Economic Survey of Europe* and *Economic Bulletin for Europe*, various issues.

[2] Joseph Stalin, *Economic Problems of Socialism*, *op. cit.*, p. 26.

[3] *Staff Papers*, *op. cit.*, p. 443.

[4] Nicolas Spulber, *The Economics of Communist Eastern Europe*, *op. cit.*, p. 452. This may be seen in the trade statistics which show that the import surplus of the CMEA countries from the West disappeared in 1948, and that trade has been either balanced or else the East has had a slight export surplus in almost every year since then.

[5] Nicolas Spulber, 'Effects of the Embargo on Soviet Trade,' *op. cit.*

Such analyses seem to omit several important factors, however. There were, of course, many short-run crises in the very beginning because certain imports were suddenly stopped. What is more important, however, is that the embargo has served to intensify the many production bottlenecks which have occurred in each Bloc nation every year by limiting the ability of the Bloc to import suddenly scarce goods and materials from the West.[1] Aside from these short-run effects, the embargo has forced the Bloc countries to invest in many extremely high cost industries in order to produce goods formerly imported.[2] If the embargo were really so economically unimportant to the Bloc, then there was little reason why the Bloc nations should have screamed so loudly and so long over the benefits to the West of increased East-West trade, and should have used such insincere arguments to further this trade.[3] Certainly the propaganda value of yelling 'blockade' to the world was severely limited since the CMEA nations were, at the same time, hanging a *complete* blockade over Yugoslavia.[4]

Taking all these factors into account, I think that the embargo hurt the East Bloc a good deal more in the long-run and the short than other Western commentators indicate. It seems to me that the embargo was the primary factor for the declining volume of East-West trade up to 1954 and that the rapid rise of East-West trade in

[1] The value of the West as an 'escape valve' for East Bloc planning blunders has been vividly described by former DDR planner Fritz Schenk, *Magie der Planwirtschaft, op. cit.*, pp. 246ff.

[2] The composition of trade shifted appreciably in the period. Western exports of machines and raw materials fell to a mere trickle from 1950–55 and intermediate and consumer goods became the predominant Western export to the Bloc.

[3] In the propaganda directed to Western foreign traders two main arguments were used: (1) The ruling classes in the Capitalist nations ordered the embargo against the real interest of the nation and of the businessmen who could earn nice profits here; (2) Trade with the East is a way to alleviate the general crisis of Capitalism. These arguments were insincere because they contradicted some of the most basic principles of Communist ideology (i.e. that the businessmen *are* the ruling classes and that there is no way to escape the general crisis of Capitalism).

[4] A wonderful example of double-thinking may be found in an article by Anton Borgmeier ('Probleme der internationalen Wirtschaftsbeziehungen der Staaten des sozialistischen Weltwirtschaftssystem,' *Wissenschaftliche Zeitschrift der Martin Luther Universität* VIII, 4 and 5/1958–59, pp. 541–60) who declared that the 'difficulties' in trade between Yugoslavia and the CMEA Bloc were caused by Yugoslavia trying to redirect her trade to the West! Speaking of propaganda, it seems somewhat strange that the Eastern counter-blockade against the West is never mentioned by the West. For example, DDR economist Rudolf Brauer ('Zur Frage des volkswirtschaftlichen Nutzeffektes des Aussenhandels,' *Wirtschaftswissenschaft*, 3/1958, pp. 389–402) reminded the CMEA Bloc members to be more careful in their prohibiting of exports of strategic value to the West.

1955–6 was due to the cutting of the embargo list. This interpretation is, however, open to question since several Bloc nations began to show a growing interest in more trade with the West during this period and it is difficult to tell if this new Bloc policy was independent of, or a response to, Western actions. From 1956 to the present, the effect of the embargo has increasingly waned since the embargo list has been progressively shortened. By 1960 the embargo was still acting as a hindrance to increased trade between the Bloc and the United States, which has maintained the most restrictive export list. However, taking the West as a whole, I believe that the embargo has served only to limit a small proportion of potential exports to the Bloc in recent years and is not now a major discouraging factor to an expansion of trade.[1]

Another political factor which has acted to discourage East-West trade from the Western side is the refusal of the Bloc to restrict itself solely to economic activities in trade. For instance, the State Secretary of Foreign Trade of the DDR declared: 'Foreign trade has not only the task of appreciably bettering the standard of living of our people; through its activity in the Capitalist world, foreign trade must also . . . support the peace-loving forces in these countries and to strengthen them in their fight against the robbing monopolists. . . . It is vitally necessary that the workers in foreign trade understand the political meaning of their work. It is necessary (for them) to see the economic tasks from a political standpoint and to recognize what type of positive and negative effects business contacts can bring.'[2] The classic case of 'supporting the peace-loving forces' was the early post-war loan of wheat by the USSR to France through the French communist leader, M. Thorez (who was then on the Cabinet of the French Government) shortly before an important French election, even though there was a wheat shortage in

[1] This opinion is shared by Nove and Donnelly, *op. cit.*, p. 43, and the various speakers at the 1961 congressional investigation of East-West trade ('Hearings before the Subcommittee on Foreign Economic Policy of the Joint Economic Committee of the Congress of the United States,' December 4–14, 1961; Washington, D.C.: Government Printing Office, 1962). For Poland, according to the Director of Export Supply of the Department of Commerce (John C. Borton, 'US Government Policies and Practices in the Control of Exports to the Soviet Bloc,' AMA Management Report No. 45, *Aspects of East-West Trade*, *op. cit.*, pp. 13–20) '. . . there is little difference in treatment between Poland and Western European countries with regard to the commodities that are approved for export.'

[2] Willy Hüttenrauch, 'Die Regierungserklarung von November 25, 1953 und die Aufgaben des Aussenhandels,' *Der Aussenhandel* III, 49/1953, p. 1173. According to another DDR economist (Heinz Brass, *Die wesentlichsten Einflüsse des Aussenhandels auf das gesellschaftliche Gesamtprodukt und das Nationaleinkommen im Sozialismus;* Doctoral dissertation, Hochschule für Ökonomie, 1959; p. 41): 'Carrying out foreign trade is not primarily a commercial affair (without wanting to underestimate this side) but is, first of all, a political activity.'

the USSR. In Iceland, Russia negotiated an agreement to buy Icelandic fish once a Communist party member was on the Cabinet; when he was ousted, the agreement was not continued; when he was reinstated, the agreement was renewed.[1] In 1958 Finland had a similar experience in her trade negotiations with the USSR.[2] Political motives played the leading role in the one-sided cancelling of the USSR-Israel trade contract by the Russians in 1956.[3] The sudden and arbitrary withdrawal from trade fairs by the USSR (e.g., the Zagreb Fair of 1959 or the Bangkok Fair in 1954)[4] and the one-sided cancelling of credits by the USSR to Yugoslavia in 1958–9.[5] Moreover, it was discovered in several Western countries that Bloc traders were in direct contact and working with the local Communist parties. Such political activities have made the Bloc foreign trade representatives and the Bloc trade offers very unwelcome in some countries.

Several political factors have acted to encourage East-West trade. First of all, some important public figures in both the East and West have declared that increased contacts and trade between the two Blocs will lead to a decrease in political tensions and lessen the chances of war. Certainly an increased economic interdependency would make an act of war more difficult, although it is doubtful that such an interdependency would be allowed by either side to become that great. Nevertheless, such motives were instrumental in the setting up of special conferences on East-West trade by such organizations as the ECE and UNESCO, as well as increasing number of analyses of East-West trade 'potential' in various trade magazines.

Furthermore, both the East and West have special political interests in East-West trade, although for the East I have never been able to find a very frank analysis of the problem. However, Western political commentators have attributed such motives to the East as: increased East-West trade allows the Bloc to present its political case to a wider audience; such trade permits an increase of Bloc influence in the West, and, at the same time, allows a widening of its knowledge of Western business activities; and this trade sets up the pre-conditions for the same type of power politics and economic

[1] Raymond F. Mikesell & Jack N. Behrman, *Financing Free World Trade with the Sino-Soviet Bloc* (Princeton, N.J.: Princeton Univ. Press, 1958), p. 28.

[2] David L. Cohn, 'Pannen bei der roten "Wirtschaftshilfe,"' *Freie Rundschau* 3/1960, pp. 29–33.

[3] *Ibid.* It is interesting to note that the DDR has completely boycotted Israel, although other Bloc nations have maintained trade relations with Israel.

[4] 'Boykott des Ostblocks gegenüber Jugoslawien,' *Neue Zürcher Zeitung* May 5, 1959; and Joseph S. Berliner, *Soviet Economic Aid* (New York: Frederick A. Praeger, Inc., 1958), Chapter V. The Russians withdrew because they were not allowed to bring along their circus and ballet troups to the Bangkok fair.

[5] 'Boykott des Ostblocks gegenüber Jugoslawien,' *op. cit.*

warfare which the Nazis used before the Second World War.[1] Undoubtedly such political ideas are entertained by Bloc officials. Nevertheless, before we arm ourselves against an invasion of Bloc foreign traders, it is well to consider several important economic influences operating on Bloc policy-makers.

B. Economic Factors

In the middle and late 1950s, economic factors began to play an increasingly important role in the decision of the Bloc nations to limit East-West trade.

(1) One of the most important economic factors acting to discourage this East-West trade from the Eastern side was the unfavourable terms of trade which the Bloc nations received with the West, in comparison with what they received from other Bloc partners. In the Table below, any percentage over 100 per cent indicates that it was more advantageous to trade with Bloc partners than it was to trade with the West.

TABLE 6–4

TERMS OF TRADE OF FOUR BLOC NATIONS WITH CMEA TRADE PARTNERS COMPARED TO TERMS OF TRADE WITH THE WEST [2]

	1952 %	*1953* %	*1954* %	*1955* %	*1956* %	*1957* %	*1958* %	*1959* %
USSR	—	—	—	123	136	134	130	—
Bulgaria								
Whole sample	99	87	102	130	161	—	150	125
Sample without tobacco	141	137	129	134	166	—	175	141
Hungary								
Whole sample	106	136	89	118	(197)	126	128	—
Sample without cokes	106	104	82	102	—	—	—	—
Poland								
Whole sample	—	—	—	—	—	—	152	—
Sample without coal	—	—	—	—	—	—	140	—

From 1952 through 1959 every CMEA nation in almost every year received more favourable terms of trade with Bloc than with Western

[1] For instance, see Samuel Pisar, *A New Look at Trade Policy toward the Communist Bloc*, Materials prepared for the Joint Economic Committee (Washington: GPO, 1961); or Jacob K. Javits, *The Political Stakes in East-West Trade*, Joint Economic Committee (Washington: GPO, 1962).

[2] Data in parentheses are of dubious quality. This table was calculated from Table 5–2 (with transportation differentials added so that import data are c.i.f.) divided by Table 5–1. For statistical details, see Statistical Appendix A.

partners. This phenomenon has not gone unnoticed in the Bloc economic Press either.[1]

The CMEA nations had a trading disadvantage *vis-a-vis* the West for several reasons:

(a) Bloc FTES and their representatives have often had great problems in operating successfully in the West. First of all, their dealings have been often hampered by a great deal of bureaucratism. For instance, negotiations between Amtorg (the Russian trading company in America) and an American firm over the import of Soviet cars lasted over a year-and-a-half before the American decided to take direct action by flying to Moscow. Another American firm has found it useful to pay a special expeditor in Russia a fee for helping them cut through the red tape (no pun intended) with FTES.[2] Furthermore, merchandising policies of Bloc FTES have often been extremely inflexible. For instance, a large Greek order of timber from Rumania was cancelled merely because the Greek businessman wanted a special pre-shipment inspection which was not included in the general bureaucratic procedures used by Rumania traders.

[1] In the DDR foreign trade literature several authors have noted that the DDR received lower prices for exports and paid higher prices for imports than most Western European nations, especially West Germany. See e.g. *Der Aussenhandel:* V, 20/1955, p. 648 or VI, 3/1956, p. 90.

In one DDR source (August Brendel, *Moglichkeiten und Aufgaben des Aussenhandels bei der Unterstutzung des Prozesses der Standardisierung und Typisierung der Produktion im Maschinenbau;* Diplomarbeit, Hochschule für Ökonomie, 1960; p. 14) I found the following plan figures for average unit prices of imports (in 'foreign exchange DMs'):

	Rolled Steel First Processing Stage	*Rolled Steel Second Processing Stage*
1960 Plan		
Socialist Countries	668	1,034
Capitalist Countries	909	1,448
1961 Plan		
Socialist Countries	673	1,046
Capitalist Countries	943	1,563
1965 Plan		
Socialist Countries	611	926
Capitalist Countries	837	1,371

The differences between the average unit price data for the imports from the two Blocs can be attributed to transportation costs, quality differences or lower prices on the CMEA Bloc market. I do not believe the first two factors could have made so great a difference, which means that the DDR planned to pay higher average unit prices from Western, rather than from Bloc trade partners. This was an excellent reason for the DDR to buy as much rolled steel as possible from the Bloc.

[2] Several case histories of American firms trading with the USSR are given in Trade Research Associates, *US-Soviet Trade: Facts for the Businessman's Appraisal* (Cleveland: 1960) or AMA, *op. cit.*

Scores of other examples of such inflexibilities have been noted in the economic literature.[1] Poor advertising, lack of awareness of Western styles, and lack of spare parts for repairs have been other common failings of Bloc traders.

One reason for these commercial failings is that the personnel in the FTES have often been quite inexperienced, since political qualifications are often more important than technical skills in positions where contact with Western nations is frequent.

(b) CMEA trade with the West has been often quite erratic. This has been due to two factors: First, when sudden production bottlenecks have occurred, Bloc nations have often pushed almost any saleable article onto the Western market in order to obtain enough currency to pay for vitally needed imports. Secondly, production for export have suffered from the same production problems, material scarcities, 'storming' phenomenon, work stoppages, etc., as production for domestic consumption, and this has caused serious difficulties in trade with the West.[2] Western traders know of these difficulties and naturally have used them to obtain more favourable terms of trade. For instance, one Western trading firm has instructed its employees not to conduct trade with Bloc FTES until just before the end of the quarter when the Bloc trader is trying to meet his quarterly plan.

(c) Finally, there is some evidence that the bilateral pattern of East-West trade has weakened the bargaining position of the Bloc nations who have been more interested in this trade than the West.[3] This must, however, remain conjectural.

Various all-Bloc efforts have been dedicated to reducing this price disadvantage with the West. In the CMEA, a work group has coordinated the exhibitions of the Bloc members in trade fairs in the non-Communist countries. Futhermore, some sort of mutual market research for important products traded on the 'Capitalist world markets' as well as a general exchange of information on trading in the Western markets (including a central catalogue of insolvent

[1] On Western views of poor Bloc sales techniques, see Robert Loring Allen, *Soviet Economic Warfare* (Washington, DC.: Public Affairs Press, 1960) Chapters XII–XIV, Pisar, *op. cit.*, or Mikesell and Behrman, *op. cit.*, pp. 74–6. For an Eastern view see Hängekorb, *Termin und Qualität-A und O unseres Exports* (E. Berlin: Verlag Die Wirtschaft, 1958: p. 5), for some DDR blunders in foreign trade.

[2] According to the DDR Minister of Foreign Trade: 'It has been ascertained that non-observance of delivery dates (in foreign trade) is a frequent occurrence. This endangers [the fulfilment of] the trade plans with both Socialist and Capitalist countries, and we run the danger of losing our markets to Capitalist competitors.' (cited by Hängekorb, *op. cit.*)

[3] *World Economic Survey for 1958*, pp. 164–5.

Western traders) seems to be carried on.[1] In March 1958, representatives from the market research institutions of the Bloc countries met in Budapest to investigate possibilities of greater co-ordination in this area. Perhaps the most important developments along this line lie in the future, and one DDR economist has observed: 'In the next years the planned division of labour will lead to the situation where each Socialist country will sell a specific assortment of goods on the Capitalist world market and competition between the Socialist nations will be avoided.'[2]

Nevertheless, it seemed that up to 1961 the expected dangers to Western foreign traders of the 'omniscient foreign trade monopolies' in the East Bloc countries did not materialize. That is not to say that this will not happen in the future. However, the more the CMEA nations withdraw from the Western markets because of price disadvantages, the less experience they will gain which will allow them to overcome these difficulties.

(2) A second economic factor discouraging East-West trade has been the predominantly bilateral character of this trade. Bilateralism was not a Russian investion and before the war, was seldom employed by the USSR. Nevertheless, since the war such bilateral East-West contacts have been the rule, rather than the exception. In many cases the Bloc nations have tried to arrange bilaterally balanced trade deals with single Western firms, e.g., between Centrosoyuz of Russia and the Scottish Co-operative Society.[3] Various proposals have been made to multilateralize East-West trade and in 1957, after years of negotiation, a multilateral clearing arrangement was finally instituted by the ECE.[4] By the end of 1957 about $50,000,000 of balances had been cleared. The chief weakness in the whole arrange-

[1] See 'Zusammenarbeit der Ostblockstaaten auf Messen im "kapitalistischen Ausland" soll verbessert werden,' *IWE Tagesbericht* April 1, 1958, and Theodor Hermes, *Der Aussenhandel in den Ostblockstaaten* (*op. cit.*), p. 88. Brzezinski, (*op. cit.*, p. 284) cited a conference in December, 1957, of Bloc representatives to evaluate their foreign trade with the 'Capitalist trade markets.' Gertrud Gräbig (*Der Sozialistische Weltmarkt, op. cit.*, p. 44) declared: 'The co-ordination of long-range plans between the Socialist countries and the international co-ordination of production, investment and foreign trade, demands also the . . . co-ordination of trade with the Capitalist nations. From these factors one sees the necessity of a common front of the Socialist nations on the Capitalist markets.'

[2] Heinz Brass, *Die wesentlichsten Einflüsse des Aussenhandels auf das gesellschaftliche Gesamtprodukt und das Nationaleinkommen im Sozialismus, op. cit.*, p. 17.

[3] From a communication from Alec Nove. See also Pisar, *op. cit.*, p. 13, for other examples.

[4] For discussions of this arrangement, see Mikesell and Behrman, *op. cit.*, pp. 55–7; and for a pessimistic Bloc view, Giersdorf, 'Fragen des Überganges zu multilateralen Clearing-abkommen zwischen der DDR und kapitalistischen Ländern,' *Der Aussenhandel* X, 2/1960, pp. 13–14.

ment has been that both the CMEA Bloc and the Western countries have wanted Western currencies and have been reluctant to accept balances in CMEA Bloc currencies.

(3) Another inhibiting factor on East-West trade has been Western apathy, or even worse, opposition. For instance, Western international oil companies have refused to process Soviet oil even though in Cuba, at least, this policy backfired. The lack of direct contact with Bloc producers and the low quality of many East Bloc goods has been another inhibiting factor. For example, in the middle of the 1950s, DDR officials declared 43 per cent of all textile machines, 58 per cent of all printing machines, and 75 per cent of all heavy machines produced in the DDR to be under world standard.[1] In addition, the dislike of Western consumers for Bloc consumer goods such as Moskovitch cars has not been caused solely by the poor distribution networks and unavailability of spare parts; it has been due to a certain orneriness of the consumer who has not wanted East Bloc goods at any price. For an entirely different type of reason, Western manufacturers have been loathe to export to the East. As succinctly stated by *The Economist*, 'For businessmen, trade with Communist countries must contain risks. No formal arrangement will change the disconcerting Communist conception that Western industrial ideas are there to be copied.'[2]

(4) A fourth factor which has made East-West trade more difficult has been the rapid change in the structure of import and export demands. The traditional pattern of trade between the East Central European nations (DDR and CSSR excluded) and the West had been the exchange of agricultural and light industry products from the East for consumer goods and machinery from the West. The very rapid process of industrialization in the CMEA countries began to disturb this traditional pattern. Previously imported machinery and consumer goods began to be produced at home. Agricultural exports fell, due to the production problems resulting from the various drives for collectivization (as well as higher food demands from an increasing population), and East Central Europe became a

[1] *Economic Bulletin for Europe* VIII, August/1956, p. 55, and Mand Pielert, *Die Werbung als Mittel zum Erweiterung des Aussenhandelsvolumens der DDR mit den sozialistischen Staaten im II Funfjahrplan* (Diplomarbeit, Hochschule für Ökonomie, 1957), p. 22. For other examples see Pisar, *op. cit.*, p. 39 or Haengekorb, *op. cit.*

[2] 'Economic Co-existence,' *The Economist* CXCV, 1/9/1960. The USSR has never joined the Berne Convention of 1870 concerning international patent protection and the position of foreign patents in the USSR is quite uncertain. According to Stephen P. Ladas ('Observations on the Trademark and Patent Systems of the USSR,' AMA Report No. 45, *Aspects of East-West Trade*, *op. cit.*), foreign patents have some protection if they are registered in the USSR but the government, by law, can still expropriate any such registered invention.

net importer of grains and other foodstuffs. Furthermore, the CMEA nations began to demand industrial raw materials which, in the first post-war decade, were quite scarce in Western Europe.[1] Making new trade contracts or trade contracts for new products with the West has taken more time than some Bloc countries have estimated.

(5) The risk factor has been a final discouraging element of East-West trade.[2] For the West, '. . . it remains true that trade with the USSR or Czechoslovakia is more hazardous, more likely to be interrupted by political difficulties, or sudden and unforeseeable changes in planning decisions, than is trade with the (British) Commonwealth or our European neighbours'.[3] What has generally not been recognized or taken into account, however, is the risk for the CMEA nations. In the East-West trade contracts, trade quotas do not usually represent a governmental commitment to buy or deliver by the West. Even for State-traded commodities, the trade agreement is ordinarily a contract not subject to legal action in the event of non-fulfilment.[4] Statistical analyses of 240 trade agreements between East and West showed that 37 per cent of total export deliveries from Western to Bloc countries were 51 per cent under the target totals; and that 36 per cent of the total imports by the West from the East were 51 per cent under the expected amount.[5] It should be added, however, that there were also many cases where trade was over 100 per cent of the amount specified in the global contract.

A closer examination of seven trade agreements and 113 specific commodity targets showed that in 34 per cent of the cases, less than half the import and export targets were met.[6] A final study of twelve Western nations which had bilateral trade agreements with the Bloc demonstrated that there were greater yearly fluctuations in total trade

[1] For a more thorough analysis of trade structure, see Spulber, *The Economics of Communist East Europe*, *op. cit.;* 'Developments in the Foreign Trade of Eastern Europe and the Soviet Union,' *op. cit.;* various issues of *Economic Bulletin for Europe* (yearly summaries of East-West trade), and for an early view, David Granick, 'The Pattern of Foreign Trade in Eastern Europe and Its Relation to Economic Development Policy,' *Quarterly Journal of Economics*, August, 1954, pp. 377–400.

[2] In a pure game situation a nation would minimize risk by trading with as many nations as possible. However, until the Soviet blockage of Albania the East Central European nations seemed to regard a trade blockade from the West as much more likely than a blockade by another Bloc nation.

[3] Nove and Donnelly, *op. cit.*, p. 42.

[4] Mikesell and Behrman, *op. cit.*, p. 66.

[5] *Ibid.*, Table 9, p. 78.

[6] *Ibid.*, Table 11, p. 82.

between these countries and Bloc countries, than between these Western countries and other Western nations.[1] Because of the inflexibilities in the present trade planning systems in most Bloc nations, these fluctuations and non-fulfilments could not easily be neutralized.[2] The ostensible security for a Bloc nation of a long-term contract with another Bloc nation whose government pledged itself to fulfil the quotas was a powerful stimulus for planners of the Bloc to continue to conduct most of their trade within the Bloc.

These five factors notwithstanding, the Bloc nations have had several very strong economic incentives for trading with the West.

(1) Most important is the factor of choice. The possessor of convertible Western currency has an extremely wide range of products to choose from, which he can obtain at almost any time. In the force-draft Bloc economies where planning is carried out by means of material balances and where attention is primarily focused on a few leading industries, scarcities arise in other sectors of the economy which must, in the short- or long-run, be alleviated in order for the economy to maintain an adequate overall growth rate. Importing such scarce goods in the short-run from other Bloc nations is often impossible because those countries had not planned a surplus of production of these goods. Often obtaining these goods from other Bloc countries in the long-run has been difficult because these countries also neglected the same industries. Therefore, in the words of a former DDR planner, 'the Communist (policy-makers) view the West as a type of reservoir which they can tap to their hearts desire whenever they have the cash'.[3] It is often possible to raise the cash for such imports by selling some exports at lower than World market prices. The overall benefits of trade could very well outweigh any adverse terms of trade.[4]

[1] *Ibid.*, Table 12, p. 84.

[2] This does not mean that the responsibility for the non-fulfilment of the trade contracts lay solely on the Western side. In an analysis of the history of many trade negotiations between CMEA Bloc and Western nations after global agreements had been signed, Mikesell and Behrman (*op. cit.*, pp. 79ff.) have concluded that responsibility in most cases is difficult to determine but that usually both partners were to blame. Often the quota was not filled for the simple reason that one side demanded too high a price.

[3] Schenk, *op. cit.*, p. 247.

[4] This does not mean that the Communist foreign traders deliberately set out to disturb Capitalist markets by dumping. Because of the shortage of Western currencies, the Bloc exporters have been interested in receiving the highest prices possible for their goods. Furthermore, they have usually received fat bonuses when such high prices have been obtained. Nevertheless, lack of real knowledge of production costs plus the occasional sudden needs for certain imports has encouraged some undercutting of the World market prices. The recent tremors in the international tin, aluminium and platinum market have been attributed to Soviet desire to disturb Western markets. Rather than malice,

(2) Many of the goods which the Bloc nations delivered to each other have been of extremely poor quality. According to a Western economist, 'Polish coke delivered to East Germany was repeatedly described as substandard; electric locomotives from the Hennigsdorf plant in East Germany soon broke down in Poland; Czech equipment for the Elblag power plant in Poland had to be replaced twice. Similar complaints were repeatedly registered, at least in Poland, about the quality of iron ore and cotton, as well as about equipment supplied by the Soviet Union; apparently there were attempts to sell used and reconditioned Soviet equipment as new. In 1958 2,000,000 Soviet clinical thermometers were scrapped as substandard. A list of defective machines supplied by Czechoslovakia to its neighbours in the area was (recently) published. . . .'[1] This poor quality of exports combined with the late deliveries and difficulties in obtaining repair parts for these goods have encouraged Bloc nations to trade with the West.

(3) The East has also been able to obtain new types of technology through trade with the West. Khrushchev himself admitted that imports from such countries as the United States, England, and West Germany would provide the USSR with 'quicker fulfilment of its programme for the construction of new chemical enterprises without wasting time on creation of plans and mastering of the production of new types of equipment.'[2] Technology has sometimes been directly obtained as, for instance, in the case where the CSSR and Italy made a production specialization agreement for knitting machine parts.

(4) Geographical contiguity has encouraged some Bloc nations to trade with the West to save high transportation costs.

From this brief review it is apparent that *both* political and economic forces have played important roles in East-West trade.[3] In any one decision these factors might be impossible to untangle, e.g.,

---

the real reson for this activity was probably stupidity, especially since the political repercussions in Indonesia and Malaya, as a result of excess Russian tin sales, were unfavourable. On this whole matter of dumping, see H. G. Aubrey, 'Soviet Trade, Price Stability, and Economic Growth,' *Kyklos* XIII, 3/1959, pp. 290–300; Nove and Donnelly, *op. cit.*, p. 25, and, for the case of oil, see Richard J. Ward, 'Soviet Competition in Western Markets,' *Journal of Industrial Economics* VIII, 2/1960, pp. 133–49.

[1] Jan Wszelaki, *Communist Economic Strategy: The Role of East Central Europe* (Washington, D.C.: National Planning Association, 1959), p. 125.

[2] Quoted by Pisar (*op. cit.*, p. 45) who has in an appendix a long list of complete factories and highly technical machines which the East Bloc has imported from the West.

[3] For other analyses of Bloc economic motives in East-West trade, see Robert Loring Allen, 'Economic Motives in Soviet Foreign Trade Policy,' *Southern Economic Journal* XXV, October/1958; R. L. Allen, 'An Interpretation of East-West Trade,' *Comparisons of the United States and Soviet Economies* (Washington, D.C.: Joint Economic Committee, US Congress, 1959), pp. 403–26.

economic motives might be the most important in the choice of the good to be traded and the choice of general trade direction and yet political factors might determine the method of handling the trade and the choice of the way in which the final contract is made. Nevertheless, I believe that such economic factors as the adverse terms of trade, the bilateralism, the difficulty in exporting some goods because of Western prejudices, the rapid shifts in trade structure, and the risk factor have discouraged East-West trade a great deal more than the blockade or the desire for economic independency. These adverse economic factors to the Bloc have been offset, to a certain extent, by the greater choice of goods in the West, their higher quality, and the innovation costs which could be saved by imports.

2. THE PATTERN OF CMEA TRADE BETWEEN ECONOMICALLY DEVELOPED AND UNDERDEVELOPED NON-COMMUNIST NATIONS

Communist trade with the underdeveloped nations has been greatly stressed since the death of Stalin, and a recent statement by the Minister of Foreign Trade of the DDR summarizes the case: 'Our deliveries in these (underdeveloped) nations has . . . not only a purely economic character, but also an important trade policy and foreign policy effect. It contributes to the struggle of the nationally conscious anti-imperialistic circles of these peoples, and to the protection and strengthening . . . of the zone of peace and the weakening of the power positions of the imperialists.'[1]

Nevertheless, it is worthwhile to look at the extent of this trade and to examine some relevant economic factors which I believe have been more important than the more obvious political factors.

The volume and growth of Bloc trade with the Western underdeveloped nations has often been exaggerated. Some idea of the extent of this trade may be gained from the following data:[2]

Although the increase in foreign trade between the Bloc and the Western underdeveloped nations has been quite impressive since

[1] Heinrich Rau, 'Zu einigen Fragen der volkswirtschaftlichen Rolle und Bedeutung unseres Aussenhandels,' *Einheit* XII, 2/1957, pp. 168–180. The second edition of the *Politische Oekonomie Lehrbuch* has a special paragraph beginning, 'The continual widening of the economic relations of the nations of the Socialist camp with the underdeveloped nations has great importance . . .' which was not included in the first edition of this work, a sure sign of a new policy.

[2] From current price data, deflated by world trade unit price index for underdeveloped countries. Estimates for 1938 were made for pre-war trade of DDR area and German area east of the Oder–Neisse but does not include intra-German trade. For definition of 'underdeveloped nations' and for sources and methods, see Statistical Appendix B, Section 2.

TABLE 6–5. VOLUME OF CMEA BLOC TRADE TURNOVER WITH THE WESTERN UNDERDEVELOPED COUNTRIES

Year	*Volume Index (1950=100)*	*Percentage of CMEA Trade with West* %
1938	550	15
1948	158	16
1950	100	14
1951	108	15
1952	100	13
1953	84	11
1954	173	18
1955	248	21
1956	278	19
1957	340	21
1958	423	23
1959	488	24
1960	571	—

1953, this must not be overrated. During the early 1950s CMEA Bloc trade with the underdeveloped nations fell considerably more than CMEA Bloc trade with the Western developed nations. As a result, by 1958 the CMEA Bloc trade with the underdeveloped countries was only about 75 per cent of the pre-war level. The great increase in trade with the underdeveloped nations was due far more to a general growth in East-West trade than to a redirection of trade, as one may see from the second column in Table 6–5.

These aggregate data hide some interesting information on the mainsprings of the so-called 'Rouble offensive', which are revealed in an examination of the sources and direction of this trade (see Tables 6–6 and 6–7 on the following page).

From these data the changing pattern of the sources and direction of trade of the CMEA Bloc with the underdeveloped countries may be easily seen. Before the war, the DDR area and German territory east of the Oder-Neisse had the most extensive trade with the underdeveloped nations. In the post-war period until 1955, Czechoslovakia and Poland played the leading roles. Since then, the USSR has been steadily increasing its trade in this direction so that after 1956 it was the largest trader with the underdeveloped nations. Indeed, since 1956 Russia has played the major role in the trade drive. Primary receivers of Bloc goods before the war were the Latin American nations. In the post-war years, however, the pattern has changed radically several times. Between 1956 and 1958 the Arab states became the largest trade partners among the underdeveloped nations with the Bloc, with the other Asian nations in second place and the Latin American nations trailing behind. In 1960 the increased trade with Cuba placed Latin America as one of the leading trade areas again.

TABLE 6–6

TRADE TURNOVER OF CMEA BLOC NATIONS WITH WESTERN UNDERDEVELOPED COUNTRIES

(million current $)[1]

Year	*Albania*	*Bulgaria*	*CSSR*	*DDR*	*Hungary*	*Poland*	*Rumania*	*Total*	*USSR*
1938	0	2	84	333	17	61	22	519	44
1948	0	4	159	—	9	44	31	247	212
1950	0	1	98	—	11	28	5	142	118
1951	0	0	142	—	19	45	22	239	103
1952	0	4	108	6	21	53	8	200	104
1953	0	7	91	4	26	48	18	192	46
1954	0	2	146	8	47	85	30	327	159
1955	0	3	217	16	69	148	35	489	213
1956	0	10	260	35	68	119	35	527	268
1957	0	14	237	63	38	134	34	519	460
1958	0	16	269	77	61	163	51	636	540
1959	0	20	259	102	72	172	47	672	645
1960	0	21	296	125	62	216	57	771	780

TABLE 6–7

DIRECTION OF CMEA BLOC TRADE WITH WESTERN UNDERDEVELOPED COUNTRIES[2]

Year	*Latin American Nations*	*Arab Nations*	*Other African Nations*	*Other Asian Nations*
	%	%	%	%
1938	46	11	8	35
1948	27	35	6	32
1950	12	41	6	41
1951	8	43	8	41
1952	6	56	7	30
1953	28	41	9	22
1954	51	28	7	14
1955	49	29	5	17
1956	30	37	4	29
1957	20	41	5	28
1958	21	48	4	27
1959	21	41	5	34
1960	32	33	5	30

Some Western economists have attributed the especially favourable terms of trade as a prime motive for the Bloc trade offensive in the underdeveloped nations. Their opinions have been based on various well-known statements by political leaders in several underdeveloped nations. For instance, the Indonesian Cabinet Minister Harshap declared before the Indonesian Parliament on October 24, 1955: 'With barter trade and compensation transactions (with the CMEA Bloc) our exports are usually sold at a lower price than that obtained

[1] 1938 trade of DDR includes German territory east of Oder-Neisse. For sources and cautions, see Statistical Appendix B.

[2] For sources and cautions in using this table, see Statistical Appendix B.

on the World market. Losses suffered are "compensated" by increasing prices of articles imported under the transactions. Thus the country loses doubly; on the one hand, it receives less foreign exchange, on the other hand, Indonesian customers have to pay heavily for increased prices of imported goods.'[1] In Burma, U Nu said that Burma was losing from 10 per cent to 20 per cent in the clearing arrangement with Bloc nations. He also complained of the limited choice of goods, their poor quality, inflated prices and irregularities in deliveries.[2]

Some statistical evidence reinforces these claims, e.g., a recent study of USSR trade with Egypt showed that the USSR received much better terms of trade with Egypt, than in its trade with Western Europe.[3] On the other hand, Ceylon generally has received more than World market prices for its rubber exports to China, and Yemen is reported to have received many machines from the Bloc at especially low prices.[4]

Such isolated incidents do not, however, prove the case one way or the other. For the Soviet Union, enough average unit price data are available to compute some terms of trade comparisons. In the table below any result over 100 per cent indicates that it was more profitable for the USSR to trade with the underdeveloped nations than with other trade partners (as a group).

TABLE 6–8

TERMS OF TRADE OF THE USSR WITH THE WESTERN UNDERDEVELOPED NATIONS COMPARED TO TERMS OF TRADE WITH ALL OTHER TRADE PARTNERS[5]

('Combined Import and Export Relations')

1955	*1956*	*1957*	*1958*
%	%	%	%
118	100	119	116

[1] Quoted by Mikesell and Behrman, *op. cit.*, p. 88.

[2] *Ibid.*, p. 92.

[3] Horst Mendershausen, *The Terms of Soviet-Satellite Trade: A Broadened Analysis*, *op. cit.* In regard to Egypt, Berliner (*op. cit.*, p. 146) reported that on several contracts the Soviets underbid Western offers and then, after the preliminary contracts and technical plans had been drawn up, raised their prices by 40 per cent.

[4] Mikesell & Behrman, *op. cit.*, p. 91 and Berliner, *op. cit.*, Chapter VIII.

[5] Prices were computed at border of exporting country. Even if import data were converted to c.i.f. data by adding a 10 per cent transportation charge, Russia would still have received more favourable terms of trade with the underdeveloped nations than with all other trade partners, except in 1956. (The nature of transportation costs between the underdeveloped nations and Russia is unknown. Many of the Russian imports from underdeveloped countries came from middlemen in Europe, although the imports were classified according to country of origin.) The sample used is almost the same as that of Olivér von Gajzágó,

These data show that the USSR, except in 1956, had a considerable price advantage in trading with the underdeveloped countries in relation to all other trade partners, and I suspect that the other CMEA nations had a similar advantage.[1]

CMEA Bloc nations had other economic advantages in trading with the Western underdeveloped nations. Since the East Central European nations had relatively neglected agriculture and the extractive industries, and relied quite heavily on the USSR for these products, they could reduce their dependency on Russia by obtaining these products from the underdeveloped nations. Moreover, there is some evidence that the production costs of manufactured good in the CMEA Bloc has declined relative to the production cost of agriculture and raw materials. Since this shift in opportunity costs has not been offset by a shift in the terms of trade, the Bloc nations have additional incentives to obtain minerals from the nations outside the Bloc.[2]

The Western underdeveloped nations have several incentives for trading with the Bloc. First of all, the Bloc has been willing to buy up many agricultural surpluses, e.g., coffee from Colombia, cotton from Egypt, tobacco from Greece, fish from Iceland, cocoa from Ghana, cashew nuts and mica from India, hides from Argentina, rice from Burma, jute from Pakistan, and so forth. Indeed about 90 per cent to 95 per cent of Soviet imports from the underdeveloped nations have fallen into three categories: textile raw materials and half finished materials; leather and rubber; and foodstuffs.[3] Over 90 per cent of the DDR imports from Egypt have consisted of cotton. Since the underdeveloped nations have been so dependent on a few such exports, Bloc imports of these goods have been very welcome. Moreover, trading with the Bloc puts the Western underdeveloped countries in a stronger bargaining position with other Western

---

'Der sowjetische Aussenhandel mit den Entwicklungsländern,' *Vierteljahrshefte zur Wirtschaftsforschung*, 4/1959, pp. 435–50, and I must thank Herr v. Gajzágó for the use of his work sheets which permitted these indices to be calculated. For further statistical details, see Statistical Appendix A.

[1] At a conference 'Criteres economiques de la division internationale du travail' in Brussels (October 17–21, 1960). Professor Minc from Poland said in a speech that the CMEA nations sometimes deal with the underdeveloped nations as a homogeneous Bloc without inner competition, which 'guarantees' that the underdeveloped nation will always buy from the best producer at the lowest price. This 'guarantee' seems somewhat dubious. It must be noted that the Western underdeveloped nations may not necessarily lose in trading with the Bloc since their bargaining position *vis-a-vis* the Bloc may be stronger than *vis-a-vis* the Western international market.

[2] Robert Loring Allen, 'Economic Motives in Soviet Foreign Trade Policy,' *Southern Economic Journal* XXV, October/1958.

[3] Gajzágó, *op. cit.*

nations since they have alternative trade partners. Finally, because the underdeveloped nations have a great shortage of capital, it makes good economic sense to import machines which are less 'capital intensive' and not up to world standards (but which cost less) than the highly automatic machines which are offered by the USA, England or West Germany.[1] The CMEA Bloc nations, having gone through the industrialization process much later than the Western nations, have a greater sensitivity concerning the machinery wants of the labour intensive, economically underdeveloped countries.

Several economic factors discouraged trade between the Bloc and the underdeveloped nations. First, the USSR and the Bloc nations have had a limited capacity to absorb some of the primary products which the underdeveloped nations have had to offer. Once the saturation point is reached, Bloc policy-makers face the dilemma of cutting off such imports or else re-exporting. Disregarding some possible adverse political consequences, the latter alternative has often been chosen. In Indonesia, Minister Harshap complained: 'It is an open secret that parallel transactions with the East European countries have brought about a reduction in the overall sale of our foreign exchange. Raw materials we have sold these countries are usually re-traded in other markets . . . with the result that in our World markets we have had to compete with goods originating in our own country. In other cases, parallel transactions have resulted in surplus credit in the form of money which does not serve our purposes well, because imports of goods from the countries concerned do not meet the need of the producing sector of our country. . . .'[2] Evidence is available that the USSR and other Bloc countries have re-exported Egyptian cotton, Ghanese cocoa, and some Greek products, the latter below the normal selling price.[3] In the cases where the imports from the Western underdeveloped nations have been absorbed by the Bloc nations, difficult problems have arisen, e.g., imports of Burmese rice by the USSR, where this food is eaten by only a very small segment of the population.[4]

Second, the lack of hard Western currencies by both Bloc nations and the underdeveloped nations has had an adverse effect on the trade between the two areas. Bloc currencies have been transferrable only with great difficulties: for instance, in 1957 Argentina accumul-

[1] Some Bloc exports are cheap because their quality is very poor. See examples cited by Pisar, *op. cit.*, p. 40.

[2] Quoted by Mikesell and Behrman, *op. cit.*, p. 88.

[3] Pisar, *op. cit.*, p. 39; and *New York Times*, Nov. 18/1962, p. 24.

[4] For some goods from underdeveloped nations, the Bloc countries do not want to increase their imports. In 1962 a US delegate to the United Nations noted that for tea, domestic prices were thirty times higher than import costs in the USSR and sixty-two times higher in Poland. Similarly for coffee, domestic prices were thirteen times higher than import costs in the USSR and ninety-seven times higher in Poland. (*New York Times*, Oct. 21, 1962.)

ated $50,000,000 of Bloc currencies which it had to peddle at a 40 per cent discount.[1] For this reason many underdeveloped nations have wanted to be paid in Western European currencies or dollars which have been very scarce in the Bloc. Similarly, if a CMEA Bloc nation exported more than it imported to an underdeveloped country, it has had either to finance this balance by a loan or demand payment in hard currencies which have been quite scarce in the underdeveloped nations.[2]

For trade to increase between the CMEA Bloc and the underdeveloped nations, both imports and exports have had to increase together, or else complicated triangular deals have had to be arranged. Although such agreements were often made, they were very difficult to conclude.

Finally, scattered evidence suggests that the USSR has not been willing to scale down investment in certain sectors to allow the underdeveloped countries to increase their exports to the USSR, especially in wool and cotton. Information for other Bloc nations is completely lacking.[3]

Notwithstanding the above mentioned factors which acted to discourage trade, I believe that it has made excellent economic sense for the Bloc to redirect more of its trade with the 'Capitalist world market' to the underdeveloped nations. The political advantages are only frosting on the cake. In view of these factors, the goal of the Bloc[4] to double trade with the Western underdeveloped countries from 1959 to 1965 seems somewhat low since Bloc trade with the Western developed nations is planned to increase by about two thirds. That is to say, Bloc trade with the Western underdeveloped nations as a proportion of total Bloc trade with the West is foreseen to rise only from 24 per cent to 33 per cent in this period. Although there has been talk in the Bloc about an all-Bloc bank to finance trade with the underdeveloped nations no action was taken on these proposals through 1960.

[1] Berliner, *op. cit.*, p. 82. More recently Uruguay faced the same problem.

[2] According to a Hungarian source: 'It is the payment situation of the underdeveloped countries, their need for credit, the long transportation routes, the relative shortcomings . . . which hinder the extension of our trade (with them).' (Cited by *East Europe* XI, 12/1962, p. 8.)

[3] For deeper analyses of Bloc motives for trade with the underdeveloped nations, see: Aubrey and Darmstadter, *op. cit.*; *Communist Economic Policies in the Less Developed Areas* (Washington: GPO, Dept. of State, 7020, 1960); *The Sino-Soviet Economic Offensive in the Less Developed Countries*, *op. cit.* and for discussions about trade and aid, Berliner, *op. cit.* and H. J. P. Arnold, *Aid for Developing Countries* (London: The Bodley Press, 1962).

[4] *Economic Survey of Europe* for 1960, pp. V-14.

3. THE PATTERN OF TRADE WITHIN THE CMEA BLOC

It is difficult to analyse the motives behind the geographical pattern of trade within the Bloc, since unknown political factors may be important. Rather than speculating on intra-Bloc politics, I concentrate exclusively in this section on several economic factors.

Some idea of the actual trade distribution of the various CMEA nations with each other may be gained from the following Tables.[1]

TABLE 6–9

PROPORTION OF THE TRADE TURNOVER OF CMEA NATIONS WITH EAST CENTRAL EUROPEAN NATIONS

Year	*Bulgaria* %	*CSSR* %	*DDR* %	*Hungary* %	*Poland* %	*Rumania* %	*Average* %	*Russia* %
1938	30	17	3(11)	23	12	25	7(15)	7
1948	23	16	37(—)	19	19	41	20	—
1950	31	25	33(39)	35	32	32	31	50
1951	33	27	28(30)	32	30	28	29	—
1952	30	31	28(30)	37	31	31	31	—
1953	33	36	26(28)	35	33	37	32	—
1954	39	30	25(27)	34	29	26	29	—
1955	38	29	26(29)	32	27	27	28	53
1956	31	27	25(28)	30	26	25	27	50
1957	28	26	22(24)	33	25	22	25	54
1958	29	28	22(25)	33	25	20	26	52
1959	27	28	23(26)	32	26	25	27	47
1960	27	29	25(28)	32	26	27	27	44

TABLE 6–10

PROPORTION OF THE TRADE TURNOVER OF CMEA NATIONS WITH THE USSR

Year	*Bulgaria* %	*CSSR* %	*DDR* %	*Hungary* %	*Poland* %	*Rumania* %	*Average* %
1938	0	3	1(2)	0	1	0	1(2)
1948	55	16	38(—)	16	22	31	23
1950	54	27	40(47)	27	27	52	33
1951	58	30	46(49)	29	25	50	35
1952	57	35	42(45)	30	32	54	38
1953	50	36	46(49)	34	34	46	39
1954	45	37	44(48)	31	38	54	39
1955	46	34	38(43)	22	32	47	35
1956	47	32	41(46)	24	31	48	36
1957	54	34	45(51)	29	31	48	38
1958	54	33	43(49)	27	26	51	37
1959	52	36	45(51)	29	30	47	39
1960	—	34	43(48)	30	30	40	36
1965 (Plan)	—	42	40(—)	—	—	—	—

[1] For statistical details see footnote 2, p. 164, and Statistical Appendix B. Percentage of DDR trade with USSR in 1965 estimated from Heiduschat, 'Zwei neue Handelsabkommen mit der Sowjetunion,' *Der Aussenhandel* IX, 23/1959, pp. 4–5.

Several conclusions may be drawn from these data. First, the most important redirection of trade has been the increase of trade between Russia and the East Central European nations. Except for the DDR, the percentage redistribution of trade of the East Central European nations with each other has been small. Second, changes in the trade pattern hit a peak in 1953, the first year of the New Course.

A more detailed analysis of the trade patterns of the individual countries shows that the predicted 'little trading circle' of Rumania, Hungary and Bulgaria, and the 'larger trading circle' of the CSSR, DDR and Poland, failed to materialize.[1]

Economic influences entering in the decision of the Bloc nations to trade with certain other Bloc nations have been of two types: the traditional economic forces, such as production patterns, prices, etc., and the factors due to the peculiar intra-Bloc institutions for conducting trade.

Obviously, the structure of production and the raw material conditions within each nation have been extremely important factors in the choice of trade partners. Raw materials and fuels have been the most important Soviet exports to the relatively mineral-poor East Central European nations. However, Poland and the CSSR are relatively more self-sufficient in basic minerals than the DDR, Hungary or Rumania. Similarly, the DDR has been in a better position to supply the USSR and Bulgaria with machinery imports than Poland. The situation facing the foreign trade planners in the various East Central European nations has not been the textbook problem of an importer-exporter confronting a perfectly competitive market with only demand and supply elasticities to worry about. In many cases one country is the only Bloc exporter of a particular good. For instance, in 1958, 50 per cent of Soviet exports to Poland were articles which Poland received from no other CMEA nation.[2] Similarly, the USSR has been absolutely dependent on the other CMEA nations for a few traded goods.

These qualitative considerations of production structure seem in some cases to be more important than the political importance of directing trade toward certain special East Bloc partners. For instance, trade with China was a stated political goal of the DDR and the directives for the Second Five-Year Plan specified that the trade with China, as a percentage of trade with all Communist nations, should rise from 10 per cent in 1955 to 17 per cent in 1960.[3] In 1958,

[1] Nicolas Spulber, *The Economics of Communist East Europe*, *op. cit.*, has been the main advocate of this 'trading circle' view.

[2] See Statistical Appendix B for details of this estimate.

[3] 'Die Aufgaben des Aussenhandels im zweiten Funfjahrplan,' *Der Aussenhandel* VI, 12/1956, p. 403–5.

however, the actual percentage had fallen to 9 per cent because, I believe, Chinese exports were of little use to the DDR.[1]

From such considerations of production structure, it seems that price considerations were important only in a relatively small area of economic decision-making in the choice of Bloc trading partners. If prices did play any role, it is reasonable to expect that the countries which were most discriminated against by the USSR would also import proportionately less goods where Russia is not the sole Bloc supplier. Unfortunately, such an hypothesis cannot be tested with existing data. From conversations in East Berlin, I was able to obtain few additional facts except for such vague statements as: 'The prices which the various CMEA nations offered us played a role in the choice of trade partners in a few cases.'

The specific institutions of intra-Bloc trade also influenced the choice of trade partners.

As I discussed in Chapter III, although trade negotiations were decentralized after 1955, the 'wants lists' and final top-level negotiations for the global trade contract have continued to play an important role. Since a very chronic sellers' market existed in the Bloc, a very obvious development took place.

Each country has tried to negotiate with its largest (or potentially largest) trade partners first, in order to be able to strike off the most items on its 'want lists'. For instance, the DDR signed the long-term contracts for both the first and second Five-Year Plan periods in almost the exact order of the rank of importance of that country in trade with them.[2] Although the final date of signing the yearly contracts has been of less importance, since price rather than quantity bargaining may have taken up most of the time, a similar phenomenon may be seen.[3] This institutional factor has had several results: First, the special type of price leadership, which I discussed in Chapter V, has been encouraged. Second, one might suspect that

[1] According to *Statystyka Handlu Zagranicznego, 1959*, Poland imported some 216,000 tons of iron ore from China in 1959, paying half the price that it paid per ton for iron ore from Finland. This could mean that China found it difficult to export any very useful commodities to the CMEA Bloc nations, except at very low prices.

[2] The relative order of importance of various trade partners for the DDR was somewhat different in these two plan periods. The order of long-range contract signing paralleled these changes, however.

[3] I constructed a matrix with the rank order of the signing of the yearly trade contract on one axis and the rank order of the value of trade turnover of the corresponding countries on the other axis for all CMEA trade partners (except Albania) of the DDR for each year from 1950 to 1958. Applying a normal chi-square test, it was found that the independence assumption had to be rejected (·95 confidence limit), i.e. that there was a significant correlation between the two variables. Less thorough investigations of the signing dates of trade contracts between the other countries showed similar results.

the countries with the smaller total trade potentials would realize a lower percentage of their trade potential since they begin their trade negotiations relatively late. Positive evidence of this hypothesis is available but is not conclusive.[1]

Many Western economists have laid great importance on the bilateral trade pattern as an influential factor in intra-Bloc trade.[2] This bilateralism is inferred by them from the system of bilateral trade negotiations and is supported by several well-known examples of Russian re-exports of raw materials.[3] I believe, on the contrary, that this whole issue has been grossly over-emphasized in the West.

Inferring that bilateral trade will come from a system of bilateral negotiations is a confusion of form and content. It is an empirical question whether the bilateral trade negotiations of the Bloc led to bilateral trade, and it can only be answered by means of empirical investigation. One method of measuring the degree of multilateral-bilateral trade is with the following simple definitions and formula:

a. 1 . . . . . n=trading partners; e=exports; i=imports

b. Degree of multilaterality in trade=

$$\frac{\sum_{1}^{n} e_j - i_j}{\sum_{1}^{n} e_j + i_j} = \frac{\text{sum of absolute value of trade balances with each country}}{\text{trade turnover}}$$

This definition of the degree of multilateral trade differs from other definitions in two respects. First, all types of multilateral trade (triangular, quadralateral, etc.), are subsumed under the classification of multilateral. Second the formula measures the degree of

[1] The total potential trade turnover as well as the percentage realization of potential trade may be calculated from Table 1–2. Calculating Kendall rank order correlation coefficients for these two variables, I obtained results of +·05 from Chenery's estimates and +·60 from my estimates. The latter correlation coefficient is statistically significant, the former is not.

[2] See especially the discussion of Erich Klinkmüller, 'Das Prinzip der Bilateralität,' Chapter IX, *Die gegenwärtige Aussenhandelsverflechtung der sowjetischen Besetzungszone Deutschland, op. cit.*

[3] According to the ECE ('Developments in the Foreign Trade of Eastern Europe and the Soviet Union,' *op. cit.*, p. VI–10, footnote 13) one-fourth of Soviet oil exports to the other CMEA members are re-exports; and two-thirds of Soviet coal exports to these nations are similarly re-exports. However, some of the coal which Russia exported to Poland was a special quality of coking coal which Russia lacked. Some parts of the USSR are closer to the Polish coal mines than the Soviet coal areas. Therefore, the Soviet imports and exports of coal to Poland were not completely irrational. Nevertheless, since the USSR exported so much hard coal across Poland to the DDR, I suspect that great transportation savings could have been achieved here through a more multilateral trading arrangement.

multilateral trade only from the end results. For instance, French traders may deal with German and English traders without restriction; if, however, the final French trade is balanced with each country, then according to the formula, trade is bilateral.

The characteristics of the formula may be illustrated with two extreme cases:

Case 1:
Complete multilateral trade

Country A

Partners	*Exports*	*Imports*
Country B	—	100
Country C	100	—
	100	100

Degree of multilaterality=1·00

Case 2:
Complete bilateral trade

Country X

Partners	*Exports*	*Imports*
Country Y	50	50
Country Z	50	50
	100	100

Degree of multilaterality=0·00

Applying this formula to trade between the East Central European countries and to trade between the Common Market nations yields surprising results:

TABLE 6–11

DEGREE OF MULTILATERAL TRADE IN TWO TRADING AREAS[1]

Year	*East Central European Nations*	*Common Market Nations*
1948	·09	·13
1950	·11	·20
1951	·08	·15
1952	·08	·11
1953	·08	·15
1954	·08	·16
1955	·10	·14
1956	·09	·15
1957	·12	·15
1958	·10	·11
1959	·09	·09
1960	·08	·10
Average 1950–55	·09	·15
Average 1955–60	·10	·12

[1] Trade for calculation of both indices was valued f.o.b. border exporting country (or closest approximation thereto). USSR trade was omitted in calculation of index for Bloc because of importance of invisibles (services, troop costs, etc.) which were not included in the trade statistics. (However, inclusion of USSR in the index did not change the degree of multilaterality very appreciably). Albanian trade was also omitted from index for East Central Europe because Albania had a constantly passive trade balance (due to the large amounts of development loans from other CMEA nations) and no Common Market country was in an analogous position. For further statistical details, see Statistical Appendix B.

Although the Common Market nations have had a higher degree of multilateral trade than the East Central European nations, the differences have been, in some years, quite small. Even though multilateralism was often damned by East Bloc theoreticians, the trade between the East Central European nations has been a good deal more multilateral than commonly believed.[1] An important question, of course, is how this multilateral trade occurred.

First, it is important to realize that the signing of a global trade contract was no guarantee that trade would be carried out in this fashion by the FTEs (who made the operational contracts bringing the global agreements to their most specific form). The only long series I could find to show the differences between trade contracted in the global agreements and actual trade conducted was for trade between Albania and the DDR.

TABLE 6–12

CONTRACTED AND ACTUAL TRADE BETWEEN THE DDR AND ALBANIA

(data in 1,000 roubles)[2]

	DDR Exports			DDR Imports		
Year	*Contracted*	*Actual*	*Actual/Contracted* %	*Contracted*	*Actual*	*Actual/Contracted* %
1952	9,315	9,530	102	1,160	1,890	163
1953	12,008	11,615	97	3,291	2,489	76
1954	14,179	8,622	61	3,941	2,314	59
1955	22,880	24,232	106	9,400	5,070	54
1956	15,914	16,696	105	8,074	6,612	82
1957	24,027	17,068	71	11,195	9,113	81
1958	24,668	21,969	89	18,710	10,150	54
1959	27,307	27,700	101	23,883	19,172	80

Second, multilateral trade may come about through grants of credits and the shifting of trade balances. Some credits have been

[1] Some may argue that although the trade between the East Central European nations was multilateral to some degree in each year, trade was essentially bilateral over a series of years. However, the degree of multilateral trade calculated from the total trade balances of each nation with the other nations over a five-year period was not much lower than the degree of multilateral trade in each single year.

[2] Source: Hildegard Jerke, *Zur Analyse der Aussenhandelsbeziehungen der Volksrepublik Albanien von* 1950–59 (Diplomarbeit, Hochschule für Ökonomie, 1960), Statistical Appendix. Fräulein Jerke's data on actual trade between the DDR and Albania were slightly different from the figures in the DDR *Statistisches Jahrbuch.* The existence of an extensive system of fines for various contract violations is another indication that gaps have existed between trade policy making and trade policy execution.

given between the East Bloc nations;[1] for instance, from 1951 to 1957, the DDR received from other CMEA Bloc members loans of at least 1,605,000,000 Roubles and, in turn, granted credits of at least 1,008,000,000 Roubles to Bloc members;[2] together these amounted to about 4 per cent of total DDR trade turnover. Intra-Bloc loans may rise in the near future.[3]

The CMEA nations also made many intra-Bloc arrangements for the shifting of trade balances, e.g., such agreements were made between the DDR, Bulgaria and the USSR; between the DDR, Bulgaria and

[1] For data on credits made by one CMEA nation to another, see ECE *Economic Survey of Europe in 1957*, pp. VI-56 ff; UNESCO *World Economic Survey for 1960*, p. 120; *World Economic Survey for 1961*, pp. 114ff; I. Schevel, 'Credit and Aid between Socialist Countries', *Dengi i Kredit* 9/1961. It often appears as though the USSR only gives credits to other Bloc nations and never receives any. This is not true, however. The CSSR has delivered certain machinery on credit to the USSR and will receive payments in the form of minerals delivered in future years (O. Bogomolov, *Voprosi ekonomiki* 11/1961 and S. Plaksen, *Sozialistische Planwirtschaft* 8 & 9/1962, pp. 13–15) and a consortium of Bloc nations lent the USSR capital for the building of a phosphate plant in Estonia (*New York Times*, Nov. 11/1962, p. 21). Moreover, some Western underdeveloped nations have made deliveries of raw materials for Soviet capital equipment which had not yet been sent out and thus served as a source of 'development loans' to the USSR.

Marxist theory distinguishes between two types of international loans. 'Capitalist loans' are exploitative and merely enable the creditor nations to drain off surplus value. On the other hand 'Communist loans' are always very helpful to debtor countries and a source of satisfaction to both sides. With such altruism it is difficult to understand why the USSR cancelled its credit agreements with Yugoslavia in 1947 or suddenly 'postponed' new credits to the same country in 1958; or why the promised credits of the USSR and CSSR to Albania were so suddenly withdrawn in 1961.

One could write long analyses of the metaphysical difference between 'Capitalist' and 'Communist' loans. However, the main differences seem to be that loans granted by Communist countries are usually earmarked for special projects, often have to be paid back in specific amounts of certain goods, and usually carry fairly low interest charges (although rates as high as 6 per cent have been recorded; see H. J. P. Arnold, *op. cit.*, Chapter VI, on this point). Such arrangements have acted to minimize currency problems and to eliminate uncertainty about future terms of trade and new difficulties in repayment.

[2] Siegfried Gollus, 'Kreditierung nach sozialistischen Prinzipien,' *Der Aussenhandel* VII, 20/1957, p. 718.

[3] Soviet economists have spoken for a long time about the necessity for greater intra-Bloc flows of capital to investment projects with high capital/output ratios, and long maturation periods, and which have special importance to the whole Bloc, e.g. mineral extraction projects. In 1962 Khrushchev ('Vital Questions of the Development of the World Socialist System,' *Current Digest of the Soviet Press*, XIV, 35 & 36/1962) spoke of the need of an all-Bloc investment bank to facilitate such flows of capital. Moreover, officials and economists from other Bloc nations have made similar suggestions. The mechanics of such an arrangement have not yet been very carefully spelled out, however.

Rumania; and between the DDR, CSSR and Hungary.[1] One DDR economist wrote, 'The three-sided balancing of accounts which equalizes the balance of payments between the Socialist countries has often been used in the past....'[2]

In addition to these intra-Bloc triangular deals, various trilateral treaties and agreements for the shifting of trade balances have been arranged with non-Communist countries. Since 1949, triangular deals were made between Finland, the USSR and the following countries: China, the CSSR, DDR, Poland and Rumania.[3] Other triangular trade deals have been made between Burma, the CSSR and the USSR; Japan, the CSSR and North Vietnam; Egypt, the CSSR and the USSR; Egypt, Rumania and the USSR.[4] Moreover, various Bloc nations co-operated in delivering some complete factory units to Western underdeveloped nations which also gave rise to intra-Bloc balances.[5]

All of these credit programmes and agreements for the shifting of trade balances have been difficult to arrange for administrative reasons, and after 1954, Bloc economists began to demand a formal multilateral clearing arrangement. Finally, in the Eighth Plenum of the CMEA in 1957, an intra-Bloc clearing bank was created. According to the Director of the Polish Ministry of Foreign Trade, Bidzinski, 'The Settlement Department of the Gosbank in Moscow will act as the clearing bank, setting up the accounts for the individual countries. The clearing operations of the Settlement Department will be carried out monthly. Each country is required to grant a credit of 3 per cent of its foreign trade turnover to all clearing partners and has the right to receive such a credit from all of its clearing partners. The tendency to reduce the debt of a nation is encouraged through a progressive interest charge. At the end of the year a country can carry forward 25 per cent of its balance [up to 0·75 per cent of the trade turnover with its partners]. This amount is to be paid off by a specified date

[1] Erich Klinkmüller, *op. cit.*, p. 134; G. Popissakoff, 'Volksrepublik Bulgarien-DDR eine Untersuchung ihrer wirtschaftlichen Beziehungen,' *Der Aussenhandel* VI, 19/1956, p. 667; Erike Dally, 'Ein Jahr Zahlungsverfahren des RGW,' *Der Aussenhandel* VIII, 8/1958, pp. 14–15.

[2] Burgemeister, *op. cit.;* see also A. Altschaler, 'The Clearing Forms Used between the USSR and the People's Democracies,' *Dengi i Kredit*, 7/1957.

[3] Mikesell and Behrman, *op. cit.*, Appendices and, for a summary of the sad end to the Finnish arrangements, pp. 54–5; see also J. Slobin, 'The Soviet Rouble: The Most Stable Currency in the World,' *Voprosy Ekonomiki*, 5/1951, for a Russian view of these triangular deals.

[4] Mikesell and Behrman, *op. cit.*, Appendices.

[5] Gerd Friedrich and Lothar Roucik, 'Die Spezialisierung und Kooperation der Produktion im sozialistischen Weltwirtschaftssystem,' *Wissenschaftliche Zeitschrift der Hochschule für Ökonomie*, 3/1958, pp. 189–97.

through additional deliveries [of goods]. If this does not happen, the balance must be paid off in an additional period with priority goods (coal, oil, sugar, metals).'[1] The accounts carried over have been charged with a 2 per cent interest and the over-limit balances have had to be paid off in three months. The clearing has not followed automatically, as in the EPU, but has had to have the permission of all parties involved.[2]

According to one DDR economist, 'The primary goal [of the clearing bank] is to encourage the exchange of goods which are not covered in the bilateral global agreements. These include . . . goods from above-plan production, from above-plan inventories of traded goods, . . . from articles [usually] traded with Capitalist nations . . . and from the domestic consumer market. . . . The multilateral clearing agreement between the CMEA nations has not been able to facilitate the multilateral exchange of goods corresponding to the above requirements.'[3] Another DDR economist declared: 'It is important to emphasize that the multilateral exchange of goods and the multilateral clearing resulting from this agreement are only additional elements to the bilateral trade and payment arrangements at the present stage of development. The heavy weight will—at least for the next few years—lie on the bilateral trade.'[4] I believe that both of these authors underestimated the possibilities of this 'additional trade' and how it could add up to impressive sums. As I mentioned in Chapter III, in 1958 in Poland, $50,000,000 of trade was handled in this way.

Since 1959, the multilateral clearing has been implemented by 'trade meetings' of representatives for all Bloc nations, who have come together with lists of desired and surplus commodities and who tried to make multilateral trade deals. The trade volume of goods traded in this multilateral exchange in the first half of 1960 was 450 per cent of the volume of trade concluded in a similar meeting

[1] Quoted by 'Oststaaten im Multilateral Clearing,' *Osthandel* 3/1958, p. 11.

[2] See F. Bystrov, *Voprosi ekonomiki* 2/1960, pp. 112–9, or, for a copy of the original agreement, Zsoldas, *op. cit.* Appendices. In 1962 a great deal attention in the CMEA Bloc press was focused on the need for greater multilateral trade and multilateral balancing of intra-Bloc payments. (See, e.g. 'Principles of the Socialist Division of Labor, *Current Digest of the Soviet Press* XIV, July 11/1962, pp. 3ff, or Oskar Lange, 'New Answers for New Questions,' *Meshdunarodnaya shisn* 5/1962.)

[3] Gertrud Gräbig, *Der Sozialistische Weltmarkt* (East Berlin: Lehrbrief für Fernstudium, Hochschule für Ökonomie, mimeo., 1959).

[4] Rudolf Trebuth, 'Das mehrseitige Clearing zwischen den sozialistischen Staaten,' *Der Aussenhandel* VII, 18/1957, pp. 652–3. O. Bogomolov in *Mirovaia Ekonomika i Mezhdunarodnya Otnoshenia* (cited by Alfred Zauberman, 'Economic Integration: Problems and Prospects,' *Problems of Communism* VIII, 4/1959, pp. 23–9) said that the Clearing Bank was a failure.

in the previous year. Bloc policy-makers became more enthusiastic and decided to hold regularly such meetings at least twice a year in the future.[1] Rules and special procedures for these conferences have been drawn up and the DDR Ministry of Foreign Trade gave instructions to all FTEs to increase the trade handled in this way.

Several major forces have worked against the increase in multilateral trade within the Bloc. The lack of unified prices in foreign trade and the presence of price discrimination has discouraged the transfer of active balances in the currencies of countries with whom it has been possible to obtain particularly favourable terms of trade.[2] Moreover, as some Western economists have noted, the administrative problems involved in increasing the degree of multilateral trade and the uncertainties of the planners concerning how the various active and passive accounts would finally be balanced, has also discouraged multilateral clearing.[3] Finally, several of the smaller Bloc nations have feared that multilateral trade would give rise to chronic debtor and creditor positions in the same way as in Western Europe.[4]

It is difficult to evaluate all these factors and since it is impossible to estimate the 'optimum degree of multilateral trade' I can only make several tentative qualitative conclusions.[5]

First, a certain degree of multilateral trade has existed within the Bloc and has been aided by various institutions (e.g., the 'trade meetings') and by certain arrangements (e.g., triangular trade deals, international clearing bank, etc.) for the shifting of trade balances.

Second, although many proposals for the widening of the powers of the clearing bank have been made in the past few years, the need

[1] E. Burgemeister and F. Pörtner, 'Handelstreffen dienen dem multilateralen Warenaustausch,' *Der Aussenhandel* X, 22/1960, pp. 22–4.

[2] This factor is discussed by Klinkmüller, *op. cit.*, Chapter IX, and was also mentioned to me by an East Berlin Economist.

[3] For a long discussion of these problems, see Klinkmüller, *op. cit.*, pp. 60–5.

[4] 'Der Aussenhandel der DDR,' Informationsbüro West *Tagesbericht*, April 14, 1959, IV/108/1959.

[5] After this analysis of multilateral trade was completed, an empirical study of the whole subject of multilateral-bilateral trade was published. (Michael Michaely, 'Multilateral Balancing in International Trade,' *American Economic Review* LXX, Sept./1962, pp. 685–703). The author concluded that multilateral trade within currency areas is considerably less than multilateral trade between currency areas and that the more underdeveloped a country was, the more it tended toward greater multilateral trade. Bearing this in mind, the similarity of degree of multilateral trade within the CMEA Bloc and within the Common Market does not seem as important as one might conclude from the data alone.

for greater multilateral trade did not impress the Bloc policy-makers enough to make any radical changes.[1]

Undoubtedly, the degree of multilateral trade within the Bloc has not been ideal. Undoubtedly, the overall trade turnover between the various Bloc nations has been adversely affected by the clumsiness of the clearing arrangements. Unquestionably some nations have been forced to lower their overall trade with one country in order to have enough exports to pay for vitally needed imports from another country. Nevertheless, for the reasons presented in the above discussion, I think that these factors may have been overrated by Western economists.

Without any more specific information, it is impossible to tell exactly how the geographical trade pattern has been affected by these factors. For the DDR, I would guess that trade with Rumania, Hungary and Bulgaria has been relatively neglected in favour of trade with the USSR because of the overriding importance of obtaining as many Russian raw materials (especially coal and iron ore) as possible.

4. SUMMARY AND CONCLUSIONS

Although CMEA Bloc leaders have proclaimed the necessity for bringing political considerations into every foreign trade transaction, I have presented evidence in this chapter that a great many features of the geographical pattern of trade can be explained by economic factors.

In the choice of trade partners by the CMEA nations, the trade embargo was probably the most important factor in the decision of the Bloc policy-makers to reorient their trade to the East although, of course, the desire of the Bloc policy-makers for 'economic independence' from the West also contributed. Since 1954, however, the influence of the blockade has waned as the embargo list has been cut. The continuance of the Bloc nations to trade with each other after this action can be attributed to such economic factors as adverse terms of trade with the 'Capitalist world market', opposition in the West, and the factor of risk to the Bloc nations in trading without firm global commitments beforehand.

Within the Western markets, it has been economically rational for the Bloc nations to trade more and more with the Western underdeveloped nations for several reasons. First of all, the Bloc

[1] Criticism of the present operations of the clearing bank is often quite explicit, e.g. J. Slobin, *Voprosi ekonomiki* 2/1962, pp. 68–81; or O. Bogomolow and J. Pekschew, *Sozialistische Planwirtschaft* 8 & 9/1962, pp. 1–6. Nevertheless I have not seen any Bloc discussion of exactly *how* the bilateral trade pattern distorts trade or leads to an inefficient allocation of Bloc resources.

nations have probably obtained quite favourable terms of trade. Moreover, certain scarce agricultural and mining products could be obtained from these countries. Nevertheless, Bloc trade with these nations is planned to rise only from one-fourth to one-third of total Western trade in the period 1958 to 1965.

The choice of trade partners within the Bloc itself is more difficult to analyse. One very important factor has been the structure of resources and production in each country. Price considerations have probably played a minor role. Western commentators have stressed the importance of the system of bilateral trade negotiations although I feel that this factor has been greatly overemphasized.

CHAPTER VII

MECHANISMS IN INTRA-BLOC FOREIGN TRADE

It is an economic truism that one of the functions of a market mechanism is to bring the plans of buyers and sellers into a consistent pattern. Between the Bloc countries, however, there is not a traditional international market, and co-ordinating the separate trade plans and decisions of the various nations presents some special difficulties.

In this chapter I first show why the most important co-ordinating mechanisms in trade between market economies have not functioned in intra-Bloc trade and why the mechanisms which did co-ordinate early intra-Bloc trade had serious deficiencies. The difficulties in achieving a consistent intra-Bloc trade pattern forced attention on the possibilities of a co-ordination of Bloc production; the inadequacies of the intra-Bloc trade pattern focused discussion on the possibilities of a specialization of production. The result has been the increasing scope of activities of the Council of Mutual Economic Assistance.

1. MECHANISMS IN TRADE BETWEEN MARKET ECONOMIES

In trade between market economies, decisions are made primarily on the basis of comparisons of domestic costs, prices, and taxes with costs, prices, and taxes in other countries. If it is possible to make a monetary profit, the trader will usually try to arrange the deal. Notwithstanding this microeconomic platitude, the situation is somewhat different in the Bloc.

In the Bloc nations, domestic prices have not been necessarily related to supply and demand forces; foreign currency exchange rates have been quite arbitrarily fixed; and intra-Bloc foreign trade prices have been primarily based on Western foreign trade prices, rather than intra-Bloc supply and demand forces. An ostensibly high monetary profit (PAG) for the export of a good by one Bloc country to another can be due to either a domestic price in the exporting country which has been set much below actual production costs or a relatively high intra-Bloc price for the good which in no way reflects the relative scarcity of the good in the other Bloc nations. Indeed, comparisons of domestic production and sales costs with either domestic prices of other Bloc nations or intra-Bloc foreign trade prices can lead to very uneconomic trade (from the standpoint of the economy as a whole) in many cases. To be sure, foreign trade prices have played a role in the decisions concerning the structure of domestic production (through the use of foreign trade profitability coefficients for production and investment). As I discussed in Chapters V and VI, prices have played a very secondary role in intra-Bloc trade negotiations and the allocation of Bloc resources. It is not worthwhile, therefore, to focus more attention on the traditional (i.e. 'Capitalist') microeconomic responses in foreign trade.

On the macroeconomic level, Western foreign trade theorists have focused particular attention on the equilibration mechanisms by which exports and imports are brought into equality after certain price or income changes have occurred in the economies of the trading nations. In the CMEA Bloc the presuppositions for these macroeconomic mechanisms have not existed.

First of all, the domestic money supply and the bank accounts of the production and trade enterprises have been carefully controlled, i.e., trade surpluses or deficits have had little direct effect on the money supply or the overall level of prices; and the money supply and the overall level of prices have had little or no effect on trade. Therefore, the macroeconomic equilibrating forces in market economies, which are generated by a change in the terms of trade caused by a trade surplus or deficit, have been missing in the Bloc economies.[1]

Secondly, since the early 1950s no Bloc nation has suffered from any Keynesian-type unemployment. Therefore, the macroeconomic equilibrating forces in market economies, which are generated by a change in national income and employment caused by a trade surplus or deficit, have also been missing in the Bloc.

From these factors it is clear that traditional macroeconomic foreign trade models which have been so useful in analysing trade problems between market economies are of little help in examining intra-Bloc trade.

2. CO-ORDINATION OF PRODUCTION AND TRADE IN THE BLOC

A. The 'Russian Embassy System of Co-ordination'.[2]

Evidence is available that the USSR played an important *direct* role in the economies of the various East Central European nations from the immediate post-war years through 1954. The Soviets made

[1] See Appendix F for a more complete analysis of these factors.

[2] Material in this section comes from Fritz Schenk, *Magie der Planwirtschaft* (Köln: Kiepenheuer & Witsch, 1960), pp. 81–124 and from an interview with

decisions concerning which countries should produce certain articles (this was brought to light by Yugoslavia after the Tito-Stalin break in 1948); assisted in the drawing up of long-range plans in most Bloc nations; and chose important governmental officials in various countries.[1] The USSR also operated certain enterprises in every country (except Poland) and participated in policy-making in other firms in these nations which were producing goods for reparations. In the DDR after 1945, all high economic functionaries had their 'partner' in the Soviet embassy whom they consulted for every important move, e.g., the head of the DDR State Planning Commission, Bruno Leuschner, consulted with the Assistant Soviet Ambassador Miroschnitschenko. In later years, according to one observer: 'Over its economic section in the embassy the Russians exercise immediate influence on the chiefs of the Planning Commission and work out all controversial problems which might give the Russians difficulties in the Plenum meetings of the CMEA. Leuschner knows that he must negotiate with Miroschnitschenko over all points which will come on the agenda of the CMEA beforehand.'[2] After 1956, the direct role of the USSR in the economies of the East Central European nations seems to have decreased although little information is available on this politically sensitive subject.

Through the collection and the central analysis of production and trade information from all Bloc countries, the Soviet Union could have provided the various planners in the East Central European nations with extremely useful information on Bloc supply and demand forces. If it had been well operated, the 'Soviet embassy system of co-ordination' could have helped to prevent the occurrence of parallel investments and all-Bloc deficits of raw materials and could have acted to encourage the growth of trade and an efficient all-Bloc division of labour. However, as I noted in the first chapter, all-Bloc material deficits and parallel investments were common phenomena and the allocation of Bloc productive resources was very inefficient. These deficiencies of the 'Russian embassy system of co-ordination' had, I believe, four main causes:

First of all, many Soviet officials advising the Bloc planners were

---

Schenk on December 4, 1960. Herr Schenk was the personal assistant of the Chairman of the State Planning Commission, Leuschner, from 1953 to 1957 and, in this position, was able to obtain a unique view of the economy. See also Klinkmüller and Ruban, *op. cit.* or Alfred Zauberman, *Economic Imperialism: The Lesson of Eastern Europe*, *op. cit*.

[1] Imre Nagy, *On Communism: In Defense of the New Course* (New York; Frederick Praeger, 1957), pp. 250–1, 280–1, declared that the Russians placed him as Premier in Hungary in 1953.

[2] Schenk, *Die Magie der Planwirtschaft*, *op. cit.*, p. 90.

acting under instructions from different production ministries, within the USSR, which had not always co-ordinated their separate programmes.[1] Moreover, the Russians were often greatly resented; many times the Russian advisory teams were looked upon as spies; and some officials in the East Central European nations attempted to withhold information. Additional hostility was generated because the high salaries of many Soviet advisers were usually paid by the recipient nations. Furthermore, there is evidence to suggest that up to 1954, the Soviet Union did not want the East Central European nations to co-operate with each other and to build up a power base which would rival Russia's. The Soviet policy of encouraging each nation to build giant iron-steel combines, regardless of whether the requisite raw materials such as coal or iron ore were at hand, may have been based on a desire to force these countries into economic dependency on Russia for the needed raw materials. Finally, it is highly doubtful that the USSR collected, analysed and evaluated these Bloc data very systematically. At its best, the 'Russian embassy system' of production co-ordination was ineffectual; at its worst, exploitative.

B. An 'Iteration Mechanism'

It has been noted by John M. Montias that the balancing of the material balance system in the State Planning Commission of a single nation is formally similar to the solving of an input-output matrix via an iteration process.[2] The basic idea of this argument is very simple.

Let us suppose that each worker in the State Planning Commission is in charge of balancing one material balance, and that this worker has a series of input coefficients for the making of this product. If the demand is greater than the supply of this article in the drawing up of the plan, the worker will go to the other workers in the State Planning Commission and try to obtain the requisite inputs. And they, in turn, will go to other workers to obtain the additional inputs for their production. If this process is repeated a sufficient number of times, under certain conditions the matrix (material balance system) will be balanced and the State Planning Commission acts, in effect, as a gigantic iteration machine. That is to say, through a certain type of bureaucratic mechanism, which resembles the solving of an input-output table by an iteration method, the State Planning Commission

[1] The classic case of Soviet economic advisors working against each other was in Germany from 1945 to 1948. See Robert Slusser, ed., *Soviet Economic Policy in Post-war Germany* (New York: Eastern European Fund, Inc., 1953).

[2] John M. Montias, 'Planning with Material Balances in Soviet Type Economies,' *American Economic Review* XLIX, 5/1959, pp. 963–85.

can plan a consistent pattern of production. In this respect it serves the same function as a market mechanism in Capitalist economies although this does not mean that the bureaucratic methods bring about very efficient use of productive resources.

In the negotiations within the State Planning Commission, difficulties are introduced when production of a certain good cannot be increased (i.e., a bottleneck is reached) so that special techniques must be used in order to bring the system into balance. Other problems occur when alternative production functions are substituted into the matrix of material balances,[1] which may increase or decrease the difficulties in balancing the matrix, depending on how and when they are introduced into the planning system.

If a centrally planned economy were facing a foreign trade market with infinite demand and supply elasticities, introducing foreign trade into the system would then ease the problem of capacity constraints and simplify the problem of bringing the whole material balance system to a consistent solution. However, this is not the case, since about 70 per cent of the trade of the CMEA Bloc nations has been within the East Bloc where the demand and supply elasticities have not been infinite.

Nevertheless, the process of balancing the material balances in each Bloc nation by means of exports and imports via the five-step foreign trade contract system is analogous, in many respects, to the balancing of the I–0 matrix in a closed economy by an iteration process, where each step of the contract system represents one 'iteration'. At each step of the contract system each nation moves closer to a completely balanced material balance system which is consistent with the plans of the other Bloc nations. Balancing the system by trade is more complicated than through a closed iteration system because the planners have not only a matrix of domestic technological coefficients to worry about, but also another matrix of tentative price ratios which show how many foreign articles can be obtained from various home-produced goods, and vice versa.

In each of the five steps of the foreign trade contract negotiations, the two trade partners have tried to obtain as much from their 'want lists' as possible and, in turn, dispose of their 'surplus goods'. Since the 'want lists' and lists of disposable goods of the partner nations invariably have not completely coincided, some of the material balances in both nations have not been balanced and the planners have faced the following choices:

[1] This may be the formal substitution of new types of production functions (e.g. making pumps from bronze rather than iron) or the 'squeezing' of the coefficients of the old production function (e.g. demanding more pumps from the same amount of iron) which has been discussed by Herbert S. Levine, 'The Centralized Planning of Supply in Soviet Industry,' *Comparisons of the United States and Soviet Economies*, *op. cit.*, pp. 151–75.

(1) They could try to re-balance their own matrix (material balance system), using as capacity constraints domestic production plus maximum obtainable imports.

(2) They could try to re-balance their own matrix by changing their production goals.

(3) They could put further pressure on their trade partners to increase production of certain goods, so as to be able to obtain the good in the next step of the negotiation process, promising in turn to export more of some good greatly desired by the partner. This would mean that both nations balanced their matrices by means of a co-ordinated change of production goals.

(4) They could try to obtain the needed goods and dispose of their surplus goods on the Western markets.

However, this iteration process has had three important mechanical difficulties. First, four or five iterations have not been sufficient to bring about a consistent production pattern. Second, capacity constraints and supply inelasticities have played an important role and have greatly limited the scope of the intra-Bloc iteration. For instance, many raw materials such as coal and iron have been in chronic deficit. When the supply constraints for these products have been reached in the iteration process (which, because of the importance of these materials has occurred quite early), further iterations have been limited to those goods which were not made from these raw materials or which could be made from substitute materials. Third, uncertainties have been introduced because prices have not been established until quite late in the planning and balancing process.

Two additional difficulties have also occurred. First of all, the existence of independent units in the iteration process with changing policies (and political objectives) have created certain frictions which have not been present when the iteration took place in the State Planning Commission, e.g., decisions and actions could not be forced by higher authorities, bureaucratic procedures have not been as standardized, and so forth. These frictions have not been often discussed in the Bloc economic literature, but probably contributed to encouraging autarkic tendencies. Second, balancing the national material balances by means of an international iteration process does not necessarily lead to the most optimal trade pattern or the most efficient Bloc division of labour, any more than balancing the material balance system in a single nation leads to the most profitable commodity structure of trade or the most efficient allocation of national production resources.

In the intra-Bloc iteration process leading to the balancing of the material balances in each Bloc nation, communication between nations has been quite incomplete and limited primarily to the most basic information; response to communications has often been uncertain; and profitability considerations have been neglected. The system has 'worked' in the same way that any system 'works' when all participants obtain some advantages in maintaining the system. Nevertheless, the disadvantages of this system have been long apparent to East Bloc economists.

C. Problems of Trade Co-ordination Re-defined

In addition to the problems of co-ordinating the trade plans of the different Bloc nations into a consistent whole, certain economic forces have disrupted the carrying out of trade agreements. Perhaps the greatest difficulties have been caused by the inflexibilities of the domestic economies of the Bloc nations, so that plan failures in one country would set off a chain reaction of plan failures in other nations.[1] One well-known case of such a chain reaction occurred in late 1956 and early 1957 when Poland reduced coal exports to the Bloc and caused serious tremours in the economies of the other Bloc nations, especially the DDR, until the USSR was able to produce an additional amount of coal to cover a part of what Poland had failed to deliver. To a lesser degree, such a mechanism has operated quite often in the Bloc.[2] To stop such chain reactions, a nation which did not receive its expected imports would either have to obtain these imports on other markets or else produce a substitute good.

The problems of co-ordinating trade plans into a consistent whole and of fulfilling these plans have focused attention on several main policy issues. The Bloc leaders have wanted to avoid all-Bloc surpluses and deficits without relying on a 'Capitalist-type' market mechanism to regulate trade. They have wanted a more optimal

[1] In a remarkably prescient statement in 1925, Stalin remarked: 'There, in the Capitalist countries . . . the errors of single Capitalists, trust, syndicates, or this or that Capitalist group are corrected through the elementary force of the market . . . No really important error, no considerable overproduction, no appreciable discrepancy between production and . . . demand can occur in the Capitalist countries without the mistakes, errors, and discrepancies being corrected by this or that (partial) crisis . . . With us it is quite different. Every important disturbance in trade or in production, each error in calculation in our economy does not end with just a partial crisis, but effects the whole economy.' (Quoted by 'Soll oder Muss,' *Der Aussenhandel* III, 22/1953, pp. 507–8.)

[2] For instance, the DDR Hauptverwaltung Kraftverkehr was supposed to set into operation 120 cement-mixing train cars which were previously produced in the DDR but which, after 1960, were supposed to be manufactured in the CSSR and exported to other CMEA nations. However, after the DDR had stopped production of these cars, the CSSR declared itself unable to meet its export quota to the DDR. Because of a chronic shortage of hard currencies, the DDR State Planning Commission would not permit the Hauptverwaltung Kraftverkehr to import these cars from West Germany. I suspect that the lack of these cars played an important role in the failure to meet the building and investment plan in 1959–60. (Example from Klinkmüller and Ruban, *op. cit.*, p. 179.)

pattern of allocation of Bloc resources without abandoning the physical type of planning to which they are ideologically committed. They have wanted to keep their centralized decision-making systems while avoiding the dangers of chain reactions of plan failures, which have stemmed from the inflexibilities caused by over-centralization. Finally, they have wanted to co-ordinate trade plans more thoroughly than it was possible in the global trade negotiation discussions while, at the same time, preventing authoritarian decisions by one nation as was the case in the Stalin era.

Several conclusions became apparent to Bloc policy-makers. First of all, it was not enough to concentrate only on the co-ordination of trade; attention had to be paid to the underlying forces of production. Second, new types of international institution had to be created which would attack these problems on a supra-national level. Throughout the post-war years, various experiments in voluntary multi-national planning began to be made and have become quite important in recent years.

3. JOINT PLANNING EFFORTS[1]

The first forms of joint planning were primarily bilateral. During the early post-war years, nations would occasionally meet to discuss possibilities of co-operation in production and investment in specific areas. For instance, in 1947–8 Poland and the CSSR carried on a series of negotiations and issued an interesting communiqué, although other positive results from these discussions were meagre. In 1952, several nations began bilateral discussions for the specialization of production of several large items, primarily in the fabrication of steel beams and forms. 'Industrial Treaties', which specified goods which one country should produce and which another country agreed not to make, appeared in 1953. However, in some cases it appears that these 'Industrial Treaties' were merely a safeguarding of the traditional export industries of one country from over-ambitious planners in another. At any rate, such treaties were not very common before 1956.

Another form of bilateral aid in planning was the exchange of technical documents, blueprints, and description of manufacturing processes which was begun in 1949 and which expanded at a very rapid pace in the next decade. This programme provided a means for the Bloc nations to economize on scarce technical skills and must be

[1] See also Informationsbuero West, '10 Jahre Rat fuer gegenseitige Wirtschaftschilfe,' *IWE Sonderdienst* (West Berlin; 1959); Frederic L. Pryor, 'Forms of Economic Co-operation in the European Communist Bloc: A Survey,' *Soviet Studies* XI, 2/1959, pp. 173–94; or 'Integrating the Satellites—The Role of Comecon,' *East Europe* 11/1959, pp. 3–11.

viewed as highly important. Some idea of the growth of the programme may be gained from the following data:

TABLE 7–1

EXCHANGE OF TECHNICAL DOCUMENTATION BETWEEN THE DDR AND OTHER CMEA NATIONS[1]

Year	*Requests of the DDR filled by other CMEA nations*	*Requests of other CMEA nations filled by DDR*
1949	—	60
1950	40	170
1951	120	150
1952	170	180
1953	340	400
1954	395	470
1955	470	480
1956	600	850
1957	690	890
	2,825	3,650

Another facet of the exchange of technical information was the flood of bilateral and multilateral conferences (outside of the realm of the CMEA) which discussed technical problems, e.g., conferences of central bankers, postmasters, etc. In 1958 at least fifty-nine such special conferences took place.[2]

Nevertheless, these various forms of intra-Bloc co-operation and attempts to co-ordinate production planning in specific areas were quite limited. Clearly, institutions of wider scope and greater permanence were needed.

A. The Council of Mutual Economic Assistance: Chronology and Functions

The Council of Mutual Economic Assistance, the first important innovation for increasing multilateral economic communication between the various Bloc economies, was founded in Moscow on January 21, 1949, by Bulgaria, the CSSR, Hungary, Poland, Rumania and the USSR. The original purposes of the organization, as expressed in the various vague articles and communiqués later in the year, were to organize foreign trade in raw materials, foods, and industrial equipment; to further the exchange of technical and economic experiences; and to act as a counter-force to the Marshall

[1] Kurt Opitz, 'Die ökonomische Zusammenarbeit der Länder des sozialistischen Lagers,' *Die Arbeit*, 3/1959, pp. 38–40. Data for selected years for the USSR may be found in Pryor, *op. cit.*

[2] Fifty-nine conferences are listed by Klinkmüller and Ruban, *op. cit.*, pp. 156–8.

Plan.[1] Other friendly nations were invited to join and the Council subsequently accepted Albania (February, 1949) and the DDR (September, 1950).[2] The Asian Communist nations have not yet joined but have sent delegates to the Plena and 'the most important committee meetings' since 1955.[3]

Up to 1954, the CMEA was quite inactive and made few direct suggestions for changing the Bloc trade or production pattern. Aside from small service tasks, such as the 1951 recommendations for a unified foreign trade contract,[4] the CMEA did very little.

In late 1953, after the 'New Course' had begun, criticism of the autarkic planning systems started, and demands for a wider Bloc specialization of production increased. In the fourth and fifth Plena of the CMEA (March 26–7, 1954, and May 26, 1954) discussion ranged over possibilities of increased co-operation and specialization in production goods, consumer goods, and agricultural items. Several recommendations to 'eliminate parallel investments' in some industrial sectors were made, the first important CMEA decisions. In 1955 the CMEA nations signed a few 'Contracts for Mutual Co-ordination of Investment and Production Plans for 1956–60' which have never been mentioned since and which were probably a transitional step to further intra-Bloc co-operation.[5] 1954 and 1955 were prim-

[1] A great deal of effort has been dedicated by Western commentators to guess the 'real reasons' for the founding of the CMEA. A more interesting question is why had not an intra-Bloc economic organ been founded before. Tito and Dimitrov (Bulgaria) had great plans for a Balkan Union in 1946–7 and the Poles and the Czechs had high hopes for a close economic union in 1947–8. It was the policy of atomization of the East Central European nations set by Stalin which effectively stalled these movements (Brzezinski, *op. cit.*, pp. 123ff.) In 1949, a clear need for an international economic organ was obvious to all.

[2] Yugoslavia's first attempt to join the CMEA in 1949 was bruskly turned down by the USSR. According to a speech by Tito in December, 1960, Yugoslavia's attempt to regain its previous observer status in the CMEA was rebuffed twice in 1959 (although the nature of the request is not known). In 1960 a Yugoslav request for observer or full member status in CMEAS Transportation Commission was not answered. (My thanks to William D. Broderick for this citation.)

Albanian representatives have not attended the 15th, 16th or 17th Plena of the CMEA. It is not known whether they were kicked out of the CMEA or chose not to attend because of their tensions with the Soviet Union.

[3] Starting in May, 1956, China and (later) other Asian Communist nations have sent observers to CMEA Plena. In June, 1962, Outer Mongolia was accepted as the first full Asian member of the Council. This seems to me to have more political than economic significance.

[4] The form of the 'General Conditions of Trade' contracts were finally completely unified in 1958 when a CMEA-recommended statute was made into part of the civil law in each Bloc nation.

[5] See Pfuhl, *Das Recht der allgemeinen Lieferbedingungen im zwischenstaatlichen Aussenhandel des Ostblocks*, *op. cit.*

arily years of discussion, and very little concrete action was taken. Nevertheless, the way was being prepared for some important organizational changes which would, in turn, greatly increase the sphere of the activities of the CMEA.

In 1954 and 1955, several *ad hoc* committees were set up to work on special problems of the Bloc industrial production. In the seventh Plenum (May 18-25, 1956, in Berlin) the Council created twelve Standing Commissions in the various industrial areas to bring together for the first time on a permanent basis representatives from the various Ministries of the CMEA nations.[1] In the next years more Commissions as well as special work groups and committees were also added. The Standing Commissions have had three functions: making recommendations on specialization and standardization of production; suggesting various measures for the co-ordination of the national production plans; and acting as centres for the multilateral exchange of technological and scientific information.[2] With these specialized committees, the scope of CMEA decisions greatly increased after 1955.

The first function of the Commissions, the making of standardization and production specialization agreements, gained momentum quickly. The multilateral specialization recommendations which started with several products (rolled steel goods, tractors, and other types of agricultural machinery; sixth Plenum, Budapest, December, 1955), progressed to large industrial segments (machine goods; seventh Plenum, Berlin, May, 1956), to entire industries (chemical industry; tenth Plenum, Prague, December, 1958).[3] The standardization work of the Standing Commissions began immediately after their formation and has been carried on not only in conjunction with the specialization discussions but also in other industrial areas. (Scattered data of this specialization and standardization work are presented in Table 1–4). In addition to these standardization measures

[1] According to Manfred Haseneyer (*Die Möglichkeiten für die Erweiterung des Anlagenexports der DDR durch Kooperation mit sozialistischen Ländern und die Gestaltung der organisatorischen Zusammenarbeit;* Diplomarbeit, Hochschule für Ökonomie, 1960) various countries also set up special work groups in 1956 to make recommendations for co-operation between enterprises and for specialization of production (e.g., for the sugar refining industry, the CSSR, DDR, Hungary and Poland formed such a committee). These work groups proved ineffectual for several reasons: first, they had no power or sanctions to enforce their decisions: second, their work overlapped and conflicted with the work of the various CMEA Commissions.

[2] For a description of these Commissions and the general organizational structure of the CMEA, see Appendix D.

[3] For an interesting study of specialization in the chemical industry, see Ernst Liening, 'Die Zusammenarbeit der Ostblockländer auf dem Chemiesektor,' *Ost-Europa Wirtschaft* V, 1/1960, pp. 112–120.

O

the Bloc nations have started to build up a common set of production norms, technical standards, and measurements.[1]

It must be noted, however, that the making of specialization and standardization recommendations does not mean that these recommendations were intelligent, workable, or actually carried out. And, as I discussed in Chapter I, the results of the new production specialization have left much to be desired.

The second function of the Commissions, the co-ordination of the production plans of the Bloc nations, was relatively neglected until the late 1950s since in the beginning the Council operated more on a project than plan orientation. Methods and problems of all-Bloc planning are discussed in detail in a later section of this chapter.

The third function of the Commissions was the exchange of technical information, and was, according to several DDR economists with whom I spoke, the most important activity of the Council up to 1960. Moreover, the Soviet Union participated much more actively in this phase of the CMEA activity than in the standardization or specialization work.

Unfortunately, information concerning the many aspects of this information exchange is fragmentary. Within the Commissions the members have compared data on various production coefficients, e.g., the Ferrous Metals Commission analysed the blast furnace performance information from each country and worked out recommendations for improving blast furnace efficiency. Exchange of technical and scientific information has also been facilitated through special all-Bloc conferences sponsored by the CMEA Commissions on special production problems, e.g., the series of conferences on cement production technology which were held by the Building Industry Commission. A true picture of the extent of such activities can only be gained through case studies of each Commission.[2] A third facet of this mutual technical aid programme has been the assigning of special research and development tasks to the various Bloc nations. For instance, Rumania was supposed to conduct research on oil refining machinery and the DDR was supposed to test

[1] For details on some of the technical standards which have been agreed upon, see Karl Krüger, 'Die Integration,' Chapter V, *Der Ostblock: Die Produktion* (West Berlin: Safari Verlag, 1960). One difficulty concerning norms was that the GOST norms of Russia were not as good as the DIN norms of the DDR, and, according to one East German economist with whom I spoke, neither nation wanted to adopt the norms of the other. I do not have space to discuss the Bloc standardization in fields such as patent law or law for co-operatives (see Klinkmüller and Ruban, *op. cit.*, pp. 203–5).

[2] For a case study of the Building Industry Commission, see Appendix D; for the Chemical Industry Commission, Liening, *op. cit.;* for the Agriculture Standing Commission, see the magazine *Internationale Zeitschrift der Landwirtschaft.*

certain types of chemical production equipment. A final aspect of this work has been the co-ordination of current research projects, and elimination of parallel research. For instance, by the spring of 1960, the Commission on Machine Building had examined 6,300 research projects and had been able to weed out 900 as duplicating too closely the work in other Bloc nations.[1]

The work of the Standing Commissions of the CMEA in the areas of production specialization, planning, and exchange of technological information seems to be increasing each year. Since the CMEA, contrary to the practices of such Western institutions for international economic co-operation as the OEEC, has chosen to hide the extent of its activities, a more exact evaluation is impossible.[2]

B. Political Problems and Methods of Operation of the CMEA

The East Central European nations have had a long history of antagonism towards each other and, whatever their relation with Russia might be, they were very jealous of each other in the past. Since such attitudes do not disappear overnight, the degree of authority of the CMEA has been an extremely sensitive issue.

Concerning the method of operation of the CMEA, a prominent Bulgarian economist wrote: 'The socialistic world economy has no planning centre and no unified long-range plan. The planned development of the Bloc is achieved because the various countries willingly co-ordinate their long- and short-range plans with each other. Through such discussions the growth of material production is given a planned direction on the basis of the mineral structure and the work force reserves in the whole Socialist camp.'[3] The concrete

[1] K. Vinogradov, 'Collaboration of the Socialist Countries in the Development of Machine Building,' *Problems of Economics* III, June/1960.

[2] More than 10,000 specialists were working in the CMEA Commissions in 1961, according to *Neues Deutschland* (Special Edition for Leipzig Spring Fair 1961, p. 4). This figure must not be taken too literally, however. The Building Commission, for instance, has 20 full time workers but has held conferences attended by several hundred experts. I imagine that those who attended the occasional conferences which each Commission held during the year were included in the 10,000. According to several foreign trade experts in East Berlin, 'less than 100 people' worked in the CMEA central offices in Moscow in 1959.

[3] G. Popissakoff, 'Zur Entwicklung der internationalen Arbeitsteilung im Sozialismus,' *Der Aussenhandel* X, 10/1960, pp. 17–20. DDR economists reacted strongly to my suggestion that the CMEA prepare a master plan for the whole Bloc since, as they declared, 'This would be a violation of national sovereignty.' The determination of where sovereignty begins or ends is, perhaps, a metaphysical question; nevertheless, it is a prickly issue in the Bloc. Knud Erik Svendsen ('Notes on the Economic, Relations between the East European Countries,' *Statøkonomisk Tidsckrifts* 1/1961) cites one Soviet author who wrote that 'for the moment' the CMEA does not prepare an all-Bloc plan.

institutional manifestation of these sentiments has been the requirement for unanimous approval for all Council recommendations. As far as I have been able to determine, this has also been carried out in practice.

However, unanimity can also be forced, and several CMEA nations have not hesitated to go against Council suggestions. Between 1956 and 1958, the Poles not only broke their coal delivery agreements with the DDR (and sent this coal to the West) but also produced a great many machines which, according to the specialization recommendations of the CMEA and the bilateral specialization agreements, they should have imported.[1] Even after the end of the political thaw in 1958, they still continued to produce goods which violated CMEA suggestions, e.g. telautographic machines.[2] Other nations have acted similarly. For instance, the CSSR was supposed to produce 25-horsepower tractors and export these to other nations. The DDR was not able to obtain enough of these tractors from Czechoslovakia and had to start producing such a model themselves. A DDR commentator remarked: 'In the concrete case of the Zetor (25 HP) which is produced in the CSSR, I must agree with the foreign traders that the behaviour of the CSSR is not right, since the CSSR sells large amounts of these tractors especially on the Capitalist world market. For each Socialist country the maintenance of the principles of mutual advantage and brotherly aid must take first place.'[3]

In another case it was observed, 'The first organizational presupposition for a strong international production specialization is . . . the acceptance of the specialization agreements in the export and import plans. Up to now these obvious measures were not in all cases observed. For instance, due to the non-observance of co-ordination talks concerning the specialized production of ball bearings, disturbances arose . . . in trade and production between various Socialist partners. . . .'[4] Other examples of such behaviour have filtered out

[1] According to Werner Föster, *Die Notwendigkeit der Koordinierung der Produktion bei Werkzeugmaschinen zwischen der Volksrepublik Polem und der DDR und ihre Auswirkung auf den Aussenhandel* (Diplomarbeit, Hochschule für Ökonomie, 1958; p. 33): 'The reduction of the imports [from the CMEA Bloc] by Poland is the effect of their disregard of the programmes for the co-ordination of [Bloc] production.'

[2] Jochen Teubel, *Die Bedeutung der Perspectivplanung im Wirtschaftzweig Aussenhandel und ihre Auswirkung auf die Arbeitsweise im Aussenhandelsunternehmen, inbesondere auf die Jahres- und Operative Planung* (Diplomarbeit, Hochschule für Ökonomie, 1960), p. 13.

[3] Hanni Mothes, *Probleme der Spezialisierung der Produktion und des Aussenhandels bei Landmaschinen zwischen der DDR und den Ländern des RGW* (Diplomarbeit, Hochschule für Ökonomie, 1958), pp. 15–16.

[4] Gertrud Gräbig, *Internationale Arbeitsteilung und Aussenhandel im sozialistischen Weltsystems*, *op. cit.*, p. 69.

from time to time.[1] It does not seem unnatural that some of the CMEA's recommendations have been disregarded, but, unfortunately, I have no way of determining the extent of this disobedience.

It should also not be surprising that informal pressures have been brought to bear upon various countries to enforce obedience to CMEA recommendations. During the last months of 1956 and the early months of 1957, the DDR, USSR and CSSR joined together to withhold certain chemicals, fertilizers, tyres and raw materials such as cement from Poland, in order to encourage Poland to adhere more closely to previous agreements.[2] Such sanctions have also been applied to other Bloc nations from time to time.[3]

It is very important to realize that Russia does not completely control the CMEA. In the formal Council meetings, Russia has only one vote (in other international groups in the Bloc, such as the Danube Commission, Russia has several votes). In the Commissions the countries where the Commission is permanently located usually plays the major role. Of course, in the most important decisions it is obvious that Russia had (and has) the most power. The most important Commissions are located in Moscow and the Russian delegations on the other Commissions are very large (e.g. in the Building Industry Commission in the East Berlin about eight members come from the DDR, five from the USSR, and one or two from the other nations). In case of disputes between East Central European nations, Russia has often been called in to mediate. And, as I indicated before, through the 'Russian embassy system' the USSR was able to obtain much more information about the East Central European nations than these nations were able to obtain about the USSR or each other.[4]

Finally, because all East Central European nations have been much more economically dependent on the USSR than the reverse, all have had to take into account the difficulties which would occur *if*

[1] Information concerning these 'contraditions' between Bloc nations is difficult to secure. I have heard stories of the USSR refusing to supply raw materials to the Rumanians to build a new truck factory because the CMEA had already assigned such production to Poland. According to *Der Tagesspiegel* ('Widerstand gegen Comecon,' July 5, 1960) great disputes have occurred between the various Bloc nations concerning the production of tractors, and, between Hungary and several other countries, concerning exports of cars to Yugoslavia. Köhler (*op. cit.*, p. 106) notes that the DDR refused to give up production of heavy caterpillar tractors and that Khrushchev, at the June, 1960 Communist Party meetings at Bucharest, is known to have reprimanded the Bulkan nations for their resistance to specialization decisions. Schenk, (*Magie der Planwirtschaft*, *op. cit.*, pp. 103ff) also has some very interesting anecdotes concerning similar problems.

[2] Interview with Fritz Schenk.

[3] e.g. see 'Integrating the Satellites—The Role of Comecon,' *op. cit.*

[4] Schenk, *op. cit.* p. 86.

the Soviet Union decided to withhold certain raw materials in punishment of some transgression. All this notwithstanding, there has been an element of voluntariness and of mutual responsibility (and profitability) in the work of the CMEA that is enabling the CMEA to succeed where all measures backed by force had failed. Political tensions still exist and have been manifested in peculiar ways, e.g. the withholding of certain statistical information. Nevertheless, such tensions seemed to be becoming less acute after 1956.

C. Problems of Decision-making in the CMEA

The growth of the CMEA has been the growth of an organization which has tried bureaucratically to co-ordinate production decisions in the various Bloc nations. Due to its voluntary nature, the CMEA has had to develop special methods of making decisions which would not only bring about a more optimal allocation of Bloc resources but which would also be accepted by the various participating nations.

The first major problem of decision-making was the gathering of information and the development of a statistical reporting system which would permit meaningful comparisons between data from the various CMEA nations. The co-operation between statisticians in the member nations of the CMEA has been, until recent times, slight.

In 1952, the CMEA sponsored a conference which attempted to work out some common definitions for foreign trade statistics. Although the exact recommendations of this conference are not known, one participant told me that 'a few, but not all, of the suggestions were adopted by the various member nations.' After a lapse of six years, the 'First Conference of Statisticians' met in Berlin to make recommendations for a common industrial classification for statistical reports. In working out such a nomenclature (which was adopted by the DDR State Planning Commission for use in the planning of the new Seven-Year Plan several months later) the conference did not grapple with the much more difficult problems concerned with measurement of physical production within the various industrial areas, or of the value measurements of production.

In a second conference in Moscow in November, 1958, Bloc representatives discussed problems concerning comparison of living standards and real wages. They did not reach agreement and set up a subcommittee to study the problem further. In March, 1959, Bloc statisticians worked out additional details of a product nomenclature for foreign trade as well as a standard methodology for calculation of trade price indices and volume indices.[1]

[1] Gunter Hartig, 'Die Bedeutung einheilicher statistischer Unterlagen für die planmässige Zusammenarbeit der sozialistischen Länder,' *Statistische Praxis*, 10/1958, pp. 217–20; details of the various statistical conferences mentioned

In 1960 the nomenclature of products in foreign trade statistics was unified, but aside from a general classification system, production statistics in the Bloc varied widely and made comparisons for accurate planning difficult.

In the early 1960s CMEA subcommittees began working out a product nomenclature with common physical and value measurements for all countries to use, as well as common macroeconomic accounting procedures and definitions for national income calculations.[1] These are ambitious projects which, while offering few theoretical problems, are very difficult to do. Plan periods have also been co-ordinated.[2]

To facilitate this work, in June, 1962, the CMEA established a special Standing Commission for Statistics—an extremely important step toward effective all-Bloc planning.

Working out common statistical and planning nomenclatures has not been the only problem of intra-Bloc planning. Because the Bloc policy-makers have rejected co-ordinating production and trade decisions by a market mechanism, some special methods have had to be developed for the CMEA to compare cost and price data. In the conference of Communist party leaders in Moscow in May, 1958, the problems of making valid international comparisons were discussed and in November, 1959, the Standing Commission on Economic Questions drew up a long-range programme for research on these problems. At the same time, prominent Bloc economists such as Ostrovitianov began to demand a reform in cost calculations in the whole Bloc so that a single yardstick could be developed for the comparison of long-term production costs in the various CMEA

---

may also be found in Helmut Michael, 'Brüderliche Zusammenarbeit der Statisker in RGW,' *Statistische Praxis*, 9/1959, pp. 166–8; D. Albrecht and G. Otto, 'Die Vereinheitlichung der Aussenhandelsstatistik zwischen den Teilnehmerländern des RGW,' *Der Aussenhandel* IX, 8/1959, pp. 17–18; Hans Schönherr, 'Einige Probleme bei der Durchführung internationaler Vergleiche,' *Statistische Praxis*, 2/1958, pp. 42–4.

[1] In June, 1958, Bloc statisticians met to clarify such problems as where the border should be drawn between 'productive' and 'nonproductive' economic activities, and at what degree of 'grossness' industrial production should be calculated. The ECE has also sponsored a conference between statisticians in East and West to clarify differences in national accounting methodology. For details on these macro-accounting problems, see 'A Note on Some Aspects of National Accounting Methodology in East Europe and the Soviet Union,' *Economic Bulletin for Europe*, 3/1959, pp. 52–68.

[2] In 1956 all CMEA nations except Bulgaria began a new five-year plan. This lock step was somewhat interrupted by the changeover to a seven-year plan by the USSR in 1957 (which was subsequently followed by many East Central European nations). Nevertheless, each Bloc country will end a long-range plan in 1965 and will march together again.

nations.[1] A Western expert commented: 'Sets of "maximalists" and "minimalists" . . . are fighting somewhat confused battles, the significance of which transcends the boundaries of the Soviet Bloc. The "maximalists" proceeded the Council's Tirana Plenum (May, 1959) . . . with a whole barrage of new demands. They asked for uniform price fixing procedures and methods of accountancy throughout the . . . Bloc' as well as stricter and more extensive intra-CMEA standardization of engineering and other manufactured goods, and strengthening of the CMEA's authority.[2]

In 1960 the Standing Commission for Economic Questions was working on four main problems:

1. Comparable methods for the calculation of coefficients of production and the distribution of national income.
2. Main principles and coefficients of the international division of labour in the Bloc.
3. Methods of comparison of economic profitability of investments.
4. Methods of comparison of coefficients for production cost (including accounting and pricing procedures).[3]

This work included derivation of methods of calculating both value and quantity coefficients, not only for such coefficients as capital-output ratios and labour productivity but also for capacity measurements, and so forth.

As I discussed in the chapters on planning in the DDR, collecting adequate information is only one-half of the task of planning; our the other half consists of the problems of analysing, evaluating, and using these data to make decisions. Two main planning methods have been employed by the CMEA commissions: material balance techniques and the 'method of coefficients.'

The all-Bloc material balances, which were first calculated late in 1955, were the most important early planning tools of the CMEA and

[1] K. V. Ostrovitianov, *Pravda*, 2/8/1959, cited by *World Economic Survey in 1958*, *op. cit.*, p. 163.

[2] Isaac Deutscher, 'Communism's Common Market,' *New Statesman*, 11/7/1959, pp. 37–8.

[3] *Der Aussenhandel* X, 4 & 5/1960, pp. 5–7. According to Terechow and Shastitko, *Planovoe khozyaistvo* 11/1961, the following major intra-Bloc differences exist: investment costs in the USSR exclude capital repair on fixed assets while in the DDR and Hungary, such costs are included; costs of testing and commissioning enterprises are included in current operating costs in the USSR while they are considered part of investment costs in Rumania; surveying and designing costs are included as part of investment costs in the CSSR, but not in other countries; DDR has a turnover tax on producer goods while other Bloc countries do not; Hungary does not tax wage earnings, while other countries do to varying degrees; free services are about one-quarter of real earnings in Hungary and the USSR, while in the other Bloc countries this percentage is different (and thus wage rates are not directly comparable).

were made for some raw materials, machines, and agricultural goods. As far as I have been able to find out, technical coefficients linking outputs with inputs have not been made, which greatly limits the use of these balances by making it impossible to construct any type of input-output matrix to test the consistency of the projected goals. Moreover, not only have all problems of national planning been transferred to the international level, but additional problems have arisen. For instance, one Bloc economist has summarized the situation in the following way: 'The necessities for rational specialization and co-operation of production or for other forms of division of labour between the Socialist countries are, at the present time, ascertained with the aid of the balance method, i.e. through comparisons of material balances for the various goods in the Bloc. In these balances, production and demand for different types of goods are drawn up, not only for the whole Socialist camp, but also for the CMEA nations. . . . However, these methods do not give any directions for the elimination of deficits and surpluses. Moreover, such methods say nothing about the way in which one can bring about the international division of labour or give any basis for deciding which variants are the most advantageous from the standpoint of economic and natural conditions in the different countries. All of these problems are subject to broad and special additional investigations.'[1]

Little has been written in the Bloc press about the intra-Bloc material balances or how these balances have been actually used and how conflicts have been resolved in bringing the supply and demand sides into balance. As far as I know, only the most important minerals and agricultural goods have been 'officially' balanced by the CMEA; each Commission has made its own balances for special products, but these seem to have a somewhat 'non-official' status. The actual methods by which the CMEA or the Commissions have decided how the discrepancies in all-Bloc demand and supply (as reflected by the material balances) are to be eliminated, is still a mystery.

The intra-Bloc material balance system has not lacked critics. In 1958 a DDR economist demanded that not only raw materials and fuels be balanced but also intermediate products and labour supplies.[2] The Czech economist Kaigl suggested an intra-Bloc balance of production sectors I and II (production and consumption goods).[3]

[1] Grigor Popissakoff, 'Zur Entwicklung der internationalen Arbeitsteilung im Sozialismus (II),' *Der Aussenhandel* X, 11/1960, pp. 22–5.

[2] Gunther Kohlmey, *Entwicklungsprobleme des sozialistischen Weltwirtschaftssystems* (East Berlin: Akademie Verlag, 1958), p. 64.

[3] Cited by Karl Morgenstern, 'Zur Preisbildung auf dem sozialistischen Weltmarkt,' *Wirtschaftswissenschaft* VI, 3/1958, pp. 442–8. I have not seen the original suggestion and do not, therefore, know the full extent of Kaigl's programme.

In 1960, a Russian economist suggested that a unified system for material balances be used by all countries in the Bloc to simplify the making of all-Bloc balances.[1] Nevertheless, none of these economists attacked the problem of how the system was to be used.

The problem of deriving suitable coefficients to test the relative profitability of production in the various Bloc countries and to make use of them in making specialization decisions has been a great deal more difficult to solve than the problem of making all-Bloc material balances.

In the beginning, specialization decisions seemed to be made on the principle that any specialization which would lead to longer production runs was better than no specialization at all.[2] As I noted in Chapter I, a series of CMEA recommendations in May, 1956, concerning the specialization of production of six hundred different types of machine goods proved unworkable for this reason. Although the principle motive in setting up the Standing Commissions was to have technical problems solved by technicians (rather than politicians), one DDR author said in early 1958: 'The work of the Standing Commissions for Economic and Technical-Scientific Mutual Aid of the CMEA has been characterized up to now by the fact that the recommendations were not based on scientific rules for specialization.'[3] Nevertheless, inadequate theoretical methods for decision-making did not discourage the Commissions from making detailed plans and decisions for Bloc production specialization and trade from 1956 to 1960.[4]

Due to lack of any very firm theory on how specialization recommendations should be made, and lack of adequate exchange rates to compare national values, each CMEA Commission was forced to improvise. Through the years each Commission has developed a series of (physical) technical and engineering coefficients which they

[1] B. Miroschinickenko, 'Co-ordination of the National Economic Plans of the Socialist Countries,' *Problems of Economics* III, October/1960, pp. 45–53 (from *Voprosy Ekonomiki*, 3/1960).

[2] One of my DDR interviewees said that labour hours of production was the principle criterion used in these early production specialization discussions. He added that since capital intensity of production, use of materials, and comparability of final products were seldom considered, the decisions reached were not very good. Since this informant did not himself participate in the early discussions, his statement must be viewed with caution. Other interviewees criticized the early methods without, however, telling me exactly what methods were used.

[3] Walter Mosteitz, 'Spezialisierung und Kooperation im Maschinenbau zwischen den sozialistischen Ländern,' *Wirtschaftswissenschaft* VI, 5/1958, pp. 659–71.

[4] In a DDR Diplomarbeit I saw such planned trade data in great detail for each CMEA nation (except Albania) from 1956–60 for agricultural machines. These plans were probably made in 1956 and showed that at least in some areas, specialization agreements were quite extensive at an early date.

have used in place of cost comparisons. For instance, the Commission of the Building Industry, in analysing the production of cement and concrete, has used the following coefficients:[1]

(*a*) Capital/output ratios
(*b*) Physical production per 'capacity unit'
(*c*) Productivity per production worker (cubic metres of concrete per man, etc.)
(*d*) Cement per cubic metre of concrete
(*e*) Energy necessary for a cubic metre of concrete production
(*f*) Steam necessary for a cubic metre of concrete production
(*g*) Space requirements

Demand forces have been estimated from gaps in the all-Bloc material balances, market survey analyses of leading non-Communist nations, straight line extrapolations, and so forth. All these methods have been quite crude.

The 'method of coefficients' has two main defects:

1. Except for raw material extraction or extremely labour intensive industries, such coefficients are not very accurate guides to either average or marginal production costs in the Bloc nations. Another difficulty arises in the reconciliation of the various coefficients. For instance, the Commissions have had little idea of the relative values of labour skills and capital in the various countries and have had, therefore, no real method of deciding which of two countries should produce an article when one country has a lower capital/output ratio but a high labour/output ratio of production than another country.

2. The separate Commissions have had little idea of where the comparative advantage of one nation lies. For instance, the Chemicals Commission might note that the DDR has an absolute advantage in producing every chemical, but it would have no way of knowing whether or not the DDR has a real comparative (relative) advantage in production of chemicals without communication with the Commissions in all other production areas. Such overall comparative advantage estimates have not, however, been made up to 1962. Moreover, since each Bloc country has been extremely interested in increasing exports so as to increase desperately needed imports, it has not been easy to convince one country of the desirability of dropping the production of one export article without assigning this nation another export good to produce. Since this is most easily done in the same Commission, I believe that each Commission has made its specialization recommendations on the basis of 'comparative advantage' only within its own particular area.

The DDR economists with whom I spoke seemed aware of these difficulties and I believe that purely bureaucratic methods have not

[1] For source and more information, see Appendix D.

always been used in decision-making. I was told, for instance, that certain questions in the Commissions were settled by bargaining; indeed, for the production of some new articles, bids were submitted and the lowest bidders were awarded the contracts.[1] In this way the Commission has partially simulated a market mechanism!

As far as I have been able to find out, the CMEA has not focused primary attention on trade problems although, of course, trade is affected by almost every recommendation for specialization of production. The CMEA has not directly aided in the drawing up of consistent trade plans by the individual Bloc nations. Nevertheless, by making the planners in each country more aware of Bloc supply and demand forces the CMEA has played an important indirect role in the co-ordination of trade.

The increasing importance of CMEA work has been reflected in the form of the long-range global trade agreements for 1959 to 1965, in which goods in the agreement were divided into three categories:[2]

(*a*) Priority goods, such as hard coal, coke, copper, zinc, fertilizer, wheat, sugar, machines for production of energy, etc. (for which all-Bloc material balances had probably been made)
(*b*) Goods for which production specialization agreements had been made
(*c*) Other goods

This type of nomenclature has facilitated the discussions between Bloc planners trying to reach a consistent pattern of trade and production. The next logical step is the drawing up of an all-Bloc trade flow plan but up to the early 1960s this was not done.

D. Bloc Viewpoints on Production Specialization Criteria: A Digression

Within the Bloc, a great diversity of opinion has existed concerning the proper criteria to be used for making specialization agreements. Since Bloc economists have often denounced or misunderstood the Ricardian theory of comparative advantage[3] the theoretical bases of the arguments in the debate have been quite varied. There seems to be three main schools of thought.

The first group of economists may be called the 'nationalists', since they believe that if each country concentrates on the production

[1] An undocumented statement in 'The Work of Comecon,' *East Europe* IX, 4/1960, pp. 3–9, asserts also that competitive bidding sometimes occurred.

[2] Gertrud Gräbig, *Der sozialistische Weltmarkt* (Lehrbrief 3, Fernstudium der Hochschule für Ökonomie, mimeographed, 1959), p. 17.

[3] For a survey of the Ricardian ideas in the Bloc, see my 'Communist Foreign Trade Theory,' *op. cit.*

of those goods for which it has a comparative advantage (the highest profitability, measured by the profitability coefficients) then Bloc specialization can be carried out most efficiently and trade will be optimized. Two subgroups of this school exist. One subgroup believes that such a process can occur partly spontanteously: 'If each country concerns itself with the production of such goods which it can produce under more favourable production conditions than other countries and—including the essential meaning of the planned Socialist international division of labour-import those goods which these [partner] countries can produce with less expense of labour and consequently lower value and price, then both trade partners will gain.'[1] The other subgroup believes that this specialization of production on relatively more profitable items must be guided. For instance, the CSSR economist Cerniansky declared at an intra-Bloc conference: 'If all countries of the Socialist camp work out a group of such [profitability] coefficients for all or for the largest part of their [traded] goods on the basis of the same methods, then there would exist the possibility to decide together which products have the best (production) conditions in one country, in a second country, and in a third country. In this case we would have a very useful analytical tool for the investigation of the conditions of the international division of labour in the Socialist world economic system.... The methods of calculating the coefficients of economic profitability (of trade) can be used as a means for the international comparison of productivity of social labour in the Socialist world market.'[2] A joint Czech-DDR article at the end of 1960 outlines the operation of such a system in detail. Each nation would first calculate an average coefficient of profitability of all exports (similar to the 'labour coefficient' discussed in Chapter IV). Then in the all-Bloc discussions concerning production specialization, for each country, a comparison would be made between the export profitability coefficient of the good in question with the average export profitability of the same country. In this way the comparative advantage could be determined. Although there are some theoretical difficulties here, the suggestion has merit and represents a decided advance over the previously vague proposals in the Bloc literature.[3]

[1] Rudolf Thiele, 'Der sozialistische Aussenhandel als potentielle Akkumulationsquelle bei äquivalenten Warenaustausch,' *Der Aussenhandel* IX, 4 and 5 1959, pp. 53–5. This statement sounds as if Thiele does not quite understand the difference between relative and absolute advantage in trade, although in the same article he presents Ricardo's wine-cloth example.

[2] V. Cernianský, 'Hauptreferat,' *Sammelheft: Internationale Konferenz über die Rentabilität des Aussenhandels, op. cit.*, pp. 101–18.

[3] Rudolf Brauer and Viliam Cernianský, 'Die Bedeutung der Kennziffern der Rentabilitaet des Aussenhandels fuer die sozialistische internationale Arbeitsteilung,' *Wirtschaftswissenschaft* VIII, 7/1960, pp. 977–90.

On the other hand, the 'internationalists' write: 'The choice of the branches of industrial production which will be primarily developed in the different countries should be taken not only with the viewpoint of raw materials and other favourable domestic [production] conditions, but also in relation to the meaning of this or that branch, not only for the development of the economy of that nation, but also for the covering of the necessities and demands of other Socialist nations.'[1] 'Up to now the publications concerning profitability of foreign trade began from the viewpoint of one country. That *was* the correct starting point . . . Under the conditions of the Socialist international division of labour . . . however, it is not sufficient to view the possibilities for a higher profitability of foreign trade for a single country.'[2] 'The higher profitability of the Socialist camp as a whole has priority. . . .'[3] The basic analytic tools of this school are hard to ascertain since assertion rather than analysis has been the chief argumentive device. This school seems to have the same static approach of the 'nationalists' but places more emphasis on demand factors.

A third school of thought (often allied with the 'internationalists') believes that too much attention has been paid to the problem of static profitability, and that dynamic factors must be brought into consideration. For instance: 'Two basic factors must be observed in the mutual production planning between the Socialist nations: the profitability of production and the complex development of the economy. . . . Each Socialist country must have a proportional development. This includes a faster development of Section I, the manufacturing of production goods, than Section II, the production of consumer goods. The existence of a heavy industry base in each country is unconditionally necessary for the maximum development tempo of the whole economy. By the organization of the mutual production work between the Socialist nations, the most favourable conditions in each country must be used as a basis, and one must observe such factors as raw materials, demands, production experience, transport, (production) capacities, and bottlenecks.'[4] (In

[1] N. Silujanow, 'Eine neue Etappe in der Entwicklung der internationalen sozialistischen Arbeitsteilung,' *Der Aussenhandel* IX, 8/1959, pp. 8–11. For this sentiment repeated in almost the same words, see G. Popissakoff, 'Zur Entwicklung der internationalen Arbeitsteilung im Sozialismus (II),' *Der Aussenhandel* X 11/1960, pp. 22–26.

[2] Gertrud Gräbig, *Internationale Arbeitsteilung und Aussenhandel im Sozialistischen Weltsystem* (East Berlin: Verlag Die Wirtschaft, 1960), pp. 51–2.

[3] Gertrud Gräbig, 'Auswirkung der internationalen Produktionsspezialisierung auf dem Aussenhandel der sozialistischen Staaten,' *Der Aussenhandel* IX, 16 and 17/1959, pp. 9–11.

[4] Gertrud Gräbig, *Der Aussenhandel* VII, 9/1957, pp. 318–20. According to the recently published 'Principles of the Socialist Division of Labour.' (*Current*

the Bloc literature, however, the counter-argument has appeared quite often that with the development of intra-Bloc trade, this is not necessary for every country.) This school of thought has also brought other dynamic factors and goals into consideration, e.g. 'The Socialist international division of labour is not concerned with value alone. Important principles are, for instance, the equal distribution of the work force in the Socialist camp and the closing of the gap between the industrially less developed nations.'[1] The economists who discuss such dynamic factors have never been very specific about how they would accomplish their plans. The Bloc theoreticians have not yet been able to help the planners very much since they haven't been able to agree upon even the basic outlines of foreign trade theory and the theory of international production specialization. Until some theoretical issues are solved so that the commissions can have firm criteria for making specialization decisions, the quality of the plans drawn up by the CMEA will leave a great deal to be desired.

4. SUMMARY AND CONCLUSIONS

The international market mechanisms which act to co-ordinate trade and production decisions of various non-Communist nations have been missing in intra-Bloc trade. In the very beginning, some co-ordination was effected through directions from the Soviet Union, but by the end of the 1950s, several other trade co-ordinating mechanisms had been developed.

The extension of the global trade contract negotiations into a five step contract system has allowed the partial balancing of the material balance system of each nation through an international iteration process. Although this process has aided in achieving a consistent Bloc production and trade pattern, several disadvantages have existed: first, questions of optimality have been neglected; second, the system has been a clumsy method to bring about such consistency in Bloc plans.

The Council of Mutual Economic Assistance has changed from a nebulous Stalinist discussion group to an organization which draws up all-Bloc material balances, makes production specialization

---

Digest of the Soviet Press XIV, July 11, 1962, pp. 3–8) each country must develop the means of production faster than other industrial branches, must build up its agricultural sector, and must utilize all possible domestic raw materials. For application of such ideas *ad absurdum* for N. Vietnam, see A. Borgmeier, *Wissenschaftliche Zeitschrift der Martin Luther Universitaet* VIII, 4 & 5/1958–9, pp. 541–60.

[1] Gertrud Gräbig, 'Auswirkung. . . ,' *op. cit.*

recommendations, and brings together production representatives from all-Bloc nations for exchange of information. The two greatest problems of the CMEA have been the gathering of adequate information and the devising of satisfactory planning methods. Up to the early 1960s, the influence of the CMEA on foreign trade has been indirect. Nevertheless, the drawing up of all-Bloc material balances has given the planners in each nation a more accurate idea of Bloc supply and demand forces to take into account in drawing up their own plans. Moreover, bringing together representatives from all-Bloc nations on a permanent basis has facilitated intra-Bloc communication and has undoubtedly helped in this informal way to co-ordinate the trade plans of the Bloc nations. The CMEA has not yet drawn up all-Bloc trade plans or participated in the bilateral trade negotiation sessions between the various Bloc nations.

Co-ordination of trade does not necessarily bring an optimal trade pattern. The search of the CMEA for criteria for decision-making in the production specialization talks is an attempt to discover methods to bring about a more efficient allocation of Bloc resources through bureaucratic methods rather than reliance on a market mechanism in trade.

CHAPTER VIII

THE FUTURE OF COMMUNIST TRADE

The development of the Communist foreign trade system has been impressive, contrary to the expectations of many eminent Western economists.[1] The successes have been accompanied, however, by many changes in the early trade institutions and methods of conducting trade. What lies in the future?

The very long-term goals seem clear. Khrushchev, in a notable statement, outlined them in the following way. 'Communist society, which will have an abundance of material and spiritual wealth, is capable of satisfying the needs of every individual as well as of every nation. . . . In these conditions the old concepts of borders as such will disappear. With the victory of Communism on a worldwide scale, state borders will disappear, as Marxism-Leninism teaches. In all likelihood only ethnic borders will survive for a time and even these will probably exist only as a convention. Naturally these frontiers, if they can be called frontiers at all, will have no border guards, customs officials, or incidents. They will simply demarcate the historically formed location of a given people of nationality in a given territory. . . . Speaking of the future, it seems to me that the further development of the Socialist countries will in all probability proceed along the lines of consolidation of the single world Socialist economic system. The economic barriers which divided our countries under Capitalism will fall one after another. The common economic basis of world Socialism will grow stronger, eventually making the question of borders a pointless one.'[2]

In order to reach the millennium, Communist policy-makers have outlined three major middle term goals which have implications for foreign trade:

1. A greatly increased volume of trade between Bloc nations. Between 1960 and 1980 the USSR has planned a 7·2 per cent average annual rise of its total foreign trade turnover. In the same period

[1] For instance, Jacob Viner (*American Economic Review* XXXIV, March/1944, pp. 315–25) predicted that nations in a state trading system would not be able to develop objective criteria for settling economic disputes (e.g. prices) and that this would lead to an unstable situation.

[2] *Pravda*, March 27, 1959, quoted by Brzezinski, *The Soviet Bloc. op. cit.* p. 401.

P

the Czechs have planned an average annual trade increase of about 8·4 per cent. Although neither country has specified the direction of their future trade and although other Bloc countries have not yet announced their long-term trade goals, it seems reasonable to suspect that Bloc trade is planned to rise at an average annual rate of 7 to 9 per cent for the next 20 years. This goal is quite in line with the planned 8·6 per cent annual increase in intra-Bloc trade foreseen by the CMEA for the current Seven-year plan period. The necessity for this continuing expansion of intra-Bloc trade is considered a self-evident proposition in all Bloc countries.

2. A more nearly optimal allocation of productive resources withn the Bloc. This is, of course, the primary motive behind the negotiations for the all-Bloc production specialization agreements and the exchanges of technological information within the CMEA. The growing interest in foreign trade theory among Bloc economists, the increasing number of attempts to quantify 'foreign trade profitability,' and the greater attention which has been paid to foreign trade problems by Bloc policy-makers are other reflections of the efforts directed towards achieving this goal.

3. A more equal per capita production or consumption in all-Bloc nations. In 1958 Khrushchev first emphasized this target when he declared: 'In the process of the building of Communism, the Socialist economies will integrate their economies with each other and will eliminate the differences in levels of development. . . . The equalization will not occur through the sinking of the level in the economically highly developed nations. No, this equalization must and will come about through the faster development of the economically less developed countries. Thus all Socialist countries will march forward in a common, unified front on the path of Socialism, on the path of the construction of Communist society.'[1] In the bloc discussion concerning this point, data have sometimes been offered to show that this is already happening (see Table 8–1).

In none of these discussions is there ever any mention of the Asian Communist nations, nor are any comparative data for East Bloc members in Asia and Europe ever given.

The short-run economic goals which affect trade include the well-known aims of eliminating the most crass misallocations of Bloc productive resources and increasing the volume of trade (especially exports). Although much can be said about the specific short-term trade goals, I will spend the remaining few pages speculating on some of the longer term possibilities for Bloc trade and the intra-Bloc trading system.

[1] N. Khrushchev, *Neues Deutschland*, July 25, 1958. For other comments on this policy, see *Ost Probleme* XII, Sept. 16/1960, or Willi Kunz, *Wirtschaftswissenschaft* 2/1962, pp. 169–87.

TABLE 8–1

INDICES OF RELATIVE PER CAPITA INDUSTRIAL PRODUCTION[1]

Country	*Russian Estimates (Original: USSR= 100)*		*Russian Estimates (Transpose: Poland =100)*		*Polish Estimates (Poland= 100)*	
	1950	*1958*	*1950*	*1958*	*1950*	*1957*
Czechoslovakia	—	—	—	—	210	180
East Germany	—	—	—	—	155	160
Soviet Union	100	100	130	118	—	—
Poland	77	85	100	100	100	100
Hungary	—	—	—	—	80	90
Rumania	46	50	60	59	55	55
Bulgaria	35	40	45	47	40	45

If the 8 to 10 per cent planned annual rise of industrial production from 1960 to 1980 is realized,[2] I can see no *a priori* reason why the 7 to 9 per cent planned annual increase in foreign trade will also not be attained. Certainly this foreign trade goal does not seem extraordinarily high in comparison with the 10 per cent annual rise in foreign trade which the Common Market nations experienced in the period from 1950 to 1960 or in comparison with the approximate 11 per cent annual rise in foreign trade of the Bloc countries from 1955 to 1960. And, as I pointed out in Chapter I, even if industrial production increases more slowly than planned, there is still a large potential of profitable trade which has not yet been realized by the various CMEA nations.

Does this planned rapid increase in CMEA foreign trade imply a radical change in the geographical pattern of Bloc trade? Unfortunately Bloc economists have not openly discussed this prickly topic, but some guesses can be made from scattered evidence. Among the six nations now forming the Common Market, the ratio of intra-Market to total trade rose from about 23 per cent in 1950 to 30 per cent in 1955 and 34 per cent in 1960. On the other hand the proportion of trade of the East Central European nations with the CMEA Bloc to total trade has remained about the same in the past decade: 63 per cent in 1950, 64 per cent in 1955, and 64 per cent in 1960. For the USSR this ratio was 50 per cent, 53 per cent and 49 per cent respectively in these years.[3] Now it is entirely conceivable that the

[1] Soviet estimates from O. Bogomolov, *Voprosi Ekonomiki*, 1/1960; Polish estimates from Marian Kaminski, *Polityka* No. 28, 11/7/1959, cited by Knud Erik Svensen, Statsøkonomisk Tidsskrift, 1/1961.

[2] According to N. S. Khrushchev ('Vital Questions of the Development of the World Socialist System,' *Current Digest of the Soviet Press* XIV, 35 & 36/1962) for the period 1960 to 1980, Bloc industrial production will rise at an average annual rate of 9·4 per cent; agriculture, 5·6; and national income, 8·4 per cent.

[3] Table 6–2.

CMEA nations, which have a total population of over 300,000,000 people, will maintain or increase this high percentage of 'internal trade.' (I suspect that if the United States were broken up into 6 or 7 regions, the ratio of 'internal foreign trade' to total 'foreign trade' would be as high if not higher than this ratio within the CMEA Bloc.) Nevertheless, maintaining the same overall East-West geographical distribution of trade as well as the planned growth of trade implies a rapid increase in production specialization among the CMEA nations.[1] Here lies the real crux of the matter.

As I indicated in previous chapters, the forces of the intra-Bloc trade 'market' in bringing about a more rational specialization of Bloc production were very weak. This was due, among other factors, to the limited communication of economic information between Bloc nations, the planning systems which encouraged an 'institutional autarky,' and the 'explosion' type of planning. These limitations gave rise, as I have indicated, to an intra-Bloc economic institution, the CMEA, which has tried to plan a more rational distribution of Bloc productive forces. Undoubtedly the CMEA has achieved many successes and has paid a major role in alleviating some of the most crass misallocations of productive resources. Nevertheless, if this work is to continue successfully in the future, several very difficult obstacles must be overcome.

First of all, Bloc economists must develop a theory of foreign trade and economic integration and must devise a set of rational criteria to decide the most satisfactory division of labour between the individual nations. Throughout the early 1960s, foreign trade theory in the Bloc was still in a relatively underdeveloped state and there seemed to be little agreement on even the fundamentals.[2] The draft of the main principles of the 'Socialist division of labour' reveals a curious lack of incisiveness and rigour. (See translation in *Current Digest of Soviet Press* XIV, July 11/1962.)

Of course, it is quite possible to make production specialization decisions without the aid of any very developed theory or decision-making criteria. However, in such cases the decisions might be objectively impossible to carry out, which was the case with the 1956 CMEA recommendations; or the policy-makers in the individual countries might be somewhat reticent in carrying out the recommendations since they would see no very compelling reasons for the various specific proposals. If, on the other hand, the recommenda-

[1] Khrushchev, *op. cit.*, foresaw a much more rapid rise in intra-Bloc trade than total trade. This is not reflected, however, in the plans which have been announced (see Tables 1–6, 6–1, and 6–2). Furthermore, the future of CMEA Bloc trade wih the Asian Communist nations is also never discussed.

[2] For details, see my article on Communist foreign trade theory in *Soviet Studies*, July/1962.

tions were made on a sound theoretical basis, they would be more palatable for the individual planners and policy-makers in each nation. Solving these theoretical difficulties is, I believe, principally a matter of time.

Since planning a more rational specialization of Bloc production involves the national interest of relatively sovereign nations, some very prickly political problems must also be solved.

In drawing up all-Bloc development plans, the CMEA must take into consideration the fear of some of the less developed Bloc nations that they will be relegated to specialize in agricultural and mineral products while richer nations receive the major share of industrial production. This has been reflected in various articles in the Bloc economic literature which point out the static character of comparative costs as a criterion for production specialization, the need for each nation to have an industrial base, and (in a vague way) the large scope for external economies within the less industrialized Bloc nations. This concern for large-scale industrialization in every Bloc country, although often buttressed by some incorrect autarkist theories, is certainly valid.

Once production specialization agreements are made, other difficulties arise. Many Bloc countries would be asked to produce raw materials or goods for which they had a comparative disadvantage in comparison with the West. And it is quite possible that the world market price which they would receive from other Bloc countries for the product would not cover their operating costs. One obvious way to relieve the burden of these producing countries is for the other Bloc nations to pay special subsidies in the form of prices higher than those on the world market for such products. As I pointed out in Chapter V, however, this would open the gateway for every Bloc country to try to obtain such subsidies. Those countries which ended up paying, rather than receiving such windfalls, might be tempted to redirect their trade towards the West if they could receive more favourable terms of trade. As long as world market prices are used in intra-Bloc trade and as long as Bloc nations are able freely to redirect their trade, the specialization of production within the Bloc is limited.

Even if the above mentioned obstacles are surmounted, the costs of transition towards a more rational division of labour within the Bloc would give additional headaches. In all Bloc countries, uneconomic plants or, indeed, entire industries will have to be converted or scrapped. Although the DDR could afford to convert its aircraft industry to making construction goods and machines, similar action could impose much heavier burdens on the poorer nations. However, it must be noted here that the pattern of future investment is much more important than the immediate reconversion of high cost plants, since these will, in time, wear out. Moreover, some nations may not want, for instance, to scrap some of their uneconomical industries (e.g. steel), since these may be important national status symbols in this era of conspicuous production.

The development toward rationally integrated economies implies the transfer of productive factors from one nation to another and this, in turn, raises more problems. With the current political situation, it would certainly be unacceptable to any Bloc nation to transfer a significant part of its population to another. Therefore, even if a great labour scarcity continues to have adverse effects on the economic growth of the more industrialized Bloc nations such as the CSSR or the DDR, it is highly unlikely that Bloc countries with persistent labour surpluses or underemployment, such as some of the Danubian countries, would consent to any large-scale labour transfer.

A similar situation would exist in regard to capital flows. It is quite logical that the relatively mineral-rich nations such as Poland would be asked to increase greatly their production of these products. Nevertheless, such investments have relatively high capital output ratios and take many years to come into operation, and, with the great capital shortage in the Bloc, such nations would feel disadvantaged unless this burden were shared by the other CMEA members. Although this seems a simple matter and although institutional machinery within the CMEA exists for recommending and channelling such multinational loans, this has not occurred on a large scale up to now, because of the overwhelming priority in each country for domestic investments. For instance, Poland has received more loans from the United States than from the CMEA nations combined. Proletarian internationalism between Bloc nations seems to evaporate when it comes to lending money. The future intra-Bloc lending is an open political question, which, unfortunately, is impossible to answer at the present time.

From this brief survey, it should be clear that the tasks facing the Bloc planners will not be easy. On the other hand, there is no convincing evidence that the Bloc nations cannot *slowly* improve the existing pattern of production and achieve a more rational intra-Bloc division of labour. Indeed, deciding the main guidelines of this evolution was one of the main reasons for drawing up the Twenty-year plans.

The closing of the gap of per capita production and consumption between the richer and poorer Bloc nations has some interesting implications for foreign trade. According to the best estimates of level and change of industrial production, the previously presented table of relative per capita industrial production somewhat distorts the true picture:

TABLE 8–2

LEVEL AND CHANGE OF PER CAPITA INDUSTRIAL PRODUCTION[1]

Country	*Approximate 1955 Level*	*Average Annual Increase: 1950–58*
	$	%
CSSR	405	6·4
DDR	339	9·7
Hungary	189	8·4
Poland	215	5·7[a]
USSR	264	7·4

There is neither a positive nor a negative correlation between level and growth of *per capita* industrial production. Although no very accurate estimates of Rumanian and Bulgarian growth are available, their inclusion would probably make the correlation slightly positive. The diminishing of the level of *per capita* industrial production between Bloc nations is really occurring quite slowly.

With this in mind, the goal of equalization of per capita production and consumption in each East Bloc country implies one of three different alternatives:

(*a*) This is a very long-range goal which can only be reached when the more industrialized Bloc nations begin to show a retardation in their rate of industrialization.

(*b*) This is a medium-range goal in which the lagging industrial production of some of the poorer Bloc nations will be balanced by a faster-growing agricultural sector, so that trade of industrial for agricultural products becomes more extensive. This has never, to my knowledge, been suggested by any Bloc economist and does not seem very likely.

(*c*) This is a medium-range goal which will be attained by a redistribution of income among the various Bloc nations either directly or else through the setting of intra-Bloc foreign trade prices to favour the poorer nations. However, neither of these possibilities seems very likely at the present time although, of course, the situation could change in the future.

The goal of equalization of per capita production and consumption between the different Bloc nations seems to me either to lie in the distant future or else to be an empty phrase to sooth the consciences of those who are disturbed by the present inequalities.

These economic goals imply great changes in the current intra-Bloc economic institutions. Already a number of important changes have been made and, in the past few years, a great many proposals for future changes have been made.

[1] a=1949 to 1955. For sources of data, see Tables 1—2 and 1–6. It is interesting to note that in the current long-range plans (1958 to 1965) for industrial production, Czechoslovakia, the richest Bloc nation, plans an annual average increase of 12 per cent while Hungary, one of the poorest Bloc nations, foresees an annual average rise of only 7·8 per cent.

In the fifteenth CMEA Plenum (December, 1961) a 1963 deadline for the co-ordination of the national twenty-year plans was set. In the following Plenum (June, 1962) the Council established a new Standing Commission for Statistics (the nucleus for an all-Bloc central statistical agency?), a Standing Commission to Co-ordinate Scientific and Technical Research, and an Institute for Standardization, which will probably be concerned with the working out of all-Bloc production norms. Moreover, a Central Executive Committee composed of Assistant Ministers of the member states of the Council was set up to replace the former Council of Representatives. Council statutes were also changed in some important but, as yet, unspecified way.[1] Moreover, Bloc officials have made proposals for changes in CMEA planning methods which will greatly increase the Council's importance in this area. Khrushchev suggested the drawing up of all-Bloc material balances for production and consumption of all major manufactured goods for the time period up to 1970 as well as the working out of a system for multilateral trade planning.[2] Oskar Lange proposed making the Council recommendations for the specialization of production enforceable by law.[3] Other voices have been raised for common accounting methods to be used in all Bloc countries, more realistic exchange rates, and an all-Bloc input-output table.

Attention has also been focused on forms of economic cooperation outside the CMEA. New types of intra-Bloc joint stock companies are being set up with agencies of various nations as stockholders, e.g. the Polish-Hungarian Haldex Corporation for the mining of coal or the new Soviet-Mongolian companies for mineral extraction. In July, 1962, all CMEA Bloc nations (except Albania) signed an agreement for the organization of a central dispatching board for a unified all-Bloc power system, to be located in Prague.[4] In the DDR an all-Bloc research centre was established to study problems of investment

[1] According to Khrushchev (*Current Digest of the Soviet Press* XIV, 35 & 36/1962) the CMEA could not effectively co-ordinate national plans in general and investment in particular because it lacked the necessary powers under its *former* statutes. He noted that the decisions of the 16th Plenum would change this situation. According to an undocumented article in the *New York Times* (October 7, 1962, p. 24) these new (unspecified) changes in the CMEA have been hampered by lack of adequate personnel.

[2] Khrushchev, *op. cit.*

[3] See 'Wirtschaftliche Zusammenarbeit im Ostblock,' *Ost Probleme* XIV 14 & 15/1962, pp. 431–50.

[4] The CSSR, DDR, Hungary, Poland and the USSR have already linked their power grids. In 1963–4, Rumania and Bulgaria will be linked to the system.

[5] PAP *Polish Economic Survey*. 15/1962.

for all countries.[5] Proposals have been made for multilateral trade and payment agreements, rolling five-year trade pacts, and the establishments of special economic organs to co-ordinate production, consumption, and research and development for individual goods.

During the early 1960s, increasing attention is being paid to theoretical problems of foreign trade and economic integration and entire monographs on the subject are appearing for the first time.[1]

However, development of intra-Bloc trade and economic integration presupposes some political changes as well. If, on the other hand, the movement toward political polycentrism in the Communist camp develops more momentum, the trend toward economic integration might be reversed as certain nations turn more toward East-West trade. Certainly the current Soviet economic pressures on Albania illustrate the dangers of too close dependency on the USSR and reveal some of the disadvantages of 'proletarian internationalism[2].' In the case that Bloc countries begin to turn more toward East-West trade, realization of a more rational division of labour within the Bloc would have to come about through a type of market mechanism in which each country would be striving toward the most profitable exports. At the present time, however, such a political development does not seem very likely.

If the CMEA does extend its planning authority, many domestic foreign trade institutions will begin to lose their functions. For instance, the *raison d'être* of the 'foreign trade monopoly' was protection of the domestic economy against the 'anarchy of the Capitalist world market' and not against other Bloc nations. Moreover, Yugoslavia has successfully shown that it is possible for a Communist

[1] See, for instance, Rudolf Brauer, *Probleme der Ermittlung des oekonomischen Nutzens der sozialistischen internationalen Arbeitsteilung und des Aussenhandels sozialistischen Staaten* (East Berlin: Verlag Die Wirtschaft, 1962); or Viliam Cerniansky, *Ekonomika socialistického zahranicniko obchodu* (Prague: SNTL, 1961). Several interesting articles have also recently appeared about the attempts which are being made to derive criteria for a rational all-Bloc division of labour, e.g. Eva Manz, *Wirtschaftswissenschaft* X, 6/1962; Terechow and Shastitko, *Planovoe khozyaistvo* 11/1961; or J. Schukstal, *Voprosi ekonomiki* 10/1961.

[2] Great economic pressures have been exerted on Albania to make it conform to the Moscow line in the Soviet–Chinese dispute of 1961–2. In April, 1961, Khrushchev cut off Soviet aid and began to withdrawn technicians. Other Bloc countries did the same. In May, Soviet and East European tourists had ceased to come to Albania. In August, all scholarships for Albanian students in the USSR were withdrawn and Albanian students were shortly thereafter expelled. Although the Albanians had attended various meetings of CMEA Standing Commissions until November, they did not attend the December Plenum or, as far as I know, later Commission meetings. In late 1961 the Soviet Union also stopped all normal trade relations with Albania although other CMEA nations did not. China has replaced the USSR as Albania's chief trade partner but the lack of spare parts for Soviet machines became a serious economic problem in 1962.

economy to operate effectively without any such organization of foreign trade.[1] It is possible that the FTEs will increasingly direct their attention to East-West trade and that individual firms or domestic buying organizations will begin to maintain direct contact with each other or with the various CMEA organizations. Certainly the increasingly direct contact between planners, production leaders, and foreign traders in the various CMEA Bloc nations suggests such a development.

The foreign trade system of the Communist Bloc is still in its infancy. Institutions and ideas are in flux and an experimental mood prevails. The quest towards a more optimal volume and commodity structure of trade has not slackened, and such sacred institutions as the 'foreign trade monopoly' may yet fall by the historical wayside as the logic of efficiency demands closer contact between producers and buyers.

The rising generation of Bloc economists and technicians who are in contact with real trade and production problems seems to me to be less bound by the fetters of ideology than the older generation. Their success in radically improving the foreign trade system depends, in the last analysis, on their success in rising above the old Marxist foreign trade dogmas.

[1] In Yugoslavia the foreign trade monopoly as an organizational form was eliminated in 1951. Control of trade has been carried out by multiple exchange rates, quantitative restrictions and a series of indirect measures since then.

Any firm is allowed to carry out foreign trade by registering at the Federal Committee for Foreign Trade and showing that it is technically staffed for such operations. The great bulk of trade, however, is handled by twenty or so large export-import firms.

In 1962 there was a unified rate of exchange. Domestic firms were encouraged to export by means of subsidies up to 30 per cent plus partial retention of the foreign exchange which they earned abroad. They could either import or sell this foreign exchange at a special free market. For imports, certain amounts of foreign currency were distributed to the trade associations which, in turn, distributed these funds among their members. No firm was told, however, what goods it must import. The rest of the foreign exchange were auctioned off. In 1962 there were three categories of imports: a free list; those requiring licences; and those allocated. Despite the liberalization measures, more than 70 per cent of the imports were subject to some type of quantitative restriction.

The greatest difficulty in foreign trading in the early 1960s was that domestic prices were still greatly out of line with world market prices which complicated the problems of control of trade.

APPENDIX A

PRICE AGREEMENT BETWEEN USSR AND DDR

Basis for Interpretation of the Price Clause: Agreement between USSR and DDR, 1958.

1. Prices are to be set on the basis of the average 1957 world market price on the chief market of the good in question, taking into account transportation costs.

2. Speculative and discriminating factors are to be eliminated in the setting of the price.

3. The 'chief market' means the leading market for the good in question. In choosing the chief market for the good, one must take into account the economic and geographic factors of the good in question to the partner countries.

In choosing the chief market for the calculation of the basis price, one must start from the standpoint of the buyer, taking into consideration the interests of the seller. One must take into account on which chief markets the buyer, for purely economic considerations, would conduct his transaction if he were not able to buy the goods from his Socialistic partner.

4. The basis price is to be determined from the following documentation:

(*a*) Contracts and accounts of deliveries already carried through.
(*b*) Market exchange notices (effective rather than nominal prices).
(*c*) Price writs.
(*d*) Bids of serious firms.

For information purposes the following documentation is also to be considered:

(*a*) Prices from periodically appearing technical literature (lowest amount).
(*b*) Price lists and catalogues.

The validity of the documentation is to be examined and analysed. Special market deviations of a noncommercial character should not be taken into account. The contract (used to determine the basis price) must be signed under usual commercial conditions.

5. In so far as the documentation price is expressed in a clearing currency whose purchasing power deviates considerably from the purchasing power of this currency in free currencies, then either this price is not to be used as basis price or else the difference in purchasing power is to be appropriately taken into account.

6. The contract prices in trade of the Socialist nations with Capitalist nations may be used as a basis price in the case where it concerns a good which the Socialist nations sell or buy on the Capitalist world market in considerable amounts.

7. If no documentation from 1957 is available, the price is to be determined on the basis of documents from an earlier period, taking into account recognized price indices and/or other means of adjustment agreed upon by the partners.

For special equipment where no documentation can be offered, the basis price is to be calculated by comparison of prices on the chief markets of similar products.

For agricultural products with special seasonal character, the basis price is to be calculated for the season.

8. In the estimating of transporation costs, only regular transport costs are to be taken into consideration.

9. Prices for re-exports are to be set on the basis of actual buying prices previously agreed upon, including the transport cost and a 1 per cent commission.

10. When subsequent quality changes are made, prices are also be to correspondingly changed.

11. With the closing of the (yearly) contract, as many final prices as possible should be set. Only in exceptional cases are provisional prices to be permitted, which should correspond to the average world market prices. Final prices must be set three months or, in the case of complete factory units, six months after signing of the yearly contract.

APPENDIX B

A BRIEF SURVEY OF EXCHANGE RATES OF THE EUROPEAN COMMUNIST NATIONS

Western economists have neglected the whole subject of exchange rates of the Communist nations for two reasons: First, Soviet Bloc currencies are strictly domestic currencies; second, East-West trade is conducted in Western prices and currency units, and intra-Bloc trade is conducted primarily in Western foreign trade prices, converted to a special Rouble accounting unit by dividing the Western Dollar prices by the official Rouble-Dollar exchange rate. However, a brief look at the theory and practice of Bloc exchange rates illuminates several interesting aspects of their foreign trade which are worthy of Western attention.

1. EXCHANGE RATE THEORIES IN THE BLOC

Three main schools of thought have arisen in the East Bloc concerning Bloc exchange rates:

The first group of economists believes that the exchange rate is related to the gold content of the domestic currency which, in turn, is supposed to represent a certain amount of labour expanded in the production of this gold.[1] Indeed, many Bloc economists place as strong an emphasis on the gold content of the currency as conservative American bankers.[2] Opposing this view one Hungarian economist noted: 'The gold content of Socialist money is a declaration almost completely devoid of practical significance so far as the domestically circulating money and the domestic accounting unit are concerned.'[3]

A second group of Bloc economists tie the existing exchange rates directly to the relative purchasing power of national currencies. For instance, in a National Prize-winning (similar to a Stalin Prize) book, an East German economist noted: 'Another . . . characteristic of the monetary relations on the democratic world

[1] This is one of the views of money expressed by Academy of Science of the USSR, *Politische Okonomie Lehrbuch* (trans. from first Russian ed., East Berlin: Dietz Verlag, 1955). For the best summary of Marxist theory on this point, see Stefan Varga, 'Money in Socialism,' *International Economic Papers No. 8*, (London: Macmillan, 1958) pp. 200ff.

Several East German economists explained to me how practical it would be if exchange rates were to represent the value of labour in the currency units. Complications arise since, according to Marx, the reproduction value of labour is different for the various countries where education and living expenses vary. Several schemes have been suggested to get around this problem but they are extremely complicated and, I believe, of dubious value.

[2] It is interesting that most of the top Soviet leaders have not shared this gold fetish. For instance, Lenin once wrote (Über die Bedeutung des Goldes jetzt und nach dem vollen Sieg des Sozialismus; *W.I. Lenin-Ausgewählte Werke in 2 Bänden;* Moscow: Verlag für Fremdsprachige Literatur, 1947; pp. 892–99): 'When we have won on a world scale, we will, I believe build public comfort stations out of gold in the streets of some of the largest cities of the world. That would be the most suitable and best object lesson on the [proper] use of gold . . .' Khrushchev (quoted by *Time magazine*, April 4, 1960, p. 21) misquoted Lenin on this point in his pre-summit visit to Paris in 1960 and noted, 'We have a little gold, but we keep it. I don't know why.'

[3] Varga, *op. cit.*

market is that the exchange rates are stable and are being increasingly brought into alignment with the purchasing power of the single currency units . . . After the official declaration of the gold content of the DM of the DDR as 1 DM=1·8 Roubles, the following situation resulted: one could buy for, let us say, 1·8 million Roubles in the USSR the same average amount of production goods, consumer goods and services as one could buy for one million DM in our republic.'[1] Other Bloc economists have denied that the exchange rates really represent relative purchasing power[2] or that the exchange rates are related in any way to supply and demand forces.[3]

A final major group of Bloc economists believes that the exchange rates have very little meaning at all. Viewing the subject in the same way as Western economists, two East German officials were led to declare: 'For the Socialist countries between themselves, the setting of currency exchange rates has meaning only in so far as a certain mode of clearing is found. Mutual defrauding is impossible here . . . as exports and imports between two Socialist countries are balanced in a specified period of time.'[4]

Some of the Bloc ideologists have also connected the exchange rates to political phenomenon[5] but an examination of these ideas would take us too far afield.

The most vigorous critique of Bloc theorists of exchange rates has been made by a Polish economist who wrote: 'Marxist . . . economic ideas . . . on the problem of foreign currencies in general and foreign currency exchange rates in particular . . . are trivial. It appears that the considerations of exchange rate problems in the Marxist literature have been analysed up to now primarily from the viewpoint of money, without any connection with the modern theory of international trade, i.e. based on antiquated, anachronistic, old-fashioned views of the theory of money. In the area of monetary theory, the Marxist theories with the exception of the timorous attempts by Atlas, have not transcended the framework of the old

[1] Gunter Kohlmey, *Der demokratische Weltmarkt* (East Berlin: Verlag Die Wirtschaft, 1954), pp. 260–1. On page 266 of the same book he admits that the existing exchange rates did not really correspond to the purchasing power of the different currencies.

[2] e.g. Hans-Jürgen Nitz, 'Zu Fragen der Rentabilität im Aussenhandel,' *Der Aussenhandel* VII, 11/1957, pp. 400–2.

[3] e.g. '. . . in comparison to Capitalism, the exchange parity and exchange relation of the DDR Deutsche Mark is not dependent on the equilibrium of the balance of payments. Since the exchange course is not determined through the relation of supply and demand for foreign currencies on the market and because the DDR DM does not circulate in foreign countries, the exchange rate is independent of the balance of payments.' (Fritz Fabian, 'Die Zahlungs- und Verrechnungsbilanz der DDR,' *Der Aussenhandel* VI, 10/1956, pp. 363–4).

[4] H. Heuchler and L. Petzold, 'Zum Thema Preisausgleich und Subvention im Aussenhandel,' *Deutsche Finanzwirtschaft*, 6/1958, pp. 81–2. The same type of statement was more recently made in a speech by Professor B. Minc at a conference on East-West trade (Conference on 'Criteres economiques de la division internationale du travail,' held in Brussels on October 17–21, 1960).

[5] e.g. the former head of the East German Central Bank, commenting on the 1953 revaluation of the DM of the DDR (DMO) remarked, '. . . the fact that 2·22 DMO = $1·00 while 4·20 DMW (DM of the Bundesrepublik) = $1.00 is a visible expression that the DDR, as a member of the camp of freedom, has formed and developed its currency according to the needs of the daily worker while in West Germany, American and West German imperialists have carried through all possible currency manipulations to increase the exploitation and plundering of the worker.' (Martin Schmidt, 'Die Leipziger Messe und der Kurs der DM der DNB,' *Der Aussenhandel* V, 5/1955, pp. 157–8.)

quantity theory . . . The ideas of authors in East Germany . . . can serve as examples of how great the confusion of concepts and the misunderstanding of the economic nature of the exchange rate are spread.'[1]

Most Marxist economists have not understood the obvious fact that the rates of exchange represent the prices of foreign currencies and that they will have an impact on the domestic economy. For instance, let us suppose that the exchange rate in a Soviet-type economy is overvalued (which has been the case for every European communist nation). This could have two main effects on the domestic economy:

A. Given set domestic prices for imported goods, the foreign trade enterprises (FTEs) would have greater incentives to import than to export since a greater monetary profit would be earned. This, in turn, would cause a chronic balance of payments problem and Bloc nations have tried to prevent such a chronic import surplus through a variety of measures including direct import limitations of most goods and special 'shadow exchange rates' which the FTEs must use in the calculation of their overall profits (these rates are closer to 'purchasing power parity' rates than the official rates).

B. If the price for an imported article is set by the Ministry of Foreign Trade on the basis of the foreign price multiplied by the exchange rate, then the domestic price would be relatively low and would encourage consumption of the good (industrial and consumer) to a far greater extent than would, perhaps, be economic.[2] If the domestic prices of imported goods are set on the basis of domestic considerations, rather than world market prices, then a multiple exchange rate system would be, in effect, instituted. That is, the various domestic prices would have different relations to prices on the foreign markets, depending on the subsidies or profits of the foreign trade enterprise for these goods. This causes certain difficulties, e.g. if the domestic price for an article is set low in order to encourage the home use of this article, then the foreign trade enterprises will also see an opportunity for a profit and will try to obtain this article for export, thus reducing the supply available to the citizens of the country and defeating the original purposes of the low price.[3]

These two effects of exchange rates have been for the most part, ignored by Bloc theoreticians. Nevertheless, as a Polish economist concluded: 'If one drops the gold fetish which has enfettered some Marxist economists, one can use all types of exchange rates, e.g. fixed rates, changeable rates, elastic rates, unified or differentiated rates, in the Socialist economy with . . . success, if one is aware of all the economic consequences . . . of these measures.'[4] Except in Poland, no Bloc economist has, to my knowledge, attacked the problem in this way. Until this is done, domestic planning and administration of trade will leave something to be desired.

[1] Miroslaw Orlowski, 'Das Problem der Valutenkurse in der sozialistischen Wirtschaft,' *Zeitschrift für die gesamte Staatswissenschaft*, Band 116, 1/1960, pp. 83–103. This is the best Bloc treatment of the subject I've seen; I do not quite understand why the author chose a West German journal as his forum.

[2] *Ibid.*

[3] This point has been noted by the Czech economist V. Cerniansky, 'Fragen der volkswirtschaftlichen Rentabilität des Aussenhandels,' *Internationale Konferenz über die Rentabilitat des Aussenhandels: Sammelheft der Referate und Diskussionsbeiträge* (Liblice, Czechoslovakia: College of Economics, 1957), but does not seem to have made much of an impact on other Bloc economists. The problem of the domestic price of imported goods is part of the more general problem of the proper domestic price system for a planned economy.

[4] Orlowski, *op. cit.*

2. ACTUAL EXCHANGE RATES IN THE BLOC[1]

At the present time there are three different types of Bloc exchange rates, each serving a special function and/or reflecting a different phenomenon.

A. The Official Exchange Rate

In the post-war years the currencies of all the East Central European nations were defined either in terms of gold or the Rouble. However, due to the rapid price inflations, which lasted in most countries until 1952–53, these rates had little meaning. From 1953 to 1956 the general price level fell in some Bloc nations and rose in others; since 1956 prices have generally fallen in all Bloc nations.[2] With several exceptions, the exchange rates which were set in 1952–53 were maintained up to 1961.

It is a mystery how Bloc policy-makers actually set these rates and East German economists could give me few clues. The question is rarely discussed in the Bloc economic literature, except in an extremely vague way. Two facts are, however, clear:

1. The exchange rates have had nothing to do with the gold content of the currencies, since most of the East Central European nations have had very low stocks of gold, hard currencies, and Roubles.

2. The exchange rates have had little relation to relative purchasing power of the national currency units. For instance, one American economist estimated that in 1950 before the Russians upwardly revalued the Rouble, it was already overvalued by 40 per cent.[3] One Polish economist estimated that in Polish foreign trade in 1957, 50 domestic Zlotys were equal to \$1·00, although the official rate was 4 Zloty= \$1·00.[4] The East German planners have used a 'shadow exchange rate' of 4·20 DMO=\$1·00 although the official rate is 2·22 DMO=\$1·00.

Before turning to actual 'purchasing power' of the currencies, it must be noted that this is an ambiguous concept and empirical results depend very much upon the system of weights which are chosen to make the comparisons.[5] The

[1] There are really several 'official exchange rates,' the 'official gold rate' and the 'official trade rate,' which is a special rate sometimes granted in trade with certain countries. For instance, East Germany signed a contract with Great Britain in January, 1959, which contained the provision that the official 'exchange rate' was to be 11 DMOs=1 Pound, instead of the official gold rate of 6·22 DMOs=1 Pound. Since trade was conducted solely in the English currency, this was a somewhat empty measure.

[2] For a history of Bloc currency problems, see J. G. Gurley, 'Excess Liquidity and European Monetary Reform, 1944–52,' *American Economic Review* XLIV, 3/1954, pp. 339–503, or Bruno Kiesewetter, *Der Ostblock: Aussenhandel* (West Berlin: Safari Verlag 1960). See also Oscar L. Altman, 'Russian Gold and the Rouble,' *Staff Papers* (of the IMF) VII, 3/1960, pp. 416–38.

[3] Franklyn D. Holzman, 'Review of *Voprosy valiutnogo kursa rublia*' by I. Aizenberg, *American Economic Review*, L, 3/1960, pp. 481–3. In a statement before the 85th Congress ('Some Financial Aspects of Soviet Foreign Trade,' *Comparisons of the United States and Soviet Economies;* Washington, D.C., Joint Economic Committee of the Congress of the US, 1959; p. 427) Holzman noted, 'It is no exaggeration to say that over the past 30 years, the exchange rate of no Western nation has been as far out of line from its equilibrium value as the Soviet exchange note.'

[4] e.g. M. Rakowski, 'Z problemow badan efektywnosci produkcji eksportowej,' *Gospodarka planowa*, 2/1957, pp. 19–24.

[5] The sensitivity of 'relative purchasing power' to market basket changes may be seen in the following comparisons of the purchasing power of the DM of East Germany

'relative purchasing power comparisons' below must be viewed with some caution.[1]

In 1957 a system of special intra-Bloc exchange rates 'reflecting relative purchasing power' was set up for non-commercial transactions, tourism and trade in miscellaneous invisibles. From these exchange rates one may gain a rough idea on how far the various official exchange rates are out of line from the relative purchasing powers of the currency units:

TABLE B–1

OFFICIAL GOLD COURSES AND NON-COMMERCIAL EXCHANGE RATES (MIDDLE COURSES)[2]

		1960		*1961*	
Country	*Currency*	*Official Courses (Roubles)*	*Non-Com'l Exchange Rates (Roubles)*	*Official Courses (Roubles)*	*Non-Com'l Exchange Rates (Roubles)*
Albania	100 Lek	8·00	10·00	1·80	1·00
Bulgaria	100 Lewa	58·82	112·4	13·23	11·24
Czechoslovakia	100 Crowns	55·56	86·21	12·50	8·62
East Germany	100 DM	180·00	258·0	40·50	25·80
Hungary	100 Forint	34·10	71·43	7·67	7·14
Poland	100 Zloty	100·00	66·84	22·50	6·67
Rumania	100 Lei	66·67	103·09	15·00	10·31

The fact that official exchange rates do not reflect relative purchasing power of the currency units has more importance than a refutation of some theories of Bloc theoreticians.

---

to the DM of West Germany (DMO/DMW):

	MARKET High income families	*BASKET Middle income families*	*OF Low income families*
	%	%	%
September, 1950	49	58	99
December, 1952	62	67	92
December, 1954	70	75	96
December, 1956	73	79	103
May, 1958	77	83	106
June, 1959	75	80	88

Data from: 'Preis und Kaufkraft in der SBZ,' *Wochenbericht* (Deutsches Institut für Wirtschaftforschung), XXIV, 25/1957, pp. 101–2; and 'Preise und Lebenshaltung in Mitteldeutschland,' *Wochenbericht*, XXVI, 42/1959, pp. 168–70.

[1] From Rakowski, *op. cit.* $1·00 was equal (in 'purchasing power') to 50 Zlotys. DDR economists used a 'shadow exchange rate' of $1·00=4·20 DM. 50Zl=4·20 DM. However, according to the 'purchasing power comparisons' derived from the table of non-commercial rates, 50 Zl.=12·72 DMO. Undoubtedly the discrepancy is due to the difference in weights in the indices; unfortunately, however, no information is available on how any of these estimates were specifically derived. A Czech foreign trade economist complained recently: 'The methods of determining a real exchange relation in foreign trade are not very sophisticated in the current procedures of the countries of the Socialist camp.' (Jezbera, 'Eine Methods zur Ermittlung der Austauschrelationen im Aussenhandel,' *Der Aussenhandel*, IX, 3/1959, pp. 18–20).

[2] Data from letters from Banque Nationale de Bulgarie, Statni Banka Ceskoslovenska, Deutsche Notenbank, Banque Nationale de Hongrie and Narodowy Bank Polski, supplemented by material from 'Eastern Europe and the New Rouble,' *East Europe*, April/1961, pp. 18–19.

In intra-Bloc trade a great many articles for which no world price can be established (ships, complex machinery, war materials) have been traded on the basis of the domestic price (plus a small profit), converted to Roubles by the official exchange rate.[1] And, up to 1957, service payments were also paid in this manner. This means that nation whose official exchange rate is overvalued, in relation to the other Bloc currencies receives an extremely favourable deal.

From the above data it appears that the Rouble was overvalued, relative to all other currencies except the Polish Zloty. Hungary was the most discriminated against in these transactions, followed by Bulgaria, Rumania, Czechoslovakia and East Germany. Since official exchange rates of these nations did not change in the period from 1955 to the end of 1960, and since the price movements in the Bloc nations were about the same in the period, these data show that this type of Russian exploitation lasted at least five years. I strongly suspect that the discontent of the East Central European nations concerning this discrimination was a major factor in the Russian devaluation on January 1, 1961.

The whole system of official exchange rates is due for an overhaul and, according to one Bloc economist, the Standing Commission for Economic Questions of the Council of Mutual Economic Assistance has been working on the problem.[2]

B. Non-Commercial Exchange Rates[3]

Two types of non-commercial exchange rates exist: the non-commercial exchange rates between Bloc countries, and special tourist rates with the Western countries.

Special non-commercial exchange rates between CMEA Bloc nations have existed for special purposes (e.g. for Leipzig Fair) since 1954–55. In the beginning of 1957 the central banks of the various CMEA countries agreed to establish a general non-commercial exchange rate system, primarily for tourism, and set up a standard market basket of about 75 items for the computation of these rates. These rates are established bilaterally and are adjusted every year or so. Nevertheless, during the past four years, these changes have been quite small.

Two special characteristics must be noted. First, not every set of nations has made such agreements, e.g. East Germany and Albania, Czechoslovakia and Rumania.[4] Second, the rates between the various sets of countries are not completely consistent with each other. These differences are small and may reflect the fact that the different agreements have been made at different times or else that some deviations have been made from the standard market basket.

A system of special non-commercial exchange rates has also been instituted for Western tourists by all Communist nations except Albania. Sometimes these rates are differentiated (for a while it was cheaper to buy Roubles with Finnish Marks than with an equivalent amount of Dollars) but usually they are not. Moreover, these rates to Western tourists have been quite out of line with the

[1] According to the East Berlin radio (cited in *Neue Züricher Zeitung*, March 21, 1957) uranium was sold to Russia on a cost plus basis. Fritz Schenk, who was assistant to the Chairman of the East German State Planning Commission from 1953 to 1957, told me that many goods were traded on a cost plus basis. I have seen nothing on the matter in the Bloc press, however.

[2] Lothar Rouscik, 'Die Ermittlung des ökonomischen Nutzeffektes des sozialistischen internationalen Arbeitsteilung,' *Der Aussenhandel* X, 15/1960, pp. 19–25.

[3] Information for this section from previously cited correspondence, material from the Deutsche Notenbank, East Berlin; and material supplied by the Berliner Bank, West Berlin.

[4] In the case of Czechoslovakia and Rumania, the official exchange rate is very close to what the non-commercial rate should be.

intra-Bloc non-commercial and official exchange rates, and some good opportunities for arbitrage have existed:

TABLE B–2

TOURIST AND NON-COMMERCIAL RATES (1960)

Country and Currency	*National Currency Units Equal to $1·00 at Tourist Rate*	*Arbitrage Possibilities From Dollars to Roubles and from Roubles to National Currencies at Different Exchange Rates*		
		D. to R. :G R. to N.C.:N	*D. to R. :T R. to N.C.:N*	*D. to R. :T R. to N.C.:G*
Albanian Lek	—	40·00	100·00	125·0
Bulgarian Lewa	9·52	3·56	8·9	17·0
Czechoslovakian Crown	14·35	4·64	11·6	18·0
East German DM	4·20	1·55	3·876	5·556
Hungarian Forint	23·30	5·6	14·0	29·35
Polish Zloty	23·94	5·98	14·96	10·0
Rumanian Lei	12·00	3·96	9·70	15·0
Russian Rouble	10·00	—	—	—

D.=Dollar
R.=Rouble
N.C.=National Currency

T=Tourist rate
G=Gold (official) rate
N=Non-commercial rate

The third column shows that the Dollar-holding tourist received a much better deal than the Rouble-holding tourist since in every case he was better off changing his Dollars directly into the various national currencies rather than first exchanging them into Roubles. A second characteristic is that exchanging Dollars into Roubles at the tourist exchange rate and then, these Roubles into the various national currencies at the gold (official) rate (fourth column) would have been extremly lucrative for every country except Poland, if it were permitted; which, unfortunately, it was not.

C. Free Market Exchange Rates

Since it has been illegal for these various currencies to leave the Bloc, the free market exchange rates have reflected not only economic forces of demand and suppy for these currencies, but also the political factor of how tightly the currency laws have been enforced. Some idea of these rates may be gained from the table below although it must be remembered that there has seldom been one

TABLE B–3

DOLLAR VALUE OF NATIONAL CURRENCIES (MIDDLE COURSE): 1960

Country and Currency	*Official Rate*	*Tourist Rate*	*Free Market Rate at Frankfurt a.M. August 1, 1960*
Albanian Lek	50·00	—	—
Bulgarian Lewa	6·80	9·52	23·79
CSSR Crown	7·20	14·35	28·12
DDR DM (DMO)	2·22	4·20	19·11
Hungarian Forint	11·74	23·30	47·84 to 50·76
Polish Zloty	4·00	23·94	88·56
Rumanian Lei	6·00	12·00	25·38
Russian Rouble	4·00	10·00	50·76

free market rate for these currencies, and that these rates have fluctuated a great deal over time and in different locations.[1]

Relatively little trading has been done in these free market currencies and, except for the DM of the DDR, these rates have had little economic importance. In Germany, due to the particular political and economic situation and especially the economic abnormalities in East and West Berlin, free market currency transactions have played an important economic role. The centre of the exchange activity has been West Berlin:

TABLE B–4

OFFICIAL TRADE AND FREE MARKET CURRENCY TRANSACTIONS [2]

Year	*Total West German Exports to E. Germany (in million DMWs)*	*Free Market Currency Transactions in West Berlin (Million DMWs)*	*(Million DMOs)*	*Free Market Currency Transactions as per cent of W. German exports to East Germany* %	*Average Yearly Exchange Rate DMO/DMW*
1951	178	212	?	119	?
1952	165	236	999	143	4·2
1953	254	145	725	57	5·0
1954	455	196	861	43	4·4
1955	563	158	730	28	4·6
1956	699	182	726	26	4·0
1957	846	183	?	22	?
1958	800	166	662	21	4·0
1959	1,079	183	686	17	3·8

This table does not include the free market exchange transactions in the other West German Länder or the transactions which were not carried out in the licensed exchange offices. Nevertheless, it is clear that in the early years, free market transactions were a good deal higher than official trading, and that in the following years, these transactions still amounted to an appreciable sum. Since West Berliners could only buy cultural items (records, books, concert tickets) with these free market DMOs without having to show an identity card (and having to pay in DMWs), one might conclude from the data that a fair amount of smuggling was carried on.

Unfortunately, no data are available on non-official currency exchanges in the Soviet Bloc nations, but from notices appearing in Bloc press (especially in Poland), I believe that such illegal activities are far from being stamped out.

In the near future it is highly likely that the official currency rates of the Bloc nations and the intra-Bloc non-commercial exchange rates will be about the same. Different free market exchange rates will continue as long as the Bloc monies remain strictly domestic currencies or as long as supply and demand forces are not allowed to directly influence the exchange rates. Given the current Marxist theory of economic spontaneity, a difference between free market and official exchange rates should exist for a very long time.

[1] Official and tourist rates from previously cited sources. Free market rates (except DMO) from material supplied by Deutsche Verkehrs-Kredit Bank, Frankfurt a.M. Poland is the only Bloc country which has an official free market for foreign currency within the country. (See *New York Times*, July 1, 1962, p. 10).

[2] Trade data from *Statistisches Jahrbuch der BRD*, various issues. 1951–57 data from an East German source; Hans Wemmer, 'Die Freie Stadt Westberlin—die Wechselstuben-spekulation and das Grenzgänger-problem,' *Geld und Kredit* IV, 1/1959, pp. 3–28. 1958–59 data from a reliable unofficial West Berlin source.

APPENDIX C

THE 'FOREIGN TRADE MONOPOLY' OF THE DDR[1]

In this appendix two aspects of the 'foreign trade monopoly' of the DDR are examined: the role of the various institutions participating in foreign trade and the different types of foreign trade plans.

1. ORGANIZATIONS IN THE FOREIGN TRADE MONOPOLY

Properly speaking the 'foreign trade monopoly' consists of two parts: the trade monopoly and the foreign currency monopoly (sometimes a transportation monopoly is also mentioned).[2] These 'monopolies' are spread over several institutions.

A. The State Planning Commission

This is the highest planning organ of the DDR and, as such, is responsible for the co-ordination of the foreign trade plan with the plans from the other sectors. In its statute of organization, in 1959 the State Planning Commission received the additional right to co-ordinate the economic plans of the DDR with the plans of the other Bloc nations through the CMEA or by means of bilateral trade agreements although, of course, it had been doing this for years.

B. The Ministry of Foreign and Inter-German Trade (MAI)

The Ministry oversees the work of the various foreign trade enterprises (who carry on the actual commercial work of trading), sets general foreign trade policy and procedures, negotiates the global trade contracts, and fulfils an intermediary role between the domestic economy and the surrounding world economy. In planning the Ministry receives the control figures from the State Planning Commission and, in turn, sends them to the foreign trade enterprises below. It co-ordinates the various physical plans of the foreign trade enterprises and, with the Deutsche Notenbank and the Ministry of Finance, prepares the financial and foreign currency plans. The Ministry also directs market research, holding of trade fairs, foreign trade advertising and, until recently, a college for the training of foreign trade personnel.

The Ministry has had a complicated history. According to the Allied Proclamation No. 2, September 20, 1945, the trade connections of Germany with other countries were declared null and void, and permission to trade had to have Allied authority. Until the spring of 1947 the foreign trade of the Soviet Zone of Occupation was exclusively carried out by the Administration of Foreign Trade of the Soviet Military Administration (SMAD), which also co-operated with

[1] For a very thorough description of the Soviet foreign trade monopoly, see Glen Alden Smith, *Soviet Foreign Trade: Organization and Operations* (unpubl. Ph.D. dissertation, Stanford U., 1959.)

[2] After a law in 1958 (*GBl* I, 9/1958, pp. 92ff.) which unified the transportation services connected with foreign trade, the transportation monopoly was discovered. See Elisabeth Leilm, 'Das Transportmonopol im Aussenhandel gilt es konsequent durchzusetzer.,' *Der Aussenhandel* VIII, 18/1958, pp. 630–2.

the Soviet foreign trade enterprises.[1] In September 1947, the Deutsche Verwaltung für Interzonen- und Aussenhandel (DVIA) was founded, a central trade organ whose duties were: 'the administrating and regulating of trade operations of the Soviet Occupation Zone with the other occupation zones of Germany.' The DVIA was given 'the right to make trade agreements with German organizations of the other Zones within the Interzonal ration.' It was also given the authority 'to carry through the preliminary work for the conclusion of general trade agreements with foreign nations and of the business between German and foreign firms,' but, however, 'under the instruction of the Administration for Foreign Trade of the SMAD.' In other words, a German agency was created for the carrying out of the business side of foreign trade, leaving, however, the policy decisions to the SMAD. In December 1947, an Amt für Interzonen- und Aussenhandel (AIA) was founded in each Land. These were supposed to be regional agents for the DVIA but were, however, principally responsible to the German and Soviet administration in the Länder.

In 1947 a consulting German Economic Commission was formed (the Deutsche Wirtschaftskommission, the DWK) and in March, 1949, the various Zentralverwaltung were placed under the authority of this central body. The DVIA became the Hauptverwaltung für Interzonen- und Aussenhandel (HVIA) which had permission to make or approve foreign trade deals on its own authority up to $20,000 for exports and $5,000 for imports. The AIA were given similar authority up to $500.

In October, 1949, the provisional government of the DDR was formed and HVIA became the Ministerium für Aussenhandel und Materialversorgung (MAM) which handled not only foreign trade but also domestic distribution of goods. A month later MAM was renamed Ministerium für Innerdeutschen Handel, Aussenhandel und Materialversorgung (MIAM) with the same functions. In November, 1950, MIAM lost its domestic supply functions, concentrated solely on foreign trade, and became the Ministerium für Aussenhandel und Innerdeutschen Handel (MAI), the legal identity it has maintained ever since.

Although the MAI had ostensible authority, the SMAD continued to play a very important role during the early years (especially through 1951) through the Sowjetische Kontrollkommission (SKK) which had authority to 'control foreign trade,' a function which it exercised until March, 1954 (when the Soviet declared the DDR to be sovereign).[2] Afterwards, Soviet advisers played a quieter role but, nevertheless, exercised great influence.[3]

The functions of the MAI have been executive; the actual business of foreign trade was (after 1951) exclusively carried on by various Foreign Trade Enterprises which are under the general direction of the Ministry. The early structure of Ministry was quite similar to the Ministry of Foreign Trade in the USSR. In the DDR there were the following sections:

1. Hauptabteilung Trade Policy.
   (*a*) Trade with East Bloc.

[1] See Siegfried Dorn, 'Die historische Entwicklung des staatlichen Aussenhandelmonopols und seiner Organisationsformen in der DDR,' *Wissenschaftliche Zeitschrift der Hochschule für Okonomie*, 3/1959, pp. 267–86.

[2] Very little has been written on this Soviet influence during the early years. See Nykryn, et. al., *Organization und Technik des Aussenhandels* (East Berlin: Verlag Die Wirtschaft, 1956) p. 106 or Eberhard Pfuhl, *Rechtsformen, Organization und Technik des sowjetzonalen Aussenhandels* (West Berlin: Heft 16, Berichte des Osteuropa Instituts, Freie Universitaet Berlin, 1954), p. 61. In West Germany, foreign trade was quickly decentralized, especially after the 1948 currency reform, and the Allied military missions had practically no control over foreign trade after 1949.

[3] Schenk, *Die Magie der Planwirtschaft*, *op. cit.* p. 89.

(*b*) Trade with Capitalist countries.
(*c*) Trade with West Germany.

2. (*a*) Hauptabteilung Export (Administers the FTES).
(*b*) Hauptabteilung Import (Administers the FTES).

3. (*a*) Hauptabteilung Planning and Statistics.
(*b*) Hauptabteilung Finance and Foreign Currency.
(*c*) Hauptabteilung General Administration.

At one time in the early years a Hauptabteilung for Control of Trade Contracts also existed. In the USSR, the Ministry of Foreign Trade had the following structure:[1]

1. (*a*) Administration for Trade with European People's Democracies.
(*b*) Administration for Trade with the Far East People's Democracies.
(*c*) Administration for Trade with the Western Capitalist Nations.
(*d*) Administration for Trade with South East Asia and Middle East.

2. (*a*) Export Administration for Manufactured Goods (Administers the FTES).
(*b*) Export Administration for Raw Materials (Administers the FTES).
(*c*) Import Administration for Machinery and Equipment (Administers the FTES).
(*d*) Import Administration for Other Goods (Administers the FTES).

3. (*a*) Planning and Economic Administration.
(*b*) Foreign Exchange Administration.
(*c*) Financial Administration.
(*d*) Trade Agreements and Legal Administration.
(*e*) Transport Administration.
(*f*) General Administration Divisions (there were eight of these Administrations including Personnel, Business, Customs, Inspection, Export Quality Control, Archives, Library, and Accounts).

By 1957 the internal structure of MAI was somewhat different:

1. (*a*) Hauptabteilung Trade with the East Bloc.
(*b*) Hauptabteilung Trade with the Capitalist countries.
(*c*) Hauptabteilung Trade with West Germany.

2. (*a*) Hauptverwaltung Heavy Machinery (Administers FTES).
(*b*) Hauptverwaltung 'Anlagenbau' (Administers FTES).
(*c*) Hauptverwaltung General Machinery (Administers FTES).
(*d*) Hauptverwaltung Mining, Chemicals, Foodstuffs (Administers FTES).
(*e*) Hauptverwaltung Light Industry (Administers FTES).

3. (*a*) Hauptabteilung Planning.
(*b*) Chief Accountant.
(i) Abteilung Finance.
(ii) Abteilung Comptroller.
(iii) Abteilung Price Control.
(*c*) Foreign Currency Group.
(*d*) Hauptabteilung Central Control and Technical Services.
(*e*) Abteilung Legal.
(*f*) Abteilung Transportation.
(*g*) Abteilung Press-Advertising.
(*h*) General Administration.

[1] Norman Scott, Book Review, 'The Organization and Technique of Soviet Foreign Trade,' by P. A. Chervyakov, *Soviet Studies* X, 4/1959, pp. 393–400.

C. Foreign Trade Enterprises (FTES)

The FTES are the enterprises which handle the commercial side of foreign trade and administer the actual movement of goods between domestic and foreign markets. The original models for the FTES of the DDR were the Soviet FTES, which have had the following characteristics:

(*a*) They are complete economic entities, operating on 'economic accounting,' and responsible only to the Ministry of Foreign Trade.

(*b*) They deal only with domestic Ministries, Trusts, and Central Trading Organizations; contact with domestic firms is minimal and primarily indirect.

(*c*) The Director of the individual FTE has complete responsibility for the operation of the FTE and the fulfilling of the FTE plans. Only he and the Chief Accountant are appointed by the Ministry; all other personnel are appointed by the Director or his agents.

There have been three main periods in the history of the FTES in the DDR; the struggle for the establishment of complete state hegemony of foreign trade (1947–52); the shedding of domestic functions and the imitation of the Soviet FTES (1949–54); and deviations from the Soviet model (1953– present).

From 1947 to 1949 the private trading firms and capitalistic enterprises had an appreciable percentage of foreign trade, particularly for exports. Toward the end of this period the private trading firms began to be joined together into special export-import companies which limited their number and permitted greater control over their activities. 'The activity of the private Capitalists in foreign trade reached its high point in 1947–48; with the founding of the (state) Deutsche Handelsgesellschaft, in 1948, the transition period for the elimination of Capitalist elements in foreign trade began. The chief method (for this purpose) was not the expropriation of the Capitalist firms and companies in foreign trade, but rather the granting of trading licences to favour the state enterprises . . .'[1]

The first state FTES were establish in April, 1948, one in each of the Länder to handle the commercial work in trade. They also had a domestic trade function and, therefore, stood both under the authority of the Länder governments and the HVIA. As the Länder government weakened, four central foreign trade enterprises were formed, Fachanstalten Deutscher Aussenhandel (DAHA), with a total capital of 63 million DMOs and authority to sign some contracts, open bank accounts, receive credit, and so forth. These FTES had, however, to receive specific permission from the Ministry to carry on most trade. In March, 1950, the Ministry was given permission to change the structure of these FTES and in the succeeding years, a bewildering series of changes occurred. In the summer of 1951, these DAHA Fachanstalten were, with the inclusion of inter-German trade in their activity, converted into 'Deutscher Innen- und Aussenhandel' (DIAS), organizations of 'public right.' In this same year they received from the Ministry the full-right to conduct all trade with the Capitalist and Socialist countries within the foreign trade plan without specific approval; and the Ministry dropped all of its commercial activities. In 1952, in line with the general reorganization of industry, the DIAS were changed into Volkseigenes Handelsunternehmen (VEH) DIAS, operating under the principles of 'economic accounting,' and with complete legal identity and permission to act as 'trustees of people's property.'[2] In 1956 several new FTES were formed and several others reorganized in a new form, corporations with limited liability, with various production

[1] Dorn, *op. cit.*, The Deutsche Handelszentrale had, at one time, branches in Prague and Budapest. Later it dropped these foreign trade functions.

[2] Under the statute of the new VEH DIAS the Ministry had the right to hire and fire the top directorship of the FTES. Otherwise their legal identity was practically complete.

organs actings as nominal stockholders.[1] Furthermore, several foreign trade companies have the legal form of VEBS. (People's own Factory).

The FTES continued exercising domestic functions until 1954. In imports, before 1952, the DIAS 'on the basis of the foreign trade plans, had to collect the import wishes of innumerable receivers, to oversee the transportation of the imported goods to the end receiver, to arrange for payment with the end receivers, to receive complaints of defects and to manage the corresponding exchange of documents (for these functions)'. Early in 1952 these functions were dropped and the FTES had responsibility for the imported goods only until they reached the borders of the DDR where they were turned over to the various wholesale enterprises or, in exceptional cases, to the direct receiver. Furthermore, the wholesale companies collected the import wishes of the end receivers and the FTES were left to concentrate on buying of the goods abroad and transporting them to the DDR.

In exports, however, the FTES continued to play an important domestic role until 1954. Acting on the basis of the export plans, the FTES had to find producers for the exports, to help the producer find materials to produce these articles, and to sell these goods abroad. Stemming from regulations in December, 1953, and 1954, the production Ministries took over the responsibility of finding domestic producers for the export contracts and supplying them with raw materials.

The export part of the production plan of the ministries and production enterprises was not a legal part of the production plan until 1958, however.

The deviations of the FTES from the original Russian model are described in Chapter IV and need no further comment here.

The number and authority of the various FTES has been in a constant flux over the years. Usually the FTES were organized around the various production sectors (optical and precision equipment, consumer goods, chemicals, etc.) although they were also organized to handle special trade problems (DIA Kompensation, which organized all barter deals), or to trade with geographical special areas (in the USSR, the Vostogentorg company which trades with certain Asian nations; or in the DDR, Gesellschaft Innerdeutschenhandel), or according to the function (the transport companies, insurance companies etc.). Throughout the years there have been a considerable number of proposals to change the organization of the FTES. Some authors have suggested regionally oriented FTES. Other economists have proposed that instead of organizing the FTES around certain production branches they should be grouped around certain selling areas (so that one FTE sells cameras, camera film, and photographic chemicals). The disputes over the proper organization of the FTES are endemic in the DDR foreign trade literature.

The FTES are made up of various 'accounts' (the actual buying and selling groups) and certain 'cross sectional divisions' roughly paralleling those of the Ministry of Foreign Trade.[3] There have been long disputes in the DDR trade literature concerning the ideal internal structure of an FTE.[4]

D. Subsidiary Agencies

These are the other organizations under the general jurisdiction of the Ministry

[1] The first of these limited liability companies (GmbH) actually was Deutsche Buchexport- und Import GmbH, founded in 1953. This, however, was an exception. The main GmbH foreign trade companies were founded in 1956 or 1957.

[2] Wilms, 'Das neue Importverfahren,' *Der Aussenhandel* II, 2/1952, p. 46.

[3] For an organization chart of a typical FTE, see Nykryn *et. al., op. cit.* p. 547.

[4] This literature is quite long and exhausting. A short summary of the discussion may be found in Werner Kusch, 'Zur Struktur in den Aussenhandelsunternehmen,' *Der Aussenhandel*, VIII 24/1958, pp. 839–40.

for Foreign and Inter-German Trade but which maintain a separate legal identity.[1]

1. One set of subsidiary agencies have been set up to stimulate exports:
   (*a*) The main organ for this purpose has been the Chamber of Foreign Trade (Kammer für Aussenhandel), a public organization which was founded in November, 1952. Its functions, as defined by its charter of the organization, include:

   Maintaining and deepening economic relations with foreign economic organizations.

   Advising foreign traders of the DDR on all problems concerning the establishing for foreign trade relations and the carrying through of foreign trade business.

   Receiving foreign trade and economic delegations and sending out such trade delegations to foreign countries.

   Giving out information, material, and reference books concerning trade and economic life of foreign countries to economic organs of the DDR and, on the other hand, sending out such material concerning the DDR to economic organs abroad.

   Co-ordinating DDR advertising abroad.

   Organizing trade fairs and exhibitions in the DDR and sending out exhibitions to trade fairs abroad.

   Issuing certification concerning quality of goods, etc.

   Creating a court for the settling of disputes between foreign trade organizations of the DDR and their partners.

   Originating measurements for bettering the quality of DDR goods sent abroad.

The chief task of the Chamber has been the establishment of economic relations and the signing of trade contracts with Capitalist countries which do not politically recognize the DDR and who would not deal with an 'official' DDR organ. Although members of the Chamber include representatives from various DDR factories and from foreign trade delegations, the Chamber is directed by the Ministry. The most well-known activity of the Chamber is the holding of the bi-annual Leipzig fair.

   (*b*) The German Institute for Market Research (Deutsches Institut für Marktforschung-DIM) was founded in September, 1952, and is the centre for market research of the Capitalist markets. Other agencies also do market research, including the Market and Price Division in the Ministry and sections in the FTES. Nevertheless, the DIM acts as the chief co-ordinator of this work and maintains an extensive library.

   (*c*) Export Committees began to be formed in late 1953 and early 1954 to further exports on the local level. These committees consist of representatives from industry and the FTES, and have the task of hunting out 'export reserves.' By 1957, 140 such committees existed.

   (*d*) Several organs have been formed for the special purposes of co-ordinating advertising of DDR products abroad. These include DEWAG Werbung and Interwerbung.

2. A second group of agencies handles foreign trade transportation:
   (*a*) The main transport organ is VEB Deutscher Transport (Deutrans) founded in January, 1954, taking the place of a Russian-German

[1] The various organs vary quite widely between CMEA countries. For instance, each has a Chamber of Commerce. However, only the CSSR, DDR and USSR have separate market research institutes. In Hungary, Rumania and Poland, this work is carried on in a special division of the Chamber of Commerce, and in Bulgaria, in a division of the Ministry of Foreign Trade.

transportation company called Derutra A.G. and the German company VEB Deutsche Spedition (Deusped).

(*b*) Deufracht (Deutsches Kontor für Seefrachten) was founded in 1951 to administer sea transport of foreign trade. (Encouraging trade with China was the first objective of DKS.) DKS became increasingly important as the possibilities for saving scarce foreign currencies through the establishment of a DDR merchant marine became more apparent to the policy-makers.

(*c*) Deutsche Seereederei was founded to administer the renting of boats for commercial use.

In late 1958, the three transportation agencies were combined into one transportation agency, Deutrans. This was the birth of the 'transportation monopoly.'

3. A third group of agencies may be considered miscellaneous assistance agencies. They include: Deutsche Warenabnahme GmbH, which inspects export goods to see if they pass certain quality tests; Deutsche Ausland und Rüchversicherung A.G. (formerly Schwarzmeer und Ostsee Versicherung), an insurance agency for goods in foreign trade; das Amt für Zoll und Kontrolle des Warenverkehrs (AZKW) which not only levies tariffs on goods entering the DDR[1] but also serves to prevent sabotage and smuggling and so forth.

E. Financial Agencies

The group of state organs connected with foreign currency make up the 'valuta monopoly'. 'The valuta monopoly is an instrument of the Socialistic state to break the power postion of capital and to make possible the planned administration of the economy . . . by eliminating the spontaneous influences of the Capitalist world market from domestic movements of currency, by directing international payment movements, and by planning internal money relations. . . . The valuta monopoly helps to carry out the economic law of Socialism and to protect the sovereignty of the Socialist states.'[2] Other functions of the 'valuta monopoly' include the 'protection of the domestic currency' and the complete control of all foreign securities and monies within the DDR.[3] The financial agencies are:

1. *The Ministry of Finance*. The 'financial planning' comes under the review of the Ministry of Finance, and the Ministry 'is the responsible central organ for foreign currency policies . . . This is due to the necessity . . . and demands of a unified financial system.'[4]

2. *The Deutsche Notenbank* (*DNB*). The DNB is the actual administrator of the foreign currency and, until early 1958, entertained thoughts that it alone was responsible for the foreign currency monopoly. Its power was curbed by a law designating the Minister of Finance as supreme authority for the planning and controlling of Valuta movements.

3. *Deutsche Handelsbank A.G.* (*DHB*). The DHB was founded in February 1956,

[1] Nominal tariffs are levied on all imported goods which are not in the import plan as well as on goods from countries which are unfairly discriminating against DDR goods. Goods from West Germany are freed from all tariffs. Unlike Poland no export tariffs are levied. For details on tariffs, see Nykryn, *et. al.*, *op. cit.*, pp. 203–8.

[2] Karl Hercher, *Der Zahlungsverkehr der DDR mit dem Ausland*, *op. cit.*, p. 19.

[3] Since 1949 it has been illegal to export DMOs. In 1950 and 1951 the Central Bank gained the sole right to own foreign currency and securities. A whole series of currencies laws have been collected by Hercher, *op. cit.*

[4] Hercher, *op. cit*,. p. 21.

to supplement the work of the DNB.[1] It had a total capital of 30,000,000 DMO, all owned by the DNB.

4. *Other Financial Agencies.* During the first years, several other special banks existed for foreign trade. In the immediate post-war years, the SMAD founded the Garantie- und Kreditbank (Garkrebo) which, for a short while, handled all foreign currency transactions. Later the Aussenhandelsabrechnungs Kontor (AAK) and Kontroll- und Finanzkontor (FKF) were founded. All of these organizations were merged into the DNB.

F. Other Agencies in Foreign Trade:

1. The Deutsche Warenvertriebsgesellschaft (successor of Deutsche Ein- und husfuhrgesellschaft) was, according to Western sources, an organization of the SED for import of embargoed materials from Western countries. In 1957 it was disbanded.[2]

2. The Hochschule für Aussenhandel was partially administered by the Ministry (between 1954 and 1958) for the training of foreign trade personnel. This school, in 1958, was merged with the Hochschule für Ökonomie.

3. The Foreign Trade Plans.[3]

There is no single foreign trade plan but rather a series of plans, differing in content and specificity at various levels of the foreign trade hierarchy and in different time periods. Since 1953 the form of the various plans has remained about the same.[4]

The most important parts of the overall yearly plans consist of the following 'partial plans:'

1. Export-import plans. These plans are decided by the State Planning Commission, the MAI and the FTES. They are broken down into 'operative quarters' and were stated in Roubles until 1959. (The DDR was one of the few CMEA nations to draw up trade plans in Roubles rather than in the domestic currency.)[5] The export-import plans consists of several parts:

A. Primary trade plans.

(*a*) Goods/country plan. This is the plan for exported and imported goods, classified in the plan position nomenclature for the broad currency areas (country groups). It is the main co-ordination link between the trade plan and the internal material balances. Contrary to the practice in the USSR and other CMEA nations, this is the plan which is approved by the Council of Ministers as the 'state foreign trade plan.'

(*b*) Country/goods plan. This is the plan for trade with each country, with goods classified in categories much broader than the plan position nomen-

[1] See 'Ueber die Aufgaben der Deutschen Handelsbank A.G.,' *Der Aussenhandel* VI, 5 and 6/1956, p. 174.

[2] Other DDR agencies dealing in illegal trade such as Chemiepha GmbH are described by the IWE, 'Neue DDR Aussenhandelsgesellschaft zur Umgehung der Embargobestimmung gegründet,' *Tagesbericht*, July 27, 1957.

[3] This appendix from material from the following sources: Johannes Rudolph and Gerd Friedrich, Chapter 16, *Grundriss der Volkswirtschaftsplanung, op. cit.*, Nykryn, *et. al.*, *op. cit.*, pp. 220ff.; Rudolf Brauer, *Die Planung der wirtschaftlichen Tatigkeit der volkseigenen Handelsunternehmen Deutscher Innen- und Aussenhandel in der Deutschen Demokratischen Republik, op. cit.;* Karl Hercher, *Der Zahlungsverkehr der DDR mit dem Ausland, op. cit.*, 'Ergebnisse der Planerkonferenz,' *Wirtschaftswissenschaft* VI, 7/1958, pp. 1,040–53.

[4] For historical details of the DDR planning system, see Brauer, *op. cit.*

[5] *Ibid.*, pp. 94ff.

clature. It should be the main co-ordinate link between the trade plan and the trade contracts with each nation. Although this is the 'state foreign trade plan' for the USSR and many other CMEA nations, it has been quite neglected in the DDR. Indeed, until 1953 the country/goods plan came after the trade contracts were signed and until 1955 the FTEs did not really work out such a plan. Even in 1955 and 1956 this plan was quite secondary, although it was generally realized that these plans should form the basis of the trade contract discussions.

(*c*) Delivery/goods plan. This is the plan which specifies the factories producing the exported goods. It serves as the basis for making operational contracts between the FTEs and domestic firms.

(*d*) Receiver/goods plan. This is the plan specifying the domestic receivers of imports. It was discontinued in 1956.

B. Secondary trade plans.

(*a*) Plan for manufacturing on consignment (Lohnveredlung). The DDR does enough processing and manufacturing from raw materials and intermediate items to warrant constant mention and a special plan. No data are available on the amount of this special trade but one East German economist told me that it amounted to 'less than 5 per cent of total trade.'

(*b*) Plan for re-exports. This is another small item which is, nevertheless, constantly mentioned. One DDR economist told me that the re-exports play 'a certain role' in the balancing of trade with single countries.

(*c*) Plan for 'other movements of goods.' This is never explained in the literature and probably consists of trade of illegal goods and goods of military importance, such as uranium ore from Wismut A.G. (a mixed DDR-USSR concern).

2. Service plan: The service plan (in Roubles) consists of two parts, the commercial services plan which is drawn up by the FTEs and the MAI, and the non-commercial services plan which is drawn up by the Ministry of Finance.

3. Foreign currency plan: This plan (in Roubles) is drawn up by the Ministry of Finance and consists of three main parts: current operations (exports-imports, foreign currency bonuses, etc.); services (commercial and non-commercial); and credits to and from foreign countries.[1] The credit plan does not include commercial trade credits, however, and the export-import plan does not include compensation exchange (which until 1955, formed an appreciable part of DDR trade). Because of these and other peculiarities, the trade plan of the MAI and the foreign currency plan of the Ministry of Finance have often been quite discrepant. As I indicate in the text, one of the goals of the 'complex planning' movement of 1957–59 was to eliminate such differences. Another part of the foreign currency plan gives certain norms for the turnover rate of the foreign currencies.

4. Other plans: These plans are stated in DMs and include:

A. Finance plans.

1. Preisausgleich plan. This is the plan which links the prices on the foreign markets with home prices, and shows the amount of trade subsidies or profits.

2. Credit plans. The overwhelming part of the circulating capital of the FTEs is financed from the DNB through a quite complicated system. In 1953 there were five or six different types of credits which were granted the FTEs; in later years some of these complications were eliminated and the FTEs were given unlimited credit for some activities.

3. Cost of administration plan.

4. Cash on hand plan.

[1] Dieter Kuhne, *System und Organization der Valutaplanung und Bilanzierung in der DDR* (Diplomarbeit, Hochschule für Ökonomie).

B. Transport plan for foreign trade.

C. Internal administration plans. For the FTES these include:

1. Development plans (the investment, general repair, and 'technical-organizational plans').

2. Material plans (these specify materials and cost of materials used in trading and are not very important).

3. Work force plans (these include wage, work performance, and personnel training plans).

4. Culture and social plans (these include health and social, safety, building protection, etc. plans).

The long run plans are a great deal less detailed than the annual plans. Economists in East Berlin told me that the long-range trade plan in the first and second Five-Year Plans consisted of 'primary trade plans.' In the Seven-Year Plan, finance and transportation plans were added.

APPENDIX D

STANDING COMMISSIONS OF THE CMEA

1. STRUCTURE OF CMEA[1]

The Council Plenum is the highest organ of the CMEA and meets, by statute, at least twice a year in the different capitals of the member nations. The country delegations are usually composed of the Foreign Trade Minister and/or the Planning Chairman with other Ministers and party functionaries as advisers. The Plenum receives recommendations from the Representatives Council, and, in turn, makes recommendations to the member governments.

The Council Centre has two parts, the Council of Representatives and the Secretariat. These organs are located permanently in Moscow and have a total staff of about 100 employees from the various member countries.

The Council of Representatives consists of one representative from each country. It directs the Secretariat and other subordinate organs and works out policy proposals to be considered at the Council Plena. The Secretariat, headed by N. Feddejew (a Russian) and two assistants, does the actual administrative work of the Council and represents the CMEA at various East Bloc conferences.

The Standing Commissions for Economic, Scientific, and Technical Mutual Aid are located in the various capitals of the member countries and usually consist of ministry representatives. These Commissions have three main functions; to exchange technical information and to direct the all-Bloc research projects; to make standardization and specialization recommendations; and to work out recommendations for long-range plan co-ordination in their respective industrial sectors.

2. STANDING COMMISSIONS[2]

Most of the Standing Commissions were set up after the seventh Council Plenum in Berlin, May 1956. Since then, several more have been added and others have been combined. The Standing Commissions in 1961–62 were:

(*a*) Coal Commission, located in Warsaw and set up after the Seventh Plenum. The Commission has worked out plans to eliminate imports of cokes from the West, set up Bloc energy balances up to 1965, and investigated new methods of mining.

(*b*) Electricity Commission, located in Moscow and set up after the Seventh Plenum (although an ad hoc committee had existed before). The Commission has worked on the Danube River development project and the all-Bloc electricity network project, has investigated the production of electricity by atomic energy, and has made suggestions for the production of power producing equipment.

(*c*) Oil and Gas Commission, located in Bucharest, and set up after the Seventh Plenum. Until 1958 the only active members were the Rumanian and

[1] This description of the CMEA covers the period up to 1962; since then, changes have been made which, unfortunately, cannot be analysed.

[2] See 'Dokumentation' *Der Aussenhandel* X, 11/1960, pp. 33–6, for 1959 Statutes.

[3] For greater information on the work of the Commissions, see *Der Aussenhandel* X, 4 & 5/1960, pp. 5–7; 'Work of the Commissions of the CMEA,' *Current Digest of the Soviet Press* XIII, November 8, 1961, p. 18; and various communiques of the Commissions which are being published with increasing frequency in *Der Aussenhandel*, *Vneshniaia Torgovlia*, and PAP *Polish Economic Survey*.

Russian representatives, but afterwards great interest was focused on the work of this Commission because of the plans for the oil pipeline between Russia and East Europe and the building of large petro-chemical factories in the CSSR, DDR, Hungary and Poland.

(*d*) Ferrous Metals Commission, located in Moscow, and set up after the Seventh Plenum. The Commission has discussed, among other topics, the all-Bloc steel plans until 1975, specialization measures in rolled steel and other products, and the proposed Silesian iron-steel combine.

(*e*) Non-Ferrous Metals Commission, located in Budapest, and set up after the Seventh Plenum. Specialization measures have been the main theme of discussion and research.

(*f*) Chemicals Commission, located in Berlin, and set up after the Seventh Plenum.[1] This Commission has been especially active and has co-ordinated the 1960–75 national plans of the chemicals industry for the whole Bloc. The guideline of this plan provides for the setting up of basic sulphuric acid, chlorine, ammonia, nitrogen fertilizer, and plastic and resin factories in every country. Each country will also, it is foreseen, specialize in specific chemical products. Since it is planned for each country to have the same chemicals base, plans have been prepared for standardized factories. The Commission has also directed great attention toward specialization in the construction of machinery for the chemicals industry.

(*g*) Machine Building Commission, located in Prague, and set up after the Seventh Plenum (although an active ad hoc committee had previously existed). This Commission has made comparisons of machine performance, specialization recommendations, and standardization suggestions. As indicated in the text, the early work of the Commission was not entirely successful.

(*h*) Agriculture Commission, located in Sofia, and set up after the Seventh Plenum.[2] With the goal of agricultural independence from the West, the Commission has had a wide range of activity, including the direction of all-Bloc agriculture research projects; co-ordinating the work of various national agricultural institutes; making specialization measures; testing agricultural machinery; testing various chemicals for agriculture; and encouraging the exchange of information concerning experiences in administration of agricultural co-operatives and kolkhoses. It has also directed research on the storing and processing of agricultural products.

(*i*) Foreign Trade Commission, located in Moscow and set up after the Seventh Plenum (the former Complete Factories Commission was merged with the Foreign Trade Commission). In 1957 this Commission worked out a new general trade contract to contain the commercial conditions for intra-Bloc trade and has made suggestions to improve the way intra-Bloc trade is carried out.

(*j*) Economic Questions Commission, located in Moscow and set up after the Ninth Plenum. As indicated in the text, this Commission has worked on problems of price setting for intra-Bloc trade, methods for comparison of production costs, standard nomenclatures for statistical reporting, and the setting of realistic exchange rates.[3]

[1] For a detailed report of the Commission's work, as well as of the thirteen or so Bloc conferences on various aspects of the chemicals industry, see Ernst Liening, 'Die Zusammenarbeit der Ostblockländer auf dem Chemiesektor,' *Ost-Europa Wirtschaft* V, 1/1960, pp. 112–19.

[2] In the June 1962 Plenum, the CMEA set up Standing Commissions for Statistics and for Co-ordination of Scientific and Technical Research as well as a Standardization Institute.

[3] See especially, 'Aus der Arbeit einiger Standiger Kommissionen der RGW,' *op. cit.* and Lothar Rouscik, 'Die Ermittlung des ökonomischen Nutzeffektes der sozialistischen internationalen Arbeitsteilung,' *Der Aussenhandel* X, 15/1960, pp. 19–24.

(*k*) Transportation Commission, located in Warsaw, and set up after the Ninth Plenum in July, 1958 (although an ad hoc committee had existed before). The Commission has discussed the joint canal projects and standardization in transportation projects. The relation of the Commission to other East Bloc transportation commissions, e.g. the Organization for Mutual Work in Railways (OSZD) is not known.[1]

(*l*) Building Industry Commission. For details, see below.

(*m*) Light and Foodstuffs Industry Commission, located in Prague, and set up after the Tenth Plenum in December, 1958 (taking over part of the work of the former Wood, Cellulose and Light Industry Commission which was located in Budapest). This Commission has co-ordinated research work in the shoe and leather industries, and has made recommendations in the textile industry.

(*n*) Commission for Peaceful Uses of Atomic Energy, location unknown, and set up after the Thirteenth Plenum in August, 1960.[2]

3. A COMMISSION AT WORK: THE STANDING COMMISSION FOR THE BUILDING INDUSTRY[3]

The Standing Commission for the Building Industry was set up after the Ninth CMEA Plenum (June, 1958) and is located at the Ministerium für Bauwesen in East Berlin. The Commission is guided by the DDR State Secretary Kosol and directed by Herr Schneider-Ratus, both of whom are architects (the former was a long time resident in Russia). Twenty permanent employees, primarily engineers and architects, carry on the actual administrative tasks of the Commission, supplemented by special committees for specific problems. The Commission is divided into five sections:

A. Economics Sections. This section has:

Studied the methods of planning of building on country, area, and enterprise levels for each country.

Studied the price setting procedures and calculation of buildings costs for each country.

Studied the premia systems in the building industry for each country.

Studied the economic profitability (Nutzeffekt) in building. The work in this field is just beginning and, in the future, will be focused on three aspects of the problem: (1) the overall judgments of the project (function and construction of project, basic economic coefficients like cost/square foot, and so forth); (2) mechanization of production; (3) maintenance costs. In August 1960, an all-Bloc conference was held in Leipzig to work out standard methods of computing profitability and several types of capital/output ratios were adopted. A standard nomenclature for the classification of building projects was also approved.

B. Building Industry Section

One project of this Section has been a calculation of the demand for building

[1] For the activity of these other transportation committees, see Klinkmüller and Ruban, *op. cit.*, pp. 194–202.

[2] For more details on co-operation in atomic research in the Bloc see Albert Jeromin, 'Internationale Zusamenarbeit auf dem Gebiet der friedlichen Anwendung der Atomenergie,' *Deutsche Aussenpolitik* II, 11/1957, pp. 960–7.

[3] Material from Lammert, 'Fünf Sektionen für Fragen des Bauwesens,' *Die Wirtschaft* XV, 9/1960, p. 13, from notes on the Commission in *Der Aussenhandel* X, 23–24/1960, and from an interview with an East Berlin economist. On several points the interviewee differed from the published materials and, in these cases. I have taken his word. When I speak of 'the Bloc' I mean primarily the East Central European countries. The extent of Soviet participation is unknown.

in all Bloc countries until 1965. Another project was the investigation of machines for the building industry and the making of production specialization recommendations. For instance, at the beginning of 1960, the various Bloc countries (I am not sure if the USSR is included here) produced 40 different types of revolving tower cranes. The Section has proposed that the number be reduced to nine basic types.

C. Building Materials Section

Since most building materials are extremely heavy and/or bulky and may be optimally produced in relatively small amounts, the need for specialization of production of building materials is not very pressing. Some five year all-Bloc material balances have been made for special cements, etc. but the section has concerned itself primarily with production problems of building materials. In November, 1959, a large conference of experts was held in Brno to discuss cement production technology and to work out unified norms, e.g. for use of energy for cement production. The Section has also investigated possibilities of introducing new building materials.

D. Building Plans, Norms, and Standardization Section

This Section has worked out recommendations for the production and use of finished building parts and pre-stressed concrete units. In connection with the recommendations of the Chemicals Industry Commission concerning Bloc production of chemicals from 1960–75, the Section drew up plans for several types of standard chemical plans and/or module units for these plants. Several all-Bloc conferences on 'Typenprojektierung' have been sponsored. In a conference in Leningrad in the autumn of 1959 work groups were set up to draw up unified international measurements for building.

E. Area and City Planning Section

I have been able to find out very little about the work of this Section. Since this is a very new field for the DDR, I believe that the primary work of this section has been the exchange of experiences and methods.

My East German interviewee felt that the greatest difficulty for the various Sections has been deriving adequate measurements for international comparisons. In attacking this problem, Commission members have studied the methods employed by the West European Iron and Steel Community (Schuman Plan) and other Western international agencies. In the building industry two main problems have arisen.

Comparison of output. As of 1961 there was no complete overall nomenclature for building in the Bloc, and the Commission has been working on the problem.

Comparison of inputs. Here the many difficulties in the measurement of costs have come up. My interviewee felt that Western commentators have overemphasized the difficulties caused by different price structures and cost measuring procedures in the various Bloc countries. Nevertheless, instead of trying to obtain one or two overall measurements of cost, the usual procedure in the Commission has been to compare a series of coefficients of production, expressed primarily in physical terms. For instance, in comparisons of production of cement and concrete, some of the various coefficients from the DDR, CSSR and Hungary were:

Capital/output ratios.
'Self cost' of production.
Production of factory per 'capacity unit'.
Productivity per production worker (m^3 of concrete/man, etc.)

Cement per cubic metre of concrete.
Energy necessary per m^3 concrete.
Steam necessary per m^3 cement.
Hours necessary to make one cubic metre of cement, concrete.
Space requirements.

4. EVALUATION OF WORK OF THE COMMISSION

Without having more specific information on what the Commission has done, it is difficult to judge its competence. Such considerations aside, perhaps the most valuable accomplishment of the Commission has been a communications function of bringing together the representatives from the Building Ministries of the various Bloc countries on a permanent basis for a continual exchange of information and experiences.

APPENDIX E

CMEA SPECIALIZATION AGREEMENTS[1]

1. ALBANIA

Mining Products
Chromium ore

Agricultural Products
Fruits and vegetables
Early potatoes

2. BULGARIA

Mining Products
Sulphur
Lead ore
Zinc ore
Copper ore
Uranium ore

Heavy Industrial Equipment
Oil drilling equipment

General Industrial Equipment
Industrial sewing machines
Machine Tools such as simple lathes

Agricultural Equipment
Machinery for vegetable and fruit harvesting
Other agricultural machinery such as trailer combines (only for own needs)

Ships
Ships from 1,000 to 5,000 GRT

Electro-technical Equipment
Transformers
Electrical motors
Automatic telephone equipment
Storage batteries

Agricultural Products
Fruits
Vegetables
Tobacco
Early potatoes

[1] Source: Heinz Koehler, *East Germany's Economic Integration into the Communist Bloc*, *op. cit.*, pp. 131–41.

Products which are definitely known to be produced by a single country are indicated by an asterisk although absence of an asterisk does not necessarily mean that the item is produced by more than one country.

Koehler's list is in no sense exhaustive, but it is the longest available from reliable sources. A more extensive compilation from unofficial sources may be found in *10 Jahre RGW* (Informationsbuero West, *Sonderdienst*, Berlin: 1959) as well as various issues of the *Tagesdienst* of the same organization.

3. CZECHOSLOVAKIA

Mining Products

Soft coal
Uranium ore

Chemical Products

Benzol
Xylene
Naphthalene

Heavy Industrial Equipment

Equipment for cement factories with a furnace capacity up to 800 tons per day
Equipment for rolling mills such as coarse section iron rolling mill trains, iron mill trains, wire rod mill trains, medium and fine sheet metal rolling mills
Equipment for the coal industry such as multi-bucket excavators, stackers, overburden transporter bridges, as well as soft coal refining equipment
Heavy equipment for forging and pressing
Specialized machine tools for making ball-bearings, lathes, drills
Equipment for sugar factories
Blast furnaces
Large marine diesels
Large long distance gas-pipes

General Industrial Equipment

Equipment for the shoe and leather industry
Equipment for the printing industry
Equipment for the chemicals industry
Heavy caterpillar tractors
Equipment for the textile industry such as jet looms for wool and synthetic fibre machines

Agricultural Equipment

30 H.P. tractors
Caterpillar tractors
Dairy industry equipment
Equipment for cattle raising
Sugar beet combines
Flax combines

Vehicles

Rolling stock such as 2,500 kw electric trains and heavy long distance diesel locomotives
Cars, in particular 4 cylinder passenger cars
Heavy trucks above 3·5 tons
Buses, 4 tons
Specialized means of transport

Electro-technical Equipment

Small hydraulic specialized steam turbines below 100MW
Mercury rectifiers
Specialized generators
Gas turbines
Transistor radios
Refrigerators
Medium sized vacuum cleaners
Mobile power stations
High pressure aggregates

4. DDR

Mining Products

Potassium salts
Uranium ore
Lignite

Metallurgical Products

Products for the second processing stage of steel mills such as sheet metal and drawing die mill products, all cold rolled
Zinc
Nickel
Magnesium (after 1965)

Chemical Products

Calcine soda
Plastics
Synthetic fibres
Synthetic rubber
Solvents
Polyvinylchloride

Heavy Industrial Equipment

Highly mechanized automatic precision machine tools such as duplicating milling machines*, honing machines*, thread grinding machines*, gear hobbing machines*, pipe cutters*, pipe thread cutters*, ball and roller bearing machine tools*, lathes
Equipment for cement factories with a furnace capacity of 1,000–2,000 tons per day and more
Long-distance gas-pipes (small)
Equipment for rolling mills such as continuous and semicontinuous wire rod mill trains*, leaf-metal and tube rolling mill trains*, fine section iron rolling mill trains and drawing die mill trains
Equipment for the lignite industry such as multi-bucket excavators for open pit mining, briquette factories, over burden transporter bridges, stackers, conveyor bridges*, rotary bucket excavators with a cutting power of 80 kg per cm
Light equipment for forging and pressing
Equipment for sugar factories
Large marine diesels, 4–5,000 H.P.

General Industrial Equipment

Equipment for the knitwear industry
Equipment for the chemicals industry such as chemical fibre machines
Equipment for fish processing
Equipment for lifting and transporting
Equipment for the printing industry
Textile machines especially for cotton

Agricultural Equipment

Sugar beet combines
Potato combines
Grain combines
Dairy industry equipment
Equipment for cattle pig raising 15 H.P. tractors
Meat industry equipment

Electro-technical Equipment
Radio transmitters and receivers
Measuring equipment
Transformers
Small hydraulic specialized steam turbines, esp. 32 and 50 MW
Large generators
Railway signalling equipment
Refrigerators
Small and large vacuum cleaners
Gas turbines
High pressure aggregates

Ships
Sea freighters up to 15,000 GRT, especially 3,000 and 10,000 GRT
Ships with atomic power

Vehicles
Rolling stock such as 900–1,800 H.P. steam locomotives (to be later discontinued), 900–1,800 diesel locomotives, double-decker passenger cars*, refrigerator cars*, dining cars, sleeping cars
Cars, such as two cylinder cars
Light trucks up to 3·5 tons

Precision Engineering and Optical Products
Calculating machines
Accounting machines
Electric typewriters
Mirrow reflex cameras
Movie cameras and projectors

5. HUNGARY

Mining Products
Bauxite

Metallurgy
Aluminium

Heavy Industrial Equipment
Equipment for aluminium production
Equipment for rolling mills such as wire rod mill trains
Specialized machine tools such as open front vertical drills
Diesel engines (excluding marine diesels)

Agricultural Equipment
Corn combines
Grain combines
Meat industry equipment
Equipment for cattle and poultry raising
Caterpillar tractors

Vechicles
Buses above four tons
Trucks
Rolling stock, especially sleeping cars and specialized diesel locomotives (such as for the mining industry), motor trains*

Electro-technical Equipment
Generating sets
Voltage decomposition machines
Railway signalling equipment

Gas turbines
High pressure aggregates
Telephone and telegraph equipment

Agricultural Products
Early potatoes
Rice
Fruits and vegetables

6. POLAND

Mining Products
Sulphur
Coal
Zinc

Metallurgy
Products of the first processing stage of steel mills

Chemical Products
Calcine soda
Benzol
Xylene
Naphthalene

Heavy Industrial Equipment
Equipment for the coal industry including equipment for coal combines, open pit lignite, coking plants
Rolling mill equipment such as fine section iron mill trains, small rolling mill trains
4,000–5,000 H.P. ship diesel engines
Complete factories for light reinforced concrete
Specialized machine tools such as complete wheel set machining lathes, horizontal presses up to 250 tons, cold pressure automatics, horizontal face plate lathes, roller grinding machines, toothed-wheel grinding machines for ball-bearings
Heavy forge-presses
Blast furnaces
Equipment for sugar factories

General Industrial Equipment
Cables and ropes
Small mining machines
Textile machines especially for wool

Agricultural Machines
Potato combines
One type of grain combine
Flax combines
Equipment for pig and poultry raising

Ships
Sea-going vessels, especially from 1,000 to 5,000 GRT and 15,000–25,000 tdw and specialized ships

Vehicles
Rolling stock such as sleeping cars, coach cars for wide gauge, steam locomotives, tank cars, self-unloading freight cars
Cars
Lorries up to five tons
Buses of four tons
One axle tractors

Electro-technical Equipment
Steam turbines under 100 MW, especially 25 MW
Medium generators
220 kw transformers

7. RUMANIA

Mining Products
Oil

Chemical Products
Sulphur
Soot
Calcine soda
Caustic soda
Oil products

Heavy Industrial Equipment
Equipment for cement factories with a furnace capacity of 400–450 tons per day
Equipment for oil drilling and refining
Specialized machine tools such as knee and column type milling machines, transverse planing machines, long planing machines with wide bench
Long-distance gas pipes

Agricultural Machines
Corn combines
Machinery for vegetable and fruit harvesting
37 H.P. tractors

Ships
Ships from 1,000–5,000 GRT

Vehicles
Rolling stock especially 1,200 H.P. steam locomotives (to be later discontinued), 1,200 H.P. diesel locomotives

Agricultural Products
Fruits and vegetables
Early potatoes

8. SOVIET UNION

Mining Products
Potassium salts
Apetite ores and concentrates
Sulphur
Raw phosphates
Soft coal
Oil

Metallurgy
Products of the first processing stage of steel mills

Chemical Products
Synthetic rubber
Benzol
Naphthalene
Xylene
Plastics

Heavy Industrial Equipment
Equipment for oil drilling and refining
Equipment for cement factories with a furnace capacity of 1,000–2,000 tons per day and more
Equipment for coal industry such as single-bucket excavators and shovel excavators for open pit mining, coking plants, coal combines, coal cutting machines
Equipment for rolling mills such as coarse section iron rolling mill trains, heavy rolling mill trains
Equipment for forging and pressing
Specialized machine tools such as turret head lathes, long planing machines, machine tools for ball-bearings
Blast furnaces
Very large long-distance gas lines

General Industrial Equipment
Equipment for the printing industry
Small mining machines
Equipment for the textile industry, especially synthetic fibre equipment

Agricultural Equipment
Equipment for pig raising

Ships
Sea-going vessels, all sizes, often specialized such as tankers and ships with atomic power.

Vehicles
Rolling stock, in particular 4,000 and above H.P. diesel locomotives
Passenger cars

Electro-technical Equipment
Steam turbines above 100MW*
Railway signalling equipment
Large generators

Agricultural Products
Land-intensive items

APPENDIX F

A TRADITIONAL FOREIGN TRADE MECHANISM AND TRADE OF A BLOC NATION

During the last 200 years or so, a great many Western economists have discussed how unbalanced trade generates forces which affect future trade in such a way that exports and imports are brought into alignment through price and income effects. In the mechanism relying on relative changes in price levels as the equilibrating force (sometimes called the gold-specie mechanism) the three basic assumptions are: unbalanced trade will affect the money supply; changes in the money supply will affect domestic prices; a change in domestic prices, relative to world prices, will affect exports and imports in such a way that trade will become balanced. In this Appendix, I examine these assumptions in the context of intra-Bloc trade.

1. EFFECT OF TRADE ON THE MONEY SUPPLY

The effects of trade on the money supply are transmitted through the Preisausgleich which, as I noted in Chapter IV, is the main financial link in Soviet-type economies between domestic and foreign prices. The net Preisausgleich (PAG) is the net profit, or loss, in foreign trade transactions of the FTES and is part of the state budget. Some idea of the size of the PAG may be gained from the following data for the DDR.

TABLE F–1

TRADE AND PREISAUSGLEICH IN THE DDR (BILLION CURRENCY UNITS)[1]

Year	*Trade Turnover Roubles*	*(Exports+Imports) Roubles converted to DMs by official exchange rates*	*Preisausgleich DMs*
1951	5·3	4·4	1·4
1952	6·0	5·0	1·2
1953	7·8	6·5	2·1
1954	9·5	5·3	3·8
1955	9·8	5·4	3·8
1956	11·0	6·1	—
1957	13·7	7·6	3·0
1958	14·3	7·9	1·1
1959	16·5	9·1	1·2

[1] Trade turnover in domestic prices cannot be obtained by subtracting the PAG from the foreign trade turnover obtained from Rouble data since exports and imports must be treated separately. Using ECE estimates of PAG for exports and imports separately, the PAG was about 40 per cent of the trade turnover in domestic prices in 1951 and about 25 per cent in 1955.

PAG data through 1954 are actual figures; PAG data from 1955 to 1959 are plan figures.

Sources: Trade data from various DDR *Statistische Jahrbuecher*. PAG data for years 1951 through 1954 from Volkmar Girke, *Die Stellung des Aussenhandels im System der*

Several Characteristics of the PAG must be noted:

A. The exchange rate has almost no effect on the total Preisausgleich as long as trade, measured in foreign prices, is balanced. (See Chapter IV, footnote [1].)[1]

B. The primary cause of the Preisausgleich is the difference in domestic and foreign price structures.[2] Therefore, changes in the net PAG can come about for three reasons:

1. Changes in the prices obtained or paid on the world market.

2. Changes in the domestic prices due either to changes in the tax structure, in the profit structure, or in actual production costs.

3. Changes in the overall commodity structure or volume of trade.[3]

C. Due to the above factors a change in the balance of trade, measured in foreign prices, is not necessarily reflected by a corresponding change in the Preisausgleich or in the balance of trade, measured in domestic prices.[4]

D. Due to the existence of the Preisausgleich trade measured in foreign prices may be balanced while trade measured in domestic prices may not be balanced. Therefore, balanced trade (measured in foreign prices) may affect the money supply while unbalanced trade (similarly measured) may not. Whether the actual PAG does affect the money supply or not depends on whether other parts of the government budget compensate for the positive or negative PAG, i.e. if the treasury can meet this expenditure for a negative PAG without deficit financing.[5]

Geldakkumulation in der Volkswirtschaft der DDR (Diplomarbeit, Hochschule für Ökonomie, 1960), p. 12. PAG data for 1955 through 1957 from Hellmuth Kalus, *Wirtschaftszahlen aus der SBZ* (Bonn: Bundesministerium fuer gesamtdeutsche Fragen, 1958), pp. 94–7. PAG data for 1958 and 1959 from Heinz Köhler in a personal letter. Several Western sources have estimated PAG data for exports and imports separately including Klinkmüller, *op. cit.*; Kalus, *op. cit.*; *Economic Survey of Europe for 1957* (I was told in East Berlin that these data are very good); and *Der Aussenhandel der SBZ 1953, Plan 1954 und 1. Halbjahr 1954* (Bonn: Bundesministerium fuer gesamtdeutsche Fragen, 1954).

[1] Some goods are valued on a cost-plus basis, converted to Roubles via the official exchange rate and, therefore their foreign price changes as the exchange rate changes. Thus, the overall PAG changes. Nevertheless, I believe that the amount of this trade of cost-plus goods, at least in the last few years, has been small.

[2] Since every Bloc nation has followed the example of Russia and has relatively underpriced production goods and overpriced consumer goods, it is logical to suspect that the more underdeveloped Bloc nations which export raw materials and import consumer goods would show a positive PAG and that the more developed nations which have an opposite trade structure would have a negative PAG. The situation is not so simple. Unless one were quite familiar with the trade pattern and price structure of the various nations, a definite prediction on the sign and size of the Preisausgleich is difficult to make. For comments on Hungarian and Albanian PAGs, see ECE, 'Developments in Foreign Trade of Eastern Europe and the Soviet Union,' *Economic Survey of Europe for 1957*, p. VI–29.

[3] The actual effects of some of these factors on the DDR Preisausgleich are discussed by Klinkmüller, *op. cit.*, Statistical Appendices.

[4] This phenomenon was predicted in several early theoretical analyses of Bloc foreign trade by Edward Ames ('International Trade without Markets: The Soviet Bloc Case,' *American Economic Review* XLIV, 5/1954, pp. 791–807; and 'Soviet Bloc Currency Conversions,' *American Economic Review* XLIV, 3/1954, pp. 339–53).

[5] From the remarks of Franklyn D. Holzman, 'Some Financial Aspects of Soviet Foreign Trade,' *Comparisons of the United States and Soviet Economies* (Washington, D.C.: Joint Economic Committee, Congress of the United States, 1959), Part II, pp. 427–43, one might infer that even when tax revenues cover a negative Preisausgleich, an inflationary pressure is created when the labour costs of producing exports

Similarly, a change in the PAG would not cause a change in the money supply if correspondingly opposite changes occur in another sector. For instance, the domestic taxes on an exported product might be raised which, in turn, would raise the domestic price of the good. Although the foreign trade enterprise would have to pay more for this good and, therefore, receive a greater subsidy from the government (or obtain a lower net profit), this rise in the negative PAG (or fall in the positive PAG) would be compensated by a rise in government tax revenues; and the domestic money supply would remain unaffected.

If the government budget (including the PAG) is so planned that an overall monetary equilibrium will be maintained, then 'trade affects the money supply' only in so far as actual trade and PAG differ from plan goals. For instance, let us suppose that the overall import and export goals (measured in world market prices) are fulfilled. Trade acts to increase the planned money supply if the PAG plan is underfulfilled, i.e., when the FTEs earn less net profit or receive greater net subsidies than planned. This could occur for many reasons, e.g., an unplanned change in the structure of trade, or a fall in the world market price of exports so that more domestic products were required to obtain a certain unit of foreign exchange, etc. If an unplanned import surplus (measured in foreign market prices) occurs, there would probably be an unplanned decrease in the money supply although this could be offset by an unplanned change in the structure of trade so that the PAG plan would be still underfulfilled. Overall inflationary or deflationary pressures can only be analysed when information about plans and plan fulfilment in other sectors, particularly the physical production plan, are known.

2. THE EFFECTS OF A CHANGE OF THE MONEY SUPPLY ON PRICES

In the early post-war years the unplanned increases in the money supply led to general price rises. Since about 1953 it seems as if the planners in all nations have preferred suppressed rather than open inflation. Since then, excess liquidity in all Bloc countries has been mopped up by means of currency reforms, or blocked bank balances, or increased production and I believe that these methods will be continued to be used in the future. Therefore, the main effect of unbalanced trade on future trade is through a change in the money supply directly, rather than through a change in domestic prices.

3. THE EFFECTS OF THE MONEY SUPPLY ON TRADE[1]

The direct effects of an unplanned in crease in the money supply depend on where this money is located in the economic system.

---

per unit of imports decreases. (See esp. p. 429.) This is not true and may be easily demonstrated:

(a) Domestic value of exports (V_e) = labour costs (L) + turnover taxes (T_t) = real consumption by workers in export industries (C) + other taxes (T_o) + T_t.

(b) World market value of exports = V_e + Preisausgleich for exports (PAG_e).

(c) World market value of imports = domestic value of imports (V_i)—Preisausgleich for imports (PAG_i).

Assuming that the external value of exports and imports is balanced and that total negative (positive) Preisausgleich equals total tax surplus (deficit), we find that $C = P_i$; that is, that the amount spent by the workers in the export industries equals the internal value of the imported goods. In other words, no matter how much the real value of exports (in domestic prices) changes, there is no inflationary or deflationary effect or addition or subtraction from the money supply as long as trade is balanced (measured in foreign prices) and tax revenues cover the negative Preisausgleich.

[1] Since inflationary and deflationary forces are symmetric in essential aspects, and since East Bloc nations have suffered continually from suppressed inflation, I will, in the above discussion, analyse only the pressures of excess liquidity on trade.

Unplanned bank balances of the FTES, resulting from an unplanned profit due to price changes on the world market, etc., have very little economic effect in Soviet-type economies. All foreign currency must be given to the Central Bank which discourages above-plan imports. The excess profits (in domestic currency units) must either be spent or returned to the treasury at the end of the quarter or year. However, it is difficult for the FTES to buy goods on the domestic market for above-plan exports except those goods whose production targets have been exceeded.

The effect of unplanned monetary balances in the manufacturing sector depends on the planning and control of the money supply by the banking system. Some Bloc nations have a very alert and active banking system which takes these unplanned balances immediately away (under the general laws for 'control of the Rouble,' 'control of the Zloty,' etc.) If the enterprise is allowed to keep these above-plan balances, then this money remains in the manufacturing sector until: (a) it is transferred to the consumer sector by means of higher wages, etc.; (b) it is used in obtaining above-plan imports; (c) it is used in buying goods which were destined for exports. However, permission is extremely difficult to receive for above-plan imports; and absorption of planned exports by the domestic economy is prevented in most Bloc nations by giving the FTES greater economic power than domestic enterprises via special priority laws and so forth. Excess liquidity in the manufacturing sector usually remains in the sector until the end of the quarter or year when all extra funds are turned in to the treasury.

Excess liquidity in the consumer sector has few direct effects on trade. 'Above-plan consumer imports' are difficult if not impossible to obtain and spending domestic currency abroad through personal travel and so forth is limited by special exchange restrictions. It is difficult for the consumers to obtain domestic goods destined for exports for the reasons mentioned above. Therefore, the only effect of unplanned consumer balances on trade are indirect, e.g., the effect on trade when consumers substitute leisure for work which, in turn, might adversely affect production.

4. CONCLUSIONS

From this brief survey it should be clear that the 'automatic mechanism' of market economies generated by a trade imbalance is prevented from exercising much influence in trade decisions in a Soviet-type economy. This does not mean, however, that chronic deficit or credit positions are allowed to occur. Due to the limited foreign currency reserves and the special intra-Bloc payment arrangements discussed in Chapter VI, the foreign trade authorities have great incentives to use every possible measure to avoid a chronic import surplus.

STATISTICAL APPENDIX A

FOREIGN TRADE PRICE DATA[1]

1. CHOICE OF STATISTICS

Comparison of value and quantity statistics from the various OEEC and CMEA nations is almost impossible. The CMEA nations' statistics use different commodity classification systems, different physical measurements, and are a great deal less detailed. By early 1960 only four CMEA nations had published enough data to even derive very meaningful average unit prices. For the statistics in the text, I have used the following sources:

Russia: *Vneshniaia Torgovlia za 1956 god; . . . 1957 god; and . . . 1958 god* (Moscow: 1958, 1959).

Bulgaria: *Statistcheski Godishnik na Narodna Republika Bulgaria* (Sofia; 1957); *Statisticheski Sbornik 1958–59* (Sofia, 1960) (trans. by US Joint Publication Research Service, JPRS: 7862/1961).

Hungary: *Statisztikai Evokönyu 1949–55; 1957* (English edition); *1958* (Budapest: 1957, 1959, 1960).

Poland: *Statystyka Handlu Zagranicznego 1958* (Warsaw: 1959).

2. CHOICE OF GOODS

The categories of goods, especially in the Hungarian and early Bulgarian statistics were very broad and comparison of average unit prices in many cases was meaningless (e.g. 'machine tools'). Therefore, a sample had to be taken. The assumption behind the use of a sample is that the price setting process for the relatively homogeneous articles selected was the same for other goods traded. If one believes that the price setting process for, let us say, lathes was different from the price setting process for an article for which a 'world market price' was more easily established (e.g. wheat), then the statistics presented in the text have value only for the specific cases which they represent.

To choose the goods for the samples, three questions were asked:

1. Is the good in question sufficiently homogeneous that quality differences would not significantly effect the average unit price?

2. If the good in question does vary widely in quality, could these quality differences be expected to cancel out? This meant that imports were judged much more severely than exports. (Exported iron ore could be expected to have the same iron content whether exported to a CMEA or OEEC country. Iron ore imports from these two areas could not be expected to be the same in quality.)

3. If the good in question does vary widely in quality, and if these differences could not be expected to cancel out, could a physical measurement be found which would have a linear relation to price? (e.g. Lancashire boilers, measured by kilograms of steam per hour potential).

Ultimately, the choice of goods was a matter of taste. Doubtful goods (e.g. wool or cotton textiles) were tested to see if average unit price variations

[1] A much more complete description of my statistical methods with complete lists of the goods in each sample may be found in Statistical Appendix A of my PhD dissertation, *The Foreign Trade System of the European Communist Nations* at the Yale University library in New Haven, Connecticut.

were too wide to be considered due to bargaining strength differences and were, for the most part, eliminated from the samples. The final choice of goods for the various samples was made by myself and an independent observer.

3. RESULTS

For each set of price comparisons the following data are presented:

(*a*)=per cent of trade of the A market which the sample represents
(*b*)=per cent of trade of the B market which the sample represents
(*c*)=number of commodities in sample
(*d*)=1/'export relation' or the advantage of exporting to the A market (if over 100 per cent) than to the B market
(*d*[1])='import relation' or the advantage of importing from the A market (if over 100 per cent) than from the B market

For formulae for export and import relations, see Chapter IV in text).

Bulgarian Samples

My results for Bulgaria for 1958 and 1959 differ somewhat from Holzman's (*op. cit.*) results because my samples are smaller but more select.

TABLE SA–1

BULGARIAN TRADE WITH THE BLOC AND THE WEST

A market=other CMEA nations
B market=all non-Communist nations, 1948–56; all non-Communist countries in Eastern Hemisphere, 1958–59

	1948	*1952*	*1953*	*1954*	*1955*	*1956*	*1958*	*1959*
Export Sample								
(*a*)	72·8%	43·8%	39·7%	37·9%	27·6%	22·3%	35·2%	39·6%
(*b*)	13·1%	45·8%	43·7%	59·6%	47·4%	28·7%	60·0%	44·7%
(*c*)	7	12	12	15	17	18	51	52
(*d*)	82·0%	59·9%	74·3%	104·0%	115·4%	123·1%	126·4%	128·8%
Export sample without tobacco								
(*a*)	3·7%	13·4%	18·9%	18·5%	18·0%	9·4%	23·5%	23·2%
(*b*)	8·7%	44·3%	42·7%	57·6%	33·6%	22·7%	44·9%	34·2%
(*c*)	6	11	11	14	16	17	49	50
(*d*)	103·8%	85·8%	117·1%	131·0%	119·2%	127·1%	146·8%	147·5%
Import sample								
(*a*)	8·2%	7·9%	5·0%	4·5%	3·9%	6·2%	30·6%	23·9%
(*b*)	9·4%	5·5%	7·1%	1·4%	5·7%	6·6%	52·0%	45·9%
(*c*)	6	6	7	5	5	6	28	32
(*d*[1])	88·0%	159·5%	111·8%	93·4%	107·3%	125·4%	113·9%	91·7%

TABLE SA–2

BULGARIAN TRADE WITH THE USSR AND THE EAST CENTRAL EUROPEAN NATIONS

A market=USSR
B market=East Central European nations

	1948	*1952*	*1953*	*1954*	*1955*	*1956*	*1958*	*1959*
Export sample								
(*a*)	87·5%	44·4%	42·9%	40·2%	26·8%	24·1%	34·1%	41·0%
(*b*)	35·2%	35·9%	34·3%	28·6%	21·6%	17·5%	54·5%	48·4%
(*c*)	2	11	12	10	12	12	34	36
(*d*)	98·2%	97·7%	83·2%	88·5%	83·5%	74·7%	82·3%	80·6%

Export sample without tobacco								
(*a*)	—	7·3%	16·2%	11·3%	10·0%	7·7%	25·5%	26·3%
(*b*)	—	18·1%	23·3%	21·3%	10·4%	9·7%	36·4%	29·6%
(*c*)	—	10	11	9	11	11	33	35
(*d*)	—	89·0%	94·3%	91·6%	92·8%	94·9%	92·6%	92·5%
Import sample								
(*a*)	8·6%	8·5%	6·7%	8·0%	6·1%	10·9%	33·5%	26·3%
(*b*)	5·0%	5·7%	4·2%	3·6%	2·7%	2·6%	28·4%	18·8%
(*c*)	6	9	9	9	7	8	24	24
(*d*[1])	130·6%	100·7%	101·9%	97·8%	91·2%	97·0%	103·4%	104·8%

Hungarian Samples

These statistics contain one curiosity. The statistics from the earlier Hungarian statistical year-book are somewhat different from those of later years, particularly in what items are detailed, and especially for the trade with the USSR. I have therefore included the overlapping year (1955) to show the differences between the samples.

TABLE SA–3

HUNGARIAN TRADE WITH THE BLOC AND WESTERN EUROPEAN NATIONS

A market=other CMEA nations
B market=Common Market countries plus Switzerland and Sweden

	1952	*1953*	*1954*	*1955*	*1955*	*1956*	*1957*	*1958*
Export sample								
(*a*)	13·8%	10·9%	12·0%	11·5%	6·1%	11·1%	11·9%	10·7%
(*b*)	32·2%	25·4%	39·5%	39·6%	23·7%	30·4%	43·2%	33·3%
(*c*)	15	12	16	16	18	15	19	16
(*d*)	113·3%	122·9%	122·5%	114·0%	122·8%	168·3%	117·6%	133·9%
Import sample								
(*a*)	1·1%	6·5%	10·0%	10·3%	2·4%	7·9%	25·2%	9·4%
(*b*)	3·0%	5·5%	20·7%	19·5%	1·6%	2·8%	22·0%	3·7%
(*c*)	6	8	11	9	4	4	11	9
(*d*[1])	93·3%	110·9%	72·5%	103·7%	86·3%	116·9%	107·2%	95·4%
Import sample without cokes								
(*a*)	1·1%	1·2%	5·2%	3·1%				
(*b*)	3·0%	3·5%	15·1%	15·0%				
(*c*)	6	7	10	8				
(*d*[1])	93·3%	85·0%	66·7%	89·8%				

TABLE SA–4

HUNGARIAN TRADE WITH THE USSR AND THE EAST CENTRAL EUROPEAN NATIONS

A market=USSR
B market=East Central European nations

	1952	*1953*	*1954*	*1955*	*1955*	*1956*	*1957*	*1958*
Export sample								
(*a*)	13·1%	11·0%	9·5%	7·7%	·4%	7·1%	5·1%	4·0%
(*b*)	8·1%	6·9%	7·9%	8·2%	2·8%	2·3%	4·1%	3·7%
(*c*)	6	5	6	7	2	4	4	4
(*d*)	89·2%	95·0%	95·2%	93·0%	154·8%	112·9%	119·6%	112·2%

Export sample without bauxite								
(*a*)	11·4%	8·9%	6·3%	6·9%	—	—	—	—
(*b*)	6·5%	5·4%	6·7%	5·3%	—	—	—	—
(*c*)	5	4	5	6	—	—	—	—
(*d*)	108·8%	105·2%	90·9%	96·9%	—	—	—	—
Import sample								
(*a*)	12·0%	14·2%	21·0%	46·7%	22·7%	31·4%	39·2%	35·6%
(*b*)	19·5%	21·9%	13·3%	19·2%	24·2%	27·0%	26·5%	21·0%
(*c*)	6	9	9	10	9	10	11	9
(*d*[1])	91·8%	100·0%	95·8%	104·7%	100·7%	109·0%	109·8%	109·2%
Import sample without cokes								
(*a*)	—	—	—	—	14·7%	23·4%	34·0%	26·8%
(*b*)	—	—	—	—	17·5%	16·1%	17·1%	14·2%
(*c*)	—	—	—	—	8	9	10	8
(*d*[1])	—	—	—	—	103·8%	102·8%	107·0%	111·4%

Polish samples

TABLE SA–5

POLISH TRADE

	A market=other CMEA nations B market=Common Market nations	A market=USSR B market=East Central European nations
	1958	*1958*
Export sample		
(*a*)	38·5%	39·2%
(*b*)	63·6%	52·4%
(*c*)	72	28
(*d*)	132·0%	96·7%
Export sample without coal		
(*a*)	14·4%	18·3%
(*b*)	37·8%	24·7%
(*c*)	71	27
(*d*)	120·6%	99·7%
Import sample		
(*a*)	6·1%	34·8%
(*b*)	24·7%	13·2%
(*c*)	66	41
(*d*[1])	101·8%	105·3%

Russian samples

Many of the calculations below were also made by Horst Mendershausen (*op. cit.*) His calculations, particularly in the discrimination analysis, differ from mine slightly because his samples are somewhat different.

TABLE SA–6

RUSSIAN TRADE WITH THE BLOC AND WESTERN EUROPE

A market=East Central European nations
B market=Western Europe

	1955	*1956*	*1957*	*1958*
Export samples				
(*a*)	42·7%	41·1%	49·5%	49·1%
(*b*)	45·0%	56·2%	48·7%	48·5%
(*c*)	35	36	36	35
(*d*)	116·7%	112·0%	105·7%	114·4%

Import samples				
(*a*)	5·0%	7·1%	7·4%	5·8%
(*b*)	10·2%	24·7%	26·3%	24·8%
(*c*)	18	26	24	18
(*d*¹)	101·2%	116·0%	122·2%	108·4%

For my analysis of price discrimination by the USSR between the various East Central European nations, I used a slightly different procedure. I calculated an average unit export or import price from or to the other CMEA nations (excluding Albania), and computed the export or import prices of the individual countries as a percentage of this average. For all price comparisons, the following data are presented:

- (*a*)=per cent of USSR export trade with this country which the sample represents.
- (*a*¹)=per cent of USSR import trade with this country which the sample represents.
- (*b*)=number of commodities in sample.
- (*c*)='export relation' or the relative advantage of exporting to this country (if *under* 100 per cent). (Note that this is the inverse of what was previously presented).
- (*c*¹)='import relation' or the relative advantage of importing from this country (if *over* 100 per cent).

TABLE SA–7

RUSSIAN TRADE WITH INDIVIDUAL EAST CENTRAL EUROPEAN NATIONS

	1955	*1956*	*1957*	*1958*
Export samples				
Bulgaria				
(*a*)	20·2%	27·3%	36·6%	26·0%
(*b*)	27	35	35	33
(*c*)	98·6%	98·0%	103·4%	96·8%
CSSR				
(*a*)	62·1%	57·3%	63·9%	64·6%
(*b*)	43	52	49	42
(*c*)	98·9%	99·4%	98·9%	98·3%
DDR				
(*a*)	53·5%	56·7%	56·9%	55·8%
(*b*)	43	51	52	50
(*c*)	99·2%	98·8%	101·2%	102·0%
Hungary				
(*a*)	58·8%	55·2%	67·6%	61·4%
(*b*)	35	43	44	42
(*c*)	100·3%	102·2%	100·4%	98·6%
Poland				
(*a*)	35·6%	42·3%	65·7%	53·4%
(*b*)	26	31	31	28
(*c*)	103·9%	102·9%	98·6%	100·0%
Rumania				
(*a*)	31·4%	31·6%	40·3%	33·8%
(*b*)	34	35	35	33
(*c*)	97·6%	99·8%	99·3%	99·4%

Import samples

Bulgaria				
(*a*[1])	31·0%	34·9%	20·1%	21·5%
(*b*)	7	17	14	15
(*c*[1])	98·0%	97·5%	98·0%	95·9%
CSSR				
(*a*[1])	8·7%	7·4%	5·8%	8·3%
(*b*)	5	10	6	7
(*c*[1])	106·6%	104·4%	103·7%	103·6%
DDR				
(*a*[1])	6·0%	5·8%	3·4%	1·6%
(*b*)	12	15	11	5
(*c*[1])	92·3%	94·4%	94·0%	91·3%
Hungary				
(*a*[1])	7·6%	8·4%	9·2%	7·6%
(*b*)	10	16	11	10
(*c*[1])	106·0%	110·9%	107·4%	104·6%
Poland				
(*a*[1])	10·1%	9·0%	3·4%	6·3%
(*b*)	8	14	11	11
(*c*[1])	99·5%	101·3%	95·8%	103·0%
Rumania				
(*a*[1])	42·2%	42·9%	42·8%	13·7%
(*b*)	15	21	18	15
(*c*[1])	100·4%	100·6%	101·7%	101·4%

STATISTICAL APPENDIX B

1. 'TRADE POTENTIAL' (TABLE 1–2)

Comparing the industrial production per capita of the CMEA Bloc nations is fraught with statistical problems, but two difficulties stand out. First of all, there is the problem of selecting the proper weights for the estimates. Second, there is the problem of obtaining comparable data. Any estimates of comparative production must be used with great caution.

Two estimates of comparative industrial production per capita of the Bloc nations have been published in the Bloc and they are presented in Table 8–1 in the text. The methods which were used in calculating these estimates were not elucidated, however. I assume that the price weights used were prices of the country whose economists were computing the indices. The estimates are close enough so that an 'average' index of relative industrial production per capita can be estimated for 1955 (first column of Table SB–1).

Converting these estimates into dollars presents some problems, and recourse must be made to some Western estimates of Bloc production. Stolper and Roscamp[1] have estimated the DDR production per capita in 1955 as 990·4 DMs (1950 West German DM's). Using the Gilbert and Kravis estimates of relative prices in Germany and the United States,[2] this is equal to $387·00, if US prices are used as weights, or $304·00 if weighed European prices are used as weights. (1950 dollars; these data in 1955 dollars are $431·00 and $339·00 repectively). From these data and from the above index of relative industrial production per capita in the Bloc, dollar value of industrial production per capita can be calculated for each Bloc country. (second column of Table SB–1). This is, of course, a very crude method of estimation, however, and I include some independent Western estimates for purposes of comparison.

My estimate of Soviet industrial production per capita, using average European prices, is about the same as the LRS estimate, and about midway between Nutter and CIA estimates. My estimates for Czechoslovakia and Poland are considerably higher than Zauberman's; however, his estimates have received criticism for being low.

In order to make a conservative estimate for trade potential, I use my estimates with average European prices as weights. I fully realize that my statistical methods leave much to be desired but my data do indicate, I feel, the general order of magnitude of the industrial production per capita of the various Bloc nations.

The population data come from the UN *Statistical Yearbook, 1956*. I estimated the Soviet population from the 1956 figure. The trade data come from the various national statistical year-books.

Two formulae are used to estimate potential trade from per capita industrial production and population. Chenery's formula comes from his article 'Patterns of Industrial Growth,' *American Economic Review* L, 4/1960, pp. 624–55.

[1] Wolfgang Stolper and Karl Roscamp, *The Structure of the East German Economy* (Cambridge: Harvard U. Press, 1960).

[2] Milton Gilbert and Irving B. Kravis, *An International Comparison of National Products and the Purchasing Power of Currencies* (Paris: OEEC, 1954), p. 25. The price ratios used were for total GNP, but the ratios for industrial production are about the same. This may be seen in the dollar comparisons of various parts of the GNP.

TABLE SB–1

INDUSTRIAL PRODUCTION PER CAPITA OF BLOC NATIONS FOR 1955 (1955 DOLLARS)

Country	Bloc Index	My Estimates (US prices)	My Estimates (Average European prices)	Independent Estimates[1, 2]
		$	$	$
Bulgaria	46	125	99	—
CSSR	189	515	405	257
DDR	158	431	339	345
Hungary	88	240	189	—
Poland	100	273	215	126
Rumania	58	158	124	—
USSR	123	335	264	183 to 310

Definitions: I = industrial production per capita (in dollars)
Y = national income per capita (in 100 dollars)
P = population (in 10,000,000's)
i = imports per capita (in dollars)
R^2 = correlation coefficient squared
s = standard error of estimate
N = size of sample

	R^2	s	N
$\log I = \log 16{\cdot}95 + 1{\cdot}362 \log Y + {\cdot}046 \log P$	·963	·109	48
$\log i = \log 20{\cdot}40 + {\cdot}987 \log Y - {\cdot}281 \log P$	·808	·217	62

$(\log i = \log 2{\cdot}624 + {\cdot}725 \log I - {\cdot}314 \log P)$

Several sources of error exist. First of all, Chenery uses industrial production, converted to dollars with the official exchange rate. This acts as a downward bias in the data of all countries (see Bela Balassa, 'Patterns of Industrial Growth: Comment,' *American Economic Review* LI, 3/1961) and, therefore, the formula derived for the relationship between industrial production per capita, population, and trade per capita has a built-in bias. Second, his data are not completely comparable; nevertheless, the differences partially cancel each other out and it is hard to tell in which direction the results are affected.

[1] A. Zauberman, *Industrial Development of Czechoslovakia, East Germany, and Poland* (Oxford: Oxford U. Press, mimeo., February, 1958). Zauberman's methodology is open to some dispute. He calculates indices of industrial production for Czechoslovakia, DDR and Poland from a sample of 'typical products' from 10 to 16 industries. He then links these indices to ECE estimates of pre-war industrial production (weighed by US prices).

[2] Warren Nutter, Israel Borenstein and Adam Kaufman, *The Growth of Industrial Production in the Soviet Union*, (Princeton: Princeton University Press, 1962), p. 238 estimate Soviet industrial production per capita as 19·6 per cent of the US's (weighed by US prices) or 16·5 per cent of the US's (weighed by Soviet prices). In the table above I converted their estimate with US price weights to 1955 dollars. (With Rouble price weights, the Soviet industrial production per capita for 1955 was $153·00.)

On the other hand CIA economists have estimated total Russian industrial production in 1955 at about 40 per cent of the industrial production of the United States (using a geometric mean of prices) or about $310·00.

In a booklet prepared by the Legislative Reference Service for the Joint Economic Committee of the Congress (*Soviet Economic Growth: A Comparison with the United States;* Washington: Government Printing Office, 1957) Soviet industrial production is estimated as about one-third that of the US or about $260·00 (no procedure was given for this calculation. I assume that the geometrical mean of prices in the USSR and the US were used.)

My formula is based on comparable production data for eight Western European nations.

Definitions: T=trade turnover per capita (in dollars)
I=industrial production per capita (in dollars)
P=population (in 1,000,000's)
R^2=correlation coefficient squared
s=standard error of estimate
N=size of sample

	R^2	s	N
T=194·2+1·250 I—8·170 P	·805	90	8

Three main sources of error exist:

1. Although the correlation coefficient and the regression coefficients are statistically significant (·95 level of confidence) the sample is very small and the standard error of estimate is very large.

2. Since the sample is based only upon West European nations with relatively high levels of per capita industrial production, it is not completely representative and derived results for nations with lower levels of per capita industrial production may be biased.

3. My formula is linear which, over a certain range, would serve as a useful approximation. With its large population, Russia does not fall within this range.

2. STATISTICS OF THE DIRECTION OF TRADE[1]
(TABLES: 1–1; 6–1; 6–2; 6–3; 6–5; 6–6; 6–7; 6–9 AND 6–10)

A. Sources of Data and Estimation Procedures

The pre-war data came from several sources:
Foreign Trade by Areas, 1928, 1937–53 (Paris: OEEC, 1954); *The Network of World Trade; Directions of International Trade* (Statistical Papers T. Joint Publication of UNO, IMF and IBRD)
'Pre-war Regional Interdependence and Post-war Interzonal Trade in Germany,' *Economic Bulletin for Europe*, 3/1949.

The greatest difficulty in calculating pre-war trade patterns is estimating the trade of the area of the present DDR. The above cited *Economic Bulletin for Europe* contains estimates for foreign and inner-German trade of each area of Germany for 1936. To calculate the trade of the current DDR for 1938 I computed the 1936 trade of the Soviet Zone of Germany plus the trade of one-half of Berlin as a percentage of total German trade for that year. I then multiplied total German trade of 1938 by this percentage. Trade for the area of Germany east of the Oder-Neisse River for 1938 was calculated in a similar way.

Data for 1948 to 1954 for the Bloc nations are quite skimpy and must, in several cases, be estimated from scattered sources. I have used the estimates from the very complete survey by the ECE, 'Developments in the Foreign Trade of Eastern Europe and the Soviet Union,' *Economic Survey of Europe for 1957*, supplemented (for trade between the USSR and Rumania) by data from Bruno Kiesewetter, *Statistiken zur Wirtschaft Ost- und Südosteuropas* Vol. III, *Handel und Verkehr* (West Berlin: Duncker und Humbolt, 1957). It must be noted that

[1] For more complete details, see my dissertation, *op. cit.*

other estimates vary somewhat with these, especially for 1948. For instance, Köhler, *op. cit.* estimates DDR trade with the Bloc as 41 per cent instead of 75 per cent although I've seen the latter figure in the DDR literature.

Data for 1955 through 1960 came from 'Developments in the Foreign Trade of Eastern Europe and the Soviet Union,' *op. cit.*; 'Foreign Trade and Economic Development in Eastern Europe and the Soviet Union,' *Economic Bulletin for Europe*, 1/1959; *International Trade Statistics for 1960;* and following national sources:

Bulgaria: *Statistitchesky Godishnik na Narodna Republika Bulgaria* (Sofia: 1957) and *Vneshna trgoviya*, 9/1958, pp. 2 and 18.

Czechoslovakia: *Statistická Rocenka Republiky Ceskoslovenské* (Prague: 1958) and *Statisticke Zpravy*, 8/1959.

DDR: *Statistisches Jahrbuch der deutschen demokratischen Republik* 1958, 1960–61 (East Berlin: 1959, 1960).

Hungary: *Statisztikai Havi Közleményck* 5/1959.

Poland: *Rocznik Statystyzcny, 1956; 1957; 1958* (Warsaw: 1956, 1957, 1958) and *Biutetyn statystyczny*.

USSR: *Vneshniaia Torgovlia SSR za 1956 god; za 1957 god; and za 1958 god, op. cit.*

Estimations were quite straightforward except for Rumania which has published almost no trade data up to 1958. For total trade turnover up to 1958 I used estimates of above cited ECE sources. For percentage distribution of trade, I used data of world trade with Rumania, adjusting these data with reference to 1956 percentage data which have been published (cited by Klinkmüller and Ruban, *op. cit.*, p. 235).

B. Trade with Underdeveloped Nations

Calculation of CMEA trade with the Western underdeveloped nations from Eastern data is impossible because of the large 'miscellaneous nations' categories in the trade data. Therefore, I have used the data from the underdeveloped nations, as summarized in:

Directions of International Trade (various issues) supplemented by *International Trade Statistics for 1960*.

In the table I categorized the underdeveloped nations in the following way:

Latin American nations: all nations in the Western Hemisphere (including Trinidad, Tobago and North Antilles) except the USA and Canada.

Arabic nations; Aden, Algeria, Egypt (UAR), Iran, Iraq, Jordan, Kuwait, Lebanon, Libya, Morocco, Saudi Arabia, Sudan, Syria (UAR) and Tunisia.

African nations: all African nations except the Union of South Africa and those included as Arabic nations.

Asian: all Asian nations except Japan, Israel, the Asian Communist countries, and those included as Arabic nations.

Several difficulties occurred in the calculation. First, the valuation of trade (f.o.b. or c.i.f.) differ between countries. I have made no allowances for these differences, however.

Second, several important trade partners of the Bloc do not report any trade (Afghanistan and, for exports, Iran) or have reported for only some years (Argentina after 1952). Most countries reported trade quite fully after 1952 and, therefore, these data reflect the actual events somewhat more accurately. The changes in the geographical direction of trade between 1952 and 1953 may be attributed primarily to the increased coverage. The increase in Bloc trade with Asia in 1956 is also partially due to this statistical factor.

Third, data for 1960 were not entirely complete and, therefore, some small estimates had to be made.

3. GRADE OF IMPORT SPECIALIZATION OR 'SINGLE SUPPLIER PHENOMENON' (TABLE 1–7)

An import is 'specialized' for one CMEA nation, when another CMEA nation supplies 95 per cent or more of its imports of that good from the Bloc.

Whether or not an import is 'specialized' depends very much on the form of the data which are available. If the imports are lumped together into large categories then the 'grade of specialization' will be quite low. Detailed data were available only for Russia (*Vneshniaia Torgovlia, op. cit.*) and Poland (*Stakystyka Handlu Zagranicznego, op. cit.* up to 1960). These data are classified in the same way as the USSR data, but in somewhat greater detail.

TABLE SB–2

PERCENTAGE OF TOTAL 'SPECIALIZED IMPORTS'

	1955	*1956*	*1957*	*1958*
	%	%	%	%
USSR with all CMEA nations	33	30	29	24
USSR with all CMEA nations except Poland	26	24	22	21
Poland with all CMEA nations	—	—	—	40
Poland with all CMEA nations except USSR	—	—	—	29

Noteworthy is the fact that although the percentage of 'specialized imports' has been steadily decreasing over the past four years in the USSR, the absolute amount has remained about the same.

TABLE SB–3

PERCENTAGE OF 'SPECIALIZED IMPORTS' OF THE USSR FROM VARIOUS CMEA NATIONS

	1955	*1956*	*1957*	*1958*
	%	%	%	%
Albania	36	29	24	12
Bulgaria	48	35	32	32
CSSR	8	10	10	10
DDR	36	32	26	27
Hungary	14	16	7	6
Poland	63	61	75	48
Rumania	33	22	26	27

TABLE SB–4

PERCENTAGE OF 'SPECIALIZED IMPORTS' OF POLAND FROM VARIOUS CMEA NATIONS

	1958
	%
Albania	40
Bulgaria	47
CSSR	14
DDR	42
Hungary	25
Rumania	29
USSR	51

In calculating the degree to which the four broad categories of Russian trade (machinery, raw materials, foodstuffs, and consumer goods) are specialized, I ran into the problem of conflicting sources of data. The original USSR source only separates machinery fom the other broad categories. A later article in the same magazine presents slightly different amounts for machinery as well as a complete breakdown for the other broad categories.[1]

In the table below, I present both sets of data.

TABLE SB–5

PERCENTAGE OF 'SPECIALIZED IMPORTS' OF THE USSR FROM CMEA NATIONS FOR BROAD TRADE CATEGORIES

	1955 %	*1956* %	*1957* %	*1958* %
Original source:				
Machinery	23	28	29	26
Later source:				
Machinery	—	25	24	22
Raw materials	—	45	43	37
Food and Live Animals	—	17	40	32
Manufactured consumer goods	—	5	7	4

4. DDR TRADE ESTIMATES (TABLES 2–1 AND 2–2)

Heinz Köhler (*East Germany's Economic Integration into the Communist Bloc, op. cit.*, p. 481) made the following estimates of the changes of DDR trade volume:

TABLE SB–6

ANNUAL CHANGE IN DDR TRADE VOLUME

Year	*Exports* %	*Imports* %
1951	26·0	9·9
1952	10·2	18·3
1953	13·3	34·3
1954	59·3	14·2
1955	—1·0	7·7
1956	15·6	5·4
1957	9·8	16·2
1958	8·2	8·8
1959	14·3	20·0

Since he used West German trade prices as weights, there is no very satisfactory method by which these data may be combined to estimate the annual growth of the total trade turnover (exports+imports). In the text I used a simple arithmetic average.

5. DDR NATIONAL INCOME AND INDUSTRIAL PRODUCTION STATISTICS (TABLES 2–1 AND 2–2)

One must use some caution with DDR statistics. The DDR, like all East Bloc nations, uses a gross-gross (Brutto) calculation for estimations of total national income and industrial production, which includes a great deal of double accounting. Net national income and an industrial production index are calculated but

[1] A. Ketkowitsch and J. Romanow, 'Warenaustausch zwischen den Mitgliedländer des RGW im Jahre 1958,' *Der Aussenhandel* IX, 21/1959, p. 6–9; (a translation from Vneshniaia Torgovlia).

these are also not very satisfactory. Wolfgang Stolper has made an extensive analysis of the DDR statistical methodology.[1]

Several Western economists have estimated industrial production and national income of the DDR. The differences between the various DDR and Western calculations may be seen below.

TABLE SB–7

ANNUAL CHANGES IN DDR NATIONAL PRODUCT

DDR data:	*1950–55*	*1955–58*
Bruttoprodukt (gesellschaftliches Gesamtprodukt) current prices[2]	13·4	6·1
Nettoprodukt (Nationaleinkommen) current prices[3]	11·2	7·4
Bruttoprodukt, constant prices (Messwerte)[4]	11·2	—
Nettoprodukt, constant prices (Messwerte)[5]	10·2	—
Nettoprodukt plus depreciation[6]	11·3	7·5
Western estimates:		
Stolper estimates, 1950 prices, Marxist definition GNP[7]	8·7	4·7
Stolper estimates, 1950 prices Western definition GNP[7]	7·7	4·8

TABLE SB–8

ANNUAL CHANGES IN DDR INDUSTRIAL PRODUCTION

DDR data:	*1950–55*	*1955–58*
Bruttoproduktion, current prices[8]	14·7	9·5
Nettoproduktion, current prices[9]	15·4	9·5
Bruttoproduktion, constant prices[10] (Messwerte and unchanged plan prices)	13·7	8·3
Nettoproduktion, constant prices[11] (Messwerte)	14·8	—
Western estimates:		
Stolper estimates[12]	11·5	5·4
Zauberman estimates[13]	8·9	—
Germanicus estimates[14]	7·7	—
Abeken estimates[14]	8·3	—

[1] Wolfgang Stolper and Karl Roskamp, *The Structure of the East German Economy op. cit.* Chapter III.

[2] *Statistisches Jahrbuch der DDR, 1958*, pp. 172–3.

[3] *Ibid.*, pp. 174–5.

[4] *Statistisches Jahrbuch der DDR, 1955*, p. 90.

[5] *Ibid.*, p. 90.

[6] *Statistisches Jahrbuch der DDR, 1958*, pp. 176–7.

[7] Stolper and Roskamp, *op. cit.*

[8] *Statistisches Jahrbuch der DDR, 1958*, p. 5.

[9] *Ibid.*, pp. 174–5.

[10] *Statistisches Jahrbuch der DDR, 1955*, pp.90ff; *Statistisches Jahrbuch der DDR 1958*, pp. 272–3.

[11] *Statistisches Jahrbuch der DDR, 1955*, pp. 90ff.

[12] Stolper and Roskamp, *op. cit.*

[13] A. Zauberman, *Industrial Development in Czechoslovakia, East Germany and Poland, 1937–56, op. cit.*, p. 38.

[14] Cited by Zauberman, *op. cit.*, p. 38.

For comparison, the national income of the Bundesrepublik Deutschland (West Germany) grew at an annual average of 9·4 per cent (Western definition) or 10·3 per cent (Marxist definition) between 1950 and 1955 and the industrial production grew in the same period at an annual rate of 12·2 per cent (1950 prices).

6. SOURCES OF DDR PLAN DATA (TABLES 2–1 AND 2–2)

The main source of plan information is, of course, the *Gesetzblatt der DDR;* however, many figures are not contained here. In the tables I used the following additional sources:

Der Aussenhandel der SBZ, 1953, Plan 1954, und 1. Halbjahr 1954 (Bonn: Bundesministerium fuer gesamtdeutsche Fragen, 1954).

Der Aussenhandel der SBZD im Jahre 1952 und Plan 1953 (Bonn: B. f.g.F., 1953).

'Bericht der Staatlichen Plankommission,' *Statistische Praxis,* 2/1951.

Economic Survey of Europe, various issues.

'Erfüllung des ersten Fünfjahrsplanes der industriellen Bruttoproduktion,' *Statistische Praxis,* 5/1956.

Willi Huttenrauch, 'Zu neuem Erfolg,' *Der Aussenhandel* VII, 1/1957, pp. 3–5.

Heinrich Rau, 'Der Volkswirtschaftplan 1950,' *Volkswirtschaftplan* 1950 (East Berlin: Deutscher Zentralverlag, 1950).

Kurt Richter, 'Der Fünfjahrplan,' *Statistische Praxis,* 9/1950.

Karl C. Thalheim and Peter Propp, *Die Entwicklungsziele fuer die gewerbliche Wirtschaft der sowjetischen Besatzungszone in der zweiten Fünfjahrplan Periode* (Bonn: B.f.g.F., 1957).

'Volkswirtschaftplan 1955: Aufgaben des Aussenhandels,' *Der Aussenhandel* V, 10/1955.

7. DISTRIBUTION OF TRADE OVER THE YEAR (TABLE 2–3)

Data for Bulgaria from *Statisticheski Sbornik 1958–59* (*op. cit.*) are also available to illustrate this annual 'trade cycle.'

TABLE SB–9

PERCENTAGE OF BULGARIAN TRADE FALLING IN SPECIFIC TIME PERIODS

	Exports		*Imports*	
Period	*1958*	*1959*	*1958*	*1959*
	%	%	%	%
First Quarter	18·5	17·6	23·9	20·3
(March)	(8·5)	(9·2)	(10·2)	(9·4)
Second Quarter	22·8	19·4	25·3	27·8
(June)	(10·5)	(7·7)	(10·2)	(12·4)
Third Quarter	25·9	23·1	23·0	24·6
(September)	(11·7)	(9·7)	(9·6)	(10·3)
Fourth Quarter	32·7	39·9	27·8	27·3
(December)	(14·5)	(19·6)	(13·8)	(13·5)

8. GM AND THE DDR (CHAPTER III, FOOTNOTE 2)

Data for GM from 'The Fortune Directory: The 500 Largest US Industrial Corporations,' *Fortune* LXII, July/1960, pp. 131–50 and information supplied to me by General Motors.

DDR data from Stolper and Roskamp, *op. cit.* for 1958, converted to dollars from geometric mean of DM/$ price comparisons of Gilbert and Kravis, *op. cit.* Capital/output ratio for 1958 from *World Economic Survey for 1959*, p. 128. Using data from Ernst Lange, *Die Investitionen in der volkseigenen Industrie der DDR im ersten Planjahrfünft* (East Berlin: Verlag Die Wirtschaft, 1958), p. 138, I estimated the same figure.

9. INDICATIONS OF THE CENTRALIZATION OF THE PLANNING SYSTEM (CHAPTER III, FOOTNOTE 3, p. 81)

TABLE SB–10

DEGREE OF DETAIL IN THE PLANNING PROCESS

Year	*Industrial Planning Positions*[1]	*Industrial Quota Goods*[2]	*Positions in State Plan*[3]	*Material Balances (Central)*[4]
1950	—	—	—	—
1951	—	—	—	—
1952	—	—	—	—
1953	—	—	—	—
1954	2,288	330–483	—	—
1955	—	688	955	—
1956	—	—	810	1,000
1957	2,279	553	440	—
1958	—	397	—	—
1959	2,485	408–426	560	570
1960	—	363	—	—

10. POPULATION AND LABOUR FORCE DATA OF THE DDR (TABLE 4–4)

1939–58 populations data from *Statistisches Jahrbuch der DDR, 1958*. Working age for men from 15 to 65, and for women, from 15 to 60. 1965 estimate a. from Hans-Gert Tönjes, 'Bevölkerungsentwicklung und Arbeitskräftepotential in Mitteldeutschland,' *Vierteljahrshefte zur Wirtschaftforschung*, 2/1959, pp. 210–19. 1965 estimate b. from ECE, 'Manpower and Employment in Eastern Europe and the Soviet Union,' *Economic Survey of Europe for 1957*.

Overall labour force data for 1939, 1950 and 1951 from Stolper and Roskamp,

[1] These are the number of categories of goods for which enterprises must state their needs while drawing up their annual plan from the control figures. These data from various *Schlüsselliste des Volkswirtschaftsplans* (East Berlin: Zentralverwaltung der Statistik, various years).

[2] These are called Kontingentierte Gueter (or funded goods) and were obtained from various *Schlüsselliste* and laws in *Gesetzblatt der DDR*. The number of quota goods varied throughout the year because of the many changes in the list.

[3] 1955–57: 'Zur Diskussion über die weitere Verbesserung der Leitung der volkseigenen Industrie,' *Wirtschaftswissenschaft* VII, pp. 346–61; 1959: Hugo Meiser, 'Zu einigen Fragen der Durchführung des Volkswirtschaftsplans 1960,' *Sozialistische Planwirtschaft* I, 1/1960, pp. 4–6.

[4] 1956: Hans Fülle, 'Zur Rolle der Materialbilanzen in der Wirtschaft der DDR, *Wirtschaftswissenschaft*, IV, 4/1956, pp. 495–504; 1959: Heinz-Werner Hubner, 'Aktuelle Probleme der Planung der Industrieproduktion,' *Sozialistische Planwirtschaft* I, 1/1960, pp. 8–15.

op. cit. Data from 1952 to 1958 from various *Statislche Jahrbuecher*. In the DDR data, labour force does not include employees of the Ministry of Interior (and workers in the Ministry factories), members of the armed forces and police, employees abroad, and employees of the uranium mines (SMAG Wismut). Men and women as proportion of labour potential from various *Statistische Jahrbuecher*. Women in labour force as proportion of total labour force, 1939 and 1590 from Stolper, *op. cit.;* from 1952 and afterwards from *Statistisches Jahrbuch* 1958, p. 202 (includes apprentices). Unemployment data for DDR from various *Statistische Jahrbuecher;* Western estimate from Bruno Gleitze, 'Das Problem der gespaltenen Wirtschaft Duetschlands,' Wirtschaftswissenschaftliches Institut der Gewerkschaften, *Mitteilungen* VII, February–March, 1954, p. 30, quoted by Stolper, *op. cit.* Gleitze was former head of the DDR Statistical Administration and has a deep insight into DDR statistics.

11. PRICE LEADERSHIP CALCULATIONS (TABLE 5–7)

The samples were taken from *Vneshniaia Torgovlia za 1958 god* (*op. cit.*) and *Statystyka Handlu Zagranicznego 1958* (*op. cit.*)

Out of the hundreds of export and import goods traded by the USSR and Poland with the rest of the Bloc, I was able to find only a small sample of similar goods which both countries traded with the same Bloc partners. Moreover, I had to cut this list considerably to eliminate those goods which were not easily comparable because of possible quality variations. (A full listing of the goods is given in my dissertation, *op. cit.*)

The samples were the following sizes:

TABLE SB–11

PRICE LEADERSHIP SAMPLES

	Number of Commodities	*Proportion of USSR Trade with B.C. D.H.R.*[1] %	*Proportion o, Polish Trade with B.C.D.H.R.*[1] %
Imports	11	8·8	8·7
Exports	10	8·2	43·9

12. DEGREE OF 'TRIANGULATION IN WESTERN AND EASTERN EUROPEAN TRADE' (TABLE 6–11)

The sources for the data for Western Europe are: *Foreign Trade by Areas, 1928, 1937–53* (Paris: OEEC, 1954); various issues of *Direction of International Trade* and *International Trade Statistics 1960*. The sources for data for the Bloc, see sources listed in Section 2A of this Statistical Appendix.

In calculating the degree of 'triangulation' for the Bloc, several difficulties occurred. First, the data available for Eastern Europe, especially for the early 1950s, are not uniform. Some countries value both imports and exports f.o.b.; others value imports c.i.f. Hungary between 1951 and 1956 valued goods at the point of transfer of ownership. Moreover, certain nations (e.g., Russia) include re-exports in the trade statistics while other (e.g. the DDR) do not. Furthermore, the nations differ in their practices of including or excluding certain goods in their trade balances. I also do not know exactly how the line is drawn between goods and 'invisibles.' Finally, some countries have not listed their trade with other countries (e.g. Rumania up to 1958) or have only listed their trade in percentage form. I have used ECE estimates of the network of trade within the Bloc from

[1] B. = Bulgaria; C. = Czechoslovakia; D. = DDR; H. = Hungary; R. = Rumania.

1948 to 1956 and have made estimates from the national sources from 1955 to 1960. In the ECE data, exports are valued f.o.b., imports are valued f.o.b. up to 1951 and f.o.b.+transportation costs from 1952 to 1955. In my estimates, both imports and exports are valued f.o.b. exporting country.

I have excluded trade between the East Central European countries and Albania because Albania has been running a chronic trade deficit and no nation in Western-Europe is in a comparable position. I've also omitted the trade between the East Central European nations and the USSR because some Western economists feel that a great many invisibles are not included in the trade statistics which might make a difference. Actually, including the USSR in the calculations makes very little difference at all.

For Western Europe I've chosen the Common Market Countries as a comparable trading Bloc. I've calculated the degree of triangulation for Western Europe using two different ways for valuing imports. Exports are valued f.o.b.

TABLE SB–12

'DEGREE OF TRIANGULATION' IN TWO TRADING BLOCS[1]

	East Central Europe		*Western Europe*	
Year	*From ECE Trade Estimates*	*My Trade Estimates*	*Imports valued f.o.b.*	*Imports valued c.i.f.*
	%	%	%	%
1948	9	—	13	19
1950	11	—	20	18
1951	8	—	15	16
1952	8	—	11	12
1953	8	—	15	17
1954	8	—	16	16
1955	11	10	14	14
1956	11	9	15	15
1957	—	12	15	16
1958	—	10	11	11
1959	—	9	9	8
1960	—	8	10	11

[1] Countries included in sample for East Central Europe: Bulgaria, CSSR, DDR, Hungary, Poland and Rumania. Countries included in sample for Western Europe: Belgium-Luxembourg, France, Italy, Netherlands, and the German Federal Republic.

MISCELLANEOUS STATISTICAL DATA

A. *Export Ratios of East Central Europe*[1]

Commodities	1956 %	1960 %
Solid fuels[2]	6·3	7·5
Electrical energy[3]	0·7	2·0
Wood[4]	0·4	0·9
Pig iron[5]	1·6	2·2
Steel products[6]	12·0	13·0

B. *Export Ratios of CMEA Bloc*[7]

Commodities	1950 %	1959 %	1960 %
Pig iron	1·63	1·35	1·65
Rolled steel	2·65	2·46	4·80

C. *Types of Machines produced in CMEA countries before and after Standardization and Specialization Agreements*[8]

Commodities	*Types before Agreements*	*Types after Agreements*
Open pit mining equipment	63	34
Canning industry equipment	108	71
Machines for milk industry	297	52
Sugar factories	32	17

[1] Ratio of total exports of the commodity to total production in all the East Central European nations except Albania. Inclusion of the USSR or comparison of imports to total production changes the raios slightly but, on the whole, displays the same general magnitude and trends. A more meaningful comparison would be the ratio of products traded between the East Central European nations to total production but unfortunately such data were only available for solid fuels and yielded ratios of 2·5 per cent 2·8 per cent in the respective years. For other data, see ECE *Economic Survey of Europe for 1957.*

[2] Numerator includes coal, coke, briquettes, and patent fuels; denominator, hard and brown coal mined. Data are for 1957 and 1960 and are from various issues of ECE *Quarterly Bulletin of Coal Statistics for Europe.*

[3] Excludes Bulgaria. Data from ECE *Quarlerly Bulletin of Electrical Statistics for Europe.*

[4] Wood includes only pitprops. broadleaf sawnwood, and plywood. Data from ECE *Timber Bulletin for Europe.*

[5] Excludes Bulgaria and Rumania. Pig iron includes ferro-alloys for blast furnaces. Data from ECE *Quarterly Bulletin of Steel Statistics for Europe.*

[6] Excludes Bulgaria and Rumania. Numerator includes 'steel products'; denominator, rolled steel products, finished steel castings, and steel forgings. Data from *ibid.*

[7] S. Plaksen, 'Die sozialistische Zusammenarbeit in der Schwarzmetallurgie', *Sozialistische Planwirtschaft* III, 8 & 9/1962.

[8] Ladislav Smit, 'Die sozialistische Zusammenarbeit im Maschinenbau', *Sozialistische Planwirtschaft* III, 8 & 9/1962, pp. 9-13.

SELECTED BIBLIOGRAPHY

A. FOREIGN LANGUAGE: PERIODICALS CITED

Die Arbeit. East Berlin: Freier deutscher Gewerkschaftsbund, Verlag Tribüne, monthly.

Der Aussenhandel. East Berlin: Verlag Die Wirtschaft, twice monthly.

Aussenpolitik. Stuttgart: Deutsche Verlags-Anstalt, monthly.

Biuletyn statystyczny. Warsaw: Glówny úrzad statystyczny, monthly.

Dengi i Kredit. Moscow: Gosudarstvenny bank S.S.S.R., monthly.

Deutsche Aussenpolitik. East Berlin: Gesellschaft zur Verbreitung wissenschaftlicher Kenntnisse, Rütten & Loening, monthly.

Deutsche Finanzwirtschaft. East Berlin: Verlag Die Wirtschaft, twice monthly.

Deutscher Export. East Berlin: Kammer für Aussenhandel, Verlag Die Wirtschaft, monthly.

Economia Internazionale. Genoa: Bank of Genoa, quarterly.

Einheitliche Transittarife zum Abkommen über den internationalen Eisenbahn und Guterverkehr. Dresden: VEB Landesdruckerei, irregular.

Ekonomista. Warsaw: Komitet nauk ekonomicznych Polskiej Akademii Nauk i Polskiego Towarzystwa Ekonomicznego, 6 times yearly.

Einheit. East Berlin: Zentralkomitee der Sozialistischen Einheitspartei Deutschlands, Dietz Verlag, monthly.

Freie Rundschau. Munich: Zentralverband Politischer Emigranten aus der USSR, ZOPE Verlag, 6 times yearly.

Geld und Kredit. East Berlin: Akademie Verlag, quarterly.

Gesetzblatt der DDR (GBl). East Berlin: Büro des Präsidiums des Ministerrates der DDR, irregular.

Gospodarka planowa. Warsaw: Polskie wydawnictwa gospodarcze, monthly.

Handel zagraniczny. Warsaw: Polska Jzba Handlu Zagranciznego, monthly.

Internationale Zeitschrift der Landwirtschaft. East Berlin: Ständige Kommission für Landwirtschaft des Rates für gegenseitige Wirtschaftshilfe, Deutscher Bauernverlag, quarterly.

Közgazdaśági szemle. Budapest: Közgazdaságtudományi intézet, monthly.

Kyklos. Basel: List Society, Kyklos-Verlag, quarterly.

Die Materialwirtschaft. East Berlin: Verlag Die Wirtschaft, twice monthly.

Ministerialblatt der DDR (MinBl). East Berlin: Regierungskanzlei der DDR, Deutscher Zentralverlag, irregular.

Neues Deutschland. East Berlin: Zentralkomitee der Sozialistischen Einheitspartei, daily newspaper.

Neue Zuricher Zeitung. Zurich: daily newspaper.

Nová mysl. Prague: Ústredni výbor komunistické strany Ceskoslovenska, monthly.

Ost Chronik. West Berlin: Deutsches Institut für Wirtschaftsforschung, quarterly.

Ost-Europa Recht. Bergisch-Gladbach: Deutsche Gesellschaft für Ost-Europakunde, e.V., Heider Verlag, quarterly.

Ost-Europa Wirtschaft. Bergisch-Gladbach: Deutsche Gesellschaft für Ost-Europakunde, e.V., Heider Verlag, quarterly.

Osthandel. Vienna: Oberösterreichischer Wirtschaftsverlag Gesellschaft GmbH, monthly.

Plánované hospodárstvi. Prague: Státni úrad plánovaci, 10 times yearly.

Politiká okonomie. Prague: Vydává Ekonomický Ústhv Ceskoslovenské Akademie ved, 10 times yearly.

Pravda. Moscow: Communist Party of the Soviet Union, daily newspaper.
Die Presse der Sowjetunion. East Berlin: Amt für Information der DDR, VEB Deutscher Zentralverlag, irregular.
Probleme economice. Bucharest: Institutul de cercetări economice, monthly.
Rocznik statystyczny. Warsaw: Glówny úrzad statystyczny, yearly.
Schlüsselliste des Volkswirtschaftsplanes für Industrie, Landwirtschaft, Materialversorgung, Aussenhandel. East Berlin: Staatliche Zentralverwaltung für Statistik, yearly.
Sozialistische Planwirtschaft. East Berlin: Verlag Die Wirtschaft, monthly.
Statisticheski Sbornik. Sofia: irregular.
Statistická ročenka Republiky Ceskoslovenské. Prague: Státni úrad statistiký, yearly.
Statistische Praxis. East Berlin: Staatliche Zentralverwaltung für Statistik, VEB Deutscher Zentralverlag, monthly.
Statistisches Jahrbuch der DDR. East Berlin: Staatliche Zentralverwaltung für Statistik, VEB Deutscher Zentralverlag, yearly.
Statistitchesky godishnik na Narodna Republika Bulgaria. Sofia: Tsentralno statistichesko upravlenie pri Ministerskiya savet, irregular.
Statisztikai Évokönyv. Budapest: Központi statisztikai hivatal, yearly.
Statisztikai havi közlemények. Budapest: Központi statisztikai hivatal, monthly.
Statsøkonomisk Tidsskrift. Oslo: quarterly.
Statystyka Handlu Zagranicznego. Warsaw: Nakiadem Glównego Urzedu Statstycznego, yearly.
Tagesbericht. West Berlin: Informationsbüro West (IWE), daily newsletter.
Der Tagesspiegel. West Berlin: daily newspaper.
Vierteljahrshefte zur Statistik der DDR. East Berlin: Staatliche Zentralverwaltung für Statistik, VEB Deutscher Zentralverlag, quarterly.
Vierteljahrshefte zur Wirtschaftsforschung. West Berlin: Deutsches Institut für Wirtschaftsforschung, Duncker & Humblot, quarterly.
Vneshna trgoviya. Sofia: Ministerstvo na turgoviyata, monthly.
Vneshniaia torgovlya. Moscow: Ministerstvo veneshnei torgovli S.S.S.R., monthly.
Voprosy ekonomiki. Moscow: Institut Ekonomiki Akademii Nauk S.S.S.R., monthly.
Die Wirtschaft. East Berlin: Verlag Die Wirtschaft, weekly newspaper.
Wirtschaftswissenschaft. East Berlin: Verlag Die Wirtschaft, 6–8 times yearly.
Wissenschaftliche Zeitschrift der Hochschule für Ökonomie. East Berlin: Hochschule für Ökonomie, 5 times yearly.
Wissenschaftliche Zeitschrift der Martin Luther Universität. Wittenberge: Martin Luther Universität, 5 times yearly.
Wochenbericht. West Berlin: Deutsches Institut für Wirtschaftsforschung, weekly.
Zeitschrift für die gesamte Staatswissenschaft. Tübingen: J. C. B. Mohr, quarterly.
Zentralverordnungsblatt (ZVOBl). East Berlin: Deutsche Zentralfinanzverwaltung in der SBZD, irregular.

B. MOST IMPORTANT BOOKS AND PAMPHLETS CITED

Akademie der Wissenschaften der USSR, Institut für Ökonomie, *Politische Oekonomie Lehrbuch*. (trans. from first Russian edition) East Berlin: Dietz Verlag, 1955.
Allen, Robert Loring. *Soviet Economic Warfare*. Washington, D.C.: Public Affairs Press, 1960.
American Management Association, Inc. *Aspects of East-West Trade*. New York: AMA Report 45, 1960.

Balassa, Bela. *The Hungarian Experience in Economic Planning.* New Haven: Yale University Press, 1960.

Baykov, Alexander. *Soviet Foreign Trade.* Princeton: Princeton U. Press, 1946.

Bergson, Abram, ed. *Soviet Economic Growth: Conditions and Perspectives.* Evanston and White Plains: Ro Peterson and Co., 1953.

Berliner, Joseph. *Soviet Economic Aid.* New York: Frederick A. Praeger, Inc., 1958.

Brauer, Rudolf. *Die Planung der wirtschaftlichen Tätigkeit der volkseigenen Handelsunternehmen Deutscher Innen- und Aussenhandel in der DDR.* (Unpublished Doktorarbeit) East Berlin: Hochschule für Ökonomie, 1956.

Brzezinski, Zbigniew K. *The Soviet Bloc: Unity and Conflict.* Cambridge, Massachusetts: Harvard U. Press, 1960.

Caves, Richard E. *Trade and Economic Structure.* Cambridge, Massachusetts: Harvard U. Press, 1960.

Cooper Charles A. *Agriculture, Labour Surplus and Foreign Trade in Bulgaria.* (Unpublished PhD Thesis) Massachusetts Institute of Technology: Department of Economics, 1960.

Dewar, Margaret. *Soviet Trade with Eastern Europe.* London: Royal Institute of International Affairs, 1951.

Figurnov, P. K. *Stroitel'stve socizlisticeskoj ekonomiki i razivike vnesney torgovli evropejskich stranach narodnoj demokratii.* Moscow: Vnestorgizdat, 1955.

Graebig, Gertrud. *International Arbeitsteilung und Aussenhandel im sozialistischen Weltsystem.* East Berlin: Verlag Die Wirtschaft, 1960.

Grossman, Gregory, ed. *Value and Plan.* Berkeley: U. of California Press, 1960.

Haengekorb, Karl. *Termin und Qualität- A und O unseres Exports.* East Berlin: Verlag Die Wirtschaft, 1958.

Heiduschat, Franz. *Wirtschaftswerbung: Bedeutung und Nutzeffekt.* East Berlin: Verlag Die Wirtschaft, 1958.

Hercher, Karl. *Der Zahlungsverkehr der DDR mit dem Ausland.* East Berlin: Verlag Die Wirtschaft, 1958.

Hermes, Theodor. *Der Aussenhandel in den Ostblockstaaten.* Hamburg: Cram-De-Gruyter & Co., 1958.

Hirsch, Hans. *Mengenplanung und Preisplanung in der Sowjetunion.* Basel: Kyklos Verlag, 1957.

Kaestner, Joachim. *Die finanzpolitischen Massnahmen zur Exportförderung.* East Berlin: Verlag Die Wirtschaft, 1959.

Kaigl, Vladimir, ed. *Czechoslovak Economic Papers.* Prague: Nakladatelstvi Ceskoslovenské akademie věd, 1959.

Kiesewetter, Bruno. *Der Ostblock: Aussenhandel.* West Berlin: Safari Verlag, 1960.

Klinkmüller, Erich. *Die gegenwärtige Aussenhandelsverflechtung der sowjetischen Besatzungszone Deutschland.* West Berlin: Duncker & Humblot, 1959.

Klinkmüller, Erich and Ruban, Maria. *Der wirtschaftliche Zusammenarbeit zwischen den Ostblockstaaten.* West Berlin: Duncker & Humblot, 1960.

Köhler, Heinz. *East Germany's Economic Integration into the Communist Bloc.* (Unpublished PhD Thesis) University of Michigan: Department of Economics, 1961.

Kohlmey, Gunther. *Der demokratische Weltmarkt.* East Berlin: Verlag Die Wirtschaft, 1954.

Kohlmey, Gunther. *Entwicklungsprobleme des sozialistischen Weltwirtschaftssystem.* East Berlin: Akademie Verlag, 1958.

Kornai, János. *Overcentralization in Economic Administration.* (transl. by John Knapp) Oxford: Oxford University Press, 1959.

Kronsjö, Tom. *Optimization of Foreign Trade Policy for a Planned Economy by Mathematical Programmes.* (Unpublished dissertation) Lund University: Institute of Economics, 1960.

Krueger, Karl. *Der Ostblock: Die Produktion.* West Berlin: Safari Verlag, 1960.

Mendershausen, Horst. *The Terms of Soviet-Satellite Trade: A Broadened Analysis.* Santa Monica: The RAND Corporation, Paper P–1,873, January, 1960.

Mendershausen, Horst. *Terms of Trade Between the Soviet Union and Smaller Communist Countries, 1955–57.* Santa Monica: The RAND Corporation, January 18, 1959.

Mikesell, Raymond F.; and Behrman, Jack N. *Financing Free World Trade with the Sino-Soviet Bloc.* Princeton: Princeton U. Press, 1958.

Nagy, Imre. *On Communism: In Defense of the New Course.* New York: Frederick A. Praeger, 1957.

Nebenzahl, Leon, (trans.) *Traitscho Kostoff und seine Gruppe.* East Berlin: Dietz Verlag, 1951.

Nykryn, Jaroslav; Herman, Karel; Stěpán, Karel; Heiduschat, Franz. *Organization und Technik des Aussenhandels.* East Berlin: Verlag Die Wirtschaft, (first edition), 1956.

Nove, Alex and Donnelly, Desmond. *Trade with Communist Countries.* London: Hutchinson, 1960.

Oelssner, Fred. *Die Uebergangsperiode vom Kapitalismus zum Sozialismus in der DDR.* East Berlin: Akademie-Verlag, 1956.

Pfuhl, Eberhardt. *Das Recht der allgemeinen Lieferbedingungen im zwischenstaatlichen Aussenhandel des Ostblocks.* West Berlin: Heft 27, Berichte des Osteuropa Instituts, Freie Universität Berlin, 1956.

Pfuhl, Eberhardt. *Rechtsform, Organisation und Technik des sownjetzonalen Aussenhandels.* West Berlin: Heft 16, Berichte des Osteuropa Instituts, Freie Universität Berlin, 1954.

Pisar, Samuel. *A New Look at Trade Policy toward the Communist Bloc.* (Materials prepared for the Subcommittee on Foreign Economic Policy of the Joint Economic Commission of the US Congress) Washington: Government Printing Office, 1961.

Prozess gegen die Leitung des staatsfeindlichen Verschwörerzentrums mit Rudolf Slánsky an der Spitze. Prague: CSSR Ministry of Justice, Orbis, 1953.

Remer, C. F. *Three Essays on the International Economics of Communist China.* Ann Arbor: University of Michigan Press, 1959.

Roginski, G. S.; Rolpakow, B. T.; Bakulin, S. N.; Paromow, M. J. *Grosse Sowjet Enzyklopaedie: Der Aussenhandel.* East Berlin: Verlag Die Wirtschaft, 1953.

Rudolph, Johannes and Friedrich, Gerd. *Grundriss der Volkswirtschaftsplanung.* East Berlin: Verlag Die Wirtschaft, 1957.

Sammelheft: Internationale Konferenz über die Rentabilität des Aussenhandels. Prague (Liblice): Hochschule für Ökonomie, 1957.

Schenk, Fritz. *Die Magie der Planwirtschaft.* Köln: Kiepenheuer & Witsch, 1960.

Schultz, T. Paul. *The Process of Adjustment to the Change in Relative Prices of Oil and Coal: Case Study Poland.* (Unpublished B. A. Thesis) Swarthmore College: Department of Economics, April 1961.

Simon, Herbert. *Models of Man.* New York: John Wiley & Sons, Inc., 1957.

Smith, Glen Alden. Soviet Foreign Trade: organization and operation. (Unpublished Ph.D. Thesis.) Stanford University: Department of Economics, 1959.

Slusser, Robert, ed. *Soviet Economic Policy in Post-war Germany.* New York: East European Fund, Inc., 1953.

Spulber, Nicolas. *The Economics of Communist Eastern Europe.* Cambridge, Mass. and New York: Wiley and the Technology Press, 1957.

Staff Papers (Presented to the Commission on Foreign Economic Policy). Washington, D.C.: Government Printing Office, February 1954.

Stalin, Joseph. *Economic Problems of Socialism in the USSR*. New York: International Publishers, 1952.

Studiengesellschaft für wirtschaftliche Entwicklung e.V. *Entwicklungshilfe innerhalb des Ostblocks:* Frankfurt a.M. and West Berlin: Alfred Metzner Verlag, 1960.

Stolper, Wolfgang; and Roskamp, Karl. *The Structure of the East German Economy*. Cambridge, Mass.: Harvard U. Press, 1960.

Trade Research Associates. *US-Soviet Trade: Facts for the Businessman's Appraisal*. Cleveland: 1960.

U.S. Congress, *Comparisons of the United States and Soviet Economies*. (Papers Presented to the Joint Economic Committee). Washington, D.C.: Government Printing Office; 1959.

Vaganov, B. S. *Voprosy organizacii vnecnej torgovli strannarodnoj demokratii*. Moscow: Vnestorgizdat, 1954.

Wszelaki, Jan. *Communist Economic Strategy; The Role of East-Central Europe*. Washington, D.C.: National Planning Association, 1959.

Zauberman, Alfred. *Economic Imperialism: The Lesson of Eastern Europe*. London: Ampersand Ltd., Bellman Books, 1955.

Zauberman, A. *Industrial Development in Czechoslovakia, East Germany and Poland*. Oxford: Chatham House Memorandum, Oxford University Press, mimeo., February 1958.

Zehn Jahre RGW. West Berlin: Informationsbüro West Sonderdienst, 1959.

Zehn Jahre Rat fur gegenseitige Wirtschaftshilfe. East Berlin: Dietz Verlag, 1960.

Zsoldos, Laszle, *The Economic Integration of Hungary into the Soviet Bloc: Foreign Trade Experience, 1950–1958*. (Unpublished Ph.D. Thesis.) Ohio State University: Department of Economics, 1961.

INDEX